LOBBYING AND POLICYMAKING

To Kenneth G. Ainsworth, Jennifer Godwin,
Sen. Marshall Rauch, D-NC, and Neal Tate

LOBBYING AND POLICYMAKING

The Public Pursuit of Private Interests

KEN GODWIN

UNIVERSITY OF NORTH CAROLINA CHARLOTTE

SCOTT H. AINSWORTH

UNIVERSITY OF GEORGIA

ERIK GODWIN

TEXAS A&M UNIVERSITY

 |

Los Angeles | London | New Delhi
Singapore | Washington DC

Los Angeles | London | New Delhi
Singapore | Washington DC

FOR INFORMATION:

CQ Press
An Imprint of SAGE Publications, Inc.
2455 Teller Road
Thousand Oaks, California 91320
E-mail: order@sagepub.com

SAGE Publications Ltd.
1 Oliver's Yard
55 City Road
London, EC1Y 1SP
United Kingdom

SAGE Publications India Pvt. Ltd.
B 1/I 1 Mohan Cooperative Industrial Area
Mathura Road, New Delhi 110 044
India

SAGE Publications Asia-Pacific Pte. Ltd.
3 Church Street
#10-04 Samsung Hub
Singapore 049483

Printed in the United States of America

Library of Congress Cataloging-in-Publication Data

Godwin, Ken.

Lobbying and policymaking : the public pursuit of private interests / Ken Godwin, Scott H. Ainsworth, Erik Godwin.

p. cm.
Includes bibliographical references and index.

ISBN 978-1-60426-469-2 (pbk.)
Lobbying—United States. 2. Pressure groups—United States. 3. United States—Politics and government—20th century. I. Ainsworth, Scott H. II. Godwin, Erik. III. Title.

JK1118.G62 2013
324'.40973—dc23   2012024334

This book is printed on acid-free paper.

Certified Chain of Custody
Promoting Sustainable Forestry
www.sfiprogram.org
SFI-01268

SFI label applies to text stock

Acquisitions Editor: Charisse Kiino
Associate Editor: Nancy Loh
Production Editor: Laureen Gleason
Copy Editor: Megan Markanich
Typesetter: C&M Digitals (P) Ltd.
Proofreader: Barbara Johnson
Indexer: Karen Wiley
Cover Designer: Janet Kiesel
Marketing Manager: Jonathan Mason
Permissions Editor: Adele Hutchinson

12 13 14 15 16 10 9 8 7 6 5 4 3 2 1

CONTENTS

TABLES, FIGURES, AND BOXES

Tables

Figures

Boxes

Ten years ago, two of the authors of this book were discussing lobbying. One of the participants was a lobbyist and the other participant taught a course on interest groups. The lobbyist observed that if he were to attend the professor's class he would be unlikely to recognize that it dealt with what lobbyists actually do. The dissimilarity between teaching and practice raised the following question: "Was political science missing some key aspects of the interactions between lobbyists and policymakers?" If so, what were the implications of these omissions? For the past decade, the authors of this book examined these questions.

Our research discovered that few scholars studied two of lobbyists' most important activities. First, previous research often ignored the lobbying of regulatory of agencies. This oversight occurred despite evidence indicating that lobbying the rulemaking process constituted almost half of all lobbying.[1] Second, scholars had concentrated on issues involving such highly collective goods as universal health care and the appropriate tax rates for individuals and corporations. Our interviews with more than 100 lobbyists discovered, however, that lobbyists for producer organizations generally concentrated their efforts on obtaining goods that benefitted only their employer or their employer and a small number of other organizations. *Lobbying and Policymaking* demonstrates that paying greater attention to rulemaking institutions and to the public provision of private goods significantly changes the standard picture of lobbying and the policymaking process. More important, attention to these aspects of policymaking changes our understanding of the strengths and weaknesses of American democracy.

This book differs from most other textbooks concerning lobbying and policymaking in several ways. First, we examine what interest organizations actually seek from policymakers. This emphasis corrects the picture of lobbying as primarily a struggle among competing interests over highly collective goods. Second, this book gives more emphasis to the regulatory process. This greater emphasis accurately reflects the importance of regulatory agencies in policymaking. Third, the book takes advantage of the practical lobbying experience of one of the authors. We believe this makes the book more enjoyable to students and increases the verisimilitude between theory and practice. Fourth, unlike most other books on lobbying or policymaking, we present a formal model reflecting key aspects of the policymaking process. Critics of formal models of lobbying have argued that such models treat policymaking as an event that occurs at a single point in time while policymaking actually is a process that continues through time and requires multiple lobbying strategies.[2] One goal of our research project was to address this problem. The formal modeling in this book is kept within a single chapter, and we have summarized in prose all aspects of those models. The model, however, is essential to the theory of policymaking we present. Interested readers can see the more formal presentations of the model in our journal articles.

We have attempted to write a book that is accessible to undergraduate students and is useful to scholars. The pedagogical approaches we employ reflect our belief that metaphors, case studies, models, and quantitative data are important to understanding the policy process. We use metaphors to assist readers in gaining intuitive insights into lobbying and policymaking. We use eight case studies to analyze, test, and illustrate concepts and hypotheses. We use two large datasets to compare competing explanations of lobbying influence and to test the formal model we develop.

The reader will discover that this book often is in a dialog with *Lobbying and Policy Change: Who Wins, Who Loses, and Why* by Frank Baumgartner, Jeffrey Berry, Marie Hojnacki, David Kimball, and Beth Leech. That work is a decade-long study that examines what interest groups want and how successful they are in achieving their goals.[3] We believe that *Lobbying and Policy Change* constitutes the most comprehensive account of lobbying available to scholars of interest groups and public policy. We show, however, that their research design led them to ignore important lobbying activities and goals. We demonstrate how this problem affected their conclusions about interest-group influence on policy outcomes. We believe that our book provides a more balanced view of the influence process and outcomes. We hasten to add that it is not necessary to read *Lobbying and Policy Change* to appreciate the arguments we make in this book.

Lobbying and Policymaking is a product of ten years of research and writing. To have the time to devote to such a project required the support of external funding as well as our universities. The National Science Foundation (NSF) provided the external funding. UNC Charlotte received NSF grant SES-0752212, and the University of Georgia received the grant SES-0752245. Our thanks go to Brian Humes and NSF reviewers for their support of the project. Ken Godwin also received financial assistance from the Department of Political Science at the University of North Texas and the College of Arts and Sciences at the University of North Carolina Charlotte (UNCC). Scott Ainsworth and Erik Godwin received support from their departments at the University of Georgia and Texas A&M University.

We are grateful to our interviewees who provided us with numerous insights into the policy process and made us better political scientists. Their contributions made the book possible. We are grateful to Karen Godwin, who achieved an amazing 80-percent success rate in obtaining interviews with lobbyists and congressional staffers. On several occasions, interviewees commented that her determination and tact were the reasons that they ultimately granted an interview.

Our colleagues Austin Clemens, John Green, Ed Lopez, and Barry Seldon are not listed as coauthors, but they coauthored research that was essential to this book. We also are appreciative of the assistance of the late Robert Salisbury, who helped us conceptualize and measure lobbying for private goods. We are grateful to the authors of *Lobbying and Policy Change* for generously making available much of the data from their project. Frank Baumgartner provided useful suggestions throughout the research process. Eric Heberlig of UNC Charlotte provided numerous useful comments and suggestions. Erik Godwin thanks Virginia Gray and David Lowery, his mentors at UNC-Chapel Hill. Although they and he are unlikely to agree on the degree of rationality in the lobbying and policymaking, their instruction greatly informed his contributions to this book.

Several students were intimately involved in the research and writing process. At UNC Charlotte, Lawson Seropian played an important editorial role. His most difficult task was to ensure that the authors wrote in a manner accessible to undergraduate students. Lawson also was a valuable research assistant in tracking bills and participants in the policies included in our analyses. Other students working on the project included Kathryn Clifford, Perry Joiner, Ruoxi Li, and Hongu Zhang at the University of Georgia and Amanda Rutherford and Jamie Smart at Texas A&M.

We appreciate the comments of Don C. Baumer, Smith College; Julio Borquez, University of Michigan-Dearborn; Andrienne Fulco, Trinity College; Paul Lewis, Arizona State University; Jason MacDonald, Kent State University; Jennifer Miller, UNC-Chapel Hill; Laura Olson, Clemson University; Donald Stenta, The Ohio State University; and Stephen Weatherford, University of California, Santa Barbara, the reviewers of our proposal or an earlier draft of the manuscript. Our editor Charisse Kiino was helpful throughout the writing process and remained supportive even when we missed deadlines. We are grateful to Megan Markanich, Laureen Gleason, and Nancy Loh, the editorial and production team at CQ Press. As much as we would like to blame any errors on the people who were previously mentioned, those errors remain our own.

ENDNOTES

1. Scott R. Furlong and Cornelius M. Kerwin, "Interest Group Participation in Rule Making: A Decade of Change," *Journal of Public Administration Research and Theory* 15, no. 3 (2004): 353–370.

2. David Lowery and Virginia Gray, "A Neopluralist Perspective on Research on Organized Interests," *Political Research Quarterly* 57, no.1 (2004): 164–175.

3. Frank R. Baumgartner, Jeffrey M. Berry, Marie Hojnacki, David C. Kimball, and Beth L. Leech. *Lobbying and Policy Change: Who Wins, Who Loses, and Why* (Chicago: University of Chicago Press, 2009).

Ken Godwin is the Marshall Rauch Distinguished Professor of Political Science at the University of North Carolina Charlotte. He previously taught at the University of North Texas, the University of Arizona, and Oregon State University. He also served as the Rockefeller Environmental Fellow at Resources for the Future. Godwin is the author or coauthor of seven books concerning public policy issues and interest groups. His articles have appeared in numerous journals including the *American Political Science Review*, the *Journal of Politics*, the *Southern Economic Journal*, *Public Choice*, and *AI*. From 2000 to 2006, he served as the coeditor of *Political Research Quarterly*.

Scott H. Ainsworth is professor of political science in the School of Public and International Affairs at the University of Georgia. His work on lobbying, interest groups, and the U.S. Congress has appeared in numerous outlets, including the *American Journal of Political Science*, *Journal of Politics*, and *Legislative Studies Quarterly*. He is the author of *Analyzing Interest Groups* and coauthor of *Abortion Politics in Congress: Strategic Incrementalism and Policy Change*.

Erik Godwin is assistant professor of political science at Texas A&M University. His research interests focus on policy design and its implementation by the federal bureaucracy. Godwin received his Ph.D. from the University of North Carolina at Chapel Hill, and he holds a Master of Public Policy from the University of Michigan. Godwin previously conducted financial and economic analyses for the U.S. Environmental Protection Agency and the U.S. Department of Justice. He joined the Office of Information and Regulatory Affairs in the Clinton White House. After leaving the White House, he spent six years as an executive-branch lobbyist on environmental, energy, and health issues.

Key Concepts and Ideas

One of the authors of this book invited a **lobbyist** for a major defense contractor to speak to his interest group class. After the lobbyist finished speaking, the instructor asked her, "What was the most important vote you influenced in the last Congress?" She[1] responded, "Do you mean, 'What was the most important vote?' or 'What was the most important thing I did for my firm last year?'" The lobbyist went on to explain that her most significant achievement was obtaining a 25-percent price increase for the guided air-to-ground missile her firm produced for the **Department of Defense (DoD)**. This increase boosted her firm's profits by more than $50 million over a five-year period. No congressional vote ever took place on that specific price change. The 25-percent price increase occurred without any record of legislators' yeas and nays. The price increase took place during a committee markup of an omnibus defense appropriations bill.

Omnibus bills typically are hundreds of pages long, address a wide range of programs, and frequently address budget issues. With such voluminous legislation, small changes often remain overlooked by all but the most attentive legislators. During a committee markup, committee members consider various proposed changes to a bill, but they never vote on the final bill in committee. Instead, the committee members vote on a motion to report the bill to the floor with the committee recommendations. The missile price increase was just a very small part of a much larger piece of legislation. There were no media campaigns or grassroots mobilization efforts. The lobbyist's efforts were low-key, designed to raise little public or media scrutiny, and very effective.

The number of Americans who believe that money in politics presents a significant problem for democracy is growing. For fifty years, public opinion polls have asked the question, "Generally speaking, would you say that this country is run by a few big interests looking out for themselves or that it is run for the benefit of all the people?" In 1964, fewer than 30 percent of Americans believed that a few big interests ran the government.[2] By 2008, the figure rose to 80 percent.[3] Books and newspaper articles with clever titles such as "The Best Congress Money Can Buy" and "Democracy on Drugs" claimed that special interest money undermines the American political process. Americans' concerns about the influence of special interests reflect the rapid growth of **lobbying.** From 2000 to 2010, federal lobbying expenditures grew from *only* $1.56 billion to more than $3.5 billion.[4] Certainly, the organizations spending these resources expected to achieve policy goals important to them. They did not believe they were wasting their money.

Many citizens and journalists believe that special interests have too much influence on **public policy.** Certainly prominent lobbying scandals such as those portrayed in Hollywood movie *Casino Jack*[5] skew our sense of what normally occurs. Political scientists are not as certain that special interest monies buy policies. Highlighting the standard scapegoats—big business, special interests, unions, the Washington establishment—is relatively easy, but finding clear patterns of inappropriate behaviors is hard. In 2009, a comprehensive study by five eminent political scientists found that when opposing interests face each other on an issue, the side with greater political resources was no more likely to win than the side with fewer resources.[6] Money did not translate into regular or repeated wins. The following paragraph summarizes their findings:

> The results [of our study] are striking in that the usual types of resources that are often assumed to "buy" public policy outcomes—PAC donations, lobbying expenditures, membership size, and organizational budgets—have no observable effect on the outcomes. . . . Thus, at the issue level, *there seems to be no relationship between the level of these types of resources that a side controls and whether it obtains its preferred outcomes. The wealthier side sometimes wins and sometimes loses.*[7]

In other words, money and other lobbying resources appeared not to matter. These scholars do not suggest that nothing bad ever happens, that all policy outcomes are sound, or that money never influences policymaking. The study's authors showed, however, that it is exceedingly difficult to tie policy wins and losses to money when one records, as they did, the efforts of hundreds of lobbyists on dozens of issues. Some scandals might occur and money might be used occasionally to achieve undue advantages, but when considering a large number of cases, it is difficult to demonstrate that special interest money leads to undue influence.[8]

Some research has found that organizations that are active politically benefit from lobbying efforts. For example, recent studies indicate that corporations that lobby and contribute to political campaigns pay lower taxes and experience fewer problems with regulatory agencies than firms that are not politically active.[9] Nonetheless, several expansive reviews of research over the past thirty years have failed to uncover a consistent pattern of lobbying impact. In one review of forty-four published studies concerning the effects of lobbying and campaign contributions, the authors discovered that twenty-two studies showed a significant relationship between lobbying expenditures and legislators' behavior. The other twenty-two studies found either no relationship or a very weak relationship between lobbying and behavior.[10] In short, the only consistent finding about the relationship between lobbying and legislators' behavior is that the relationship is not consistent.

The goals of this book are to identify when, where, and how special interests influence policymaking and to examine the implications of this influence for American democracy. To achieve these goals, we study numerous issues on their journeys through the policymaking process. Some of the issues received repeated attention; others never became law. One of the most important goals of any study of interest group influence is to explain why some efforts to change policy succeed while others fail. Our study focuses on four questions: (1) What goals do interest organizations seek? (2) Which strategies do they use? (3) When during the policy process are different types of interest organizations most successful? (4) What factors influence a group's success or failure?

Why should you care about how, when, and where special interests influence policymaking? Because the answers to these questions indicate the health of democracy in America. The answers also provide you with insights concerning how you can influence the policy process as an individual citizen or as a member of an interest group. Should you become a corporate leader or the head of an interest organization, the answers suggest how you can further your organization's goals through political action. Most important, the answers may provide insights concerning how citizens and political leaders can improve the American political system.

WHAT DO LOBBYISTS DO?

Lobbying is an effort used to influence public policy. But what do lobbyists actually do? One popular image of lobbyists calls to mind expensively dressed people meeting with slightly frumpish legislators. The clever lobbyist convinces the legislators of the righteousness of the lobbyist's cause. Mark Twain envisioned lobbyists as scurrilous connivers, with devil's tails twitching excitedly under their pants. Other images portray lobbyists and policymakers cutting deals that help special interests and the legislator's reelection, even as they harm the public. Perhaps the most popular image is that of a person passing a bag full of campaign contributions to an elected official, hoping to "buy" favorable policies.

Some scholars use "vote buying" as an analogy to simplify their models of strategic interactions between lobbyists and legislators.[11] For these scholars, "vote buying" is a shorthand term that describes a wide array of such lobbying activities as supplying policymakers information, generating letter-writing campaigns, paying for television ads that support or oppose a policy, testifying before Congress, and meeting with public officials. Maybe unmarked hundred-dollar bills are exchanged, but it is more likely that lobbyists provide policymakers with background information, policy research, and legal campaign contributions that are fully recorded by the Federal Election Commission. To understand how individuals exert influence, it is best to consider how those attempting to exert influence use their resources.

Regardless of whether a lobbyist is attempting to influence a legislator, a bureaucrat, or the president of the United States, three activities take up most of a lobbyist's time. The first is monitoring what policymakers are doing.

Governments in the United States are active, and the federal government is the most active of all. Unlike state legislatures, with their sessions often limited to just a few months each year, the U.S. Congress is generally in session every month of the year. Congress often passes as many as 1,000 new statutes during each congressional session. Because congressional committees and subcommittees maintain their own agendas and often make critical policy decisions, lobbyists must monitor the activities of committees important to their clients. If congressional leaders choose to use special task forces or bypass committees, lobbyists must monitor these additional venues.[12] Recall the discussion at the beginning of this chapter concerning the missile price increase during a committee markup session. Markup sessions are part of the regular legislative process, but they are not widely advertised, so lobbyists must remain at the ready.

The U.S. Congress is not a lobbyist's only area of concern. Every year, the federal bureaucracy generates thousands of new **rules** and interpretations of past statutes. These rule and interpretations have the status of laws. Indeed, some legal scholars are decidedly concerned about the extensiveness of bureaucratic lawmaking.[13] In addition to bureaucratic rules, the president can issue executive orders that also have the status of laws. The White House also prepares the preliminary national budget that sets the nation's spending priorities. Keeping up with all of these activities requires enormous effort for any lobbyist.

Consider General Electric (GE), a corporation that manufactures products in numerous industries from lightbulbs to jet engines. The corporation provides various services including business and consumer finance, aircraft maintenance, health care, and entertainment. GE generates electric power using oil, gas, wind, and nuclear energy. In 2010, to keep up with new statutes, regulations, and executive orders, GE employed thirty in-house lobbyists and hired lobbyists from twenty-nine contract lobbying firms. The company reported lobbying expenditures of almost $40 million.[14] GE spent a large percentage of those funds simply monitoring the government activities that affect its multitudinous economic activities.[15] As Box 1.1 indicates, lobbyists believe that effective monitoring is critical to policy success.

BOX 1.1   "Oh, S——t" Moments: The Importance of Monitoring

Using colorful language, a lobbyist for a Fortune 1000 company explained why monitoring is so important. "There almost always are 'Oh, S——t' moments in policymaking. For several months, nothing may happen. Then, suddenly, a deal will be made or a compromise struck in committee. You have to know when this happens and be ready to defend your client's interest. If you weren't watching, if you were not ready when the deal happened, you lose and your client loses." Monitoring is equally important for lobbying the bureaucracy. Lobbyists routinely contact agency personnel to discover the new initiatives that an agency plans. Forewarned is forearmed.

The second major task of lobbyists is to supply information to policymakers. Legislators are often generalists.[16] Legislators who develop expertise in one or two issue areas remain concerned with many different issues, and they need information about all of them. Members of Congress and their staff members are among the world's busiest people, often working seventy to eighty hours per week when Congress is in session. In contrast to members of Congress, lobbyists typically are issue specialists. They know a great deal about one issue area such as pesticides, wind energy, or farm subsidies. Lobbyists' expertise is often finely nuanced. For instance, the safety of pesticides is related to their decomposition—that is, the poison is not meant to last forever. A lobbyist's expertise related to pesticides likely includes information on their biological composition, chemical composition, and photodecomposition. Few, if any, legislators would know the half-life of various chemical compounds, but lobbyists concerned with pesticide regulation would. To obtain information on all of the issues that they must address, members of Congress turn to lobbyists.

Suppose an energy issue comes up; a legislator might request a lobbyist for an energy company or a lobbyist for an environmental group to prepare a background paper on the issue. In this situation, the lobbyist is providing labor and expertise that the legislator needs to be effective.[17] The lobbyist also is signaling to the legislator that her interest group is sufficiently interested in the issue to spend substantial resources to influence the policy outcome.[18] In addition to technical information, lobbyists also supply political information. They frequently receive requests from legislators for information concerning how particular bills might affect their district or state. Lobbyists also supply the legislator with information concerning which other congressional districts might be affected as well as the legislators who are likely to be allies and those who are likely to be opponents on the issue.

The third time-consuming task of lobbyists is maintaining good relations with public officials and with other lobbyists. Scott Ainsworth has argued that legislators and lobbyists often form "**lobbying enterprises.**"[19] A lobbying enterprise consists of an informal group of lobbyists and legislators who have repeated interactions and share common goals. The repeated interactions increase a legislator's effectiveness by reducing his uncertainty about which lobbyists can be trusted and by facilitating the coordination of important policy actors inside and outside of government. Coordinating inside and outside activities is crucial because to be successful, legislative proposals need a supportive coalition within the Congress as well as the support of individuals and groups beyond the confines of Congress. A lobbying enterprise helps the lobbyist by giving her regular access to legislators who can lobby other legislators on behalf of her group's legislative priorities. The enterprise also facilitates interactions among lobbyists when they are drafting proposals for legislators.

Lobbyists must maintain good relationships with bureaucrats in the relevant agencies. For example, a lobbyist for a pesticide manufacturer must establish effective links with officials in the **U.S. Department of Agriculture (USDA)** and the Environmental Protection Agency (EPA). Those bureaucrats are on the frontlines of making, interpreting, and enforcing the regulations governing pesticides. As we will emphasize throughout this book, the bureaucracy makes far more laws than do elected officials. Bureaucrats are, therefore, a major target of lobbying activity.

In summary, lobbyists spend their time monitoring what the government is doing, providing information to policymakers, and maintaining relationships with government officials and other lobbyists. Repeated interactions make cooperation within lobbying enterprises more efficient, thereby helping the public officials and the lobbyists. Public officials benefit from the substantive and political information and other resources they need to be effective policymakers and to represent their constituents. Organized interests benefit by having easier access to the policymakers and by learning the policy preferences of other interests.

KEY TERMS

Before continuing our study, we define a few key terms. The most important of these are the terms *lobbying, lobbyist,* and *public policy.* Lobbying is any effort used to influence public policy.[20] Lobbying includes campaign contributions and the various activities of paid lobbyists as well as efforts by citizens and public officials to influence policy outcomes. Although anyone can lobby, we restrict the term *lobbyist* to those nongovernment actors who earn their living attempting to influence public policy. Public policy is "a course of action (or inaction) that government chooses when dealing with a social, economic, or political problem."[21] To place these terms in context, assume that the EPA is deciding whether to ban all insecticides containing chlorine. Lobbyists employed by the American Chemistry Council, Dow Chemical Company, the Clean Water Coalition, and the Sierra Club might attempt to influence the EPA's decision. Others who approach the EPA to influence its decision might include a deputy secretary in the USDA or the director of the North Carolina Department of Fish and Wildlife. A senator from Iowa could write a letter to the director of the EPA to oppose the chlorine ban, arguing it would reduce the agricultural productivity of farmers in his state and increase the cost of food. By our definition, all of these individuals are lobbying. If the lobbyist for the Sierra Club organizes a letter-writing campaign by Sierra Club members, the persons writing those letters are lobbying, but they are not lobbyists. Whether the EPA chooses to ban the insecticides or chooses not to ban them, its decision yields a public policy.

Types of Lobbyists

There are several ways to categorize lobbyists. In his book *Total Lobbying,* Anthony Nownes differentiated lobbyists by the organizations for which they lobby. For example, there are lobbyists for corporations, trade associations, unions, citizens' groups, governments, churches, charities, and universities.[22] Another way to categorize lobbyists is by their employer. **Internal (or in-house) lobbyists** work directly for the organization that they represent. Catherine

Robinson, for example, lobbies for Amgen Corporation, a large pharmaceutical company. She is a salaried employee of Amgen. **External (or contract) lobbyists** are individuals who work for a lobbying firm. Courtney Johnson also lobbies for Amgen, but she is employed by the Alpine Group, a lobbying firm that represents many interest organizations. (See Box 1.2.)

BOX 1.2   Biographic Sketches for Internal and External Lobbyists for Amgen

Catherine Robinson, Senior Manager, International Corporate Affairs, Amgen Corporation

Previous Appointments

Director, High Tech Trade Policy, National Association of Manufacturers

International Trade Associate, American Association of Exporters and Importers

Lawyer, House Committee on Ways and Means, Subcommittee on Trade

International Trade Fellow, United Nations

Legislative Research Assistant, Global USA, Inc.

Staff Assistant, Rep. Kevin Brady, R-TX

Named by *The Hill* as a top business lobbyist: http://thehill.com/business-a
-lobbying/102691–2010-top-lobbyist

Education

BS Political Science and Communications, Texas A&M University

Law Degree, University of Maryland

Courtney Johnson, Health Care Lobbyist, Alpine Group

Previous Appointments

Vice President, Public Affairs, Boston Scientific Corporation

Lobbyist, Council for Responsible Nutrition

Lobbyist, Jackson National Life Insurance Company

Senior Staff Member, House Committee on Energy

Staff Member, House Commerce Committee

Education

BA, Political Science, University of Tennessee

MA, Legislative Affairs, George Washington University

A third way to categorize lobbyists is by the knowledge and skills they possess. In the Appendix, "So You Want to Become a Lobbyist," we write that most successful lobbyists have three important characteristics. They have **substantive expertise** in a specific policy area, strong **personal contacts** with key policymakers, and **procedural knowledge** of the process of policymaking. While lobbyists must have all three characteristics, most are stronger in some areas rather than others. For example, lobbyists who previously were scientists working in the EPA or the **U.S. Food and Drug Administration (FDA)** generally have exceptional substantive expertise on issues related to their scientific specializations. In contrast, lobbyists who were high-level political officials in those agencies typically excel in personal contacts and procedural knowledge. They have close personal relationships with many employees in their previous agency (they may even have hired some of those employees), and they have excellent knowledge of the formal and informal procedures used in making policy decisions. Former legislators and high-ranking congressional staffers obviously have close contacts with key policymakers in Congress. This allows them privileged access to current representatives, senators, and congressional staffers. Ex-legislators also have substantial knowledge of congressional procedures.

As we will see throughout this book, the policy process can be Byzantine. There are numerous ways to slow down or stop a policy proposal. There are also ways to make a (seemingly) small change in a proposed policy that will have a major effect on its success or failure. Knowledge of the policy process and the procedures of institutions allows lobbyists to identify who, where, when, and how to lobby successfully.

Types of Policies

Public policies create benefits and costs to individuals and institutions. These benefits and costs differ in a very important fashion, and that difference is illuminated by the distinction between **private goods** and **collective goods**. Two features characterize private goods. A private good is **excludable.** The owner of a private good can exclude others from using it. Private goods also have **rivalrous consumption**, which means that as one person uses the good, its value to others is diminished. Your lunch is a private good. A collective good has **nonrivalrous** consumption, and there are no means to exclude people from using it. National Public Radio (NPR) provides a collective good. As more and more people tune in, the radio reception of other listeners is unaffected. The consumption is nonrivalrous because additional consumers do not reduce the value of the good to other consumers. Although NPR stations ask for contributions from listeners, there are no means to exclude noncontributors from listening.

Many goods have some private aspects and some collective aspects to them. Suppose that you subscribe to Sirius Satellite Radio and you also listen to NPR. The broadcasts from Sirius have a key characteristic of a private good because Sirius can exclude those who do not pay for its service. Of course, Sirius broadcasts remain nonrivalrous for subscribers to their service. NPR broadcasts are a collective good; they are available to anyone with a radio.

Other examples of collective goods are clean air and national defense. Other examples of private goods are a personal bodyguard, an air purifier for your house, and your dinner tonight.

Goods with some private and some collective attributes include toll roads, cable TV broadcasts, and public swimming pools. Even if they are "public" in the traditional sense of the word, the value of those swimming pools begins to diminish as they become increasingly crowded. Pure collective goods are invulnerable to **crowding effects** because they have nonrivalrous consumption. Most goods, however, are at some point vulnerable to crowding effects. Crowding effects occur when the value of a good or service diminishes as more and more people use the good. Public parks, free concerts, and roads are all vulnerable to crowding effects. Exclusion is used to protect pure private goods from crowding effects. Your backyard pool is not vulnerable to crowding because access to it is limited.

One way to think of the difference between private and collective goods is whether a benefit is concentrated on only a small number of individuals or organizations or whether the benefits are diffuse, allowing numerous individuals and organizations to receive them. For example, the benefits of national defense are diffuse; everyone residing in the U.S. receives them. Of course, some citizens value defense more than other citizens, but the benefits from national defense are diffuse, affecting young and old, citizen and noncitizen all across the states. In contrast, the price increase for producing the air-to-ground missile provided greater profits to a single firm. The production and deployment of the missiles yielded benefits beyond the firm, but the price increase for those missiles was a private good to the firm. The goods and services that governments provide lie on a continuum from purely private (highly concentrated) goods to purely collective (highly diffuse) goods such as national defense.

To illustrate the private–collective continuum, we explore four tax breaks included in the American Jobs Creation Act of 2004 (jobs act). (See Figure 1.1.) One tax break went to four construction companies that were using green technology to build a specific shopping center. The tax break applied only to one shopping center. Future shopping centers built with green technology would not receive the same benefits. As no other construction firm or shopping center could receive a similar tax break, this government-provided benefit was a private good for the four construction companies.

At a slightly higher level of collectiveness, the jobs act provided a tax break to all U.S. manufacturers of certain recreational fishing products. Only about a dozen U.S. companies manufactured these products and received the tax reduction. The tax break would be available to other firms, however, if they decided to produce the fishing products. Moving toward the collective end of the continuum, a provision in the jobs act legislation reduced the tax rate on the profits U.S. corporations had accumulated in foreign countries and wished to bring back to the United States. This tax break affected hundreds of multinational corporations based in the United States. The tax reduction was worth billions of dollars to the firms that brought their foreign profits back to the

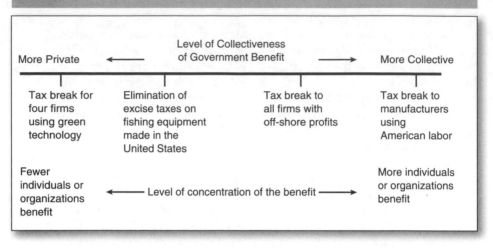

FIGURE 1.1 Provisions in the American Jobs Creation Act of 2004

United States. Finally, the provision that had the greatest level of collectiveness (was the most diffuse) gave a tax credit to all U.S. manufacturers that used any American workers to produce their goods. This last provision reduced the taxes on all American manufacturers and saved them an estimated $76 billion.[23] Figure 1.1 showed these different tax provisions.

Two concepts closely related to collective goods are **free rider** and the **collective action problem**. In his justly famous book *The Logic of Collective Action,* Mancur Olson demonstrated that an economically rational individual generally would not contribute to a group lobbying for a collective good that benefits a large number of people. Even if the individual wanted the collective good, it was not rational to contribute to its provision.[24] NPR membership drives demonstrate the collective action problem. Each year, local NPR stations have fund-raising drives and plead with the station's listeners to make a donation to support the station. If you make a donation, you probably experience a good feeling for doing your part to pay for the programming. If you do not make the donation, however, you will have more money to spend on other goods and services. Because the station has no way to prevent you from listening to its broadcasts, you will continue to receive the collective good of NPR programs. Will you donate? Olson argued that economically rational people will not contribute. We refer to people who enjoy a collective good but do not help to provide it as free riders. The collective action problem (often called the "free rider problem") occurs when rational, self-interested people free ride rather than help provide the collective good. Interest group scholars disagree about the extent to which the collective action problem creates a bias in our interest group society. For the moment, just remember the concept and the logic behind it.

APPROACH OF THIS BOOK

This book examines competing theories of interest group influence and develops a model that explains how interest organizations allocate their resources to achieve their political goals. Three central hypotheses guided our research. First, lobbying and policymaking are multistage processes. Second, all other things equal, interest organizations prefer to lobby for benefits that are private rather than collective. Third, the lobbying strategies that interest organizations employ vary systematically with the stage of the policy process and with the degree of collectiveness of the desired benefit.

We organize the book around two broadly applied approaches to understanding interest group influence: (1) **neopluralism** and (2) **the exchange model.** To assist the reader in understanding these approaches and our model of interest group influence, we make extensive use of case studies and specific examples. We also use metaphors to improve readers' understanding of policymaking and lobbying. We portray the neopluralist approach to the policy process as a tug-of-war among competing organized interests. We contrast that view of lobbying with the metaphor of the Middle Eastern bazaar, where numerous buyers and sellers exchange goods and services. We use case studies to illustrate important strengths and weaknesses of the neopluralist and exchange approaches. The case studies include policy decisions reached in federal agencies, Congress, and the White House.

In some respects, our book creates a dialogue with *Lobbying and Policy Change: Who Wins, Who Loses, and Why* by Frank Baumgartner, Jeffrey Berry, Marie Hojnacki, David Kimball, and Beth Leech. Published in 2009, *Lobbying and Policy Change* is the most comprehensive study of lobbying at the national level ever conducted. It makes a powerful and persuasive case for neopluralism. Although we began our research project before Baumgartner and his colleagues began publishing their results, the two studies complement one another. Our research demonstrates both the value of *Lobbying and Policy Change* and the limits to its generalizations.

Data

The data we use to test the competing models of lobbying influence come from several sources. The first consists of sixty-two interviews with lobbyists working on behalf of Fortune 1000 firms and includes 386 issues. These interviews contain information concerning the following six issues: (1) what issues were important to the firm, (2) on which of those issues the firm chose to lobby, (3) whether the firm's goal was a private or a collective good, (4) where in the policy process the firm spent its resources, (5) whether the firm lobbied alone or as part of a coalition, and (6) the value of the policy to the firm. An important attribute of this dataset is that it includes issues that were important to the firm but on which the firm chose not to lobby. The inclusion of these issues allows us to identify the factors that encourage a firm to spend its lobbying resources and the factors that encourage it to free ride. Another important aspect of these data is the inclusion of policies made by Congress and policies decided by the bureaucracy. One of the major weaknesses of past research on interest groups has been its almost exclusive focus on legislative institutions. A limitation of this first dataset is that it includes only lobbyists for large corporations and issues that had an impact on those corporations.

A second dataset consists of interviews and archival data related to our eight case studies. For five issues—the **Data Quality Act (DQA)**, the regulation of perchlorate, drug reimportation, the jobs act, and the **Energy Policy Act of 2003**—we conducted extensive interviews with lobbyists and government officials involved in the policy process. For the **North American Free Trade Agreement (NAFTA)**, the estate tax, and the cleanup of toxic sites, we relied largely on archival data and previous in-depth case studies. The case studies allow us to examine how lobbying strategies change as an issue moves through the policy process. Finally, the case studies allow us to investigate causal relationships and to understand how contextual factors affect lobbying success and failure.

The third dataset consists of the written documents requesting changes or opposing changes in proposed regulations. These documents are known as "**comments**" or "**comment letters**," and they constitute a major form of lobbying the bureaucracy. We have collected the comments filed on all economically significant regulatory rules proposed in 2007 by the EPA, the Department of Energy (DOE), the Department of Education, and the Department of Transportation (DOT). For each *rule*, we examine which organizations and individuals submitted comments and whether the agency responded positively to those comments.

The last set of data comes from the authors of *Lobbying and Policy Change*. These data include the lobbying efforts and policy outcomes for ninety-eight policy issues that took place during the period from 1999 to 2002.[25] Because of confidentiality issues, we did not have complete access to all of the data collected, but the authors of *Lobbying and Policy Change* generously made available substantial parts of their data. This allowed us to examine the selection of issues, interviewees, and policy goals.

Theoretical Rigor and Practical Politics

Although all three authors of this book teach in political science departments, they bring different orientations and training to this project. Scott Ainsworth's academic areas are interest groups, Congress, and formal modeling. He has published extensively on interest groups, sometimes using signaling games to highlight strategic interactions between legislators and lobbyists. Erik Godwin brings an applied orientation to the project. He spent several years working as a policy analyst in the White House **Office of Management and Budget (OMB)**. He then became a lobbyist with the EOP Group, a Washington lobbying firm that specializes on energy and environmental issues. His academic specialization concerns policymaking by the bureaucracy. Kenneth Godwin combined work as a policy consultant in health care and environmental policy with an academic career. He has advised state and national governments concerning how to design policies for effective implementation. His academic research focuses on lobbying strategies and public policy. By bringing diverse perspectives to this study, we hope to strike a useful balance between the rigor and discipline of theory-driven social science and the practical politics of how lobbyists actually attempt to influence the policy process.

In summary, the goals of *Lobbying and Policymaking* are to understand how interests influence the policymaking process and the implications of that influence for American democracy. To achieve these goals, we combine portions of the neopluralist and exchange approaches to build a model of the influence process. We test these approaches and our model using quantitative and qualitative methods and multiple datasets.

ENDNOTES

1. To help protect the anonymity of lobbyists and policymakers, throughout this book we use female pronouns to refer to lobbyists and male pronouns to refer to government officials.
2. See Joseph Nye, Philip Zelikow, and David King, *Why People Don't Trust Government* (Cambridge, MA: Harvard University Press, 1997).
3. WorldPublicOpinion.org, "American Public Says Government Leaders Should Pay Attention to Polls," March 21, 2008, www.worldpublicopinion.org/pipa/articles/governance_bt/461.php?lb=btgov&pnt=461&nid=&id=
4. OpenSecrets.org: Center for Responsive Politics, "Lobbying Database," March 26, 2012, www.opensecrets.org/lobby/index.php
5. *Casino Jack* portrayed the illegal activities of high-powered lobbyist Jack Abramoff.
6. Frank R. Baumgartner et al., *Lobbying and Policy Change: Who Wins, Who Loses, and Why* (Chicago: University of Chicago Press, 2009).
7. Ibid., 208–209, emphasis added.
8. Elected officials are able to "wheel and deal" among themselves for votes and favors. Legislators use earmarks and redistribute campaign contributions to curry legislative support. See, for example, Jeffery Jenkins and Nathan Monroe, "Buying Negative Agenda Control in the U.S. House" (paper prepared for the annual meeting of the American Political Science Association, Toronto, Canada, September 2009).
9. See Sanford Gordon and Catherine Hafer, "Flexing Muscle: Corporate Political Expenditures as Signals to the Bureaucracy," *American Political Science Review* 99, no. 2 (2005): 245–261. Brian Richter, Krislert Samphantharak, and Jeffrey Timmons, "Lobbying and Taxes," *American Journal of Political Science* 53, no. 4 (2009): 893–909.
10. See Frank R. Baumgartner and Beth L. Leech, *Basic Interests: The Importance of Groups in Politics and in Political Science* (Princeton: Princeton University Press, 1998). Other comprehensive reviews are more inclined to see interest-group influence, but there are always caveats. See, for example, Jan Potters and Randolph Sloof, "Interest Groups: A Survey of Empirical Models That Try to Assess Their Influence," *European Journal of Political Economy* 12 (1996): 403–442. See also Douglas Roscoe and Shannon Jenkins, "A Meta-Analysis of Campaign Contributions' Impact on Roll Call Voting," *Social Science Quarterly* 86, no. 1 (2005): 52–68. One reason there are disputes among the scholars who review the interest-group literature is that there is no clear baseline for assessing influence. Suppose the empirical results in a study

indicate that only twenty legislators were swayed. Now suppose that number is ten, five, or one. When is vote buying widespread enough to raise concerns, and when is it inconsequential? A second reason for disputes is that some scholars focus on legislators' individual votes while other scholars focus on policy outcomes.

11. As examples, see Timothy Groseclose and James M. Snyder, Jr., "Buying Supermajorities," *American Political Science Review* 90, no. 2 (1996): 303–315; and Gene M. Grossman and Elhanan Helpman, *Special Interest Politics* (Cambridge, MA: MIT Press, 2002).

12. Barbara Sinclair, *Unorthodox Lawmaking: New Legislative Processes in the U.S. Congress,* 3rd ed. (Washington, DC: CQ Press, 2007).

13. Jamison E. Colburn, "Agency Interpretations," *Temple Law Review* 82, no. 3 (2009): 657–702.

14. OpenSecrets.org: Center for Responsive Politics, "General Electric," March 26, 2012, www.opensecrets.org/lobby/clientsum.php?id=D000000125&year=2011

15. Personal interview with a previous lobbyist for General Electric.

16. Richard L. Hall and Alan V. Deardorff, "Lobbying as Legislative Subsidy," *American Political Science Review* 100 (2006): 69–84.

17. Raymond A. Bauer, Ithiel de Sola Pool, and Lewis Anthony Dexter, *American Business & Public Policy: The Politics of Foreign Trade* (Chicago: Aldine Atherton, 1972).

18. A wide array of interest-group scholars in political science and economics has used signaling games to model the strategic interactions between legislators and lobbyists. Interested readers can begin with David Austen-Smith and John R. Wright, "Competitive Lobbying for a Legislator's Vote," *Social Choice and Welfare* 9, no. 3 (1992): 229–257. For more recent work, see Morten Bennedsen and Sven E. Feldmann, "Lobbying Bureaucrats," *Scandinavian Journal of Economics* 108, no. 4 (2006): 643–668.

19. Scott Ainsworth, "The Role of Legislators in the Determination of Interest Group Influence," *Legislative Studies Quarterly* 22 (1997): 517–533.

20. This definition is adapted from Frank R. Baumgartner and Beth L. Leech, *Basic Interests*, 33.

21. This definition is adapted from James E. Anderson, *Public Policymaking,* 4th ed. (Boston: Houghton Mifflin, 2004), 4.

22. Anthony J. Nownes, *Total Lobbying: What Lobbyists Want (and How They Try to Get It)* (New York: Cambridge University Press, 2006).

23. Chris Atkins, "FSC/ETI Transition Relief in the New JOBS Act: Does the U.S. Have to Quit Cold Turkey?" Tax Foundation, Special Report, no. 133 (2005), www .taxfoundation.org/files/47eb8eba52aa64fc8a21688e81500b3c.pdf

24. See James E. Alt, "Thoughts on Mancur Olson's Contribution to Political Science 1932–1998," *Public Choice* 98 (1999): 1–4.

25. Readers can access these data at http://lobby.la.psu.edu/. The website includes summaries of the ninety-eight issues, congressional hearings related to the issues, and relevant news articles. Because of confidentiality restrictions, the 300-plus interviews with lobbyists active on the issues are not available. We have updated some of the Lobbying Advocacy Project issues and collected and coded data concerning what types of organizations lobbied on each issue. In particular, we have updated the data for issues that continued past the 107th Congress.

chapter 2

Models of Influence

To help describe complex, strategic interactions, social scientists often use models to focus attention on the most crucial elements of an interaction. Sometimes these models are very complicated and formally presented using tools more common to economics and mathematics. Sometimes the models are more loosely presented. With more mathematical rigor, the development of testable hypotheses is often easier. One of the most powerful means of evaluating a model is to test its implications empirically. Less mathematically rigorous models are easier, at first blush, to represent and to understand. There are fewer barriers to a reader when exposition is less mathematically oriented. The extent of rigor appropriate for any model is often a matter of individual taste. Mathematical exposition can reduce miscommunication because of its precision, but it also reduces one's overall readership. Most social scientists would agree that models should be no more complicated than necessary and that—across the board—scholars must strive to be precise in their language. This chapter does not use mathematical models, but we often base our discussion on research that employs such models.

TWO MODELS AND TWO METAPHORS

This chapter presents the two dominant models of interest-group influence: (1) exchange and (2) neopluralism. The exchange model emphasizes the interactions between legislators and organized interests (see Box 2.1).

BOX 2.1   Policy Issues

A policy issue is a social, political, or economic problem that the government considers acting upon. You may have numerous problems. You may be short of funds for college, have difficulty breathing on days where the air pollution is high, need transportation for traveling from home to work, lose your job when the textile plant where you work moves to Mexico, be extremely sad because your boyfriend or girlfriend left you for another person, and you may be less attractive than you would like. Today, all but the last two of these problems is a policy issue. There is debate on each concerning the appropriate government policy.

The neopluralist model argues that most policy issues involve competition among organized interests and that each side has sufficient resources to lobby successfully. The emphasis is on interests and interest competition. The metaphor of a tug-of-war best describes the neopluralist model of lobbying and group influence. Each side attempts to move public policy closer to its desired position. For example, government regulation of water pollution is a policy issue. The current level of regulation is the result of past battles between environmental groups that prefer more strict regulation and polluting industries that prefer less strict regulation. Lobbyists on both sides use their resources to change the policy in their preferred direction.[1] A difference between political tugs-of-war and those on the playground is that there may be more than two sides in a political tug-of-war. (See Figure 2.1.)

FIGURE 2.1   **Tug-of-War With Three Sides**

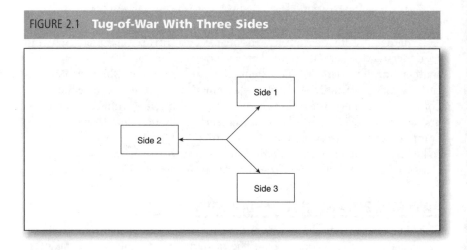

An important aspect of the tug-of-war is that the political terrain can change quickly. If a national election replaces a Republican majority in Congress with a Democratic majority, the environmental side gains the advantage of pulling downhill while the industry side must pull uphill. If public opinion shifts toward industry, perhaps due to high unemployment levels, this can tilt the terrain in favor of industry. If new interest groups join the industry side, they may provide the resources necessary to pull the policy toward less regulation. If interests leave the industry coalition, this may allow the environmental side to move policy toward greater regulation. Many actors and external events can affect which side of the tug-of-war has an advantage. Everything from 100-year floods, nuclear catastrophes in foreign lands, and economic recessions can affect the policymaking terrain. For instance, if one considers energy policy issues, the nuclear power plant meltdowns in Japan can affect the policymaking terrain because the meltdowns heightened the public's awareness of the risks of nuclear power.

For any moment in time, the tug-of-war between competing interests is likely to be at **equilibrium,** where neither side can pull the policy away from its current position. If a system reaches a steady state—the ball stops bouncing, the chemical reaction stops fizzing, the policy remains unchanged—then it is in equilibrium. Some equilibria are fragile—a slight bump starts the ball rolling again. Some equilibria are virtually invulnerable to all but the most extreme shocks. Modern skyscrapers are designed to sway but not topple. Except when under extreme duress, skyscrapers return to their equilibrium, which is standing tall and proud. Policy equilibria are vulnerable to change, but change often is difficult. In other words, there is policy inertia, which we will discuss in later chapters. The side opposing change has an advantage over the side desiring change because of the presence of policy inertia. Obviously, the tug-of-war metaphor works only when there is competition between sides. There is no tug-of-war if only one side is pulling.

The exchange model of interest-group influence assumes that participants in the political process—interest groups, public officials, and citizens—engage in exchanges to improve their economic, social, or political welfare. For example, a senator may agree to support a corporation's request for an increase in the price of a missile in hopes of having the corporation's support in the next election. The senator and the corporation believe the "exchange" will make both better off. Similarly, another senator may oppose gay rights legislation because he believes that the majority of his constituents oppose that legislation. The citizens opposing gay rights legislation "exchange" their vote for the senator in return for his siding with them on the issue. Finally, the Senate majority leader may offer that same senator a construction project in his state if the senator will support the majority leader's effort to overcome a filibuster by the opposition party.

To understand the connection between exchange theory and lobbying, consider the metaphor of the open-air, Middle Eastern bazaar. In the bazaar, interest groups and officials are buyers and sellers. An interest organization comes to the market, decides which policy option it wants to purchase, and bids for it. The bid might include electoral support, campaign contributions, or information that is valuable to the policymaker. As in the case in economic markets, competition among interest groups drives up the price of an official's policy support.[2] For example, if both sides on an issue are bidding for a legislator's support, the price he can demand for his support is higher than if only one side requests his assistance. An interesting aspect of the bazaar is that policymakers can charge different prices to different interest groups. If a buyer is from a legislator's district, the legislator might charge that interest group a lower price than he charges buyers who are not in his district.[3] A one-time purchaser of policy for an interest that is not part of the legislator's electoral constituency is treated differently than a regular, repeat customer from one's own state or district. Similarly, organized interests pay different prices to policymakers. If a policymaker has greater influence over a particular issue, his time is worth more than the time of a policymaker who has less influence.

Party leaders and committee chairs possess greater influence over the legislative process, so they can command higher prices.[4] Keeping these metaphors of interest-group influence in mind, we examine a case study of government policymaking.

THE NORTH AMERICAN FREE TRADE AGREEMENT[5]

When governments negotiate trade agreements, the policymaking process involves **rent seeking**, lobbying the government to improve an interest's economic position. What does rent seeking mean? There are two general ways that a firm can increase its profits. It can improve its productivity by adopting new technologies, organizing more efficiently, improving the skill and dedication of its workforce, and by expanding into new markets. We refer to these increases in profits as **economic rents**. The second way a firm can improve its profits is through political activity. A firm can lobby for a lower tax rate, a subsidy for its products, a waiver from a costly regulation, or for government to restrict the competition among firms in its industry. When firms look to improve profits through government actions, this constitutes rent seeking, and we refer to these additional profits as **political rents**.[6] Oftentimes, when scholars speak of rents or rent seeking they refer exclusively to political rents.

Economist and philosopher David Ricardo showed 200 years ago that eliminating trade barriers among nations generally improves the net welfare of all countries.[7] Free trade reduces the prices consumers pay, expands markets for producers, and increases overall economic efficiency. In his classic work, *Politics, Pressures and the Tariff,* E. E. Schattschneider—one of the most widely cited political scientists of the 1900s—explained that the benefits of free trade are difficult to realize.[8] The domestic interests that free trade will harm are organized and intense in their opposition while the supporters of free trade are less well organized and less intense. The reason for this imbalance is easy to see. If a trade agreement will destroy your business or eliminate your job, you are losing something of great value. In this situation, you are likely to try to punish the public officials who are responsible for your loss. In contrast, the interests that will benefit from free trade are often unaware that the agreement will help them. The future owners of new businesses that the agreement will create and the workers who will be hired because of the agreement often do not know who they are. Consumers, the largest set of beneficiaries, generally are unaware that free trade will benefit them. Members of Congress are likely cognizant of the benefits that free trade creates, but they also know that supporting free trade can cost them their job at the next election.

In various policy areas, members of Congress delegate authority to others to develop policy.[9] In matters of trade, members of Congress passed legislation that gave much of the authority to write free trade agreements to the president. The legislation enabled the president to act resolutely and limited the ability of legislators to block those agreements by adhering to **fast track** procedures. Congress and the president agreed in 1974 that the president would negotiate trade agreements using the following procedures. The president negotiates a trade agreement with other countries and transmits it as a bill to Congress. The House and Senate must introduce the president's bill on the first day their chamber is in session and must refer the bill to the committees that will hold hearings on the bill. *Congress cannot change the president's bill.* The committees have forty-five days after the bill's introduction to send the bill to the floor with their recommendation to pass or to defeat the trade agreement. Each chamber must vote within fifteen days after the bill is reported to the floor. The House and Senate can debate the bill for no more than twenty hours, and senators cannot filibuster the bill. The bill passes or fails by a simple majority vote. These procedures allow members and senators to tell their constituents who oppose the agreement, "It's not my fault. It's the president's bill." The procedures also substantially reduce the influence of special interests during the legislative process. Legislators and special interests cannot "pick apart" the agreement with exceptions for particular firms or industries. As Congress cannot change the president's bill, there is less reason to lobby Congress—the open-air bazaar is closed.

In 1990, Mexican president Carlos Salinas initiated discussions with the United States to pursue a comprehensive free trade agreement between the two countries. Salinas began those discussions in an unusual way. He requested the Business Roundtable, an organization made up of the chief executive officers of the largest U.S. corporations, to examine the benefits of a free trade agreement between the two countries.[10] Salinas was no stranger to U.S. institutions and politics. He completed a master's degree in public administration and a PhD in political economy from Harvard. Knowing that business interests in the United States generally supported freer trade, Salinas used the Business Roundtable to develop evidence that would convince President George H. W. Bush that a free trade agreement with Mexico would be beneficial to the United States. When negotiations between the two countries began, Canada, the largest U.S. trading partner, requested that the trade agreement include all three countries.

Each country expected to gain from increased trade. Mexico would gain as manufacturing and capital moved from Canada and the United States to Mexico to take advantage of lower wage rates and weaker environmental restrictions. All three countries expected that the free trade agreement would attract capital from Europe and Asia because goods manufactured in North America could be sold in all three countries without paying tariffs. The United States and Canada expected that their technology and more highly trained workforce would allow their firms to supplant Mexico's less productive firms. Finally, consumers in all three countries would gain as greater competition would exert downward pressure on prices. But the North American Free Trade Agreement (NAFTA) also would impose costs on some groups. Vegetable, fruit, and flower growers in the United States would experience stiff competition from growers in Mexico. NAFTA was likely to complete the destruction of the U.S. textile and glass making industries. Some workers in the manufacturing plants north of the Rio Grande would lose their jobs if corporations relocated their plants south of the border.

Despite the fact that the Democratic Party controlled Congress, President Bush did not expect substantial opposition to the trade agreement.[11] Bush believed that almost all manufacturing and commercial interests in the United States would gain from freer trade with Mexico. Although organized labor would oppose NAFTA, the White House believed that the unions would be unable to stop an agreement that would benefit so many economic sectors and would lower prices to consumers.[12]

Much to the administration's surprise, environmentalist, human rights, family farm, food safety, worker rights, and civil rights organizations joined labor unions to oppose any trade agreement with Mexico. The coalition took the name **Mobilization on Development, Trade, Labor, and the Environment (MODTLE).** As organized labor and environmentalists constitute two of the largest constituency groups for the Democratic Party, MODTLE made rapid progress in its efforts to stop the passage of NAFTA. House majority leader Dick Gephardt opposed NAFTA and pressured Democrats in the House to fight the agreement.

The swift mobilization of an opposing coalition led the White House to adopt a two-pronged strategy to obtain the agreement. First, the administration needed to neutralize the environmental groups so that legislators did not see a vote in favor of NAFTA as a vote against the environment. Second, a pro-NAFTA coalition had to mobilize rapidly and begin pressuring Congress. Daniel Esty, an assistant to Environmental Protection Agency (EPA) administrator William Reilly, was convinced that negotiations over NAFTA provided an excellent opportunity to insert environmental considerations into trade discussions. Reilly agreed and contacted **U.S. Trade Representative (USTR)** Carla Hills to set up a joint EPA–USTR trade and environmental working group. The goals of this group were to integrate environmental considerations into any trade agreement. In his book *Interpreting NAFTA,* Frederick Mayer quoted Esty, "We had a very clear strategy to neutralize the [environmental] issue."[13] That strategy involved splitting the environmental groups into those more radical groups that were close allies of organized labor and those groups that were more moderate.

President Bush began courting the more moderate environmental groups by inviting the heads of the Natural Resources Defense Council, the National Wildlife Federation, the Environmental Defense Fund, and The Nature Conservancy to a meeting at the White House. Bush indicated that he was in favor of making environmental issues part of NAFTA negotiations and would give environmental considerations a high priority. EPA administrator Reilly convinced the leaders of several environmental groups that NAFTA provided an opportunity to force Mexico to enforce its environmental laws and that NAFTA could have a positive impact on the environment. President Bush ordered his NAFTA negotiators to develop an action plan for cleaning up the environmental mess along the border. The Business Roundtable also encouraged the more moderate environmental groups to support NAFTA. Eastman Kodak CEO Kay Whitmore, the cochair of the Business Roundtable task force on NAFTA, was on the **World Wildlife Fund's (WWF)** board of directors. She arranged for Kodak to give WWF $2.5 million in 1992. The Business Roundtable took the lead in building the pro-NAFTA coalition that would lobby Congress. Jim Robinson of American Express and Kay Whitmore of Eastman Kodak led the effort. In a speech to his fellow CEOs, Robinson dramatized the issue by putting on a combat helmet and stating, "I want 2,000 sorties a day." He assigned each CEO the task of personally seeing three members of Congress. Robinson saw almost 200 members of Congress.[14] The Business Roundtable also put together and coordinated an ad hoc coalition of more than 2,000 companies and trade associations to lobby for the trade agreement. Robinson and Whitmore also were the cochairs of the **Advisory Committee on Trade Policy and Negotiations (ACTPN).** ACTPN coordinated the activities of thirty advisory committees that helped develop the U.S. negotiating positions.[15]

Despite the efforts of Robinson and Whitmore to develop a broad-based lobbying coalition, the anti-NAFTA coalition was well ahead of the pro-NAFTA coalition. Fortunately for the White House, the Senate Committee on Finance and the House Committee on Ways and Means were the congressional committees that would work with Bush in drafting NAFTA. The chairs of these committees, Sen. Lloyd Bentsen, D-TX, and Rep. Dan Rostenkowski, D-IL, strongly supported free trade. Bentsen was particularly interested in helping Mexico achieve rapid economic growth.[16] To prevent the anti-NAFTA coalition from defeating the agreement, Bush requested that Bentsen and Rostenkowski write all House members and senators to urge them not to take a position on NAFTA until after the White House had an opportunity to work out its action plan. The Bentsen–Rostenkowski letters bought the time the Business Roundtable needed to mobilize the pro-NAFTA forces.

When President Bush released his action plan for environmental protection and worker safety, environmental organizations found the plan unacceptable. Several of the previously pro-NAFTA groups switched sides. Almost simultaneously with the release of Bush's action plan, an event occurred that nearly ended the NAFTA negotiations. The U.S. Marine Mammal Protection Act prohibits U.S. fishers from using purse seine fishing nets to catch tuna because the method kills too many dolphins. The legislation also prohibits the importation of tuna caught using purse seine nets. In 1991, Mexico asked an arbitration panel of the **General Agreement on Tariffs and Trade (GATT)** to rule that the United States violated its GATT obligations when it embargoed Mexican tuna. Mexico argued that GATT rules do not allow one country to restrict trade by forcing other countries to obey a U.S. law—even to protect animal health or exhaustible natural resources. On September 3, 1991, the GATT arbitration panel ruled that the United States was in violation of GATT agreements.

Congress was furious with the GATT decision. It appeared to confirm everyone's fears that NAFTA would lead to environmental degradation. Although President Salinas quickly announced that Mexico would ignore the GATT ruling and announced a new law prohibiting purse seine nets by Mexican fishing boats, the GATT decision was a major blow to the pro-NAFTA effort. The decision made it difficult for Democrats to support a trade agreement with Mexico. The GATT ruling strengthened the lobbying position of environmental groups. The groups enlisted Sen. Max Baucus, D-MT, the chair of the international trade subcommittee, to press the Bush administration for more concessions for environmental interests. Rep. Bill Richardson, D-NM, a Latino and a strong supporter of NAFTA, warned President Bush that NAFTA would "go down the tubes" unless the environmental concerns of Democrats in the House were met. Richardson asserted that the environment was the issue that would determine the future of NAFTA.[17]

As already noted, President Bush had not expected the economic interests that NAFTA might harm to be effective in the lobbying of Congress. Bush miscalculated. Hundreds of interests in all three countries wanted protection. Two economic interests in the United States were causing the president special problems. The first was Florida's fruit, vegetable, and flower growers. Florida's position as a swing state in U.S. presidential elections is longstanding, and neither political party could afford to ignore Florida's interests. The president would need to negotiate a side agreement with Mexico to protect Florida's growers. U.S. automakers presented another obstacle to NAFTA. Bush had expected strong support for NAFTA from automakers and auto parts corporations as U.S. companies produce almost 70 percent of cars sold in Mexico. The auto industry, however, was not supporting NAFTA. Any trade agreement that threatened the industry threatened the largest U.S. manufacturing sector and its labor force. The potential problem with NAFTA from the auto industry's perspective was that Canada and Mexico assemble a large number of cars and trucks with Japanese, Korean, Italian, French, Swedish, and German parts. Although workers assemble the vehicles in North America, the parts come largely from outside of North America. U.S. automakers and auto parts manufacturers wanted the trade agreement to treat as an import any vehicle with more than 30 percent of its parts made outside of North America. Restricting access to imported parts would force Mexico and Canada to rely on parts made in the United States. Mexico and Canada found the 30-percent figure unacceptable and wanted the percentage of foreign parts allowable to be at least 65 percent.

By the end of 1991, it became clear that the final NAFTA agreement among the three nations might not receive congressional approval. President Bush's approval rating dropped throughout 1992, and the election of a Democrat to the White House looked likely. An incumbent president holds considerable advantages, but an event beyond Bush's control hurt his reelection chances. Third-party candidate H. Ross Perot helped to make NAFTA a highly visible issue as he had staked his political future on defeating the agreement. Unlike so many third-party candidates, Perot had a personal fortune that he freely used to maintain a professional, high-profile campaign. In a presidential debate with Bush and Democratic presidential candidate Bill Clinton, Perot gave the most memorable quote of the 1992 election campaign: if NAFTA became law, Americans would "hear a giant sucking sound of jobs being pulled out of this country." Democratic presidential candidate Jerry Brown and Republican candidate Patrick Buchanan also made defeating NAFTA a major part of their campaigns. In a campaign speech before young conservative activists, Buchanan declared that America was in the grips of the greatest invasion in history, the invasion of illegal aliens from Mexico. Buchanan further asserted that the invasion was eroding America's tax base, swamping social services, and undermining America's social cohesion. Perot garnered almost 19 percent of the popular vote in the 1992 presidential election, and newcomer Clinton won the election with 43 percent.[18]

Before he clinched the Democratic nomination, Clinton had supported NAFTA. After his nomination, however, Clinton said little on the issue. He did not want to alienate two of his party's major constituencies: (1) organized labor and (2) environmentalists. Clinton did not renounce his support of NAFTA, but he maintained that it must be changed in ways that protected the environment and workers' rights. Several of Clinton's key advisors urged him to abandon NAFTA because the issue would split the Democratic Party. Clinton, however, decided to support the agreement. His position led to the unusual situation of a majority of a president's own party opposing him on a major piece of legislation. For NAFTA to pass in the U.S. House of Representatives, Clinton needed approximately 100 Democrats to vote for the agreement. In the winter and spring of 1993, this looked highly unlikely. Democrats in Congress experienced heavy lobbying from the Citizens Trade Campaign, a well-funded coalition of grassroots organizations including labor, environmental, farm, consumer, human rights, and religious groups.[19] To overcome this opposition, President Clinton negotiated side agreements with Mexico concerning NAFTA's implementation. The most important of these would create an international enforcement agency to oversee Mexico's compliance with its own labor and environmental laws.

Even with these side agreements, NAFTA appeared dead. Public opinion had swung sharply against NAFTA. More and more people believed Ross Perot's message that NAFTA was a conspiracy between the Mexican government's corrupt politicians and Wall Street. Issues with extremely high symbolic meanings including illegal immigration, environmental degradation, Mexican drug cartels, and government corruption became highly salient. By July 1993, the support among the American public for NAFTA had dropped to 25 percent. The AFL–CIO's vote count in the House of Representatives in July showed the anti-NAFTA forces had a majority of legislators committed to voting against the agreement.[20] Organized labor confidently announced that they would defeat any Democrat who voted in favor of NAFTA.

Another obstacle the White House faced in getting Congress to approve NAFTA was the unwillingness of many pro-NAFTA coalition members to lobby for the agreement. These members wanted to wait until particular provisions were included in the side agreements that the Clinton administration was negotiating. For example, U.S. automakers agreed to support NAFTA, but that support was contingent on limiting the percentage of non-North American parts that Canadian and Mexican vehicles could include. Moderate environmental groups would support NAFTA only if the side agreements included sufficient funding and regulatory enforcement to clean up the border pollution caused by the **maquiladora** factories.[21] Clinton also had to deal with disagreements among members of the pro-NAFTA coalition. Sugar and corn interests in the United States fought over how Mexico's use of corn syrup sweeteners in food processing would affect the amount of Mexican sugar that the United States could import. The Business Roundtable tried to assist the White House by pressuring businesses to lobby their legislators. The Business Roundtable increased its efforts and formed another special lobbying organization, **USA*NAFTA,** giving it $2 million to organize business lobbying for the treaty. Despite its resources, USA*NAFTA had little success getting corporations to do anything more than add their names to the organization's membership.

The White House attempted to overcome the obstacles to NAFTA by creating a set of positive symbols. Clinton highlighted the bipartisan nature of support for the agreement by bringing former presidents Ford, Carter, and Bush to the White House to speak on the benefits of NAFTA to Americans. President Carter reinforced the use of symbolic politics when he criticized Ross Perot as "a demagogue" with unlimited financial resources who preyed on the fears and the uncertainties of the American public. Clinton also brought every American Nobel Prize winner in economics to Washington to talk about NAFTA's importance to the American economy. Clinton used his own fear-based message when he argued that if the United States did not enter into this agreement, Mexico and Canada would form agreements with America's key economic competitors: Japan and the European Common Market.

The White House also took a very high-stakes gamble. Vice President Al Gore challenged Ross Perot to a televised debate on CNN. Media experts predicted that Perot, a master of televised town hall meetings and thirty-minute political infomercials, would trounce the "wooden" Gore. The opposite occurred: Gore trounced Perot. Gore arrived well prepared and practiced. When Gore gave Perot the "gift" of a picture of former representatives Reed Smoot and Willis Hawley, Perot was visibly flustered. Smoot and Hawley had devised the most economically devastating tariff policy of the 1900s, a policy that many economists link to the onset of the Great Depression. Perot was obviously ill prepared, and he remained uncomfortable throughout the debate with Gore. The fallout from the debate largely eliminated Perot's ability to influence the outcome of NAFTA.

President Clinton moved forward with the side agreements covering pollution, worker health and safety, and workers' rights. The president promised hundreds of millions of dollars in worker retraining programs for anyone who lost their job because of NAFTA. The United States and Mexico created the North American Development Bank and pledged $8 billion over ten years to finance projects that would clean up the environment along the United States–Mexico border.

Clinton then began using pork barrel projects to buy the votes of individual legislators. As Diana Evans showed in her case study of Clinton's actions, the president provided numerous legislators special benefits for their districts.[22] For example, provisions in the side agreements with Mexico protected Florida's sugar, citrus, and tomato farming interests for fifteen years. Other concessions covered peanut farmers and flower growers. Clinton promised the government's purchase of two additional C-17 cargo planes to obtain the vote of the House member where the planes were built. Ultimately, the pro-NAFTA forces won the vote in the House 234–200. The Senate voted 61–38 to pass NAFTA. On January 1, 1994, NAFTA became law.

COMPETING MODELS OF GROUP INFLUENCE ON POLICY

Political scientists disagree over the extent to which organized interests help or harm the democratic process and the degree to which inequalities in the resources of competing interests bias the policy process. The exchange and neopluralism models of interest-group influence reviewed in this book reach nearly opposite conclusions. The exchange model describes a political process in which organized interests "buy" policies by providing resources to policymakers in exchange for favorable policy decisions. Resource-rich interests can make more and better exchanges than can resource-poor interests. The exchange model also indicates that many interests are unrepresented because large groups such as consumers, taxpayers, and low-income populations cannot overcome the free rider problem. Unorganized interests and interest groups with few resources cannot shop for policies, so they are unable to make exchanges. The general conclusion of exchange theory is that interest organizations harm the democratic process because the uneven distribution of resources among interests will bias the political process in favor of resource-rich interests.[23]

Neopluralist theory views the political process in a more favorable light. It argues that almost all interests can influence policymakers either directly through lobbying or indirectly through political parties and elections. Although interest organizations have different levels of resources, for most issues the competing sides receive adequate representation. In addition, political parties and elections can tilt the political terrain in favor of broader public opinion, and this helps to offset the greater resources of better-organized and wealthier groups. Indeed, Mark Smith notes that a powerful business interest is readily checked when the policy issue at stake is salient and public opinion runs counter to business interests.[24] For neopluralists, interest groups are democratic institutions that help link citizen preferences to policy outcomes.

How did these two very different views of interest-group influence evolve? We consider that next.

Pluralism and Elitism

For almost four decades, a majority of political scientists taught the pluralist model of interest-group influence. The theory dates back to the 1951 publication of *The Governmental Process* by David B. Truman.[25] Truman maintained that interest groups form when an economic or social disturbance adversely affects people or institutions. For example, when industrial pollution created severe health problems for many Americans, environmental interest groups formed and demanded that government develop regulations to reduce pollution. Government responded by creating the EPA and by passing such laws such as the Clean Air and the Clean Water Acts. Truman predicted that when new groups mobilize and achieve a policy change, that change will disturb other interests, and they will mobilize their own interest groups. For example, the government's regulation of pollution negatively affected numerous industries. These industries responded by forming trade associations and business coalitions to fight further regulation. The effective mobilization of one interest encourages countermobilization by other interests, so Truman expected groups to form in waves until all those interests affected by an issue organize for political action. Once all interests were mobilized, a new policy equilibrium would result. Pluralist theory fits the tug-of-war metaphor of the policymaking process. *Pluralists emphasized competing interests.*

A great advantage of an ideally functioning pluralist democracy is that as the importance of an issue to a group increases, its levels of effort and influence increase as well. Policymakers respond not only to the number of people affected by a disturbance but also to the level of harm that the disturbance creates. When those who care more about an issue expend more resources lobbying than those who care less, the policies resulting from interest-group competition will come closer to maximizing net social welfare than would policies that reflected only the number of individuals on either side of the issue. To see intuitively how this might work, assume that you and two friends are choosing a restaurant for tonight's dinner. Two of you prefer the local Chinese restaurant, but Chinese food makes the third person ill. Even though a majority favors the Chinese restaurant, the intense preference of the third person means that you probably would choose not to eat Chinese.

The observant reader might wonder whether all interests will mobilize after a disturbance. Free riding does not magically disappear in the wake of a disturbance. Even those individuals most severely affected by a policy change might have difficulty mobilizing. A strong incentive to mobilize is not the same as an actual mobilization. If we look at the policymaking process in NAFTA, Truman would likely have argued that the process worked exactly as he predicted. Business interests in all three countries saw free trade as being in their interest. These groups formed a powerful coalition that was able to defeat the groups attempting to defeat the agreement. Many of the groups that NAFTA would have harmed most, however, secured political rents. Flower growers and carmakers secured protection from competition. In addition, environmental groups received assurances that Mexico would enforce its pollution laws. In short, pluralists would argue that the final agreement reflected the relative size and the intensity of the affected interests.

While Truman was developing the pluralist model, sociologists were constructing an alternative explanation of how governments make policy. Many prominent sociologists argued that a wealthy elite decided every important policy. In other words, while there may be many interest organizations, there is only one group that really matters: the rich. Two early proponents of elite theory were Floyd Hunter and C. Wright Mills. In his 1953 book *Community Power Structure,* Hunter investigated the politics of Atlanta, Georgia. Hunter asked people who he considered knowledgeable about Atlanta's politics to identify the city's politically powerful people. He then interviewed those individuals and asked who else should be on his list. By securing interviews in this fashion, Hunter could uncover the network of political movers and shakers. If the same names came up in almost every interview, the network would look very different than if new names popped up. Hunter's study indicated that the same people were named over and over, suggesting that a relatively small group of people controlled Atlanta's policy process. The most important of these policymakers was the head of Coca-Cola, Atlanta's largest private sector employer. The other persons identified as powerful were major landowners, top business and industry executives, and corporate lawyers. Almost all of these individuals had attended elite colleges and universities, lived in the same neighborhoods, belonged to the same social organizations, and sat on the boards of directors of each other's companies. Hunter believed that his book demonstrated empirically that political power in America's cities was concentrated in an elite based on wealth.

Another book, *The Power Elite* by C. Wright Mills, looked at national policymaking. It also concluded that a narrow elite controlled the national policy process. Mills demonstrated that the individuals who occupied the powerful positions in the nation's military, industry, and government had similar backgrounds, education, and wealth. What did it matter, Mills asked, if there are competing political parties when the candidates of both parties are multimillionaires who share the same social and economic background? Mills would no doubt have noted that the 2004 Democratic and Republican presidential nominees were wealthy Yale graduates and were members of the same secret society while at Yale. The Democratic nominee in 2008 was a multimillionaire who attended Harvard Law School; his Republican opponent attended the United States Naval Academy and was married to one of the richest women in America. In 2012, the Democratic and Republican candidates graduated from Harvard Law School. According to Mills, the owners of America's giant corporations are able to put their family members and friends in the key policymaking positions.

Hunter and Mills would have no problem explaining NAFTA: the dominant capitalist class obtained exactly what it wanted—the ability to expand its
profits by reducing labor costs and avoiding environmental regulations. Elite
theorists would argue that NAFTA is just another part of capitalist globaliza-
tion that drives wages down to the lowest possible levels. The hard-won gains
that unions had achieved in the United States and Canada would be lost to
low-cost laborers in Mexico. Research by Michael Dreiling and Brian Wolf uses
elite theory to explain which environmental groups supported NAFTA and
which opposed it.[26] Their research shows the corporate contributions to the
environmental groups that supported NAFTA. Recall that Kay Whitmore, the
CEO of Eastman Kodak and cofounder of the lobbying coalition USA*NAFTA,
held a seat on the WWF board of directors. Eastman Kodak gave a $2.5 million
contribution to WWF during the NAFTA debate. In a separate article, Dreiling
showed that the most active corporations were closely linked through inter-
locking memberships on their boards of directors, membership in the Business
Roundtable, and close personal ties.[27]

Elite theory cannot explain how unions in the United States and Canada
obtained high wages in the first place. Some policy outcomes seem to corrobo-
rate the elite rule, but the elite model fails to explain the policy process. What
was the *process* that allowed for the creation of labor unions and environmental regulations that reduced corporate profits in the United States and Canada?
If wealthy capitalists actually rule, how did such issues as consumer protection
and occupational safety legislation become part of the political agenda and
succeed in becoming law?

Robert Dahl, a political scientist at Yale, wrote the pluralist response to
elite theory. In his book *Who Governs?*, Dahl points out a key weakness in the
method elite theorists used to reach their conclusion. By asking people, "Who
rules Atlanta?" Hunter assumed that there was ruling elite. The question, "Who
is influential in [your hometown]?" is framed in a way to encourage you to
provide a name or names. You are likely to respond with the name or names of
people such as the town's wealthiest citizens. In addition, because Hunter then
asked the individuals named to identify other important decision makers, it
should not surprise us that the first interviewees named persons whom they
knew and with whom they socialized. Similarly, C. Wright Mills' demonstra-
tion that the wealthiest people in the United States were closely connected did
not demonstrate that these persons use their wealth for political influence or
that they agree concerning which policy options the nation should choose.

Dahl argued that a better method for determining who influences policy
outcomes in a city is to first discover which policy issues received the greatest
political attention in the city and then find out who participated in deciding
those issues. When Dahl used this approach to study policymaking in New
Haven, Connecticut, he discovered that many organized interests participated
in politics and were influential. Each interest, however, had influence only in
their **issue arena.** For example, organizations representing teachers were influential in education policy, and organizations representing realtors were influential

in New Haven's urban planning decisions. Because different interests were influential in different policy arenas, Dahl concluded that political power in New Haven was widely dispersed. In addition, Dahl's research showed that interest groups were not the only institutions that mattered in policymaking. Elections forced policymakers to be accountable not only to organized interests but also to the preferences of voters who were not members of organized interest groups. Political parties competed for the votes of these individuals by offering those policies they desired.

Dahl also argued that to understand policymaking, researchers must study it as a process that occurs over time rather than as a decision reached at a single point in time. The policymaking process involves mutual adjustment among many individuals, groups, and institutions. Interest groups might be important in the policy process but so were political parties and competitive elections.

The politics surrounding NAFTA support many of Dahl's expectations. NAFTA became an issue when a Republican was president. Republicans are generally more responsive to business concerns than to labor concerns. Because the Business Roundtable strongly supported NAFTA, a Republican administration was more likely to initiate a free trade agreement. NAFTA also illustrates the process of mutual adjustment among interest organizations. Ultimately, NAFTA passed only when Clinton, a moderate Democrat, became president and convinced enough Democratic legislators to vote for the agreement to gain its passage. Clinton's success stemmed from his ability to satisfy a critical Democratic constituency group: environmentalists.

For several years, proponents of elite theory and pluralism fought over which model of group influence best described policymaking in the United States. Within political science, pluralism won the battle. Numerous studies of individual issues found that different interests were active in different policy arenas. The research also found that on important issues, there generally were competing policy alternatives and each side had sufficient resources to lobby effectively. Whether the research examined local, state, or national politics, parties and elections were critical in determining which problems governments would address and which policy choices government would make.

Although pluralist theory won its battle with elite theory, two important critiques of pluralism remained valid. As E. E. Schattschneider pointed out, "The flaw in the pluralist heaven is that the heavenly chorus sings with a strong upper-class accent."[28] In other words, although multiple groups may compete over issues, most group leaders and members active in interest organizations have an education and income well above the national average. Even among citizen action groups, the interests represented are predominantly those of the upper middle class.[29] In other words, poor people are not at the forefront of policymaking even when their own interests are at stake.

A second problem with pluralism concerns its research method. If the elite method of asking who rules was flawed, so was Dahl's method. Dahl urged political scientists to study who participates in deciding the important policy issues in a city, state, or country. Peter Bachrach and Morton Baratz showed in their article "The Two Faces of Power" that if political scientists study only issues that government addresses, they may miss the most important political decisions—the decision to squelch entirely some issues.[30] For example, if researchers studied the policies addressed in Birmingham, Alabama, in 1950, they would have missed the fact that whites enjoyed rights and privileges denied to blacks. Segregation and the unequal opportunities of whites and blacks were not issues that reached the political agenda. The pluralist method would have missed these issues because no one in the South who opposed segregation could get local government officials to consider changing the laws. Bachrach and Baratz argued that perhaps the most useful power an elite can have is the power to prevent government from considering issues. In other words, power has two faces. We see one face when studying issues that reach the political agenda. The other face, however, is hidden, and the pluralist methodology cannot uncover it or observe it. Yet this other face of power may be the more important one.

The Challenge of Exchange Models

Although pluralist theory emerged largely intact from the challenges of elite theorists, a more serious test comes from political economy. In his highly influential book, *The Logic of Collective Action*, Mancur Olson demonstrated that pluralism's most important assumption contains a logical flaw. Pluralism assumes that when an economic, social, or political disturbance negatively affects people, they would see that the best way to influence government was to form an interest group. "Not necessarily," said Olson. "A rational person would do nothing if he could free ride on the efforts of others."

To see Olson's point, assume that you attend a public university and the State Board of Higher Education asks the state legislature to raise the tuition at your college by $400 per year. You think to yourself, if each student donates just $20, we can hire a lobbying firm that may be able to prevent the tuition hike. Now ask yourself, how difficult will it be to contact all the affected students? Even if you can figure out an inexpensive way to contact them, can you convince them to donate to the cause? If someone contacted you and asked for a $20 donation, would you contribute? Olson argued that if you are rational, you will not contribute. Suppose there are 20,001 students at your school. If everyone donates, the group will have $400,020 to pay for the lobbying effort. If you choose not to contribute, the group will have $400,000. As a rational individual, you know that the probability is nearly zero that your $20 will determine whether the lobbying succeeds or fails (see Box 2.2). If your contribution is not going to make a difference, why contribute? If the lobbying effort is successful, you will pay the lower tuition whether or not you contributed. Being rational, you will free ride and hope that your fellow students are irrational.[31]

Olson argued that as the number of people desiring a collective benefit grows larger, it becomes harder to overcome the collective action problem. Consider recent events. The near collapse of numerous large investment banks in 2008 caused a worldwide recession that caused millions of workers to lose their jobs and cost investors trillions of dollars. After that debacle, a large

BOX 2.2   **Corporate Versus Individual Lobbying**

Congress passed the Dodd–Frank Wall Street Reform and Consumer Protection Act in July 2010. The legislation gave the Federal Reserve substantial new power to regulate investment banks. Among the law's provisions were new measures to prevent future government bailouts, rules concerning the trading of derivatives and other complex financial instruments, and new trading standards for hedge funds. The law's provisions significantly affected how the largest investment banks do business.

During the fifteen months that Congress considered the bill, JPMorgan Chase, Goldman Sachs, Wells Fargo, Bank of America, and Citibank spent a total of $24.7 million lobbying Congress. JPMorgan Chase spent the most ($7.4 million) while Bank of America spent the least (*only* $3.86 million). The American Banking Association spent an additional $7.5 million lobbying Congress. The banks used more than 130 lobbyists to influence the legislation.[32] The obvious question for Mancur Olson's theory of collective action concerns why some banks did not choose to free ride on the efforts of the others. For example, Bank of America was having severe financial difficulties. Free riding would have saved it almost $4 million.

There are several reasons that the banks chose to lobby. First, each of the banks had access to different sets of public officials. Bank of America, for example, had large corporate offices employing thousands of people not only in its home office in Charlotte but also in Boston, Atlanta, New York, and San Francisco. Each of these offices gave the bank a lobbying advantage with the members of Congress who represented those cities. Second, the CEO of Bank of America believed that the expected marginal benefit from its lobbying was greater than $3.8 million. The bank expected that its lobbyists would address provisions of the legislation that were more important to Bank of America than to the other banks. In other words, Bank of America lobbied not only for collective goods but also for private goods. Third, the five largest banks often coordinate their lobbying. If Bank of America became a free rider on the Dodd–Frank legislation, the other four banks might refuse to cooperate with it in the future. The $3.8 million spent on Dodd–Frank may have been a small price to pay for continuing cooperation.

Notice that the three reasons that encouraged Bank of America not to free ride did not apply to individuals who supported the Dodd–Frank legislation. Regardless of where an individual lived, it is unlikely that *her* influence with a representative or senator was sufficiently large to affect the legislator's behavior on a major issue. Second, any contribution an individual might make to a citizen action group lobbying for strong regulations was unlikely to have an expected marginal benefit greater than the cost of her contribution. Even if she gave $1,000 to a group for the specific purpose of lobbying on Dodd–Frank, the likelihood that the additional $1,000 would affect the policy outcome would not differ significantly from zero. Third, a person who contributed to lobbying on Dodd–Frank did not have an ongoing cooperative lobbying relationship with other citizens. They were unaware of her contribution. In the language of game theory, the banks were involved in a repeated game while the individual was involved in a onetime game. As we will discuss in chapters 6 and 8, cooperative behavior in a repeated game with the same partners often is rational while cooperation in a onetime game is irrational. (For a discussion of continuing versus onetime games, see Box 8.1 in chapter 8.)

percentage of Americans probably supported greater government regulation of the financial institutions. Few people, however, contributed to the efforts of citizen action groups that pushed for stricter regulations. In contrast to the tiny percentage of people who contributed to lobbying for increased regulations, the largest investment banks easily mounted a massive lobbying effort to oppose new regulations. From January 2009 to March 2010, the five largest investment banks in the United States spent a total of $24.7 million lobbying officials in the federal government (see Box 2.2). Why did the supporters of stricter banking regulation free ride while the investment banks contributed to their collective effort? Olson argued that small groups have several advantages. First, the small number of people or institutions that share the benefit makes it easier for them to coordinate their lobbying strategy and to pressure each other into contributing to the collective effort. Second, while an average citizen's contribution to a citizen action group almost certainly will not affect the success or failure of the lobbying effort to impose new regulations, the contribution of each bank could make a substantial difference in the success of their lobbying effort. Third, each bank probably calculated that stricter regulations could cost it hundreds of millions of dollars. For example, if the Wall Street investment bank Goldman Sachs expected that weakened regulations would improve its profits by $400 million and the probability that its $3.98 million contribution would successfully weaken those regulations was just .01, then its expenditure of $3.98 million on lobbying was rational. The expected value of the contribution (.01 * $400 million = $4 million) was greater than the cost of its contribution. A rational individual or a profit-seeking firm surely will contribute to a lobbying effort if the expected gain is greater than the cost of the contribution.

In summary, Olson's analysis demonstrates that Truman's assumption that economically rational individuals will participate in a large interest group pursuing collective goods is incorrect. Olson's analysis also suggests why the few individuals who have a large stake in a policy outcome are likely to organize and lobby while many individuals who have a small stake in a policy are unlikely to organize and lobby. Olson's analysis leads to a paradoxical conclusion: in a democracy where interest groups are influential, the few are likely to defeat the many.

At this point, an attentive reader might be thinking that while Olson's argument may be consistent with the economists' vision of how rationally self-interested individuals should act, groups representing large sets of people do exist and lobby effectively. If Olson was right, why are there groups of workers, environmentalists, consumers, opponents of abortion rights, proponents of abortion rights, and taxpayers? These are large groups. Olson responded that groups representing such interests generally provide their members private goods that are worth the cost of becoming a group member. Olson labeled the benefits that only group members receive **selective incentives**. John Chubb and Kenneth Godwin have shown that the citizen action groups that survive and prosper are those that provide the most valuable selective incentives relative to the cost of group membership.[33] For example, the Consumers Union, a citizen action group with more than a million members, provides its members the magazine *Consumer Reports*. The magazine supplies valuable information about the quality and safety of consumer products and probably saves its readers hundreds of dollars each year. Similarly, the **AARP (formerly known as the American Association of Retired Persons),** one of Washington's most powerful lobbying organizations, has a low membership fee ($16) and provides its members discounts on hotels, rental cars, car insurance, and a host of other benefits. AARP members also receive *AARP The Magazine* and *AARP Bulletin,* publications that provide information useful to older adults. Sometimes these selective incentives actually generate profits for the group. *AARP The Magazine* and the *AARP Bulletin* are the two most widely distributed magazines in the United States.[34] Any widely distributed magazine going to a niche audience generates most of its revenues from advertising. Indeed, AARP materials are heavily laden with advertisements for goods and services aimed at older Americans.

Olson maintained that when groups use selective incentives to overcome the free rider problem, the group's lobbying is a **by-product** of the organization. In other words, members do not join a group like the National Rifle Association (NRA) to help pay for lobbying; they join to obtain the private goods that only NRA members can receive. To the extent that selective incentives provide valuable benefits, group members who disagree with the NRA's policy priorities are likely to overlook a group's political stance. Certainly, a portion of the AARP's membership does not agree with the organization's lobbying efforts on behalf of liberal policies.

Olson was not the only economist in the 1960s and 1970s exploring the intersection between politics and economics. The Nobel laureate George Stigler examined the rent seeking opportunities for firms and interest groups. In "The Theory of Economic Regulation," Stigler claimed that regulations do not exist to protect workers, consumers, or the general public.[35] Rather, producers demand regulations that will increase their profits and decrease competition. Stigler wrote, "[My] general hypothesis is: every industry or occupation that has enough political power to utilize the state will seek to control entry and restrict competition."[36] For example, sugar farmers in the United States have organized and lobbied Congress to regulate sugar production and set the wholesale price for sugar. The regulations limit how much sugar the United States can import and how much sugar American farmers can grow. These regulations increased sugar growers' profits and kept sugar prices in the United States substantially higher than sugar prices on the world market. It is highly unlikely that sugar consumers demanded regulations so that they could pay higher prices.

At the same time that Olson and Stigler were arguing that organized producers typically will defeat unorganized consumers, political scientists were developing a parallel theory based on political institutions that came to similar conclusions. Theodore Lowi, a political scientist at Cornell University, developed one of the more important explanations of why the few defeat the many.

Lowi argued that the design of America's political institutions—specifically the interrelationships among congressional committees, executive agencies, and interest groups—helps producer interests and harms the public. Sugar growers are not the only farm group that receives government subsidies. Corn, wheat, rice, soybeans, and timber receive similar subsidies. In 2009, the U.S. government provided more than $200 million in subsidies to tobacco farmers, a group whose product causes cancer and kills people all around the world.[37] The ability of agricultural interests to use the political system to gain higher prices and restrict competition does not fit easily with pluralist theory. For example, several government policies such as government guaranteed prices for corn and subsidies for ethanol made from corn keep the price of corn artificially high. These high prices affect many other interests. Livestock producers depend on corn to feed their cattle, pigs, and chickens; producers of candy and many other processed foods use large quantities of high fructose corn syrup; households consume significant amounts of corn and products that use corn syrup; and the import tax on ethanol produced from sugar cane raises energy costs for everyone. Pluralist theory would predict that producers of livestock and processed foods as well as household consumers would organize and lobby against high corn prices. If Truman was right about mobilization and countermobilization, why have those interests harmed by high corn prices failed to lobby to reduce or eliminate government policies that increase the price of corn?

Lowi maintained that opponents of high corn prices have not been able to reduce the price of corn because farm subsidy policies are made in **policy subsystems.** The opponents of subsidies do not participate in these subsystems. These subsystems, sometimes called **iron triangles,** consist of congressional subcommittees that decide the policies that regulate and subsidize a product, the bureaucratic agency that implements the regulations and subsidies, and the interest organizations that represent the producers. For example, the iron triangle for corn policy would consist of (1) the congressional subcommittees that make the policies that affect corn production and corn prices; (2) the U.S. Department of Agriculture (USDA), which provides loans, scientific research, and other benefits to corn growers; and (3) the corn producers' trade associations. Lowi argued that the three corners of the triangle engage in mutually beneficial exchanges. The congressional subcommittees give subsidies to corn producers and determine USDA budgets. USDA provides farmers low-cost loans, influences the amount of corn grown, and provides corn farmers with research and other forms of assistance. The corn farmers and their interest organizations provide campaign contributions, votes, and other resources to the members of the subcommittees. The corn producer groups also lobby in support of greater funding for the USDA.

A key characteristic of Lowi's policy subsystems is that the beneficiaries in one subsystem do not challenge policies of other subsystems. Congress avoids conflict between corn farmers and livestock producers by providing subsidies to both groups. From Lowi's perspective, policy subsystems are like office holiday parties. Each subsystem (or office) holds its own party, and everyone in the subsystem—the producer groups, bureaucrats in the relevant agency, and the legislators on the subcommittees—gets an invitation to the party and receives valuable presents. No one who attends one office party objects to the gifts that attendees at other parties receive. The best part of this system of expensive parties is that the people not invited to the party—consumers and taxpayers—pay the bills. Among the results of this mutual noninterference are an increase in the size of government and a reduction in economic efficiency. Lowi named the entire policymaking process "**interest-group liberalism**." It is liberal in that it maintains a clear role for government and that the government offers "solutions" to policy failures. The solutions, however, are largely favors distributed to organized interests.

The exchange model and interest-group liberalism argue that the interests that benefit from a political rent know that they have received the political rent and reward the officials who provided it. At the same time, those who pay the costs of the rent often are unaware of the policies they are funding. This is the best of all possible worlds for policymakers. The abundant protections for various interest groups in NAFTA illustrate the exchanges inherent to interest-group liberalism. Numerous analyses of the relationship between an interest group's campaign contributions and a legislator's position on the agreement support the exchange perspective.[38] In addition, studies of union campaign contributions to individual legislators before and after Congress voted on NAFTA show that unions withdrew support from legislators who voted in favor of the trade agreement.[39] President Clinton clearly used the provision of private goods to interests in legislators' districts to "buy" those legislators' votes. Clinton's actions caused a lobbyist opposing NAFTA to comment, "Clinton won the [NAFTA] vote the old-fashioned way. He bought it."[40]

Some of the exchanges that occurred in NAFTA were between elected officials and outside interests, but there were also exchanges among various outside interests working to develop lobbying coalitions. Exchanges also occurred among elected officials as they jockeyed for more legislative support. In fact, the Middle Eastern bazaar with hundreds of buyers and sellers and thousands of exchanges portrays well the multitudinous deals made during the NAFTA policy process.

In summary, the exchange model of interest-group influence yields five major arguments:

1. Participants in the policy process—officials, organized interest, and voters—make rational exchanges.

2. The free rider problem makes it difficult for large sets of individuals to organize and enter the political marketplace. In contrast, institutions such as corporations, trade associations, and state and local governments are structured in a way that facilitates political action.

3. Two of the most important resources in politics—information and the ability to monitor the policymaking process—are expensive. Smaller,

wealthier organizations, therefore, have a considerable advantage. Most citizens cannot afford to generate information or monitor closely the policy process. They remain "rationally ignorant" of most policymakers' activities.

4. An elected official is more responsive to those organized interests that have concerns congruent to those of his constituents. If an elected official does not "charge lower prices" to his constituents, his opponent in the next election can call this to the attention of voters. Thus, politicians indirectly "sell policies" for constituents' votes. This is particularly true where the policy conflict is over highly collective goods that are highly visible to voters.

5. Bargaining takes place among all participants in the policymaking process. Interest groups bargain not only with policymakers but also with other interest groups. For example, the WWF appears to have given its support for NAFTA in exchange for a large gift from Eastman Kodak and a pledge by President Bush to force Mexico to pursue more environmentally sound policies. Similarly, policymakers make exchanges with each other. President Clinton exchanged a contract for two C-17 airplanes for a House member's vote in favor of NAFTA. The House Member was representing workers in his district while the president was furthering the interests of all consumers who would benefit from freer trade.

Taken together, these five arguments indicate that if individuals and organizations act rationally, small, wealthy, and organized producer groups will have a substantial advantage in American politics. "Organization represents concentrated power, and concentrated power can exercise a dominating influence when it encounters power which is diffuse and not concentrated."[41]

Issue Networks

At the same time that free riders and iron triangles were gaining popularity as critiques of the pluralist model, political institutions were changing in ways that did not fit with Mancur Olson's expectations or with interest-group liberalism. The number of citizen action groups representing large groups of people exploded in the 1960s and 1970s.[42] In addition, studies of individual issues showed very few iron triangles. In most cases, the subsystem surrounding an issue had many more participants, especially citizen action groups, than Lowi and others had predicted.[43] These facts led pluralist scholars to argue that the problem posed by free riders posed was exaggerated. The facts also suggested that policy subsystems were far more open to opponents of producer groups than Lowi had predicted and were not as biased in favor of producer groups as Stigler expected.

In an influential essay, public policy analyst Hugh Heclo argued that iron triangles may have been typical of policy subsystems in the 1950s and 1960s, but by the late 1970s most policy subsystems included a much wider set of participants. Heclo labeled these expanded policy subsystems "**issue networks**."[44] Issue networks include not only competing producer interests such as importers versus exporters in trade policy but also groups that oppose producer interests. Representatives from federal agencies and state and local governments, congressional committee staff, and policy experts located in universities and think tanks participate in the issue networks and often lobby successfully against producer interests. The ability of environmental organizations to participate in the NAFTA debate illustrates the argument Heclo was making. Prior to the debate over NAFTA, the trade policy subsystem was largely a battle within the business community and between business and labor. When environmental organizations joined a coalition with labor, this radically changed the trade policymaking process and opened the trade issue network to many more participants.[45]

The interests participating in issue networks generally have extensive knowledge about the technical, social, political, and economic characteristics of a policy arena. All participants in a network typically agree on which issues are the most important, and the participants share a common vocabulary when debating those issues. This shared understanding, however, does not extend to an agreement on which policies are best for society. For example, advocates for and against NAFTA knew a great deal about international trade, pollution issues along the border, and the priorities of other groups participating in the policy debate. The participants did not agree, however, on whether the implementation of the agreement would result in more or less pollution, whether NAFTA would result in more or fewer jobs in the United States, or whether the lower wages paid to skilled labor in Mexico would result in lower average wages for U.S. workers.

Water policy in the Southwest provides an example of how an iron triangle can evolve into an issue network. Prior to the emergence of the environmental movement, "water conservation" in the western United States meant building dams and reservoirs to provide additional water to agriculture and to the growing cities in Arizona, California, and Nevada. The policy subsystem consisted of the natural resource committees in Congress; the executive agencies of the Army Corps of Engineers, the Bureau of Land Management (BLM), and the Bureau of Reclamation; and interest groups demanding more water. Congress provided the funding to the Army Corps of Engineers and Bureau of Reclamation to build and maintain the projects. The resulting system of dams and reservoirs greatly expanded the water available to farmers and cities in the Southwest, provided cheap electricity to the region, and allowed extensive population growth.

Beginning in the 1970s, environmental groups forced their way into the policy subsystem and lobbied for policies that would reduce water use. The groups urged public officials to adopt programs that encouraged agricultural crops appropriate to arid lands, reduced water use by increasing its price, and encouraged sustainable ecosystems. In addition, some residents of such rapidly growing cities as Los Angeles and Phoenix wanted to curtail urban growth and the problems it created. Economists from universities and think tanks advocated market solutions to the water shortages. Urban commercial interests and state and local governments pushed for tradable water rights to encourage greater economic efficiency, and Native Americans demanded the water promised to them in treaties.[46]

An important aspect of issue networks is that officials from government agencies play an active role in lobbying for one policy alternative over others. In the battles over water for the Southwest, officials from the USDA lobbied on behalf of agricultural interests. The EPA supported the interests advocating greater water conservation and dryland agriculture. The Bureau of Indian Affairs lobbied for providing water to Native Americans. Each agency provided its client group (farmers, environmentalists, and Native Americans) information and access to the public officials who ultimately made the policy decisions. In short, the participation in issue networks looks a lot like the pluralist description of policymaking and group influence.[47]

Can We Reject the Exchange or Pluralist Models?

Given the explosion of citizen groups and the evolution of iron triangles into issue networks, can we conclude that the pluralist model of group influence is generally correct? No. Research on the influence of interest organizations refuses to support completely either the pluralist or the exchange model of interest groups in the policy process. A substantial number of studies have found that when producer organizations lobby they receive significant benefits. Politically active firms within an industry achieve higher profits, achieve greater increases in stock values, pay lower taxes, and experience less regulatory oversight than less politically active firms.[48] There is also indirect evidence that legislators receive financial advantages for supporting various interests. Over a four-year period, U.S. senators turn out to be much more savvy investors than Warren Buffett or the most successful hedge fund managers. The investments of U.S. senators beat the stock market by an average of 12 percent per year. The stocks that senators bought showed an average gain of 25-percent during the next twelve months; the stocks that senators sold averaged a 0-percent gain during the next twelve months.[49] It would appear that the senators' "blind trust investments" allow some peeking under the blindfold (see Box 2.3).

BOX 2.3 **Legislators Can Peek Into Their Blind Trusts**

With a truly blind trust, the individual owning the trust does not know what investments she owns. People have blind trusts to avoid any conflict of interests between their decisions and their financial well-being. For example, if you get tapped to serve on a corporate board, the company might require that you divest yourself of all investments in other firms in that industry. You might not want to sell off all the stock you happen to own in rival companies. So you enter a blind trust, where your money is managed by someone else. You do not even get quarterly statements concerning those investments. If a blind trust is to work properly, the person who owns the assets should not know the assets in the trust or how those assets are used. This is important for public officials as the public wants to be sure that the official is looking out for the public interest rather than for her own financial interests.

Congress, however, defines "blind trust" a little differently. Legislators receive regular (as many as 15 per year) reports from the manager of their trusts concerning the stocks they own. In addition, congresspersons can direct the managers of their trusts to buy and sell individual stocks. This is pernicious in that the public believes that the legislators are unaware of their investments and cannot gain from their decisions. This clearly is not the case.

Source: Mike Pesca, "Bill Frist, Blind Trusts and Conflicts of Interest," National Public Radio, Oct. 25, 2005, www.npr.org/templates/story/story.php?storyId=4973742&ft=1&f=17

Other research supports the pluralist perspective. Groups that Olson predicted would have difficulty forming, such as consumers, environmentalists, and taxpayers, have hundreds of thousands of members. In addition, these groups also have proven to be formidable advocates for their causes.[50] Researchers have found relatively little support for the idea that producer groups use their campaign contributions to buy outright policy outcomes on highly visible or highly partisan issues.[51] In addition, the exchange model's prediction that regulation is the result of producers' demands to reduce competition cannot explain the deregulation of the airline and trucking industries during the Carter administration or the anti-industry regulations of the EPA and the Occupational Safety and Health Administration (OSHA). Perhaps the greatest support for the pluralist perspective comes from the recent book *Lobbying and Policy Change* by Frank Baumgartner and his colleagues. That massive study of ninety-eight issues found no relationship between the lobbying resources of groups and their likelihood of winning a policy struggle.[52]

In summary, neither the pluralist nor the exchange approach has proven to be an unqualified success in explaining interest-group activity and predicting policy outcomes. Both approaches, however, make numerous accurate predictions. We turn now to a more recent theory that attempts to revise the basic pluralist model by adding important insights from the exchange model and including contributions from recent theoretical and empirical research.

NEOPLURALISM: IT ALL DEPENDS

Pluralism and exchange theory explain some policy outcomes well and others poorly, so it is not too surprising that interest-group and public policy scholars have built a descriptive model of interest-group politics that attempts to combine elements from both theories. The descriptive model is neopluralism.[53] Neopluralism builds on four basic ideas from pluralism:

1. Policymaking is a process that occurs through time and involves multiple decisions.

2. The influence of organized interests generally is limited to a single substantive policy arena and its associated issue network.

3. Major policy changes involve multiple competing groups.

4. Political ideologies, political parties, and elections constrain interest-group influence and often are more important than organized interests in determining policy.

Although neopluralism is much closer to pluralist theory than to the exchange model, neopluralism includes two central tenets of exchange theory. First, most neopluralists recognize that the collective action problem is real and sometimes biases the political process in favor of producer interests. Second, some institutional arrangements, such as the subcommittee system in Congress and the rulemaking process in regulatory agencies, favor interest organizations with extensive resources. In short, neopluralism recognizes that although there generally are competing interests on major policy issues, this does not mean that the influence of the competing interests is equal or that policy outcomes are "fair."[54]

The development of the neopluralist model includes several new insights developed since Truman, Dahl, and other researchers developed the original pluralist models. Robert Salisbury noted a flaw in the both the pluralist and exchange models. Salisbury argued that there was a general failure to recognize that groups with individuals as members do not conduct much lobbying.[55] Instead, institutions such as corporations, trade associations, hospitals, universities, and state and local governments dominate lobbying at the federal level. Salisbury wrote that a central distinction between an institution and a membership-based interest group is that institutions have interests that are independent of the interests of particular individuals. For example, when a university seeks to affect public policy, it does not justify its effort by alleging that it is reflecting the values of its students, employees, or professors. Their interests are not crucial. It is the judgment of organizational leaders about the needs of the institution that matters. In addition, because an institution has no members per se, there is not a collective action problem.

Tim Cook, the CEO of Apple, can decide to spend more money lobbying without worrying about getting shareholders' permission or raising new money from Apple's shareholders. If Cook believes that money spent on lobbying will lead to greater profits than alternative uses of that money, he can increase the size of his lobbying efforts. The assets of a large corporation, its expectation of a very long life, and its flexibility give it tremendous lobbying advantages. In contrast, when the Sierra Club lobbies, it must consider whether its lobbying on an issue will increase or decrease its donations and membership rolls.

A second advance of neopluralism is that distinguishes between **high politics** and **routine politics**.[56] High politics involve nonincremental policy changes and modifications in who participates in an issue network.[57] Routine politics occur when policymakers follow standard operating procedures and make incremental changes in policies. NAFTA is an example of high politics. It not only constituted a substantial policy change in U.S. trade relations with Mexico and Canada but it also changed the composition of the issue network. Prior to NAFTA, environmental issues received little attention in trade agreements, and neither environmental interest groups nor the EPA was an active participant in the issue network. NAFTA changed that. The EPA and environmental interest groups played influential roles in shaping the agreement. Interest-group scholar Andrew McFarland suggested that ideology, political parties, and elections are important factors in determining the policy outcomes of high politics.

Examples of routine politics would include congressional subcommittees making small increases or decreases in the farm subsidy programs and the transportation committees in Congress making incremental changes in the allocation of federal monies between highway and light rail projects. Routine politics also include the administration of existing law and the bargaining that takes place among established actors in a policy subsystem.[58] While these decisions can have extremely important consequences, they do not involve a redistribution of power within a policy subsystem or a radical change in policy.

McFarland argues that producer groups are more likely to be powerful in routine politics because public opinion, political parties, and elections are less likely to restrain group influence. Membership-based citizen action groups are unlikely to become involved in routine politics because their low visibility does not attract new members. Political scientist John Chubb shows that producer organizations are particularly likely to influence policy implementation decisions because the implementation process is less salient to the public.[59] Producer groups also have the technical expertise and monetary resources necessary to lobby the bureaucracy.

Perhaps the key characteristic of neopluralism is its stress on the highly contingent nature of group influence on policy.[62] Environmental organizations, for example, clearly influenced the final provisions of NAFTA and its side agreements, but the extent of their influence was contingent on Democrats controlling Congress. It is certainly the case that the influence of environmental groups increased dramatically when the GATT panel decided that trade agreements took precedence over the requirements of the U.S. Marine Mammal Protection Act and the lives of smiling dolphins. The panel's decision gave environmental groups a powerful symbol that made environmental protection more salient to the public. John Kingdon, in his book on agendas and policymaking, argues that interests wait patiently until events are so fortuitous that policy change is likely.[63] Kingdon likened the waiting interests to surfers waiting for the next big wave. Surfers ignore the smaller waves and wait for the wave that yields a big ride. In short, environmental groups were ready to move as soon as the GATT panel made a large wave.

Certainly, neopluralism provides an in-depth or "thick" description of the policy process for NAFTA. Neopluralism's emphasis on policymaking as a process involving multiple decisions occurring over time rather than as a single policy choice gives us an appreciation of the messiness of policymaking. Neopluralists' emphasis on process also alerts us to the importance of examining interest-group influence through the entire policymaking process. Some types of groups are more influential when issues are highly visible and salient to the public. Other interests have greater influence on less visible, less partisan, and more routine issues. The strength of neopluralism is its inclusion of numerous variables in explaining why a particular policy outcome occurred and why particular groups were (or were not) influential on an issue. These strengths of neopluralism, however, come at a cost. It is not as useful as exchange models in making testable hypotheses or in making predictions about the policy process. *If everything is contingent on a large set of unpredictable factors, prediction is not possible.*

INTEREST GROUPS, PARTIES, AND POLITICAL REPRESENTATION

The key normative question concerning interest-group influence is whether it encourages or discourages democratic representation. In other words, do interest groups help policymakers link the demands and interests of all citizens to policies, or do interest organizations heavily bias representation in favor special interest groups? It is not reasonable to write about linking public preferences to public policy without including political parties in the discussion. Our view of the relationship between parties and interest groups is consistent with the argument of Marty Cohen and his coauthors that interest organizations are **intense demanders** who use their resources to nominate candidates who share their policy preferences.[64] Parties are, therefore, long-term coalitions of intense demanders who lobby the people they elect by providing those individuals with the resources they need to be elected and to be effective after they gain office. The elected official's first loyalty is to this coalition of interests. Other interest groups may also lobby the officials after the election. These officials then decide whether to work on behalf of those groups, but their first obligation is to the groups that are part of their party's long-term coalition.[65] This view of the relationship between interest groups and political parties goes back to E. E. Schattschneider's classic work *Party Government,* and is consistent with the pluralist, neopluralist, and exchange models of group influence.[66]

Parties, interest groups, and elections are three key institutions in linking citizens' preferences to public policy. Two ideas are important in understanding this linkage. First, a long and distinguished literature shows that public officials see representing the interests of their constituents as one of their key duties, even in situations where voters have no knowledge of their actions and cannot hold them accountable.[67] Although models of interest-group influence are unlikely to capture this important influence on the behavior of officials, the reader should remain cognizant of its importance.

The second point is that the neopluralist and exchange models are not mutually exclusive when describing how representation and group influence occur. As economists Arthur Denzau and Michael Munger have shown, both models accept that elections encourage officials to represent unorganized constituents.[68] Neopluralist models emphasize the competition among interests and the contingent nature of influence and policy outcomes. Exchange models emphasize that interest organizations provide resources to a policymaker, and that policymaker then supports that organization's desired policies. The predictions of the two models are similar if all sides of an issue have sufficient resources to influence parties' nomination of candidates and to bid for policy support after the election. The models make different predictions when one side of an issue does not have sufficient resources to compete in the political marketplace.

SUMMARY

In this chapter, we set forth two metaphors of the policymaking process, the tug-of-war and the Middle Eastern bazaar. We used the passage of NAFTA to examine how various models of interest-group influence might explain the politics and policy outcomes of those issues. We briefly explored the pluralist and elite approaches. We then moved to the two approaches that are the focus of this book: (1) exchange and (2) neopluralism. The exchange model makes the crucial assumption that those who participate in the policy process—public officials, interest organizations, political parties, and citizens—act rationally. They make exchanges that increase their well-being. Incorporating utility maximizing assumptions allows the exchange model to use the tools of microeconomics and mathematics to analyze and predict political behavior. Neopluralism attempts to combine many of the insights of the pluralist and exchange models. Among the key contributions of neopluralism are its recognition of the institutional character of lobbying organizations, its distinction between high politics and routine politics, and its emphasis on the contingent nature of interest-group influence. While neopluralism helps us to appreciate the complexity of the policy process and aids us in explaining past policy outcomes, it has limited usefulness as a predictive model.

ENDNOTES

1. Hugh Ward wonders whether the forces at play pull in opposite directions. For issues with two or more dimensions, interests may compete with one another even if they are not pulling in exactly opposite directions. If the pressures from the varied

interests are vectors, then the sum of those vectors can be found using the parallelogram law. Under this scenario, interests exaggerate their positions because they recognize that the resulting policy will be a compromise found by the parallelogram law. Hugh Ward, "Pressure Politics: A Game-Theoretical Investigation of Lobbying and the Measurement of Power," *Journal of Theoretical Politics* 16 (2004): 31–52.

2. Gene Grossman and Elhanan Helpman, *Special Interest Politics* (Cambridge, MA: MIT, 2002). Suppose policy can be split into several parts. Consider tariffs, some industries are protected and others are not. The affected interests bid on different parts of the overall tariff policy. Each firm wants low tariffs on its imports so that manufacturing costs are kept low and high tariffs on its exports to limit the competition from foreign producers. Firms place bids to alter separate elements of the tariff policy.

3. Arthur Denzau and Michael Munger, "Legislators and Interest Groups: How Unorganized Interests Get Represented," *American Political Science Review* 80 (1986): 89–106.

4. The loss of majority party status could be linked to a $60,000 decrease in PAC contributions for the typical Democratic legislator. See Gary Cox and Eric Magar, "How Much Is Majority Status in the U.S. Congress Worth?" *American Political Science Review* 93, no. 2 (1999): 299–309.

5. This section depends heavily on Diana Evans' analysis of the lobbying on NAFTA found in chapter 5 of *Greasing the Wheels: Using Pork Barrel Projects to Build Majority Coalitions in Congress* (New York: Cambridge University Press, 2004); and Frederick W. Mayer, *Interpreting NAFTA: The Science and Art of Political Analysis* (New York: Columbia University Press, 1998).

6. These terms come from nineteenth-century political economist David Ricardo. Ricardo argued that the import tariffs that England placed on imported grains raised the rents English landlords could charge the tenants who farmed the land. Ricardo defined rent as "that portion of the produce of the earth which is paid to the landlord by the tenant farmer for the use of the land." The Corn Laws benefitted landowners because the increased price of grains to English consumers allowed for an increase in rents that were unrelated to the quality of the land per se. See David Ricardo's *On the Principles of Political Economy and Taxation* (London: John Murray, 1817).

7. Ricardo, *On the Principles of Political Economy and Taxation.*

8. E. E. Schattschneider, *Politics, Pressures and the Tariff: A Study of Free Enterprise in Pressure Politics as Shown in the 1929–1930 Revision of the Tariff* (New York: Prentice Hall, 1935).

9. David Epstein and Sharyn O'Halloran, "Divided Government and the Design of Administrative Procedures: A Formal Model and Empirical Test," *Journal of Politics* 58 (1996): 373–397; and Epstein, David and Sharyn O'Halloran, "The Nondelegation Doctrine and the Separation of Powers: A Political Science Approach," *Cardozo Law Review* 20 (1999).

10. The corporations included in the organization represent more than one-third of the value in the New York Stock Exchange.

11. Michael J. Graetz and Ian Shapiro, *Death by a Thousand Cuts: The Fight over Taxing Inherited Wealth* (Princeton, NJ: Princeton University Press, 2005).

12. See Mayer, *Interpreting NAFTA.*
13. Ibid., 83.
14. Ibid., 87.
15. Ibid., 114.
16. Rapid economic growth in Mexico would ease the immigration strain on Texas and make a stronger trading partner for the state. Bentsen recognized that wealthier neighbors provided greater benefits to Texas than poorer neighbors.
17. Mayer, *Interpreting NAFTA,* 134.
18. Patrick Buchanan, "Remarks Made to the Conservative Political Action Conference" (paper presented at the Conservative Political Action Conference, Omni Shoreham Hotel, Washington, DC, 1992).
19. Mayer, *Interpreting NAFTA,* 226.
20. The AFL–CIO is an organization composed of numerous separate labor organizations. It is generally considered to be the **peak association** for organized labor.
21. Maquiladora factories are located in Mexico near the United States–Mexico border. The plants can import parts and other raw materials from the United States duty free, and the goods produced and assembled in these factories are treated as if they were produced in the United States.
22. See Evans, *Greasing the Wheels.*
23. Denzau and Munger, "Legislators and Interest Groups." Denzau and Munger saw opportunities for the unorganized or latent interests to secure representation in an exchange-based model. For another view, see Morten Bennedsen and Sven E. Feldmann, "Informational Lobbying and Political Contributions," *Journal of Political Economics* 90, no. 4/5 (2006): 631–656.
24. Mark Smith, *American Business and Political Power: Public Opinion, Elections, and Democracy* (Chicago: The University of Chicago Press, 2000).
25. David B. Truman, *The Governmental Process: Political Interests and Public Opinion* (New York: Alfred A. Knopf, 1951).
26. Michael Dreiling and Brian Wolf, "Environmental Movement Organizations and Political Strategy: Tactical Conflicts over NAFTA," *Organization and Environment* 12 (2001): 34–54.
27. Michael Dreiling, "The Class Embeddedness of Corporate Political Action: Leadership in Defense of NAFTA," *Social Problems* 47 (2000): 21–48.
28. E. E. Schattschneider, *The Semi-Sovereign People* (New York: Holt, Rinehart & Winston, 1960), 34–35.
29. Dara Z. Strolovitch, "Do Interest Groups Represent the Disadvantaged? Advocacy at the Intersections of Race, Class and Gender," *Journal of Politics* 68, no. 4 (2006): 894–910. Strolovitch argued that this happens even with groups that represent the most disadvantaged in society.
30. Peter Bachrach and Morton S. Baratz, "The Two Faces of Power," *American Political Science Review* 56, no. 4 (1962): 947–952.
31. Suppose no one else contributes. Should you choose to contribute? Twenty dollars is unlikely to fund a successful lobbying effort, so once again a rational individual will not contribute. Coordinated solutions do exist, but they are particularly hard to engineer in large groups. In coordinated solutions, just the right number of

people contributes to ensure a successful lobbying effort. Fewer contributions would sink their efforts, and more contributions would not be crucial to success. The problem with coordinated solutions is that they are so hard to coordinate. There are numerous discussions of coordination problems and their relation to collective action problems. Thomas R. Palfrey and Howard Rosenthal, "Private Incentives in Social Dilemmas: The Effects of Incomplete Information and Altruism," *Journal of Public Economics* 35, no. 3 (1988): 309–332.

32. The authors gathered these data from OpenSecrets.org and the lobbying disclosure reports that lobbying organizations must file with Congress.

33. John Chubb, *Interest Groups and the Bureaucracy: The Politics of Energy* (Stanford, CA: Stanford University Press, 1983); Kenneth Godwin, *One Billion Dollars of Influence: The Direct Marketing of Politics* (Chatham House, NJ: Chatham House, 1988).

34. Magazine Publishers of America, "Top 100 Magazines," The New York Job Source, http://nyjobsource.com/magazines.html

35. George Stigler, "The Theory of Economic Regulation," *Bell Journal of Economics and Management Science* 2, no. 1 (1971): 5.

36. A minor example of producers demanding regulation was the fee airlines charged to coach passengers who wanted to hear the audio for in-flight movies. Prior to the deregulation of the passenger airline industry by President Carter in the 1970s, flight attendants announced over the intercom, "The Federal Aviation Authority requires us to charge you for the audio headsets." It is unlikely that coach passengers asked for this regulation.

37. See the following on subsidies: Environmental Working Group, "Tobacco Subsidies in the United States Totaled $1.1 Billion from 1995–2010." http://farm.ewg.org/progdetail.php?fips=00000&progcode=tobacco. Lowi also noted the irony in the fact that the U.S. government often assists interests that directly or indirectly compete with one another. For instance, the U.S. government has also forced tobacco companies to spend millions on antismoking campaigns.

38. Robert Baldwin and Christopher S. Magee. "Is Trade Policy for Sale? Congressional Voting on Recent Trade Bills." *Public Choice* 105 (2000): 79–101; and Eric Uslaner, "Let the Chits Fall Where They May? Executive and Constituency Influences on Congressional Voting on NAFTA," *Legislative Studies Quarterly* 23, no. 3 (1998): 347–371.

39. Steven T. Engel and David J. Jackson, "Wielding the Stick Instead of the Carrot: Labor PAC Punishment of Pro-NAFTA Democrats," *Political Research Quarterly* 51, no. 3 (1998): 813–828.

40. Evans, *Greasing the Wheels*, 147.

41. Earl Latham, *The Group Basis of Politics: A Study in Basing-Point Legislation* (New York, Octagon Books, 1965), 387.

42. Jack L. Walker Jr., "The Origins and Maintenance of Interest Groups in America," *American Political Science Review* 77 (1983): 390–406; and Jeffrey Berry, *Lobbying for the People: The Political Behavior of Public Interest Groups* (Princeton, NJ: Princeton University Press, 1977).

43. Jeffrey Berry, *The New Liberalism: The Rising Power of Citizen Groups* (Washington, DC: Brookings Institution, 1999).

44. Hugh Heclo, "Issue Networks and the Executive Establishment," in *The New American Political System,* ed. Anthony King (Washington, DC: American Enterprise Institute, 1978).

45. Mayer, *Interpreting NAFTA,* 76–81.

46. Helen M. Ingram and R. Kenneth Godwin, eds., *Public Policy and the Natural Environment* (Greenwich, CT: JAI Press, 1985).

47. Even within an agency, a similar phenomenon can occur. Latham, *The Group Basis of Politics,* documents instances when bureaus within the USDA worked at cross-purposes. One division or bureau within the agency was charged with promoting fiscal responsibility while other bureaus were focused on the distribution of benefits without regard to fiscal concerns.

48. Brian Shaffer, Thomas J. Quasney, and Curtis M. Grimm, "Firm Level Performance Implications of Nonmarket Actions," *Business & Society* 39, no. 2 (2000): 126–143; Hui Chen, David Parsley, and Ya-Wen Yang, "Corporate Lobbying and Financial Performance," Social Science Research Network Working Paper, 2010, http://papers.ssrn.com/s013/papers.cfm?abstract_id=1014264; Brian Richter, Krislert Samphantharak, and Jeffrey Simmons, "Lobbying and Taxes," *American Journal of Political Science* 53, no. 4 (2009): 893–909; and Stanford C. Gordon and Catherine Hafer, "Flexing Muscle: Corporate Political Expenditures as Signals to the Bureaucracy," *American Political Science Review* 99, no. 2 (2005): 245–261.

49. Alan Ziobrowiski et al., "Abnormal Returns from the Common Stock Investments of the U.S. Senate," *Journal of Financial and Quantitative Analysis* 39, no. 4 (2004): 661–676.

50. Frank R. Baumgartner et al., *Lobbying and Policy Change: Who Wins, Who Loses, and Why* (Chicago: Chicago University Press, 2009).

51. For a review of this research, see Frank R. Baumgartner and Beth L. Leech, *Basic Interests: The Importance of Groups in Politics and in Political Science* (Princeton, NJ: Princeton University Press, 1998).

52. Baumgartner et al., *Lobbying and Policy Change.*

53. Two of the best descriptions of neopluralism are Andrew S. McFarland, *Neopluralism: The Evolution of Political Process Theory* (Lawrence: University of Kansas Press, 2004); and David Lowery and Virginia Gray, "A Neopluralist Perspective on Research on Organized Interests" *Political Research Quarterly* 57, no. 1 (2004): 164–175.

54. McFarland, *Neopluralism.*

55. Robert H. Salisbury, "Interest Representation: The Dominance of Institutions," *American Political Science Review* 78, no. 1 (1984): 64–76.

56. McFarland, *Neopluralism,* 51; Kent R. Weaver, *Automatic Government: The Politics of Indexation* (Washington, DC: Brookings Institution, 1988) details the extent to which some political and policy decisions become routinized.

57. Chubb, *Interest Groups and the Bureaucracy.*

58. Mark Smith, *American Business and Political Power.*

59. Chubb, *Interest Groups and the Bureaucracy*; Jason Webb Yackee and Susan Webb Yackee, "A Bias Towards Business? Assessing Interest Group Influence on the U.S. Bureaucracy," *Journal of Politics* 68, no. 1 (2006): 128–139; and Scott Ainsworth, Erik Godwin, and Kenneth Godwin, "Rulemaking and Interest Group Dominance" (paper presented at the annual meetings of the American Political Science Association, Toronto, Canada, 2009).

60. Mark Smith, *American Business and Political Power*.

61. Chubb, *Interest Groups and the Bureaucracy*; Yackee and Yackee, "A Bias Towards Business?"; and Ainsworth, Godwin, and Godwin, "Rulemaking and Interest Group Dominance."

62. See Baumgartner and Leech, *Basic Interests*, p. 134; and Lowery and Gray, "A Neopluralist Perspective on Research," 171.

63. John Kingdon, *Agendas, Alternatives, and Public Policies*, 2nd ed. (Reading, MA: Addison-Wesley, 1995).

64. Marty Cohen et al., *The Party Decides: Presidential Nominations before and after Reform* (Chicago: University of Chicago Press, 2008).

65. Our view of lobbying after the election is consistent with looking at lobbying as signaling and seeing lobbyists as providing a legislative subsidy. For the signaling perspective, see Scott H. Ainsworth and Itai Sened, "The Role of Lobbyists: Entrepreneurs with Two Audiences," *American Journal of Political Science* 37 (1993): 834–866. For the legislative subsidy view, see Richard L. Hall and Alan V. Deardorff, "Lobbying as Legislative Subsidy," *American Political Science Review* 100 (2006): 69–84.

66. E. E. Schattschneider, *Party Government: American Government in Action* (Westport, CT: Greenwood Press, 1977).

67. See for example, Heinz Eulau et al., "The Role of the Representative: Some Empirical Observations on the Theory of Edmund Burke," *American Political Science Review* 53, no. 3 (1959): 742–756; Richard Fenno, *Congressmen in Committees* (Boston: Little, Brown, 1978); and John Wahlke, "Policy Demands and System Support: The Role of the Represented," *British Journal of Political Science* 1, no. 3 (1971): 271–290

68. Denzau and Munger, "Legislators and Interest Groups."

chapter 3

The Policy Process

I n chapter 2, we examined the ability of pluralist, elite, exchange, interest-group liberalism, and neopluralist models to explain the content and passage of the North American Free Trade Agreement (NAFTA). The issue demonstrated the complexity of the policy process and some of the difficulties involved in measuring the influence of interest organizations. In this chapter, we provide a method for breaking down the policy process into several stages so that we can analyze when interest organizations are most likely to be influential and how lobbying strategies change as policy proposals move from one stage to the next.[1] We use NAFTA and three additional case studies to introduce key concepts of the policy process. The three cases are President George W. Bush's comprehensive energy proposal, the American Jobs Creation Act of 2004 that provided $140 billion in corporate tax breaks, and the Data Quality Act (DQA) that was passed in 2001.

MAKING SENSE OF THE POLICY PROCESS

Making sense of such diverse policies as international trade, tax reform for individuals, corporate taxation, and energy policy is a daunting task. An approach that has proven useful is to divide the policy process into five conceptually distinct stages: (1) **agenda setting,** (2) **policy formulation,** (3) **policy legitimation** or **decision making,** (4) **policy implementation,** and (5) **evaluation and feedback** (see Table 3.1). Agenda setting concerns how an issue comes to the attention of public officials, how the public and policymakers perceive the issue, and the decision by public officials to address the issue.

Some issues reach the political agenda because of a crisis or focusing event. For example, the collapse of the housing market and the collapse of Lehman Brothers investment bank in 2008 moved bank bailouts, financial sector regulations, and home foreclosures to the forefront of the public's attention. The economic collapse of 2008 refocused our attention on those issues. Other issues reach the agenda automatically. Every few years, Congress must pass an increase in the U.S. debt ceiling. This allows the federal government to borrow the funds necessary to pay its creditors and to continue funding the government. Numerous regulations contain **sunset provisions** that require Congress to reauthorize the regulations or to end them. Congress must also reauthorize many specific programs such as the Elementary and Secondary Education Act.[2] The reauthorizations provide Congress the opportunity to evaluate the effectiveness of the programs and to make major changes in the regulatory statutes.

TABLE 3.1 The Policy Stages Model Applied to the North American Free Trade Agreement

Stage	What It Means	Example
Agenda setting	How problems are perceived, defined, command attention, and reach the agenda of policymakers	President Salinas perceives that a trade agreement with the United States would benefit both countries. He asks the Business Roundtable to determine if the agreement would be good for U.S. business and consumers. The Business Roundtable convinces President George H. W. Bush to pursue the agreement. The problem is defined as one of economic inefficiency caused by trade barriers.
Policy formulation	The drafting of alternative policy options to resolve the problem that has reached the agenda	President Bush forms the Advisory Committee for Trade Policy and Negotiations that drafts the U.S. positions on the trade issues among the United States, Mexico, and Canada. The Environmental Protection Agency (EPA) adds provisions to ensure that Mexico implements environmental regulations.
Policy legitimation (Decision making)	Includes the mobilization of support for the various policy alternatives and public officials following the legitimate procedures for reaching a decision	President Bush and Congress follow the procedures outlined in fast track trade legislation. In the case of NAFTA, Congress also passes legislation dictating how the three countries would implement the free trade agreement.
Policy implementation	Government allocates the resources to the bureaucracy to implement the legislation. This stage also includes the bureaucracy making and implementing the rules and regulations necessary to clarify and carry out the legislation	Mexico, Canada, and the United States set up an international body to investigate whether all of the countries are abiding by the environmental and labor requirements of the agreement.

Stage	What It Means	Example
Evaluation and feedback	Efforts to determine whether the policy had the expected outcomes. Did the policy succeed or fail? What marginal utility did each component of the policy contribute?	Numerous organizations study the effects of NAFTA on their interests. Think tanks, university researchers, and official government agencies such as the Government Accountability Office also study the effects of NAFTA and disseminate the information to the government and the public.

Source: Adapted from Table 3.1 in Michael Kraft and Scott Furlong, *Public Policy: Politics, Analysis, and Alternatives* (Washington, DC: CQ Press, 2004), 78.

Most policy issues, however, must compete for a place on the agenda. There are thousands of social and economic problems that government could address. In his classic book *Agendas, Alternatives, and Public Policies,* University of Michigan political scientist John Kingdon argued that for an issue to reach the political agenda, three relatively separate "streams" must converge and form a **policy window** (see Figure 3.1). The political stream consists of the political climate or public mood. Which party's political ideology is congruent with the prevailing public attitudes? The second stream consists of the problems on which policymakers have information that indicates that government might solve the problem. For instance, if a large proportion of unemployed persons are over fifty and previously worked in factories that relocated abroad, policymakers might have information concerning the effectiveness of job training programs for such workers. If the programs have been successful, the policymakers are more likely to see the problem as one government can resolve.

FIGURE 3.1   John Kingdon's Policy Streams

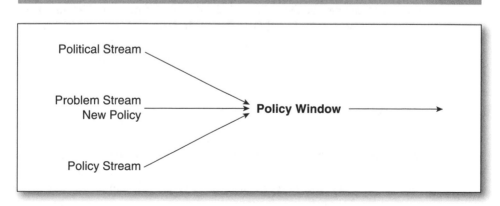

The policy stream constitutes the third element in determining whether an issue is likely to obtain a place on the political agenda. This stream consists of alternative policy tools. Kingdon maintained that certain policy solutions exist separately from policy problems. For example, the Richard Nixon and Gerald Ford administrations saw increased regulation as a policy solution to numerous environmental issues, workplace safety, and economic problems. The Reagan and both Bush administrations, however, used regulations to address other policy areas such as U.S. foreign trade. As Figure 3.1 indicates, a policy window occurs when the three streams converge. For example, during President Nixon's first term, the environmental movement became an important political and social force. The public believed that air and water pollution were creating substantial environmental and public health problems, and the public mood supported government intervention to reduce pollution. President Nixon viewed federal regulations as useful tools to reduce the harms created by the polluting industries. There was, therefore, a convergence of the political, problem, and policy streams. This convergence led to the creation of the Environmental Protection Agency (EPA) and the passage of the historic Clean Air Act Extension of 1970 and the amendments to the Federal Water Pollution Control Act of 1972. These two acts are sometimes referred to as super statutes because of their sweeping impacts.[3]

A key factor influencing which issues will reach the political agenda is **problem definition.** In politics, the side that gets to define the problem has a tremendous advantage. For example, if the "unemployment problem" is defined as one in which persons who want to work are unable to find employment because of a temporary economic downturn then government can pass policies such as extending unemployment compensation until the downturn is over. If, however, the unemployment problem is defined as one created by the laziness of the unemployed, then government is more likely to curtail unemployment benefits.[4]

In the 2011 decision concerning whether to raise the debt ceiling, Republican members of Congress defined the problem as one of too much government spending. They demanded that in return for their support of raising the debt ceiling, the Democrats had to agree to future cuts in the major entitlement programs of Social Security, Medicare, and Medicaid. Democrats defined the debt problem differently. They argued that the causes of the huge deficit were the tax cuts to the wealthy passed during the George W. Bush administration, the Iraq and Afghanistan wars, and the recession created by the financial crisis of 2008. The Democrats would consider reforming the entitlement programs only if the Republicans agreed to raise the tax rates on the wealthiest Americans. Ultimately, the Republican-controlled House and the Democratic-controlled Senate could not agree on a policy. To avoid default, Congress passed a short-term increase in the debt and formed a bipartisan twelve-member congressional committee to work on reducing the long-term deficit. That committee, however, failed to develop a solution and left the issue until after the 2012 national elections.

The second stage of the policy process is policy formulation. It refers to the development of policy proposals to resolve an issue. There are many ways that the government might address an issue. Often everyone agrees that there is a problem, but they disagree about its causes and possible solutions. Republicans formulated a solution to resolving the government's debt based on the idea that government was too large and promised to do too much. Their policy alternative was to cut the federal budget and reduce the size of government. Democrats formulated a solution to the debt problem based on the idea that President George W. Bush had recklessly reduced revenues. Their solution was to end the Bush tax cuts for persons with higher incomes and to close many of the existing tax loopholes that benefitted such special interests as the oil companies.

Policy legitimation[5] is the stage of the policy process that refers to the process of choosing among alternative policy proposals. For instance, legitimation in Congress typically begins with the mobilization of support for a particular policy alternative and involves numerous decisions. Hearings in subcommittees and committees occur in both chambers of the legislature. The House and the Senate must agree on the same version of a bill. The president must sign the bill, or Congress must override his veto. Legitimation in the bureaucratic rulemaking process requires that an agency (1) give notice that it is considering making a particular rule, (2) publish a preliminary version of the rule, (3) allow those whom the rule affects to provide comments on the proposed rule, (4) publish its response to those comments, and (5) issue the final rule.

Once Congress passes a statute, the president issues an executive order, or the bureaucracy issues a rule, officials make decisions concerning how to **implement** the chosen alternative. Few laws are self-implementing. An Apple product might work immediately upon removing it from its box, but legislators do not pass "iBills." Implementing legislation is more like setting up a wireless router that conceivably can work with Apple, Blackberry, PC, and Roku devices. Indeed, implementation is much more complex. Federal legislation often requires implementation decisions that work across fifty unique states and hundreds of industries. The role of implementation is particularly vital for regulatory policies where Congress passes laws that specify particular outcomes but allows the bureaucracy to decide the specific regulatory rules that will achieve those outcomes. For instance, the amendments to the Federal Water Pollution Control Act of 1972 require that all navigable waterways be sufficiently pollution free to allow swimming and fishing. The act left it to the EPA to set standards for what constitutes safe levels for swimming and fishing and to develop the mechanisms for achieving that goal.

The last stage of the policy process is evaluation and feedback. Policymakers and the public continuously evaluate a policy's effects. That evaluation provides feedback to decision makers who may then choose to place the issue back on the agenda. For example, Congress used evaluations of the benefits and costs of the Federal Water Pollution Control Act to amend the act on several occasions. In the 2012 presidential elections, several Republican candidates believed that the feedback and evaluation related to the EPA were sufficiently negative to justify the abolition of the agency.

Although the idea of *stages* in the policy process suggests a unidirectional, systematic process moving from agenda setting through formulation, decision making, implementation, and evaluation, this generally is not the case. Issues come on the agenda, are pushed off, and reemerge. Policy alternatives are formulated and reformulated as the support and opposition to a policy changes. Implementation may become stalled because the original policy decision turned out to be unworkable or a court decision declared it unconstitutional. This requires government officials to choose different policy tools to implement the original legislation. For example, the evaluation stage of the policy process often leads to an issue being placed back on the political agenda. In short, the policy stages model is not unidirectional. The policy process can stop at any stage, return to a previous stage, or skip a stage entirely.

POLICY STAGES AND THE STUDY OF GROUP INFLUENCE

The policy stages model allows us to break a complex process into manageable parts and to investigate the lobbying strategies at each stage. One researcher might study agenda setting and investigate whether interest organizations requesting small policy changes are more likely to get on the congressional agenda than organizations requesting larger or more radical changes. Another scholar might examine the policy formulation stage to discover whether lobbyists who use technical information are more successful than lobbyists who do not.[6] Still other researchers might examine how business groups and citizens' groups vary in their lobbying strategies at different stages of the policy process. For example, Stanford political scientist John Chubb found that citizen groups are relatively more successful in the agenda setting and decision stages, while business groups are more successful in the formulation and implementation stages.[7]

An important contribution of the stages model is that it urges researchers to focus on both faces of power. We observe one face once an issue is on the agenda. We can compare the power of competing interests to define a problem, to obtain their desired policy alternative, and to influence the implementation process. For instance, once NAFTA was on the agenda, business interests had substantially greater power than organized labor. But there also is a hidden face of power: the ability of an interest to prevent an issue from reaching the political agenda. For example, investment banks were largely successful in preventing Congress from considering greater banking regulation of such new banking instruments as derivatives from 1976 until 2009.[8] It took a massive failure in the financial system to overcome the financial community's ability to keep the issue off the agenda. Political scientists may be severely underestimating the power of an interest group if they study only issues that have reached the agenda. By studying agenda setting, we attempt to identify when an interest is exercising power's second face.

The stages model also directs our attention at policy implementation. Bureaucrats make policy when they decide how to implement a statute and the level of resources to devote to each part of that statute. Although public policy scholars have devoted substantial resources to studying the implementation process, interest-group researchers have not. Instead, interest-group research has concentrated on the policy formulation and legitimation stages of policymaking. In addition, they have limited that research largely to formulation and legitimation in Congress. A key argument of this book is that to gauge the influence of interest organizations on public policy or to understand their lobbying strategies researchers must study both faces of power and policy implementation.

Another important contribution of the stages model is its attention to the role of policy entrepreneurs. Unless you are the president of the United States or occupy a leadership position in Congress or in the bureaucracy, the likelihood that Congress will pay attention to your issue is small. Less than 20 percent of bills introduced in Congress receive any attention from committees. Policy entrepreneurs use their knowledge of people and institutions to get their issue on the agenda and to ensure that their preferred policy alternative has the best chance of success.[9] A policy entrepreneur can be either inside or outside of government. For instance, Mexican president Salinas was a policy entrepreneur for NAFTA. He realized that the best way of organizing a broad-based coalition was to have the Business Roundtable study the issue and make recommendations to Republican president George H. W. Bush. Salinas understood that the Business Roundtable and the business community had excellent relationships with the president. If the Business Roundtable pushed for the free trade agreement, President Bush was likely to place the issue on the agenda. Salinas expected that if the free trade issue reached the agenda, fast track procedures would allow the White House to dominate the policy formulation process. For the fast track legislation, see Box 3.1.

BOX 3.1   **Fast Track Procedure**

If the president transmits a trade agreement to Congress, fast track procedures require that the bill pass or fail within ninety days. The trade agreement must be introduced and the implementing bill must be submitted by the president on the first day on which their chamber is in session. Congress cannot amend the president's bill. The committees have forty-five days to report the bill or it will be automatically discharged for consideration by the full chamber. Each chamber must vote within fifteen days after the bill is reported or discharged. If the bill contains tariffs or other revenue provisions, the bill must originate in the House. If the House passes the bill, the Senate Committee on Finance has fifteen days to report the bill or it will be automatically discharged. The Senate then has fifteen days to vote on the bill. The Senate may not filibuster the bill, and each chamber may debate the bill for no more than twenty hours. A simple majority in both chambers is necessary to pass the bill.

Representatives of interest organizations often act as policy entrepreneurs for their policy priorities. Once President Salinas convinced the Business Roundtable to evaluate how a free trade policy with Mexico would affect American business, two members of the Business Roundtable took over as NAFTA's policy entrepreneurs. American Express CEO Jim Robinson and Kodak CEO Kay Whitmore took over the task of shepherding NAFTA through the shoals of the policy process. Robinson organized the congressional lobbying efforts of all of the CEOs in the Business Roundtable while Whitmore dealt with environmental groups and the federal agencies involved in trade policy. President Bush named Robinson and Whitmore cochairs of the Advisory Committee for Trade Policy and Negotiations. That committee coordinated the thirty advisory committees that developed the initial U.S. positions on each major aspect of the treaty.[10]

Using the policy stages model as an organizing tool, we now examine three issues: (1) federal energy policy, (2) corporate taxation, and (3) changing regulatory policy. When campaigning for the White House, energy and tax cuts were George W. Bush's top priorities. These issues illustrate the ability of the president to place his priorities on the congressional agenda, and they provide examples of highly partisan policy proposals that are salient to the public. The third case study is the DQA, a major policy change that initially sparked no conflict. The DQA provides an example of a policy proposal that had no visibility and no conflict when Congress passed it. With little fanfare, President Clinton signed the statute that included the DQA. The lack of conflict over DQA, however, did not reflect broad agreement among policymakers with the policy. Instead, it reflected the ability of a policy entrepreneur to use his knowledge of congressional procedures to sneak through a radical policy change.

ENERGY POLICY

During the spring of 2004, the authors of this book conducted sixty-two interviews with lobbyists representing Fortune 1000 corporations.[11] Our first question asked the lobbyist to list the policy issues that were most important to her firm or client during the previous twelve months. The issues could be national, state, or local, and they could involve any branch of government. We discovered that two issues dominated the lobbying process in the 108th Congress (2003–2004): (1) the Energy Policy Act of 2003 (hereafter referred to as the energy act) and (2) the American Jobs Creation Act of 2004 (hereafter referred to as the jobs act). These bills directly or indirectly affected every firm in our sample. Twenty-four of the sixty-two lobbyists named either the energy act or the jobs act as one of the most important issues for their firm during 2004.[12] The *Boston Globe* reported that firms and trade associations with a stated interest in the two bills spent more than $387 million lobbying in 2003 and 2004. The firms gave millions more in contributions to congressional candidates in the 2004 elections.[13] Examining these issues should provide insight into how interest organizations lobby on highly visible bills that involve substantial group conflict.

The Arab oil embargo in 1973 made America's dependence on imported oil painfully clear. Americans over fifty remember the long lines, sometimes winding around a block, at gasoline stations. America's vulnerability to a reduction in energy supplies has led every U.S. president since 1973 to propose a program for energy development and conservation. President George W. Bush was no exception. Less than ten days after his inauguration, Bush created the National Energy Policy Development Task Force and appointed Vice President Cheney as its chair. The task force, commonly referred to as the "Cheney Task Force," produced the National Energy Policy Report in May 2001. Although only public officials were official members of the task force, Cheney held meetings with over 300 chief executive officers and lobbyists from energy companies and their trade associations. The most frequent private sector attendees at the task force meetings were lobbyists for the American Petroleum Institute, the National Mining Association, and the U.S. Oil and Gas Association.[14]

Cheney became the policy entrepreneur for the president's energy policy. The vice president's comprehensive knowledge of government institutions and energy issues made him the ideal policy entrepreneur for this issue.[15] Cheney's first decision was to invite only energy producers to the task force meetings. By doing this, Cheney ensured that the policy formulation process would give priority to increasing energy production rather than energy conservation. See Box 3.2 for a discussion of the lawsuit filed to obtain the records of the task force. Cheney did not meet with proponents of conservation policies until after his task force had completed its draft report.

BOX 3.2   **Lawsuits to Force the White House to Release the Records of the Cheney Task Force**

NRDC v. Department of Energy

The Natural Resources Defense Council (NRDC) filed a request under the Freedom of Information Act (FOIA) for the documents relating to the Cheney Task Force. The Bush administration refused to disclose the names of industry participants in the task force or what they discussed with Bush policymakers. In April 2001, NRDC filed a request under the FOIA for access to the task force's records; the Bush administration refused to comply. NRDC filed suit, and a federal judge ordered the administration to turn over the documents. On March 25, 2002, nearly a year after first requesting them, NRDC received roughly 10,000 pages relating to the task force from the Department of Energy. Subsequently the department provided another 3,500 pages, but withheld more than 16,000 others. On April 25 the Energy Department produced (again, under the judge's order) the list of task force documents the Energy Department had withheld in whole or in part. The courts held that the White House was not required to provide those documents withheld.

Judicial Watch v. National Energy Policy Development Group

Judicial Watch and the Sierra Club sued the Bush administration for violating the Federal Advisory Committee Act (FACA), which promotes open and balanced government decision-making. Judge Emmett Sullivan ordered discovery in this case. On May 9, 2005, the U.S. Court of Appeals for the District of Columbia ruled that the Vice President's Energy Task Force did not have to comply with the Federal Advisory Act.

NRDC v. Department of Interior

NRDC has also filed a FOIA case against the Department of Interior for records related to the formation and the implementation of the energy task force recommendations. DOI is already moving forward to expedite energy development on public lands across the West, yet refuses to provide basic information about the decisions the agency was making and who was influencing them.

Walker v. Cheney

For the first time in history, the Government Accounting Office (GAO) sued the White House, asserting that it has the right under the statute providing for its existence and authority (Title 31 of the U.S. Code) to investigate the activities of the energy task force because the group received federal funds. Such court action has never before been necessary because GAO has never faced such a refusal for information so basic to its oversight responsibilities. The case was dismissed on December 9, 2002.

Washington Post Obtains a List of Participants

On July 18, 2007, the *Washington Post* reported the names of those involved in the Task Force, including at least 40 meetings with interest groups, most of them from energy-producing industries. Among those corporations whose representatives met with the task force were ExxonMobil, British Petroleum, Enron, the National Mining Association, the American Petroleum Institute, Duke Energy, and Constellation Energy Group. After a draft of the National Energy Policy Report had been completed, the task force invited representatives of Friends of the Earth and of the U.S. Public Interest Group.

Sources: Michael Abramowitz and Steven Mufson, "Papers Detail Industry's Role in Cheney's Energy Report," *Washington Post,* July 18, 2007, www.washingtonpost.com/wp-dyn/content/article/2007/07/17/AR2007071701987.html; and Natural Resources Defense Council, "How NRDC Brought the Records to Light," www.nrdc.org/air/energy/taskforce/bkgrd.asp

The task force published the National Energy Policy Report in May 2001. In the cover letter sent with the report to President Bush, the vice president wrote, "We have developed a national energy policy designed to help bring together business, government, local communities and citizens to promote dependable, affordable and environmentally sound energy for the future."[16] The White House sent the report to the energy and natural resources committees in Congress with the expectation that these committees would use the report as a blueprint for a new energy policy. In 2001 and 2002, however, the Democratic Party controlled the Senate. The Democratic leadership in the Senate refused to consider President Bush's energy proposals. In 2003, this situation changed when Republicans took control of the Senate. The Republican leadership in Congress quickly addressed energy issues and used the proposals in the National Energy Policy Report as its starting point in formulating energy policy alternatives.

The Republican proposal included subsidies for almost every domestic energy source including oil, gas, nuclear, wind, solar, geothermal, biomass, coal, and hydrogen. In addition, there were tax incentives for Americans to conserve energy in their homes and businesses. The Republican leadership included subsidies for renewable as well as nonrenewable energy production. They hoped that this strategy would force Democrats with energy producers in their district or state to support the bill.[17] When the energy act passed the House of Representatives in 2003, it appeared to include something for everyone. Energy producers in every state would receive subsidies.

The House bill included four controversial provisions that most Republicans supported and most Democrats opposed:

1. Limiting the legal liability of the companies responsible for contaminating ground water with the gasoline additive **methyl tertiary-butyl ether (MBTE)**

2. Limiting the legal liability of companies that produce and distribute nuclear power

3. Authorizing the opening of the Yucca Mountain nuclear waste repository

4. Allowing oil and gas exploration in the **Arctic National Wildlife Refuge (ANWR)**

A coalition of environmental interests, liberal citizen action groups, and taxpayer organizations opposed the legislation. Environmental groups and MoveOn.org, an Internet-based liberal citizen action group, mounted a well-coordinated **grassroots campaign** to urge Democratic senators to defeat the bill. The grassroots effort stressed the four most controversial sections of the bill as well as the bill's huge cost. Democrats in the Senate decided to filibuster the bill. Despite President Bush's support for the bill and Republican majorities in the House and Senate, the energy act did not have sufficient support to overcome the filibuster.

Rather than take the issue off the agenda, the Republican leadership reformulated the bill by deleting the MBTE, Yucca Mountain, and ANWR sections of the bill. This move backfired when senators from Texas and Louisiana refused to support a bill that did not include the MBTE liability limitation. Similarly, the deletion of the Yucca Mountain provision led several senators with nuclear power plants in their states to withdraw their support.[18] These defections effectively killed the opportunity to pass an energy bill in the 108th Congress (2003–2004).

Although the energy act was officially off the congressional agenda, the White House and the Republican leadership in Congress had not given up on finding a way to pass the policy. Rather than attempting to pass the entire bill, however, Speaker of the House Dennis Hastert, R-IL, and Senate majority leader Bill Frist, R-TN, began looking for opportunities to pass the energy legislation by attaching pieces of it to other bills. The jobs act provided that opportunity.

THE AMERICAN JOBS CREATION ACT

The jobs act reached the political agenda when the **World Trade Organization (WTO)** ruled that two U.S. tax laws constituted illegal export subsidies under the General Agreement on Tariffs and Trade (GATT). The two laws were the **Foreign Sales Corporation and extraterritorial income (FSC/ETI)** provisions in the U.S. Tax Code. The WTO ruling allowed other countries to levy an import tariff on U.S.-produced goods until the United States revoked the FSC/ETI subsidies. The **European Union (EU)** decided to impose the tariff, severely reducing the sale of U.S. goods in Europe. In response to the EU's decision, President Bush urged Congress to end the FSC/ETI subsidies.

President Bush realized that ending the subsidies would increase the taxes of many U.S. corporations. During his election campaign, President Bush had promised business interests that their taxes would not increase while he was president. To keep this promise, Bush asked Congress to pass a bill that would provide new tax cuts to the corporations that were losing their FSC/ETI subsidies. President Bush, however, had a problem with the fiscal conservatives in the Republican Party. When Bush became president in 2001, the country had a budget surplus. The president used this surplus to press for sizeable individual and corporate tax cuts as well as the repeal of the estate tax. He also initiated expensive wars in Iraq and Afghanistan. The result of these actions was a rapidly growing budget deficit. To prevent further growth in the deficit, Bush asked Congress to limit the size of any new tax cuts to $70 billion. A tax cut of this size would not increase the deficit. The increase in government revenues created by closing the FSC/ETI tax loopholes would pay for the tax cut.

Although President Bush wanted to prevent additional growth in the budget deficit, members of Congress see tax cuts as opportunities to enhance their reelection prospects. If a legislator delivers a tax break to his constituents, those constituents are likely to give him credit for their improved situation. Those same constituents, however, are unlikely to blame him for the budget deficits the tax breaks create. Once it became clear that Congress was considering corporate tax cuts, numerous corporate interests not affected by the repeal of FSC/ETI subsidies began lobbying Congress for tax cuts directed to them. The debate over which interests would receive a tax cut set up conflicts among various corporate interests and between Congress and the White House. The EU and President Bush had placed the issue on the agenda, but the president left it to Congress to formulate the policy alternatives.

In the formulation stage, three interest-group coalitions emerged: (1) manufacturers of goods produced and consumed mainly within the United States, (2) multinational corporations and export industries, and (3) service corporations. Each coalition wanted different tax cuts. Domestic manufacturing corporations formed a coalition with labor unions to push for tax cuts that favored domestic manufacturers. This coalition wanted to limit tax cuts to manufacturing corporations that spent at least 50 percent of their labor costs on U.S. workers. Representatives Philip Crane, R-IL, and Charles Rangel, D-NY, introduced the bill supported by this coalition. The domestic manufacturers' coalition had the advantage of bipartisan sponsorship, and its proposed tax cuts did not exceed President Bush's $70 billion limit. From President Bush's perspective, however, the Crane–Rangel bill failed to give the tax cuts to the corporations that were losing the FSC/ETI tax loopholes.

The second coalition consisted of U.S.-based multinational corporations and foreign-owned corporations that pay U.S. taxes. The information technology (IT) industry took the lead in organizing and coordinating this coalition. The Crane–Rangel bill would provide little relief to most multinational corporations as they outsource much of their production process overseas. Outsourcing is particularly prevalent in the IT industry. The IT-led coalition had the support of several extremely powerful legislators. Rep. Bill Thomas, R-CA, chair of the House Ways and Means Committee, introduced the IT-supported bill in the House. Senators Charles Grassley, R-IA, and Max Baucus, D-MT, the chair and ranking minority member of the Senate Finance Committee, introduced a similar bill in the Senate. Although most of the proposed tax cuts in the Thomas and Grassley–Baucus bills went to firms harmed by the repeal of FSC/ETI subsidies, the bill was not revenue neutral. The Congressional Budget Office estimated that this bill would add almost $80 billion to the budget deficit. This proposed tax cut substantially exceeded the level President Bush wanted.

The National Chamber of Commerce headed a third coalition. It consisted largely of corporations in the service industry. The chamber's bill provided an across-the-board tax cut for all corporations. The coalition argued that providing tax cuts to specific interests increased the complexity of the tax code and harmed U.S. economic efficiency. This coalition fell apart, however, when the Grassley–Baucus bill added tax breaks for insurance and financial service corporations. Those industries then defected from the Chamber of Commerce coalition. Their defection doomed that coalition's chances for success.

The White House found itself in a difficult situation. The bill supported by the domestic manufacturers and organized labor would not add to the deficit. But that bill gave tax breaks to corporations that were not harmed by the revocation of the FSC/ETI export subsidies. The bill supported by the IT-led coalition gave tax breaks to the companies harmed by the elimination of FSC/ETI subsidies, but that bill also gave extensive tax breaks to numerous other interests and added billions to the deficit. The White House decided to oppose both bills, but it did not want to make its opposition public until after the 2004 elections. President Bush feared that making his opposition public would alienate the interests that expected to receive tax cuts. President Bush, therefore, asked the Republican leadership in Congress to defer action on the tax changes until after the elections.

The Republican leadership in Congress decided to challenge the president. In a surprise move, the congressional Republicans agreed to add an overtime pay amendment to the Grassley–Baucus bill in return for a promise from the Democrats not to employ a filibuster to stop the bill. The revised bill also provided limited tax credits for manufacturing firms that used American workers. The Senate approved this version of the jobs act, a bill that provided between $140 and $145 billion in new tax cuts. The House passed a slightly different version of the jobs act, and a House–Senate conference committee met on October 13, 2004, to resolve the differences between the bills. But members of the conference committee did far more than resolve the differences between the bills. The conference committee attached to the jobs act almost all the provisions of the energy act except opening Yucca Mountain and ANWR. The conference committee also added a host of other provisions. Among these were tariffs on foreign-made bows and arrows, the elimination of federal licensing fees on producers and distributors of alcoholic beverages, a tax break for recreational fishing equipment made in the United States, and an 80-percent reduction in the U.S. tax rate corporations paid on foreign-generated income brought back to the United States. Other provisions added by the conference committee paid $10 billion to owners of federal tobacco quotas and allowed U.S. racetracks to cease collecting income taxes on the gambling winnings of bets placed by foreign nationals. The final jobs act statute added approximately $100 billion to the budget deficit.

The passage of the jobs/energy bill placed President Bush in a difficult situation. If he vetoed the bill because of its impact on the budget deficit, he would anger everyone who would benefit from the bill. He also would be vetoing his own energy bill. With the 2004 elections less than a month away, the White House feared a veto could make George W. Bush a one-term president. After weighing his options, the president signed the combined jobs/energy act into law.

The winners and losers in the final bill were clear. The IT industry and other corporations that outsourced large portions of their production process overseas received tax breaks that more than equaled the tax breaks lost from the FSC/ETI subsidies. Foreign-based multinational firms with large manufacturing plants in the United States received a tax break based on their use of American workers. Energy corporations received most of the subsidies contained in the original energy act. Finally, a large number of interests such as the owners of tobacco quotas[19] and the Plano Molding Corporation—the dominant U.S. manufacturer of fishing equipment and a constituent of House majority leader Dennis Hastert—received tax breaks that were essentially private goods.[20] The big losers in the jobs act were labor unions, energy companies whose priorities were ANWR or Yucca Mountain, environmental groups that wanted the energy bill to emphasize energy conservation, and the American taxpayers.

THE DATA QUALITY ACT AND THE BATTLE OVER ATRAZINE

NAFTA, the energy act, and the jobs act are examples of policies with substantial visibility, high partisanship, and extensive group conflict. We now turn to the DQA, a policy that was invisible to the political parties, to the legislators who passed it, and to the president who signed it into law. Only *after* the DQA became law did Congress, President Clinton, and the public become aware that the DQA constituted a radical change in regulatory policymaking. To understand the DQA, we must first examine how the measure became law.

The Impact of the Data Quality Act on Regulation

Prior to the passage of the DQA, the data a regulatory agency employed to evaluate a product's registration or renewal was not required to meet the same standards of quality and replicability as the data producers provided to demonstrate the product's safety. For example, the procedures of the U.S. Food and Drug Administration (FDA) might require a drug manufacturer wishing to register a drug to have multiple studies with samples of 100 animals. Other required studies might involve a host of laboratory experiments as well as extensive experimental trials, all of which cost the manufacturer considerable time, money, and effort. If, however, a researcher opposing the drug's registration conducted a single study and used only twenty-five animals and that study found a statistically significant relationship between the drug and a potential health problem, the FDA could use that study as evidence for denying a drug's registration or renewal.

This approach to scientific evidence was not limited to the FDA. For example, the EPA requires companies wishing to register or renew a pesticide to submit scientific data demonstrating the product's safety. Producing these data is a lengthy and costly process, as manufacturers must show that their product does not harm humans, wildlife, or the quality of surface and groundwater. The manufacturers must provide studies of applicator exposure, spray drift, chemical residue, and cell toxicity. Prior to the passage of the DQA, the general public and organizations opposed to the registration of the pesticide could offer evidence that did not meet such stringent scientific standards. Not surprisingly, manufacturers believed that regulatory agencies had a double standard that punished producers.[21]

Dr. James "Jim" Tozzi—a lobbyist whose clients included pesticide, tobacco, and pharmaceutical companies—decided to eliminate this perceived double standard. Tozzi crafted two paragraphs to insert into the 712-page Treasury and General Government Appropriations Act. Those paragraphs directed the White House Office of Management and Budget (OMB) to issue general guidelines "ensuring and maximizing the quality, objectivity, utility, and integrity of information . . . disseminated by Federal agencies."[22] Tozzi convinced Rep. Jo Ann Emerson, R-MO, to slip the paragraphs into the appropriations bill. Congress did not consider that bill until very late in the congressional session, and no legislators other than Emerson in the House and Richard Shelby, R-AL, in the Senate appeared to understand the implications of those two short paragraphs that became known as the DQA.[23] See Box 3.3 for the wording of the DQA.

BOX 3.3　The Data Quality Act

(a) IN GENERAL.—The Director of the Office of Management and Budget shall, by not later than September 30, 2001, and with public and Federal agency involvement issue guidelines under sections 3504(d)(1) and 3516 of title 44, United States Code, that provide policy and procedural guidance to Federal agencies for ensuring and maximizing the quality, objectivity, utility, and integrity of information (including statistical information) disseminated by Federal agencies in fulfillment of the purposes and provisions of chapter 35 of title 44, United States Code, commonly referred to as the Paperwork Reduction Act.

(b) CONTENT OF GUIDELINES.—The guidelines under subsection (a) shall (1) apply to the sharing by Federal agencies of, and access to, information disseminated by Federal agencies; and (2) require that each Federal agency to which the guidelines apply (A) issue guidelines ensuring and maximizing the quality, objectivity, utility, and integrity of information (including statistical information) disseminated by the agency by not later than 1 year after the date of issuance of the guidelines under subsection (a); (B) establish administrative mechanisms allowing affected persons to seek and obtain correction of information maintained and disseminated by the agency that does not comply with the guidelines issued under subsection (a); and (C) report periodically to the Director (i) the number and nature of complaints received by the agency regarding the accuracy of information disseminated by the agency; and (ii) how such complaints were handled.

Source: Section 515(a) of the Treasury and General Government Appropriations Act for Fiscal Year 2001 (Public Law 106-554; H.R. 5658).

The DQA directed the OMB to write general data quality guidelines for any data used by the federal government. Tozzi wanted OMB to oversee writing the guidelines because he knew that the **Office of Information and Regulatory Affairs (OIRA)** within OMB would write the guidelines. OIRA's main job is to review proposed federal regulations and to determine whether a regulation's costs outweigh its benefits. President Reagan had one goal when he established

OIRA: to reduce the regulatory burden on business and industry. OIRA takes this goal seriously, and Washington insiders refer to OIRA as "the place where regulations go to die" and as "the black hole for regulations." President Reagan had appointed Jim Tozzi the first head of OIRA, so Tozzi was intimately familiar with how the office operated. By having OIRA write the guidelines for data quality, Tozzi guaranteed that a bureau known for its antiregulatory bias would decide the DQA's standards and procedures. Tozzi was confident that OIRA would make decisions that favored producer interests and reduced the influence of environmental and consumer interest groups.

The implementation of the DQA exceeded Tozzi's wildest dreams. President George W. Bush appointed John D. Graham as the director of OIRA. Graham interpreted the DQA as requiring each federal agency to draft rules and guidelines for ensuring data quality *and to submit those to OIRA for approval.* For example, the guidelines that OIRA approved for the EPA reduced substantially the types of information the EPA could use to keep a product off the market. The guidelines required that all data used in the EPA's decision making meet the same standards that the EPA requires of the company wishing to register or renew a product. This requirement raises substantially the costs of preventing a product's registration or renewal. OIRA forced the EPA to develop a test for each harmful outcome that might lead to the denial of a product's registration.

The Battle Over Atrazine

The first major test of the DQA came when the EPA began a review of atrazine, the most widely used herbicide in the United States. Syngenta Corporation produces atrazine and sells millions of pounds of the herbicide every year. The Clinton administration decided that atrazine's widespread use justified an early review of the product's safety. Officials within the EPA expected the agency's review would deny the product's renewal as the EU had already banned atrazine use in Europe. The EPA, however, did not complete the review before George W. Bush replaced Clinton in the White House.[24] When the Bush administration came into office, the president named Christine Todd Whitman to head the EPA. One of her first decisions was to stop the EPA's review of atrazine. In response to Whitman's decision, the Natural Resources Defense Council (NRDC), an environmental group, successfully sued the EPA and forced it to complete the review.

Three scientific studies were crucial to the EPA's review of atrazine. One study found that rats ingesting high doses of atrazine were more likely to develop cancer than rats not exposed to the herbicide. Another study showed that workers in Syngenta's atrazine plant in Louisiana experienced higher prostate cancer rates than other adults in the state. The third study was the most central to the EPA's decision. Dr. Tyrone Hayes, an assistant professor of biology at the University of California, Berkeley, observed that frogs exposed to atrazine developed abnormal sex organs. Hayes concluded that atrazine had disrupted the production of the hormones necessary for the organs to develop normally. Hayes published his study in highly prestigious scientific journals, and the research received substantial media attention. At the end of 2002, it looked as if Syngenta would lose its most profitable product.

Syngenta fought the EPA by funding the Triazine Network, a newly created interest group composed of atrazine users. The Triazine Network hired Dr. Jim Tozzi to find a way to keep atrazine on the market. Not surprisingly, Tozzi used the DQA to challenge the studies that revealed that atrazine might pose a threat to human health. Tozzi was able to show that the rat study used doses of atrazine that were far in excess of the EPA's research protocols. In addition, independent research concluded that atrazine was unlikely to have caused the cancers found in the rats. The prostate cancer study also was deeply flawed. Tozzi demonstrated that the higher rate of prostate cancer observed in Syngenta's workers occurred not because atrazine was causing cancer but because Syngenta aggressively screened its workers for all types of cancer. The prostate cancer study did not have a control group that also received cancer screening. This made it impossible to conclude that the cancer rate observed at Syngenta's plant was higher than that of the general population.

Only the frog research appeared to meet the EPA's guidelines for research quality. Tozzi argued, however, that the EPA could not use the frog data as evidence that atrazine was a hormone disruptor. The EPA's data quality guidelines stipulated that until the EPA developed an approved test to determine whether a chemical created a particular harm, the agency could not deny a product's registration based on that harm. In other words, if the EPA was going to ban atrazine because it might be a hormone disruptor, the agency had to have a test for what constitutes evidence of a hormone disruptor. The EPA had not yet developed this test. The agency, therefore, could not use the frog study in its decision on atrazine safety. Citing the absence of an accepted test for measuring hormone disruption, the EPA concluded that it could not restrict atrazine use.[25] In 2009, the EPA announced that it had developed tests for hormone disruption and planned to phase out atrazine use.[26] In 2012, however, the EPA had not yet completed all of the studies necessary to meet the requirements of the DQA, and atrazine remained on the market.[27] The DQA had bought Syngenta a decade of atrazine profits.

PLACING OUR CASE STUDIES WITHIN THE POLICY STAGES FRAMEWORK

How does the policy stages model help us to discern patterns of interest-group influence in our four case studies? The first pattern we observe is that policymaking typically is not a single exchange where policymakers and interest organizations meet a single time to settle an issue. Rather, our cases indicate that policymaking is a process that involves multiple decisions by numerous individuals, groups, and institutions. The dominant mode of decision making in three of the four cases was bargaining. Multiple actors adjusted their policy goals to achieve an acceptable policy. Only the DQA does not fit this pattern.

The DQA also provides an exception to Kingdon's theory of agenda setting and formulating alternatives and to the neopluralist theory of group influence. Unlike the other three issues, the DQA did not involve the development of a broad-based coalition that gained the attention of policymakers. The problem and the solution did not exist independently of each other, and the political mood in the Clinton administration was antithetical to the DQA. Political parties and elections played no role in getting the issue on the agenda or in formulating policy options. Instead, a single lobbyist took advantage of the processes imbedded in the American legislative institutions to make a radical change in the regulatory process.

The second pattern in our cases is that the strategies and effectiveness of those strategies vary across the stages of the policy process. The case studies demonstrate that organized interests can have substantial influence during the agenda setting and formulation stages. In every case except the DQA, interest organizations mobilized support for a policy alternative inside and outside of government. Interest groups organized coalitions of groups that supported their favored policy alternatives. The groups also helped legislators organize coalitions within Congress. In three of the issues, policy formulation involved bargains and compromises among the interest groups within each coalition. The jobs act demonstrated this process most clearly. Three coalitions emerged, each with its own policy alternative. Ultimately, a bargain struck between the IT coalition and the financial services industry determined which policy alternative would succeed. One of the lobbyists involved in the jobs act stated, "There are far more deals made on K Street than on Capitol Street" (personal communication with Fortune 1000 lobbyist). (K Street is the home of numerous lobbying firms, and the Capitol building where Congress meets is located on Capitol Street.)

Although interest organizations played key roles during the policy formulation stage of all four issues, their impact on floor votes was minimal on every issue but NAFTA. Union campaign contributions had a statistically significant impact on committee behavior, position taking, and floor votes on NAFTA, even after controlling for a legislator's party identification and ideology.[28] As Diana Evans showed in her painstaking analysis of legislators' votes, however, the variable that had the largest impact on a legislator's vote was whether the legislator received a special benefit for his constituency. Eighty-four percent of legislators who received a special provision voted in favor of NAFTA. Only 47 percent of those not receiving a special benefit voted for the agreement. In a multivariate analysis of legislators' votes, receiving a special benefit for a constituent group was a more important predictor of the vote than any other variable.[29]

The third pattern we observed in our cases was that any given stage of the policy process is likely to occur multiple times. Presidential efforts to pass a comprehensive energy plan were on the agenda of every president since Jimmy Carter. The energy act reached the congressional agenda three times. The first occurred in 2001 when Vice President Cheney sent the Energy Policy Report to

Congress. Although the proposal had the backing of the president, the Democratic-controlled Congress refused to give the issue serious consideration and it dropped off the agenda. The second time the energy act reached the agenda was in 2003 when Republicans won control of Congress. This bill fell off the agenda when Democrats in the Senate decided to filibuster the bill. The issue reached the agenda a third time when the Republican leadership in Congress attached most of the 2003 energy act to the jobs act during the House–Senate conference committee. The DQA again is an exception to the pattern of repeating stages. There was only one stealthy trip to the agenda and only one policy formulation.

Three of our four cases demonstrate the importance of policy entrepreneurs. Policy entrepreneurs often are critical to policy success, and they must spend enormous time and energy attempting to get a policy on the political agenda and to shepherd it through the policymaking process.[30] The entrepreneur has extensive knowledge not only of the issue but also of the policy process. Earlier in the chapter, we examined the roles of President Salinas, Jim Robinson, and Kay Whitmore as NAFTA's policy entrepreneurs. Vice President Cheney was ideally suited to be the policy entrepreneur for the energy act. As the ex-CEO of Halliburton, the world's second largest energy services company, Cheney had comprehensive knowledge of energy issues. As a former minority leader in Congress with ten years of congressional service and as a past chief of staff for President George H. W. Bush, Cheney had an insider's knowledge of the policy processes in Congress and in the White House. His position as vice president gave him the resources to create a comprehensive energy proposal and the political power to continue pushing for its passage. Cheney used his knowledge, skills, and power to set the agenda for energy policy. His experience in the House of Representatives taught him that despite the Democratic filibuster of the energy act, opportunities would arise for attaching his proposals to other legislation.

In many respects, the most interesting policy entrepreneur in our case studies was Jim Tozzi. The most successful policy entrepreneurs create an institutional change that will shape future policy decisions.[31] Tozzi secured his policy goals by not focusing on policy. Instead, Tozzi focused on institutional structures that could ensure a wide range of policy wins. His contacts with members of Congress allowed him to pick a legislator who was on the right subcommittee to insert his 217 carefully chosen words into a bill. He also chose the right bill as the vehicle for those words, a mammoth appropriations bill that few legislators would read. Finally, Tozzi's knowledge of the procedures, and the antiregulatory bias of OIRA were critical to the long-term effectiveness of the DQA. Tozzi's ability to sneak policies into legislation that undercut the efforts of regulatory agencies led public officials and lobbyists to give him the nickname "Stealth."[32]

One characteristic of the successful policy entrepreneurs in our cases was their ability to limit the policy alternatives that policymakers considered. Jim Robinson and Kay Whitmore used their positions as cochairs of the

Advisory Committee for Trade Policy and Negotiations to limit the options available to interest organizations in NAFTA. Vice President Cheney invited only energy producer interests to participate in designing the National Energy Policy Report. Jim Tozzi formulated the only policy option for the DQA and attempted to limit the debate over the policy by ensuring that the policy proposal would be largely invisible until after the president signed it into law.

THE ROLE OF COLLECTIVE AND PRIVATE GOODS

A fifth pattern emerged from our case studies: private goods become increasingly important as a proposed alternative moves through the policy process. Collective goods provided the official justification for all four policies in our case studies. Supporters expected NAFTA to provide greater economic growth, improved productive efficiency, and lowered prices. The energy act would provide American energy independence and lower energy costs. The jobs act would prevent an unfair tax increase to all the industries harmed by the repeal of the FSC/ETI subsidies. The DQA would improve the quality of information and decision making by regulatory agencies.

During the process of becoming law, however, private goods became increasingly prevalent. The side agreements negotiated with Mexico and Canada provided goods much closer to the private goods end of the private–collective goods continuum. These goods included textile manufacturers receiving protection from Mexican textiles, Louisiana sugar growers obtaining quotas on Mexican sugar imports, and the manufacturer of C-17 cargo planes obtaining a contract for two more planes. The jobs/energy act became a typical example of exchanges among participants in the policy process. Congress provided such private goods as $10 billion to holders of tobacco quotas and a special tax subsidy to the builders of a single shopping center. Previous scholars such as Diana Evans, Robert Stein, and Kenneth Bickers have shown that presidents and congressional leaders often offer individual legislators private goods for their constituents to ensure the passage of the bill containing the collective goods.[33] Similarly, Elaine Sharp has noted the tendency of politics involving competition among larger interest groups to move toward the distribution of private goods to various client groups.[34] As we shall show in future chapters, almost all policymaking includes a phase where collective goods dominate the policy debate and a later phase during which the focus is on securing private goods.

SUMMARY

This chapter provides an overview of the stages of the policy process and shows how breaking down the process into manageable parts can assist researchers and students. The chapter also identifies patterns of interest-group influence in different policy stages. Three of the four issues studied—NAFTA, the energy act, and the jobs act—follow a similar pattern of agenda setting and policy formulation. A policy window opens up when the problem, policy, and politics streams converged. A policy entrepreneur takes advantage of this convergence to place her issue on the agenda. The entrepreneur develops a broad coalition seeking one or more collective goods. There is competition among interest groups over these collective goods, and each side has sufficient resources to lobby effectively. This competition fits well the neopluralist analysis of interest-group influence. The analysis of our cases also showed that as the policy process entered the final parts of the decision stage, private goods emerged as critical parts of the legislation. The private goods provided by NAFTA and the final jobs act involved little conflict or competition among interest groups. The private goods phase of the decision-making stage fits the exchange model of group influence.

The DQA case study suggests that the neopluralist approach may miss some important policy issues and outcomes. The DQA had no visibility, no competition, no bargaining, and parties and elections were unimportant to the passage of the act. If researchers had searched the lobbying disclosure database, they would not have found that Jim Tozzi lobbied on the Data Quality Act or on regulatory reform. Had Jim Tozzi filed a lobbying disclosure report,[35] he would have listed "government services appropriations" as the issue on which he lobbied. There was no media coverage of the DQA until long after it became law. Had scholars conducted interviews with the lobbyists and legislators who were most involved in the passage of the appropriations bill, the respondents would not have named Tozzi as an influential actor. Yet the DQA is one of the most significant regulatory reforms over the past twenty-five years.[36] It changed the balance of power between producer groups and the interests the regulatory agencies were established to protect. Congressional scholars Roger Davidson and Walter Oleszck argued that situations similar to the DQA policy process occur frequently.[37] Their research found that it is common for legislators to sneak provisions into long, complex bills. This is particularly likely to happen with appropriations bills.

The DQA and policies achieved through similar tactics are troubling to political science and to American democracy. They present a challenge for political science because the goods provided in these situations are difficult to find and to research. The public, the media, scholars, and the policymakers themselves generally are ignorant of these provisions. In this situation, political scientists cannot evaluate effectively the influence of special interests. Policies passed through hidden procedures are still more troubling for American democracy. If an elected official is unaware that he is deciding an issue, then he cannot effectively represent the preferences of his constituents or pursue his conception of the public interest. If the public is unaware of these provisions, it is not possible for them to hold their elected representatives accountable.

ENDNOTES

1. We are not suggesting that the policy process moves through orderly stages from agenda setting to implementation. We are suggesting that lobbying strategies differ across policy stages. Therefore, when a policy moves back and forth across stages, the interest organizations active and their lobbying strategies will change in predictable patterns.

2. Elementary and Secondary Education Act of 1965, Pub. L. No. 89-10, 79 Stat. 27, 20 U.S.C. ch.70 (1965).

3. William Eskridge and John Ferejohn, "Super-Statutes," *Duke Law Journal* 50 (2001): 1215–1276.

4. For excellent discussions of why problem definition is so important, see Deborah Stone, *Policy Paradox: The Art of Political Decisionmaking*, rev. ed. (New York: W.W. Norton, 2001); and Anne Schneider and Helen Ingram, *Policy Design for Democracy* (Lawrence: University of Kansas Press, 1997).

5. Some scholars refer to the legitimation stage as the decision-making stage.

6. Kevin M. Esterling, *The Political Economy of Expertise: Information and Efficiency in American National Politics* (Ann Arbor: University of Michigan Press, 2004).

7. John Chubb, *Interest Groups and the Bureaucracy: The Politics of Energy* (Stanford, CA: Stanford University Press, 1983).

8. For example, the nation's top banker, the chairperson of Federal Reserve Board, used his position to prevent the Commodity Futures Trading Commission and other federal agencies from regulating over-the-counter derivatives, credit default swaps, and forward rate agreements. See, for example, The Federal Reserve Board, "Testimony of Chairman Alan Greenspan: The Regulation of OTC Derivatives Before the Committee on Banking and Financial Services, U.S. House of Representatives," July 24, 1998, www.federalreserve.gov/boarddocs/testimony/1998/19980724.htm. Greenspan later admitted that his views were incorrect. The absence of regulation was an important factor leading to the near collapse of the financial sector in 2008 and the recession that followed it.

9. John Kingdon, *Agendas, Alternatives, and Public Policies*, 2nd ed. (Reading, MA: Addison-Wesley, 1995), 122–130; and Michael Mintrom and Phillipa Norman, "Policy Entrepreneurship and Policy Change," *Policy Studies Journal* 37 (2009): 649–666.

10. Frederick W. Mayer, *Interpreting NAFTA: The Science and Art of Policy Analysis* (New York: Columbia University Press, 1998), 87.

11. The Fortune 1000 is an annual list compiled by *Fortune* magazine that ranks the top 1,000 U.S. private and public corporations ranked by their gross revenue.

12. Six other firms named overtime pay, an issue that later became part of the jobs act.

13. Susan Milligan, "Energy Bill: A Special-Interests Triumph," *Boston Globe*, October 4, 2004, A1.

14. Natural Resources Defense Council, "The Cheney Energy Task Force," March 27, 2002. www.nrdc.org/air/energy/taskforce/tfinx.asp

15. Vice President Cheney began his political career as a congressional intern. He later served in the White House during the Nixon administration and became President Ford's chief of staff. Cheney was elected to the U.S. House of Representatives in 1978 and served six terms, eventually becoming the House minority whip. Cheney served as secretary of defense for President George H. W. Bush. During the Clinton presidency, Cheney served as the CEO of Halliburton Company, an energy company that ranks among the 200 largest corporations in America.

16. *National Energy Policy Report* in May 2001, letter from Richard Cheney to George W. Bush accompanying the report. Washington, DC: Government Printing Office.

17. The estimated total cost of the proposed bill to taxpayers and consumers was $142 billion over ten years (Committee on Government Reform, Minority Office, 2003, http://wtrg.com/EnergyReport/National-Energy-Policy.pdf)

18. Milligan, "Energy Bill: A Special-Interests Triumph"; and Chris Mooney, "Interrogations," *Boston Globe*, August 28, 2005, www.boston.com/news/globe/ideas/articles/2005/08/28/interrogations/?page=full

19. The owners of the tobacco quotas were generally not tobacco farmers but landowners who rented their quota to the low-income tenant farmers who actually grew the tobacco. The Congressional Research Service estimated that only 14 percent of the persons who received the quota buyout actually produced tobacco. Jasper Womach, "Tobacco Quota Buyout," CRS Report for Congress RS22046 , December 31, 2005, www.nationalaglawcenter.org/assets/crs/RS22046.pdf

20. Plano Molding Company is located in the congressional district represented by Dennis Hastert, the Speaker of the House at the time the jobs act was passed.

21. Having a double standard makes sense if the primary goal of a regulatory agency is to protect public safety and the secondary goal is efficiency.

22. Rick Weiss, "'Data Quality' Law Is Nemesis of Regulation," *Washington Post,* August 16, 2004, A1.

23. Interviews with individuals who are familiar with the development of the DQA indicate that Tozzi was not paid by any of his clients to develop the amendment. He was, however, in close contact with his clients and solicited their advice concerning how the amendment should be phrased.

24. The information in this section comes in part from interviews with lobbyists who were involved with the battle over atrazine. The lobbyists were guaranteed that they would not be identified in any publication dealing with the atrazine policy process.

25. Mooney, "Interrogations."

26. Natural Resources Defense Council, "Federal Government Moves towards Potential Atrazine Phase-Out," www.nrdc.org/media/2009/091007.asp.

27. U.S. Environmental Protection Agency, "Atrazine Updates," September 2011. www.epa.gov/opp00001/reregistration/atrazine/atrazine_update.htm. The DQA has provided substantial work for Tozzi's lobbying firm. Between 2001 and 2004, industry organizations filed 39 petitions challenging information that federal agencies used to support their regulatory decisions. Almost all of these challenges hired Tozzi's firm to assist them in preparing the challenges. For a list of Tozzi's work for various clients visit Tozzi's Center for Regulatory Effectiveness website CRE.com.

28. Janet M. Box-Steffensmeier, Laura W. Arnold, and Christopher J. W. Zorn, "The Strategic Timing of Position Taking in Congress: A Study of the North American Free Trade Agreement," *American Political Science Review* 91, no. 2 (1997): 324–338; and Erik Gartzke and Mark Wrighton, "Thinking Globally or Acting Locally? Determinants of the GATT Vote in Congress," *Legislative Studies Quarterly* 23, no. 1 (1998): 33–55.

29. Diana Evans, *Greasing the Wheels: Using Pork Barrel Projects to Build Majority Coalitions in Congress* (New York: Cambridge University Press, 2004), 150–154.

30. John Kingdon, *Agendas, Alternatives, and Public Policies*, 122–124.

31. Mintrom and Norman, "Policy Entrepreneurship and Policy Change."

32. This nickname was attributed to Tozzi in an interview with one of his lobbying competitors and in an interview with a lobbyist for one of the regulatory agencies.

33. See Evans' *Greasing the Wheels;* Robert Stein and Kenneth Bickers, *Perpetuating the Pork Barrel: Policy Subsystems and American Democracy* (New York: Cambridge University Press, 1995).

34. Elaine B. Sharp, "The Dynamics of Issue Expansion: Cases from Disability Rights and Fetal Research Controversy," *Journal of Politics* 56, no. 4 (1994): 919–939.

35. Because Tozzi spent less than $10,000 lobbying on the issue, he did not need to file a report.

36. Mooney, "Interrogations."

37. See Roger H. Davidson and Walter J. Oleszck, *Congress and Its Members*, 8th ed. (Washington, DC: CQ Press, 2002).

chapter 4

Policymaking by Regulatory Agencies

While the Courts handle thousands of cases
each year and Congress produces hundreds of laws each year,
administrative agencies handle hundreds of thousands of matters
annually. The administrative agencies are engaged in the mass
production of law, in contrast to . . . Congress, which is engaged
in the handicraft production of law.[1]

This quote, from a commissioner of the Federal Communications Commission, expresses one of the unexpected realities of the American political system: the bureaucracy rather than our elected representatives make the vast majority of laws. Even if we restrict our analysis to the small percentage of regulations that are the most expensive, precedent setting, and intrusive (laws that the White House designates as "significant" or Congress identifies as "major"), the bureaucracy issues approximately twice as many significant regulations as Congress passes statutes. The Office of Management and Budget (OMB) estimates that the most expensive 105 of the nearly 38,000 regulations issued between 2001 and 2010 created between $23.3 and $28.5 billion in costs and generated benefits between $81.8 and $550.7 billion.[2] Given the stakes, it is unsurprising that interest groups spend millions of dollars to influence the regulatory process.

Ironically, interest groups, Congress, and the president encounter similar difficulties when attempting to influence the bureaucracy. The federal bureaucrats in charge of regulations are unelected, difficult to fire, and largely invisible to the public. These characteristics help to insulate the regulatory process (and the bureaucrats who run them) from elected officials and interest groups alike. Congress and the president have sought to maintain control over regulatory decisions through the application of oversight statutes, executive orders, and procedural checks. Interest organizations, in turn, exploit these windows of access for their own ends. Who successfully influences regulations—and, perhaps more importantly, who fails to influence regulations—has profound implications for representation across groups in American society. This chapter examines the rulemaking process (we use "regulations" and "rules" interchangeably), the attempts by Congress and the White House to oversee the bureaucracy and hold it accountable, and the efforts of lobbyists to affect regulations at key points. We use two case studies to illustrate bureaucratic policymaking: the implementation of the Data Quality Act (DQA) by OMB and the battle over perchlorate regulation that took place between the Departments of Energy and Defense on one side and the Environmental Protection Agency (EPA) on the other.

THE BREADTH OF THE REGULATORY PROCESS

Congress routinely delegates broad lawmaking authority to the bureaucracy. The Occupational Safety and Health Act of 1970, for example, shows the exceptional latitude granted to regulatory agencies. This act, signed into law by President Nixon, created the Occupational Safety and Health Administration (OSHA). OSHA's mission is as follows:

> To assure safe and healthful working conditions for working men and women; by authorizing enforcement of the standards developed under the Act; by assisting and encouraging the States in their efforts to assure safe and healthful working conditions; by providing for research, information, education, and training in the field of occupational safety and health; and for other purposes.[3]

OSHA has the authority to do the following:

- Set mandatory workplace safety and health standards.

- Engage in research to improve safety as well as physical and mental health.

- Discover how environmental conditions in the workplace cause diseases.

- Provide medical criteria to ensure that employees will not suffer diminished health.

- Establish an enforcement program.

- Require reporting procedures for employers.

- Oversee state and local efforts to protect worker safety and health.

The secretary of labor has the authority to propose rules and regulations to achieve all of the previously stated purposes.[4] This includes the ability to dictate everything from the shade of red of fire extinguishers to the exposure limits, ventilation procedures, and clothing worn in various manufacturing processes.

The EPA has even more extensive regulatory powers than OSHA. From 1970 to 1980, a number of broad-based antipollution acts passed Congress. These include the following:

- Clean Air Act

- Clean Water Act

- Safe Drinking Water Act (SDWA)

- Resource Conservation and Recovery Act (RCRA)

- Federal Insecticide, Fungicide, and Rodenticide Act (FIFRA)

- Comprehensive Environmental Response, Compensation, and Liability Act (Superfund)

These acts and their amendments provide the EPA with an almost unlimited scope of action in terms of reducing pollution and promoting public health. For example, the stated (but impossible) goal of the Clean Water Act is to eliminate the discharge of *all* pollutants into the nation's waterways. The SDWA sets standards that govern *all suspected* toxic chemicals that can contaminate streams and groundwater. The SDWA requires the EPA to set standards for drinking water quality, to oversee all states and localities, and to enforce these standards on more than 150,000 public water systems.[5] RCRA gives the EPA the authority to control hazardous waste from cradle to grave. This includes the generation, transportation, treatment, storage, and disposal of hazardous waste. RCRA also sets the rules for the management of nonhazardous solid wastes. RCRA requires the EPA to protect human health and the natural environment from the *potential* hazards of waste disposal. Using this act, the EPA mandates the conservation of energy and natural resources, requires reductions in the production of toxic waste, and creates guidelines for recycling.[6]

Clearly, OSHA and the EPA can promulgate federal laws across broad swathes of policy territory, and the full scope of federal regulatory activity reaches far beyond the missions of OSHA and the EPA. Regulatory influence spans virtually all of society's activities, and federal agencies add new regulations at a dizzying rate. These laws determine who gets federal funding to attend college, the types of fertilizers and pesticides a farmer can use, the workers the farmer can hire, the level of risk to workers in every industry, and which drugs consumers can buy at the corner pharmacy versus which drugs they must buy in the alley behind the drug store.

THE ROLE OF THE BUREAUCRACY IN THE CREATION OF LAW

The bureaucracy presents an important challenge to democracy. The breadth and depth of the policy problems faced by modern societies require bureaucratic expertise. Policymaking requires considerable issue-specific knowledge, research, and time. When writing law, elected officials would like to leverage the technical expertise and implementation capabilities housed within the bureaucratic agencies. Ideally, this would take the form of setting the broad normative targets and letting the agencies implement those goals. For example, it is unreasonable to expect the busy members of Congress to determine how many **parts per billion (ppb)** of perchlorate in drinking water create a toxic hazard. Congresspersons are neither toxicologists nor hydrologists, and hiring sufficient congressional staff to gain the substantive expertise on every policy issue would quickly overwhelm the capabilities of even the largest legislature. Instead, Congress passes the SDWA that directs the EPA to use its scientific experts to set safe standards for chemicals like perchlorate. The EPA then crafts the highly technical and detailed implementing regulations that ensure the safety of the nation's drinking water. Neither Congress nor the White House can efficiently duplicate that effort with their limited staff, making delegation essential to the formation and implementation of good policy.

The delegation of power to the bureaucracy and the bureaucracy's extensive technical resources create an oversight problem for Congress, the president, and the public. Generally known as the **principal–agent dilemma**, effective oversight becomes an issue whenever a principal (in this case Congress and/or the president) delegates power to an agent (the agency). Work by Marissa Golden and others has shown that agencies have their own missions and policy goals, potentially tempting them to generate laws that are more consistent with their own preferences than the preferences of Congress or the president. Elected officials, with their limited staffs, struggle to ensure that the thousands of highly technical regulations are consistent with their preferences. The public suffers from a related difficulty in obtaining information about proposed regulations. Ordinary citizens lack the information to participate effectively in the rulemaking process.

The core of the principal–agent problem is asymmetric information. The agency possesses more information about the substance, the process, and the timing of the regulation than either the public or their elected representatives. Congress and the president have the necessary procedural and political information to influence the process, but they often lack the substantive knowledge to correctly structure the rule's impacts on society. Conversely, some members of the public are likely to have the technical expertise to interpret the rule yet lack the knowledge of the policy process required to use their expertise effectively. For these reasons, the principals and their constituents may possess only a part of the information puzzle, creating a dangerous challenge for democratic representation when delegation occurs.

The tremendous informational and systemic advantages enjoyed by the agencies led American government scholars in the 1960s and 1970s to conclude that the bureaucracy had the upper hand in policymaking. What these "strong bureaucracy" theories failed to account for, however, was that elected officials get to set the rules of the regulatory game. Congress and the president make full use of their authority to design the agencies' internal structures, appoint top bureaucratic personnel, and set the procedural requirements that all regulations must meet. This latter power is particularly important. Congress and the president can use their control over the process to reduce the **information asymmetry** problem. How is this done?

Consider the design problem from the perspective of an undergraduate student who wants to ensure that the classes she selects contain the information she needs and that the instructors will grade her products fairly. Imagine if only the titles of ten potential courses are available. Could the student make an informed decision about which four classes best meet her preferences for the semester? Probably not. First, the student would like to have a bit more information about the professors' expectations, course requirements, and the grading policies. In other words, the student desires that the procedures and substance of the courses be *transparent* to all interested parties (e.g., potential students). Most universities accommodate this perfectly reasonable request by requiring professors to distribute syllabi containing the relevant information. Of course, the *timing* of the distribution of the syllabi is equally critical. It does the student no good if the course description/requirements are available only after she has chosen her courses. In the interests of fairness and full disclosure, the student should receive the information prior to agreeing to the contract (which is what most schools consider a syllabus). Next, the student would like some assurance that the requirements stated in the syllabus—the timing of exams, the number of papers, etc.—will be *consistent* with what the professor actually requires. The universities that employ the authors of this book forbid professors from grading in an arbitrary or capricious manner. Finally, the student probably desires some way to appeal the grade, just in case. Universities generally have some codified *review* process, both to accommodate grade challenges and to keep professors accountable over the long term. Taken together, these procedural requirements keep the professor accountable to the preferences of the university and to the students. More importantly, however, the requirements allow the student to represent her own interests accurately and knowledgably. In other words, the student can protect her interests using the procedural steps built into the system.

Unsurprisingly, Congress, the president, and the courts have built the same four oversight systems into the regulatory process. For any new regulation, the agency must provide a transparent road map of regulatory intent, release substantive and procedural information related to the rule in a timely fashion, remain consistent throughout the process in terms of the rule's requirements, and submit to formal reviews by all three branches of government. The resulting regulatory process is designed, therefore, to be responsive to political pressure. Lobbyists routinely make use of these oversight windows to affect regulatory policy outcomes.

THE RELATIONSHIP BETWEEN OVERSIGHT MECHANISMS AND LOBBYING

Mathew McCubbins and Thomas Schwartz distinguished between two very different types of agency oversight. **Police patrols** refer to direct oversight mechanisms such as requiring broad categories of regulations to undergo White House review or requiring weekly testimony by an agency at a Senate oversight committee. Similar in nature to policemen walking a beat, direct oversight requires significant resources (particularly time and attention). **Fire alarms**, on the other hand, only occur when an agency decision harms individuals and interest groups who then appeal to Congress or the president. The interest groups inform the elected bodies that the agency has deviated from the policy preferences of the Congress or the White House. Fire alarms are very efficient. They allow elected officials to constrain agency behavior without the costs of constant oversight. A key point here is that fire alarms depend upon lobbyists and interest groups to "pull" the alarm and to provide information about agency activities.

In addition to simply alerting Congress or the White House of agency misbehavior, interest organizations provide critical technical information in policymaking. Richard Hall and Alan Deardorff showed why lobbying information is so valuable to Congress and the president.[7] Interest groups with the most to gain or lose from changes in policy often possess excellent information regarding the issue. By listening to what these groups have to say about an agency's regulatory design, elected officials avoid the costs of developing the same information and level of expertise on the issue. In effect, the political institutions receive an information "subsidy." For example, persons who work with the toxic element beryllium have the incentive and knowledge necessary to evaluate the worker safety regulations generated by the Department of Energy and OSHA. Sharing their substantive expertise with the legislature allows the workers' union to lobby, and Congress receives a wealth of knowledge with very little effort on its part.

For fire alarms and information subsidies to occur, however, the public needs to have transparent windows through which to observe the regulatory process. As with the undergraduate example, timing is critical: the windows must open at the right time so that elected officials and the public can use the information. Figure 4.1 provides a general depiction of the regulatory process.

The generation of regulations is relatively straightforward. First, Congress and/or the president grants rulemaking authority to the implementing agency. All regulations promulgated by the bureaucracy must ultimately trace back to congressional statutes or presidential executive orders. The statute, however, may be quite old. For example, the authority for the EPA to regulate the chemical perchlorate in 2012 comes from the 1974 SDWA. The decision to go forward with a regulation is political as well as technical. The EPA could have chosen to use its resources in hundreds of other ways. As a high-level EPA official indicated to one of the authors, the EPA could use its entire budget just enforcing the Clean Air Act and the Clean Water Act. Often, the president places an item on the political agenda by directing his political

FIGURE 4.1   **The Rulemaking Process**

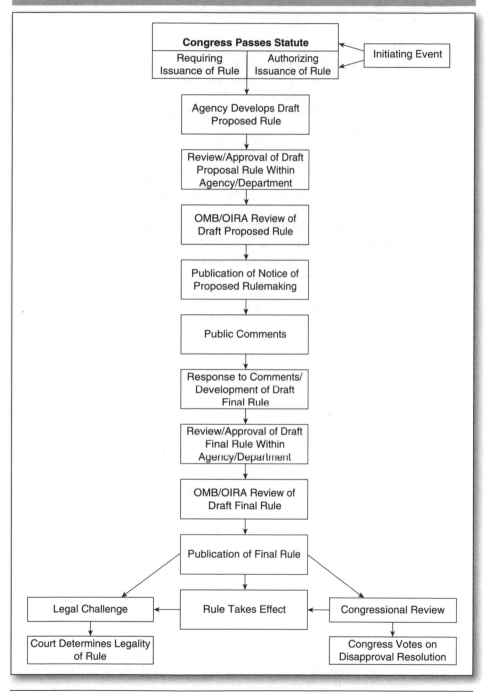

Source: Curtis W. Copeland, "The Unified Agenda: Implications for Rulemaking Transparency and Participation," CRS Report for Congress, July 20, 2009, www.fas.org/sgp/crs/secrecy/R40713.pdf

appointee at the appropriate agency to prepare a regulation. Congress also can urge an agency to give a particular issue priority. An agency's advisory committees (we will discuss these later) also may suggest that an agency develop a particular regulation.

The agency then uses its delegated authority to draft a proposed rule. Executive Order (E.O.) 12866 requires that the agencies send the most important federal regulations to the White House for review.[8] The reviews take place in the Office of Information and Regulatory Affairs (OIRA). Substantial evidence indicates that OIRA's reviews promote the president's policy agenda. When President Reagan issued E.O. 12291 requiring that all proposed regulations have greater benefits than costs, he intended it as a method of expanding presidential power over the bureaucracy: "In essence, OIRA's review institutionalizes the primacy of politics."[9] Congressional investigations have found that the review process substantially increased White House control over regulatory outcomes:

> While the informal, often secretive nature of the [OIRA] review process has made it impossible to measure the effects of E.O. 12291 with any high degree of precision, numerous documented cases of OMB influence in areas of public safety, health, and the environment strongly indicate that it has provided a very effective means of controlling policy in those instances where the administration has taken a strong interest.[10]

Although the White House has the authority to call in any regulation for review, it normally follows the criteria outlined in E.O. 12866. The thresholds for "significance" include the following criteria:

1. Have an annual effect on the economy of $100 million or more or adversely affect, in a material way, the economy, a sector of the economy, productivity, competition, jobs, the environment, public health or safety, or state, local, or tribal governments or communities.

2. Create a serious inconsistency or otherwise interfere with an action taken or planned by another agency.

3. Materially alter the budgetary impact of entitlements, grants, user fees, or loan programs or the rights and obligations of recipients thereof.

4. Raise novel legal or policy issues arising out of legal mandates, the president's priorities, or the principles set forth in this executive order.[11]

Experienced lobbyists who have access to the White House can use E.O. 12866 to delay a proposed regulation, gain another window of access, and mobilize pressure from other agencies to alter a proposed regulation.

If the proposed regulation survives White House review then the Administrative Procedure Act (APA) requires that the agency publish the full text of the proposed rule in the *Federal Register* for public comment. This **comment period** is another institutionalized oversight stage designed to reduce the information asymmetries hampering Congress, the president, and interest groups. By forcing the agency to reveal its intended regulatory language, Congress increased the likelihood that interest groups will act as a fire alarm.

The agency then drafts the final regulation, taking public comments into account. The final rule is sent back to OIRA for a second round of White House review. Again, the White House can reject the rule by returning it to the agency or forcing the agency to withdraw it. In addition, the White House can change the language here with one important caveat. The APA (5 U.S.C. §551 et seq.) requires that the final rule remain substantively similar to the proposed rule. This consistency requirement makes sense from a good governance standpoint. The regulatory process is designed to allow the public to engage meaningfully in the bureaucratic policymaking process. Rule changes between the proposed and final stages reduce the public's ability to evaluate the outcomes that the law will generate. Thus, any changes to a rule between the proposed and final stages must either come directly from the public comments or be a reasonable extension of the original proposal. If the regulation changes too dramatically then the agency must re-propose it—effectively starting the process again.

If the final rule language survives the second White House review then the agency publishes the text in the *Federal Register* as law. The public once again has an opportunity to comment, although these comments are generally made to set the stage for a court challenge. Overturning a final regulation after its publication almost always requires a successful court challenge. The courts' formal authority is limited to reviewing an agency's interpretation of congressional intent.

LOBBYING STRATEGIES

Many of the oversight and lobbying windows built into the regulatory process are visible in Figure 4.1. What the figure cannot convey adequately, however, is how readily the oversight efforts of Congress (through statutes) and the president (via executive orders) can be used by lobbyists to influence the policymaking process. For example, each agency is supposed to publish all upcoming regulatory activities.[12] Called the **Unified Agenda of Federal Regulatory and Deregulatory Actions (Unified Agenda)**, this list appears semiannually in the *Federal Register*. It serves as an early warning system for Congress, the president, and the interested public, thereby increasing transparency. It also allows lobbyists to electronically search for those regulations that will likely affect their clients.[13]

How prevalent are accountability requirements in the regulatory process? In addition to the oversight requirements listed in the APA, the DQA, and E.O. 12866, and E.O. 13563, there are numerous other regulatory oversight requirements that are specific to the policy area involved. For example, the text of a

2007 EPA final rule, "Control of Hazardous Air Pollutants from Mobile Sources," explicitly addressed oversight requirements from the following:

- The Paperwork Reduction Act (PRA)

- The Regulatory Flexibility Act (RFA), as amended by the Small Business Regulatory Enforcement Fairness Act of 1996 (SBREFA)

- The Unfunded Mandates Reform Act (UMRA)

- The National Technology Transfer Advancement Act (NTTAA)

- The Congressional Review Act (CRA)

- E.O. 12866, Regulatory Planning and Review

- E.O. 13132, Federalism

- E.O. 12898, Federal Actions to Address Environmental Justice in Minority Populations and Low-Income Populations

- E.O. 13211, Actions Concerning Regulations That Significantly Affect Energy Supply, Distribution, or Use

- E.O. 13045, Protection of Children from Environmental Health Risks and Safety Risks

Lobbyists can use any or all of these institutionalized checks on regulatory activity as levers to block a regulation or demand major changes in the proposed rule. All laws create winners and losers. As we will see in chapter 5, interest groups and government officials actively lobby regulations as no one wants to end up on the losing side of a newly codified law. Regulations are sticky policies, meaning that overturning them is difficult. This means that interest organizations have an enormous incentive to ensure that they are the winners in the new regulation.

CASE STUDIES OF A POLICE PATROL AND A FIRE ALARM

Implementing the Data Quality Act

In the previous chapter, we saw how lobbyist Dr. Jim Tozzi changed the regulatory process by adding two paragraphs to an appropriations bill. The two paragraphs became known as the DQA. Tozzi believed that the bureaucrats who develop regulations had far too much discretion to develop regulations that furthered the agencies' missions without regard to the costs of those new laws. Tozzi's solution was to give the White House greater oversight of agencies by determining and reviewing the quality of the information agencies used to develop their new laws. In other words, Tozzi wanted to provide additional police patrols to reduce agency autonomy. Because of Tozzi's intimate knowledge of the regulatory process, the two-paragraph DQA directed OMB to develop the implementation guidelines those police patrols would use.

OMB directed OIRA to write the policy and procedural guidelines to ensure and maximize the "quality, objectivity, utility, and integrity of information that is disseminated by Federal agencies?"[14] Because there were no committee hearings or other legislative history of the development of the DQA, it was not possible to determine the intent of Congress concerning what the guidelines should look like. This meant that OIRA's interpretation was binding on all major agencies.[15] The individual who oversaw the writing of the DQA guidelines was Dr. John Graham, President George W. Bush's appointee as the administrator of OIRA. Graham was widely viewed as antiregulation, and he used the DQA to expand OIRA's authority over the development of new regulations.[16]

OIRA's general guidelines for departments and agencies expanded the original DQA from less than 250 words to more than 7,250.[17] OIRA required each government department or agency to develop guidelines to ensure information quality and objectivity. The agencies then submitted those guidelines to OIRA for approval. OIRA determined that the information covered by the DQA included agency risk assessments, the formulation of potential rules, a record of the rulemaking process, the development of the information used in the rulemaking process, and all information on an agency's web page. If OIRA deemed any information as "influential" or "that [it] has or will have an important effect on the private sector," then the information must be the result of sound science, statistics, and research methods. These research methods must include an independent peer review by unbiased scientists. OIRA also required agencies to provide an opportunity for the public to comment on the peer review and its content.[18] In practice, OIRA's guidelines required that any information concerning the "environment, safety, or a health risk" must include a benefit–cost analysis of the rule that will alleviate the risk.[19] OIRA then reviewed that analysis.

Graham also decided that OIRA would oversee agencies' implementation of the guidelines. For instance, OIRA required agencies to provide it with copies of complaints the agencies received that involved major policy questions or areas of interest to more than one agency. OIRA required that agencies invite OIRA to any meetings with outside parties concerning those complaints.[20] The completion of the guidelines by agencies and executive departments spawned tens of thousands of words governing the federal government's use of information and its dissemination. The Congressional Research Service's report to Congress on the implementation of the DQA found that OIRA had established an "exceptionally broad scope" for its role in the policymaking process.[21]

When Congress became aware of how the DQA was affecting the regulatory process, it expanded its own policy oversight. Congress required OMB to submit reports indicating how the DQA had influenced the regulatory process. Congressional Democrats were concerned that the DQA was becoming a tool that business interests used to slow down or to stop regulatory policymaking.

Congressional Republicans wanted to know whether government departments and agencies had been responsive to public requests for corrections of information.[22] OIRA's first report to Congress concluded the following:

- Requests for information had come from all segments of society, not just business and industry.

- The DQA had not slowed down the regulatory process.

- The DQA resulted in only thirty-five *important* requests to agencies from the public and that the affected agencies denied a majority of these requests.[23]

A number of organizations strongly criticized OMB's report. For instance, OMB Watch, a nonprofit public interest group, published the report *The Reality of Data Quality Act's First Year: A Correction of OMB's Report to Congress.* The group's report stated that OMB's report to Congress was "seriously flawed," biased, and contained inaccurate data and misleading information. OMB Watch claimed that the actual number of important challenges to agency information was three times greater than OMB reported and that almost three-quarters of the requests came from corporations and trade associations.[24] Industry-related groups filed 133 requests while public interest groups filed only 6.

OMB Watch, environmental organizations, and press reports claimed that the DQA has substantially slowed down the issuing of new regulations.[25] Robert F. Kennedy Jr., the senior attorney for the Natural Resources Defense Council, found the following information regarding John Graham's supervision in the first two years of the DQA:

[The] Environmental Protection Agency halted work on 62 environmental standards, the Department of Agriculture stopped work on 57 standards, and the Occupational Safety and Health Administration halted 21 new standards. In the two years after the DQA, the EPA completed just two major rules—both under court order and both watered down at industry request—compared to 23 rules completed by the Clinton administration and 14 by the Bush Sr. administration in their first two years.[26]

In summary, the implementation of the DQA by OIRA successfully created the change in the regulatory process that Jim Tozzi wanted. The DQA also illustrates how a government bureaucracy, in this case OIRA, can use vague statutory language to carve out considerable discretionary authority within a policy area. It is important to point out, however, that OIRA's use of the DQA was not without significant oversight by elected officials. In particular, President George W. Bush exerted considerable influence over the policy outcomes through his appointment authority and control over OIRA's actions.

Further, President Obama did not abandon using OIRA and the DQA to oversee the regulatory process. Obama issued E.O. 13563, Improving Regulation and Regulatory Review.[27] That order reaffirmed the authority of OIRA to require a benefit–cost analysis of all proposed and *previously passed regulations.* In other words, Obama gave the White House authority to review all regulations, regardless of when they had become law.

The Environmental Protection Agency and the Regulation of Perchlorate

The DQA provided an example of how the president and Congress develop police patrol mechanisms to oversee the bureaucracy. We now turn to an example of how fire alarms create agency oversight. An important finding in Baumgartner et al.'s *Lobbying and Policy Change* was that government officials often are the most important lobbyists in the policy process. Our interviews with lobbyists for Fortune 1000 corporations uncovered an interesting regulatory issue that confirmed that finding.[28] The issue was the EPA's attempt to reduce the allowable levels of perchlorate in drinking water from 200 ppb to 1 ppb. (One ppb would be equivalent to one grain of salt in an Olympic-size swimming pool.)

Perchlorate is a component of rocket fuel where it permits combustion in environments that do not supply oxygen. Perchlorate has two undesirable characteristics. First, high levels of exposure to the chemical reduce the ability of the thyroid gland to metabolize iodine. An iodine deficiency can cause developmental disorders in fetuses and goiters in adults. Second, perchlorate is extremely persistent in the environment. This increases the toxic exposure of individuals who are repeatedly exposed to the chemical. The EPA's proposed regulation would have raised the costs of corporations in defense, energy, and aerospace industries. The regulation also would have had a substantial impact on the National Aeronautics and Space Administration (NASA), the Department of Defense (DoD), the Department of Energy (DOE), and the Department of the Navy.

The 1974 SDWA requires the EPA to determine the safe level of exposure to toxic chemicals. The level that the EPA chooses becomes the **reference dose (RfD),** and it serves as the baseline for all federal laws regulating a chemical's production, use, and cleanup. States may apply more stringent standards than the EPA, but most states do not. A change in an RfD can increase manufacturing and cleanup expenses by billions of dollars. Given the stakes, it is not surprising that organizations lobby heavily on RfD decisions. In 1985, the EPA began a study to determine a safe RfD for perchlorate and suggested a drinking water standard of one ppb.

Four private companies and four government agencies immediately sounded a fire alarm. Aerojet, American Pacific Corporation, Kerr-McGee Chemical, and Lockheed Martin formed the **Perchlorate Study Group (PSG),** a coalition that lobbied against stricter perchlorate standards. Other perchlorate producers and users later joined the coalition. The DoD and NASA worked closely with the PSG and provided it with the technical information that alerted the White House to the negative impacts of the proposed RfD on industry and government. This lobbying effort convinced President Reagan to discourage the EPA from developing new perchlorate regulations.

After the election of President Clinton, the EPA again advocated an RfD of one ppb. Our interviews with perchlorate manufacturers and users found that a one ppb standard would have substantial negative effects on at least nine Fortune 1000 companies, and the standard would have significant effects on the spending by the DoD, NASA, and the Department of the Navy. For example, the cost of cleaning up the Colorado River Basin would require that the DoD and NASA spend more than $40 billion. The DoD spent $30 million on research to demonstrate that perchlorate did not pose a significant health risk, and it issued a report indicating that an RfD of 200 ppb was sufficient to protect public health.[29] Government regulations prevent overt lobbying by federal agency officials, but federal guidelines do not consider "information sharing" to be "lobbying."[30] Therefore, although NASA and the DoD were not members of the new coalition, they provided it with substantial information.

Congress and the Clinton administration responded by asking the National Academy of Sciences (NAS), a distinguished body of the nation's top scientists, to review the evidence. In 2005, the NAS released its perchlorate report. The report concluded that the best available evidence indicated that the RfD should be no lower than 24.5 ppb. The NAS report combined with pressure from the perchlorate manufacturers, the Pentagon, and NASA forced the EPA to abandon its one ppb proposal.[31] OIRA also advocated against the one ppb standard, indicating that the costs of such a standard far outweighed its benefits. In 2005, the EPA set the RfD for perchlorate at the level recommended in the NAS report.[32] Believing that its job was done, the PSG coalition disbanded.

In 2006, however, Massachusetts and California adopted perchlorate standards of five ppb and six ppb respectively. These actions placed the perchlorate manufacturers and users of perchlorate in those states at a competitive disadvantage compared with firms in other states. The firms from Massachusetts and California lobbied their congresspersons to force the EPA to set a perchlorate RfD in line with their state standards. In 2007, two Democrats from California, Rep. Hilda Solis and Sen. Barbara Boxer, introduced legislation that would force the EPA to set a perchlorate RfD in line with the California standard. That same year, a contract lobbyist organized and coordinated a new coalition to oppose stricter perchlorate regulation. The corporations joining the perchlorate coalition paid a fee to participate in the coalition. Once again, the combination of industry and government lobbying sounded the fire alarm.

Although Boxer was the chair of the Senate's environmental committee, her bill did not reach a floor vote. A single senator placed a **hold** on Boxer's bill. Senate majority leader Harry Reid, D-NV, received pressure from perchlorate producers and users in his state to stop the Boxer bill. That pressure was successful, and Reid decided not to lift the hold. In 2008, Senator Boxer again pressured the EPA to propose a more stringent regulation. The EPA responded to Senator Boxer and her committee by proposing regulations that would reduce the RfD to five ppb. The coalition opposing a reduction in the RfD and the DoD lobbied OIRA to prevent the new standard. OIRA used the DQA to force the EPA to withdraw its proposed regulation. OIRA found that the EPA had failed to respond to a request from a perchlorate producer either to withdraw some of the data the EPA had used in determining its newly proposed RfD or to justify those data under the DQA guidelines.[33] President George W. Bush supported OIRA's decision.

In 2009, President Obama appointed Lisa Jackson to head EPA. Jackson announced her support for reducing perchlorate levels in the drinking water. The EPA once again pushed for a lower perchlorate RfD.[34] OIRA, using its authority under the DQA, called for an information meeting on perchlorate that would take place at OIRA and would include representatives from the EPA, the DoD, the Department of the Navy, and the perchlorate industry to discuss possible new perchlorate regulations. This time, the forces arguing for a stricter standard sounded the fire alarm. With the support of environmental lobbyists, EPA administrator Jackson requested that President Obama intervene on behalf of the EPA. Obama ordered that the EPA rather than OIRA organize all future interagency meetings dealing with any toxic chemical. The president also ordered that all such meetings take place at EPA headquarters and that the EPA decide who would attend. Backed by the president, the EPA announced on February 2, 2011, that perchlorate was a hormone disruptor and that the agency would "*begin* its evaluation of the feasibility and affordability of treatment technologies to reduce perchlorate levels in drinking water."[35]

The policy process surrounding the regulation of perchlorate illustrates how interest groups can use fire alarms to limit agency discretion. The perchlorate policy process also demonstrates the critical role that the bureaucracy can play as initiators of public policies and as lobbyists. Using the broad authority granted to it by the SDWA, the EPA placed perchlorate regulation on the political agenda. EPA's proposed standard of one ppb demonstrated that the agency zealously pursued its mission of protecting the public and the environment from toxic chemicals. Other parts of the bureaucracy, however, had different missions. Personnel from NASA, the Department of the Navy, the DoD, and OIRA played the key roles in preventing the EPA from achieving its goals. In short, governmental officials were the key advocates on both sides of the policy issue. Finally, the perchlorate issue shows that Congress can use its oversight authority to pressure agencies. Although Senator Boxer was unsuccessful in gaining legislation that required a stricter perchlorate standard, she showed the agency that her committee was interested in the issue and gave the EPA support to push for a lower perchlorate standard.

SUMMARY

This chapter examined the policymaking powers of the bureaucracy and the efforts of the president, Congress, and interest groups to hold the bureaucracy accountable. We saw one of the basic dilemmas of modern democratic government: elected officials (the principals) must delegate power to unelected officials (the agents) who have the resources and expertise necessary to write many public policies. Police patrols and fire alarms are two metaphors for how elected officials attempt to overcome the principal–agent dilemma. We saw how the White House has established an extensive review process to oversee proposed regulations and to ensure that those regulations reflect the president's priorities. The implementation of the DQA by OIRA provided a case study of the development of a new police patrol mechanism that the president can use to restrict bureaucratic discretion. The twenty-five-year effort of the EPA to reduce levels of perchlorate in drinking water provided an example of how elected officials used the firm alarms sounded by interest groups and other government officials to restrict agency actions.

ENDNOTES

1. Commissioner of the Federal Communications Commission, quoted in Lee J. Fritschler, *Smoking and Politics* (New York: Appleton-Century Crofts, 1969), 94.
2. Office of Information and Regulatory Assessment, Office of Management and Budget, *Report to Congress on the Benefits and Costs of Federal Regulations*, www .whitehouse.gov/omb/inforeg_regpol_reports_congress
3. Occupational Safety and Health Administration Act of 1970, Pub. L. No. 91–596, 29 U.S.C. § 651 (1970).
4. Occupational Safety and Health Administration Act of 1970, 29 U.S.C. § 655 (1970).
5. Alfred Marcus, "Environmental Protection Agency," in *The Politics of Regulation*, ed. James Q. Wilson (New York: Basic Books, 1980), 267–303; and Resource Conservation and Recovery Act, 42 U.S.C. § 6901 et seq.
6. Resource Conservation and Recovery Act, 42 U.S.C. § 6901 et seq. (1976).
7. Richard L. Hall and Alan V. Deardorff, "Lobbying as Legislative Subsidy," *American Political Science Review*, 100 (2006): 69–84.
8. Gerhard Peters and John T. Woolley, "Ronald Reagan: Executive Order 12290— Federal Exports and Excessive Regulation," The American Presidency Project, University of California, Santa Barbara, Feb. 17, 1981, www.presidency.ucsb.edu/ws/index.php?pid=43422#axzz1kwyCDn59
9. Joseph Cooper and William F. West, "Presidential Power and Republican Government: The Theory and Practice of OMB Review of Agency Rules," *Journal of Politics* 50, no. 4 (1988): 864.
10. Curtis W. Copeland, "Federal Rulemaking: The Role of the Office of Information and Regulatory Affairs," *CRS Report for Congress*, June 9, 2009, www.fas.org/sgp/crs/misc/RL32397.pdf
11. Executive Order 12866, Regulatory Planning and Review, *Federal Register*, Vol. 58, No. 190, Oct. 4, 1993, 51734-51744, http://govinfo.library.unt.edu/npr/library/direct/orders/2646.html

12. The Regulatory Flexibility Act, 5 U.S.C. § 601 et seq. (1980); The Unfunded Mandates Reform Act of 1995, PL 104–4 (1995); Executive Order 12866, Regulatory Planning and Review (September 30, 1994, 58 FR 51735); and Executive Order 13132, Federalism (August 4, 1999, 64 FR 43255)

13. Of course, agencies do not always comply with transparency requirements. A 2009 study conducted by the Congressional Research Service, the nonpartisan research arm of Congress, found that 25 percent of the proposed rules that underwent OMB review in 2008 did not appear in the Unified Agenda prior to proposal's publication in the *Federal Register*—cited in Curtis Copeland, "The Unified Agenda: Implications for Rulemaking Transparency and Participation," *CRS Report for Congress*, July 20, 2009, www.fas.org/sgp/crs/secrecy/R40713.pdf. The report went on to make recommendations for revising the Unified Agenda in ways geared toward improvements in "the transparency of the rulemaking process, or in the ability of the public to participate in that process."

14. Sidney A. Shapiro, "The Information Quality Act and Environmental Protection: The Perils of Reform by Appropriations Rider," *William and Mary Environmental Law Review* 28, no. 2 (2004), 346.

15. Curtis W. Copeland and Michael Simpson, "The Information Quality Act: OMB's Guidance and Initial Implementation," *CRS Report for Congress*, September 17, 2004, www.fas.org/sgp/crs/RL32532.pdf

16. SourceWatch, "John D. Graham," November 11, 2008, www.sourcewatch.org/index.php?title=John_D._Graham

17. For a copy of OIRA's guidelines, see www.whitehouse.gov/sites/default/files/omb/fedreg/reproducible2.pdf

18. Safe Drinking Water Act, 42 U.S.C. § 300g-1 (b) (3) (A) and (B) (1996).

19. This guideline by OIRA is likely to be challenged as portions of air and water pollution statutes mandate that the EPA not do a benefit–cost analysis; and Shapiro, "The Information Quality Act and Environmental Protection."

20. Copeland and Simpson, "The Information Quality Act," 8.

21. Ibid., 12–14.

22. Ibid., 8–9.

23. Ibid.

24. OMB Watch, *The Reality of Data Quality Act's First Year: A Correction of OMB's Report to Congress*, July 2004, www.ombwatch.org/files/info/dataqualityreport.pdf

25. Rick Weiss, "'Data Quality' Law Is Nemesis of Regulation," *Washington Post*, August 16, 2004, A-1.

26. SourceWatch, "John D. Graham."

27. *Federal Register*, Vol. 76, No. 14, p. 3821, www2.ed.gov/policy/gen/reg/retrospective-analysis/index.html

28. We discuss these interviews more fully in chapter 5.

29. David Corn, "How a Clean Water Advocate and Senator Became a Chemical Industry Lobbyist," *Mother Jones*, February 23, 2009, www.alternet.org/water/128471/how_a_clean_water_advocate_and_senator_became_a_chemical_industry_lobbyist/?page=1

30. An example of lobbying on perchlorate by the DoD can be found at www.denix
    .osd.mil/cmrmd/upload/PEERCOMMENTS.DOC

31. Corn, "How a Clean Water Advocate," 2.

32. U.S. Environmental Protection Agency: Integrated Risk Information System (IRIS),
    "Perchlorate (Cl04) and Perchlorate Salts Quickview (CASRN 7790-98-9)," April
    20, 2012, http://cfpub.epa.gov/ncea/iris/index.cfm?fuseaction=iris.showQuickView&
    substance_nmbr=1007

33. This was the second time opponents of stricter regulations had used the DQA to
    thwart EPA. The Perchlorate Study Group had earlier forced the EPA to withdraw
    information that it was using to support stricter standards. For a letter from the
    PSG to the EPA, see www.epa.gov/quality/informationguidelines/documents/13679A
    .pdf

34. Sara Goodman, "Defense Contractors Lobby to Block Perchlorate Advisory,"
    Greenwire, June 22, 2009.

35. Environmental Protection Agency 40 CFR Part 141. "Drinking Water: Regulatory
    Determination on Perchlorate," *Federal Register* 79, no. 29 (February 11, 2011),
    7762.

Interest-Group Participation, Strategies, and Success in the Regulatory Process

The previous chapter examined two cases in which Congress delegated broad powers to agencies, and then the agencies used that delegated authority to make policy. The case studies showed how Congress, the president, bureaucrats in executive branch departments, and lobbyists attempted to influence the agencies' policies. This chapter moves beyond case studies and examines quantitatively how interest groups decide the level of resources they will devote to lobbying the bureaucracy and their perceived level of success in these efforts.

INCENTIVES FOR LOBBYING THE BUREAUCRACY

Once an interest organization decides to invest in lobbying, it must decide how to allocate its resources among institutions. Will the organization focus largely on Congress, or will it also devote lobbying resources to the White House, the bureaucracy, and the courts? Twenty-five years ago, political scientist John Chubb hypothesized that groups with fewer financial resources and citizen action groups were more likely to lobby Congress than to lobby the bureaucracy. He also hypothesized that producer groups would allocate a higher percentage of their lobbying resources to the bureaucracy than would citizen groups. As recent research largely has confirmed Chubb's hypotheses, it is worthwhile to examine the reasoning behind his expectations.

Chubb studied interest organizations involved in energy policy. He observed that more groups lobbied Congress than lobbied the bureaucracy, that producer groups were more likely to lobby the bureaucracy than citizen action groups, and that resource-rich citizen groups were more likely than resource-poor citizen groups to lobby the bureaucracy.[1] Chubb argued that one reason for these patterns was that the ratio of the **marginal benefits** from lobbying to the **marginal costs** of lobbying is greater for Congress than for the bureaucracy. For this reason, organizations that have few lobbying resources will lobby Congress. Only organizations that have resources beyond those necessary to lobby Congress effectively will direct time and energy to lobbying the bureaucracy.

Chubb maintained that for most interest groups the marginal cost of lobbying on an issue begins at a high level. Getting on the political agenda is costly, and changes in the status quo are difficult. An interest organization must formulate a policy alternative and mobilize external support for that alternative. Members of Congress are unlikely to devote their scarce time to an issue unless they believe that a perceived problem has a solution, that the proposed solution has sufficient support to become policy, and that they will gain electoral support because of their efforts. As several of our case studies have shown, the benefits of a congressional decision to an organized interest can be enormous. This is true whether the good sought is private or collective.

When Congress reaches a policy decision on a broad collective good such as the Safe Drinking Water Act (SDWA) or the Data Quality Act (DQA), it delegates the implementation of the policy to the bureaucracy. This starts a second round of the policy process in which the bureaucracy writes the rules dictating how to allocate the benefits and costs among the affected interests. Chubb argued that the marginal costs of lobbying increase rapidly at the point where the congressional decision process ends and the bureaucratic decision making begins. Participation in the rulemaking process requires technical expertise, knowledge of the policymaking process, and close relationships with bureaucrats. All of these activities require extensive lobbying resources. Technical expertise and procedural information are expensive, and close relationships require regular maintenance, thereby ensuring the expenditure of substantial resources as well as a sustained lobbying effort.[2]

A huge difference between interest organizations that rely on donations and members to generate lobbying resources and corporations is the ability of corporations to borrow money. A citizen's group typically has a set budget for lobbying; corporations do not. If spending additional resources lobbying the bureaucracy will increase a company's profits, the corporation can shift resources from other corporate divisions to the lobbying effort.[3] A corporation can also approach lenders and borrow funds. Most large corporations that lobby have substantial collateral, and this provides security to lenders. This allows corporations to continue spending money on lobbying whenever the expected benefits of lobbying the bureaucracy exceed the expected costs of that lobbying.[4]

A reason that citizen action groups prefer to lobby Congress is that such lobbying is likely to have a positive impact on the organization's size and resources. Citizen groups must convince current and potential members that the group can lobby effectively on issues that are salient to them. The media give much greater attention to policymaking in Congress than to policymaking in the bureaucracy, and congressional policymaking tends to be less technical and more easily understood by the general public than the issues decided by the bureaucracy. Issues characterized by publicity and simplicity encourage new members; technical issues do not.[5] For example, while potential members and donors certainly care about safe drinking water and may support a group that lobbies Congress to pass the SDWA, those same individuals are less aware of and less concerned about whether the Environmental Protection Agency (EPA) sets the safe reference dose at 12.5 parts per billion rather than 6 parts per billion.

Producer organizations do not need to recruit new members; they need to increase profits. While citizen groups prefer media attention to attract new members and donors, producer organizations generally prefer to lobby on issues that do not attract media attention. A corporation does not want consumers to quit buying its product because they disagree with the corporation's lobbying goals. For instance, most companies would prefer that the public not know of their efforts to prevent regulations that improve worker safety or that reduce pollution. Whenever possible, corporations prefer that their trade associations take public stands on issues, allowing the corporations' lobbyists to stick to personal contacts with decision makers. Such contacts are not easily visible to the public and the media.

Citizen action groups—with their ideologically and issue-oriented members—prefer lobbying Congress. Groups with a politically active membership have a greater impact on the decisions of elected officials than on the decisions of career bureaucrats. Grassroots lobbying depends on an organization's ability to mobilize citizens to contact public officials and to vote for officials who share the group's policy preferences. Mobilization is easier when policy issues receive substantial publicity, when the issues are less technical, and when citizens can understand the implications of those policy decisions. In addition, when a citizen group mobilizes its members, this encourages those members to renew their memberships and to donate more money to the group.[6]

Members of Congress care about citizen action groups, grassroots lobbying, and voters. Elected officials often count on citizen action groups to provide not only campaign contributions but also volunteer workers. As most citizen groups affiliate more readily with one party than the other, these close alliances facilitate the mobilization of campaign volunteers, voters, and grassroots lobbying of Congress. For example, environmental groups, abortion-rights groups, and the left-leaning MoveOn.org have close ties with the Democratic Party and provide the party with large numbers of campaign workers. Similarly, the National Rifle Association (NRA), Focus on the Family, and the Christian Coalition align closely with the Republican Party, and these members are active in the campaigns of Republican candidates.

A final reason that producer organizations remain more active in bureaucratic lobbying is that corporations and industries understand how regulatory decisions affect the competitive advantages of firms and industries. For example, a decision by the EPA to reduce the arsenic reference dose (RfD) will advantage natural gas producers and disadvantage coal producers. Similarly, reducing the perchlorate RfD to 6 parts per billion (ppb) will advantage perchlorate producers and users in California and Massachusetts while a standard of 12.5 ppb will disadvantage those producers. It is not surprising, therefore, that the natural gas and coal industry's trade associations extensively lobby the EPA over the arsenic RfD or that perchlorate manufacturers in different states lobby the EPA to set a perchlorate RfD at the level that advantages their firms.

THE FREQUENCY AND PERCEIVED IMPORTANCE OF REGULATORY LOBBYING

Professors Scott Furlong and Cornelius Kerwin gathered data in 1992 and 2001 concerning the frequency with which different organizations lobbied regulatory agencies. [7] Furlong and Kerwin used the *Government Affairs Yellow Book: Who's Who in Government Affairs* to obtain their list of lobbying organizations and lobbyists. This directory contained over 20,000 government affairs personnel from businesses, trade, and professional associations; citizen groups; unions; and government institutions. [8] Producer organizations were by far the most prevalent type of lobby. More than three-quarters of all organizations in the *Government Affairs Yellow Book* represent businesses, trade associations, and professional associations. Only 11 percent of the organizations are citizen groups, 11 percent are government organizations, and 2 percent are unions.

Table 5.1 shows the rate of participation in rulemaking by different types of groups in 1992 and 2001. As Chubb had hypothesized, Furlong and Kerwin found that producer organizations were more likely than citizen groups to lobby the bureaucracy during the rulemaking process. The difference between producer organizations and citizen groups, however, declined between 1992 and 2001. When asked how important lobbying the bureaucracy was relative to other types of lobbying, more than three-quarters of the organizations rated the importance of lobbying the bureaucracy at least as important as lobbying Congress and the White House.

TABLE 5.1 Interest Organizations Reporting Participation in Regulatory Rulemaking

	Rate of Participation	
Type of Organization	1992	2001
Trade association/professional association	90	84
Business	88	87
Labor union	80	100
Citizen's group	59	75

Source: Cornelius Kerwin, ed., *Rulemaking: How Government Agencies Write Law and Make Policy,* 3rd ed. (Washington, DC: CQ Press, 2003), 183.

Table 5.2 indicates the frequency with which lobbying organizations frequently or always employ various lobbying strategies aimed at the bureaucracy. These responses show that lobbying agencies is an ongoing process. Interest groups lobby agencies prior to the agency's initiation of the formal rulemaking process, and they continue to lobby after the agency has published the final rule. Table 5.3 shows that lobbyists see informal contact before the agency publishes its proposed rule as the most effective time to influence the rule. Not only do lobbyists contact the agencies during this period but the agencies also use this period to obtain information that they need to develop a rule and to obtain the opinions of those groups the rule will affect.

TABLE 5.2   Lobbying Agencies at Various Stages of the Rulemaking Process

Frequency of Contact by Interest Organizations	Informal Contact Before Notice of Proposed Rulemaking	Attendance at Hearings	Provide Written Comments During Notice and Comment Period	Informal Contact After Notice of Proposed Rulemaking
Sometimes	50.2%	60.2%	39.9%	53.8%
Frequently	36.6%	29.2%	25.7%	25.9%
Always	10.7%	8.8%	29.2%	17.0%
Total	97.5%	98.2%	94.8%	96.7%

Source: Kerwin, *Rulemaking*, 187.

TABLE 5.3   Lobbyists' Rating of the Effectiveness of Lobbying Strategies

Frequency of Contact by Interest Organizations	Informal Contact Before Notice of Proposed Rulemaking	Attendance at Hearings	Provide Written Comments	Informal Contact After Notice of Proposed Rulemaking
Less effective	10.4%	16.9%	14.3%	22.9%
Effective	21.7%	33.0%	31.4%	35.2%
More effective	68.0%	60.0%	54.3%	41.9%

Source: Kerwin, *Rulemaking*, 190.

PERCEIVED LOBBYING SUCCESS

When Furlong and Kerwin asked lobbyists to rank their success in influencing rulemaking, they found that lobbyists saw themselves as successful about half the time. Table 5.4 shows that almost 90 percent of lobbyists see themselves as able to affect the rulemaking process at least half the time. This is a highly positive assessment. To get a different perspective, Furlong surveyed agency personnel and asked them to indicate on a scale of zero to ten the frequency with which they made changes in rules in response to comments from different types of groups. Agency personnel ranked all groups less than five.[9] Of course, just as lobbyists have an incentive to report high rates of success, agency personnel have a disincentive to indicate that they are responsive to lobbyists. Furlong also asked agency personnel to rate the effectiveness of eleven strategies interest organizations use to influence the rulemaking process. Table 5.5 shows how agency officials perceive the frequency of these lobbying strategies and the estimated effectiveness of each.

STRATEGIES FOR INFLUENCING REGULATORY AGENCIES

We are now ready to examine research concerning the four lobbying strategies that agency personnel rank most highly: (1) written comments concerning a proposed rule, (2) participation in advisory committees, (3) lobbying representatives and senators to communicate an organization's concerns to the agency, and (4) participation in public hearings.

Written Comments Concerning a Proposed Rule

It is surprising that political scientists have not examined the rulemaking process more frequently. Agencies must publish a proposed rule in the *Federal Register* and solicit comments from those whom the rule will affect. Because the proposed rule, the comments submitted, the agency responses to the comments, and the final rule are public documents, scholars can measure directly how a rule changed in response to interest-group lobbying. Researchers can see which organizations attempt to influence a rule, which parts of a rule an organization wants changed, and which parts the agency changes. The rulemaking process, therefore, allows a reasonably direct measure of an organization's success.[10] See Figure 4.1 in chapter 4 for a review of the steps in the rulemaking process.

Although elite interviews with lobbyists and bureaucrats provide a rich source of information about policy participants' perceptions of lobbying effectiveness, the interviewees are biased observers. For instance, Table 5.4 shows that lobbyists *perceived* their efforts extraordinarily effective. Bureaucrats, however, *perceived* those efforts as much less successful. These results support Marissa Golden's worries about over- and underreporting influence in survey responses.[11] Some respondents will want to appear important; others will want to downplay their role in the policy process. Although

TABLE 5.4   Lobbyists' Perception of Their Success Rates in Affecting Rulemaking

Frequency of Success	Interest Groups Reporting
Less than half the time	9.0%
At least half the time	61.9%
At least three-quarters of the time	29.2%

Source: Kerwin, *Rulemaking,* 205.

TABLE 5.5   Lobbying Strategies and Perceived Effectiveness

Lobbying Strategy	Frequency	Effectiveness
Written comments to proposed rule	8.27	6.26
Participation in advisory and alternative dispute committees	5.97	6.19
Communicating with congressional committees or staff	7.01	6.01
Participation in public hearings	7.72	6.00
Communicating informally with agency personnel	6.97	5.88
Bringing suit against the agency after an enforcing action	4.00	5.33
Bringing suit against the agency prior to an enforcing action	3.84	5.32
Mobilize grassroots drive to communicate with the agency	4.83	4.72
Contact OMB to advance a position	4.18	4.71
Petition agency for a rule	4.53	4.58
Use of another agency to advance a position	3.08	3.26

Ratings on a scale of 0 to 10.

Source: Adapted with permission from Scott Furlong, "Political Influence on the Bureaucracy: The Bureaucracy Speaks," *Journal of Public Administration Research and Theory* 8, no. 1 (1998): exhibit 5. Copyright © 1998, Oxford University Press.

perceptions of policymaking participants are interesting and important, the policy changes that lobbying creates are the best measure of lobbying success.

Three sets of scholars have examined how multiple agencies responded to comments during the rulemaking process. Marissa Golden published the first of these studies in 1998. She randomly chose rules decided by the EPA, the National Highway Traffic Safety Administration (NHTSA), and the Department of Housing and Urban Development (HUD) and examined the effects of comments on the amount a rule changed. "The dominance of business commenters in the rule-making process at EPA and NHTSA" was Golden's most striking finding:

> Between 66.7 percent and 100 percent of the comments received were submitted by corporations, public utilities, or trade associations. For five of the eight rules, citizen's groups did not submit any comments. In no case did the citizen group participation exceed 11 percent [of the comments]. Neither NHTSA nor the EPA received a single comment from an individual citizen on any of the eight rules that were examined. There was modest participation by other government agencies—including the Department of Energy and the National Transportation Board—and by a few academic experts.[12]

Even in the rulemaking of HUD, a bureaucracy designed to assist ordinary and low-income citizens obtain housing, only 9 percent of the comments during rulemaking came from individual citizens and 17 percent came from citizen action groups. The remaining comments came from producers and their organizations. Golden indicated that one reason for the dominance of producer groups is their ability to monitor the agencies. Paid lobbyists read the *Federal Register,* communicate with one another concerning agency activities, and contact agency officials on a regular basis. Few citizens or citizen action groups have the resources to monitor such agency activities.

Golden found that agencies are most responsive to comments when there is a consensus among commenters in favor of a change. If the comments conflict, however, Golden found that the agency is likely to stay with its original rule. Golden concluded that there are two clear findings from her study. First, significant influence on rulemaking is limited. Only one of the eleven rules she examined changed substantially from the proposed to the final rule. Second, with respect to whose voices are heard, no clear pattern emerges. Producers win more frequently than other groups but only because they participate more frequently.

Researchers Susan Yackee, Jason Yackee, and Amy McKay constructed a dataset that contains almost 1,700 comments on 40 agency rules.[13] Like Golden, these researchers found that business interests file far more comments than other interests do. Unlike Golden, however, Susan Yackee and her colleagues found that business interests were more successful in achieving a rule change than were other interests. This was particularly true when business interests were united in their comments.[14] The researchers also found that agencies are responsive to comments from government interests, particularly state and local governments arguing for less stringent regulation.

The authors of this book collected a dataset for economically significant rules finalized in 2008. We included three federal agencies: the Department of Energy (DOE), the Department of Transportation (DOT), and the EPA. The politics of the rulemaking process for economically significant rules differ from the politics of ordinary rules. Economically significant rules entail a greater likelihood of disputes as more is at stake and more commenters enter the fray. There are reasons to study all types of rules, and the earlier studies provide important information concerning who participates on rules of different levels of importance. By limiting our sample to economically significant rules, however, we can better examine how bureaucracies balance competing demands in high-stakes conflicts.

Our study measures policy change differently than earlier studies. Golden evaluated the level of change in an entire rule. She made an overall subjective judgment of whether a rule changed a great deal, some, minimally, or not at all. Yackee and her colleagues examined whether a comment letter was pro-regulation or antiregulation. Both types of evaluations are important, but they omit a great deal of information. Comment letters are incredibly specific. Rarely does a letter simply indicate that it wants to kill a rule or to strengthen it. Comment letters seek adjustments in specific parts of rules. Letters typically raise issues related to narrow aspects of a proposed rule. For example, the EPA may propose a fifty-page rule regulating electric power plants. On one page, there might be a provision that allows ten years for power plants using older coal-burning technologies to modernize or shut down. The National Clean Air Coalition might submit a comment letter that urges the EPA to change the rule in several places, and one of the requested changes might be to give power plants only six years to modernize or close. As the EPA publishes all submitted comments on the Internet, the industry group the Electric Power Research Institute (EPRI) will see the National Clean Air Coalition's request for a shorter period. EPRI can respond by submitting a comment letter urging the EPA to maintain the ten-year provision. The same letter might also include a request urging the EPA to leave certain other parts of the proposed rule unchanged and a request to reduce the stringency of another section of the rule. Because letters often include multiple issues, we used issues as our unit of analysis. We coded each issue into one of four categories of requests: (1) decrease the stringency of a provision in the rule, (2) increase the stringency of a provision, (3) leave a provision unchanged, and (4) provide a clarification of the meaning of a provision. We record the wins and losses by the type of issue raised and the type of organization raising the issue.

The average number of issues raised per comment letter was five. About 30 percent of all letters raised just a single issue, but several letters raised over forty issues. Table 5.6 shows that business organizations raised 64 percent of all issues. Government organizations raised 21 percent of issues, and citizen groups, individual citizens, and other types of organizations raised 16 percent. Table 5.6 also indicates that business had a significantly higher percentage of wins than did other categories of organizations. Business interests achieve their goal on more than 40 percent of the issues they raise; other groups win only about 11 or 12 percent of the time.

TABLE 5.6 Number of Issues and Percentage of Wins

Type of Lobby	Number of Issues Addressed	Number of Issues Won	Winning Percentage
Business	634 (64%)	267	42%
Government	205 (21%)	23	11%
Citizen & other	155 (16%)	18	12%

Table 5.6 obscures an important finding. The likelihood that an interest organization will achieve its desired change depended heavily on the type of change the organization requests. As Table 5.7 demonstrates, agencies were unlikely to grant requests for less stringency (33 percent) or for more stringency (5 percent). When a commenter requested that the agency keep the rule the same, however, the agency approved of this request in 94 percent of the cases. Similarly, agencies responded positively to 67 percent of requests for clarifications of proposed rules. When we controlled for the type of request commenters make, there were few significant differences in the success rates of business and government lobbying. Citizens and citizen groups won less frequently, but when their comments advocated greater stringency, they were successful on 9 percent of their efforts while business organizations were successful on only 4 percent of their requests for greater stringency.

TABLE 5.7 Issue Objectives and Issue Wins

Type of Commenter	Less Stringency % of type	% won	More Stringency % of type	% won	Do Not Change % of type	% won	Clarification % of type	% won
Business	93%	33%	33%	4%	72%	100%	83%	70%
Government	5%	53%	37%	3%	22%	96%	10%	69%
Citizen & other	2%	14%	29%	9%	6%	14%	7%	29%
Average success		33%		5%		94%		67%

When we used multivariate statistical techniques and limited our analysis to issues related only to increasing or decreasing stringency, several factors stood out. First, advocates representing business or government were more likely to win than were citizen groups or individual citizens. Second, commenters who cited past agency decisions and used agency data were significantly more likely to achieve their desired change than commenters who did not follow these strategies. Third, a consensus among commenters in favor of a change increased the likelihood of that change.[15]

To summarize the three studies of rule changes, all found that business interests predominate, and this was particularly true of comments requesting less stringency. The predominance of business interests was not surprising because most of the proposed regulatory changes affected production processes. Business interests were the targets of most of the new regulatory provisions, and the regulations were likely to increase their production costs. A second reason that business interests are predominant in requests for less stringency is that competing business interests have requested greater stringency. Many times business interests see regulations as an opportunity to gain a competitive advantage. If the EPA bans atrazine, the firms that produce other herbicides will make greater profits. We saw in the perchlorate case study that after Massachusetts and California passed stricter perchlorate standards, producers in those states demanded that the EPA pass a stricter nationwide standard. Producers in other states fought to prevent stricter standards. In short, each producer wanted the standard that would maximize its competitive position. As Table 5.7 indicates, producer interests actually file more comments to increase stringency than do citizens and citizen action groups.

All three analyses of rulemaking supported John Chubb's hypothesis that producer groups will be the predominate organization in bureaucratic policymaking. Citizen groups participated far less, even when the stakes were very high. On economically significant rules, business organizations submitted four requests for every request submitted by an individual citizen or a citizen action group. When the rules were not economically significant, business interests were even more dominant. The predominance of business interests did not mean, however, that regulatory agencies were pro-business. Business interests submitted the most comments because they bore most of the costs (or reaped the benefits) of regulations. In addition, our analysis of the issues found that when there was conflict among commenters, the conflict generally was not between business and citizen groups. Rather, the conflict was between one business interest and another business interest. The biggest surprise in studies of regulatory comments was not that business interests were active but that citizen groups were not more active, particularly in high-stakes, economically significant regulations. We turn now to methods of participation that might be more favorable to citizen group involvement.

Participation in Federal Advisory Committees

Bureaucrats rank group participation in advisory committees as the second most effective lobbying strategy. The Federal Advisory Committee Act (FACA) requires regulatory agencies to form advisory committees that include all relevant stakeholders (those interests directly affected by the agency's decisions). FACA also requires the committees to be "fairly balanced."[16] For example, we would expect the EPA's advisory committees to include producer groups, environmental groups, and state and local government agencies. In response to this requirement, regulatory agencies and executive departments have formed approximately 1,000 FACA committees with more than 40,000 members.[17] The advisory committees give the interest groups on the committees an opportunity to provide direct input into the formation and implementation of agency rules.[18]

The advisory committees can provide a valuable forum for the participation of competing organized groups, but the committees also limit participation. In their government-sponsored study of the effects of advisory committees on environmental regulation, Rebecca Long and Thomas Beierle found that advisory committees improve the representation of established interest organizations, but they limit the participation of grassroots organizations and ordinary citizens. Long and Beierle argued that procedural requirements governing how committees are formed and who may participate "draw a sharp line between FACA 'haves' and FACA 'have nots.'" Groups invited to participate enjoyed enhanced access to government decision making, but those groups that were not invited were "kept at arm's length."[19] Two studies prepared for the House of Representatives Government Reform and Oversight Committee on the effects of advisory committees show that even those agencies that strive for "fairly balanced" committees favor organizations that already were part of established issue networks.[20]

Political scientists Steven Balla and John Wright have argued that advisory committees provide an important oversight mechanism through which Congress controls the bureaucracy.[21] Balla and Wright found that the interest organizations that lobbied Congress when a statute was passed are the same organizations that dominate the makeup of FACA committees. The committees, therefore, provide continuing congressional oversight of the bureaucracy. Because the agencies rely on interest groups to nominate committee members and the interest groups making the nomination are the same groups that were active in the legislative process, Congress can expect to hear from those groups that proposed regulations harm. In other words, advisory committees provide enhanced police patrols in congressional oversight of the bureaucracy. Although there are no quantitative studies of the success rates of interest groups using advisory committees to lobby agencies, numerous case studies indicate that the groups participating in the committees have a privileged position from which to lobby.[22]

Lobbying Congress to Affect Regulatory Agencies

Numerous studies in political science suggest that the best way to lobby regulatory agencies is to lobby Congress.[23] This research revolves around the principal–agent dilemma. We discussed the principal–agent dilemma in chapter 4. It occurs when a principal (Congress) delegates authority to an agent (the bureaucratic agency) to accomplish a task. The agent typically has greater expertise and information than the principal and might even have different interests than the principal. The interest groups most affected by regulations monitor agencies closely and report attempts by agencies to deviate from the tasks and goals that Congress and the president originally set for the agency.[24] There is considerable evidence that agencies fear congressional oversight and sanctions. Because of this, agencies design their proposed rules in ways that reduce the likelihood that interest organizations will complain to Congress or the president. Such complaints might lead to statutes or executive orders that reduce an agency's authority, autonomy, and budget.[25]

In our interviews with lobbyists from Fortune 1000 firms, we asked if they requested that senators and representatives contact regulatory agencies on behalf of their firm. Eighty-seven percent answered affirmatively, and the majority of these lobbyists used this lobbying tactic frequently. Once again, a private good was likely to be the primary objective of these lobbying efforts. Sixty-three percent of the lobbying attempts were aimed at securing an agency decision that would benefit fewer than five firms. Only 38 percent of the efforts were directed at securing a decision that would benefit five or more firms. Examples of the private-good benefits they sought included:

- Asking a committee chair to write the Securities and Exchange Commission (SEC) concerning a proposed rule interpretation that affected only Freddie Mac and Fannie Mae

- Requesting several senators to write the SEC concerning a request for a regulatory waiver to obtain an extension of the bank's trading activities

- Asking home-state senators to contact the DOT to waive the restrictions on the ports that a particular cruise line could use

- Asking a House member to contact the EPA in support of a waiver for a coal-fired power plant

- Requesting a committee member to write the U.S. Food and Drug Administration (FDA) in support of a change in its proposed rule concerning the labeling of sunscreens (the proposed change would create a competitive advantage for the firm making the request)

Examples of requests involving collective goods included the following:

- Asking a committee chair to urge the SEC not to propose additional regulations on hedge funds

- Requesting a committee member to urge the SEC maintain its current definition of "banks" to prevent Wal-Mart from providing consumer banking services in its stores[26]

- Asking the House majority leader to pressure the FDA to speed up its process for licensing new products

- Asking numerous senators to pressure the FDA to weaken its proposed obesity warnings on products sold by fast-food chains

- Requesting a committee chair overseeing the DOT to ease regulations concerning the transport of nuclear waste

In summary, Fortune 1000 firms devoted significant resources to lobby Congress to influence regulatory agency behavior, and the lobbyists used this tactic more frequently to pursue private goods.

Public Hearings

Regulatory agencies increasingly use public hearings that invite all interested parties to participate. The goals of public hearings are to bring new participants and perspectives into administrative decision making, to improve the efficiency of regulations, and to increase the level of democracy in the regulatory process.[27] Two assumptions, or articles of faith, underlie the use of public hearings. First, greater citizen involvement will lead to policies that are more responsive to citizen needs, and second, the more closely the demographic characteristics of hearing participants reflect the demographics of the affected population, the more likely it is that policy outcomes will reflect the preferences of that population.[28] Are these assumptions correct?

Two academic analyses have reviewed almost 300 case studies of public participation in regulatory hearings. Jeffrey Berry, Kent Portney, Mary Beth Bablitch, and Richard Mahoney in their 1984 study "Public Involvement in Administration" examined forty-five case studies of citizen participation programs. The Berry et al. study employed three indicators of program success: (1) the case study author's overall judgment of how well the participation efforts worked, (2) whether the demographics of hearing participants were representative of the demographics of the affected population, and (3) whether the agency was responsive to the demands of participants to change the proposed policy.

Berry and his colleagues found two institutional variables were positively associated with the outcome indicators. Decision processes that encouraged early public involvement and decision processes with a greater number of opportunities for inputs had positive effects on the participation process, the representativeness of the participants, and the responsiveness of the agencies. Three political factors positively affected the indicators of success: (1) the salience of the issue to the public, (2) the scope of the policy impact, and (3) the presence of competing organized interests. One political indicator—the specificity of the legislative statute—had a negative relationship with the representativeness of the participants. Presumably, this occurred because legislative specificity reduced the flexibility of the agency to change a proposed rule. The major conclusions of the Berry et al. study were that public hearings should (1) take place as early as possible in the policy process, (2) occur at all stages of the process, and (3) include a balance of private interests and citizen groups. The study did not find that "ordinary citizens" who attend hearings as individuals have an impact on policy outcomes.

Thomas Beierle and Jerry Cayford reviewed 239 published case studies of public involvement in environmental decision making.[29] Their study included public hearings and regulatory negotiations that involved competing interests. Beierle and Cayford concluded that a structured process of dispute resolution led to better environmental decisions and increased trust in government decision making. They also concluded, however, that public hearings did not expand participation by citizens who were not members of organized groups. In fact, public hearings tended to exclude ordinary citizens—particularly citizens with lower incomes and less education.

Unfortunately, neither of the Berry et al. nor the Beierle and Cayford study examined whose participation in public hearings actually changed policy. The studies found that the presence of competing interest groups led to outcomes that responded to organized interests, but neither study measured which of those interests were more likely to succeed. What is clear from these studies is that individuals with less education, less income, and less information did not achieve policy changes. It seems reasonable to conclude, therefore, that public hearings reinforce the patterns of influence observed in comment letters, advisory committees, and lobbying legislators.

REGULATORY WAIVERS

All agencies, with the exception of the National Labor Relations Board, have policies that allow them to grant waivers, and each year the value of the waivers to recipients is many billions of dollars.[30] In many respects, regulatory waivers are the ultimate private good. A waiver not only provides an immediate economic benefit to the organization that receives it but the waiver also typically gives the recipient organization an advantage over its competition. Although agencies may grant waivers for such valid reasons as economic efficiency and equity, there is clear evidence that agencies favor some firms over others.[31] For instance, an examination of the SEC waivers by Edward Wyatt of the *New York Times* found that from 2001 to 2011 the SEC provided JPMorgan Chase, Goldman Sachs, Bank of America, and Wells Fargo nearly 350 waivers. By granting those waivers, the SEC granted those Wall Street firms powerful advantages over their competition. Investment experts estimated that these waivers netted the four corporations billions of dollars (see Box 5.1 for a condensed version of the Wyatt article).[32] In addition, Wyatt found that the SEC generally was unwilling to bring expensive enforcement actions against these same banks.

Table 5.5 showed that lobbyists rank lobbying members of Congress as a highly effective tool for affecting agency behavior. In addition, 53 of the 61 lobbyists for Fortune 1000 firms frequently lobbied Congress to influence regulatory outcomes. The examination of those efforts uncovered numerous examples of corporations requesting members of Congress to pressure agencies to grant particular waivers. This lobbying appears to have had substantial

---

BOX 5.1   SEC Is Avoiding Tough Sanctions for Large Banks

Despite numerous findings that Wall Street giants like JPMorganChase, Goldman Sachs, and Bank of America had engaged in fraudulent practices, the Securities and Exchange Commission granted them exemptions to laws and regulations that were supposed to act as deterrents to securities fraud. These exemptions made it easier for them to raise money and to avoid liability from lawsuits.

A *New York Times* analysis discovered nearly 350 instances where the SEC gave Wall Street institutions a pass on sanctions. JPMorganChase, for example, had settled 13 fraud cases, but it obtained 22 waivers, in part by arguing that it has "a strong record of compliance with securities laws." Bank of America and Merrill Lynch, which merged in 2009, have settled 15 fraud cases and received at least 39 waivers. The *Times* analysis found 49 instances in which the SEC had waived punishment to Wall Street firms since 2005. Since 2000, the agency has given 91 waivers that granted the firms immunity from lawsuits and 204 waivers related to raising money and managing mutual funds. Securities experts say that granting those waivers gave the firms powerful competitive advantages.

---

payoffs as several of our interviewees listed obtaining a waiver as one of their major lobbying accomplishments.

Scholars of public policy and of interest groups have failed to study the waiver process. The authors of this book reviewed the past twenty years of research in the five major political science and public administration journals and found no studies of which firms receive waivers, why agencies grant them, or of the impact of waivers on economic outcomes.[33] Waivers, however, are a major part of firms' rent-seeking behavior. The reason that political science has failed to study the waiver process probably reflects the fact that a company's attorneys rather than its lobbyists typically take the lead in obtaining regulatory waivers. Hopefully, future researchers will correct this important oversight.

SUMMARY

This chapter reviewed how interest organizations lobby the bureaucracy, whether producer interests dominate the lobbying efforts, and the effectiveness of different types of lobbying behavior. We had three reasons to expect that producer organizations would be more active in the regulatory process than citizen groups. First, regulations have the greatest direct impact on producer organizations, so they have the most to lose. Second, producer organizations have the resources to lobby the entire policy process, including implementation by the bureaucracy. Third, producer groups prefer to lobby when there is less media attention and where technical information often is more important than public opinion and elections. These preferences suggest that producer groups will favor lobbying the bureaucracy. In contrast, citizen groups use their lobbying to increase group membership and to solicit donations. The groups also have the greater influence when votes matter more to the policymaker than technical expertise. These factors lead citizen groups to concentrate on Congress rather than the bureaucracy.

The research of Furlong and Kerwin found that producer organizations are more likely than citizen groups to lobby the bureaucracy. Studies of the rulemaking process indicate that comments from producer groups are far more prevalent than comments from other types of groups. Studies of who files comments during the rulemaking process and the success of those comments show that producer groups comment more than citizen groups and that producer groups are, on average, more successful than citizen groups in achieving their goals. This pattern exists not only for ordinary rules but also for the most economically significant rules. Other types of lobbying the bureaucracy—participation in advisory committees, attending public hearings, and lobbying Congress to influence bureaucratic behavior—indicate that these channels of participation enhance participation by citizen groups, but they do not encourage participation by persons who are not members of organized groups.

The empirical research concerning lobbying the bureaucracy provides support for the neopluralist and exchange models. Despite the predominance of producer groups in the regulatory process, all types of *organized* groups participate in bureaucratic lobbying. Federal advisory committees and public hearings help balance the predominance of producer groups in the comment stage. In addition, organized groups also lobby Congress to influence the bureaucracy. Citizen groups have a comparative advantage in this type of lobbying as elected officials respond to grassroots efforts and electoral participation. The patterns of regulatory lobbying also support the exchange model. The currency of bureaucratic lobbying is information and producer organizations have the resources to produce the information that bureaucrats need. This may encourage regulators to be more responsive to producer interest organizations than to citizen organizations. The success rates of business comments are substantially higher than the success rates of citizen group comments. Comments on proposed rules are specific in nature and often contain requests for private goods. The frequency of private good requests in comments on proposed rules and in requests to legislators to influence bureaucratic behavior supports the exchange model of interest-group influence.

ENDNOTES

1. John E. Chubb, *Interest Groups and the Bureaucracy: The Politics of Energy* (Stanford, CA: Stanford University Press, 1983), 36–45.
2. Ibid., 40.
3. The political action committees (PACs) tied to corporations are similarly advantaged. Corporations are able to foot all of the overhead costs of their PACs and shift resources into and out of their PACs. Stand-alone PACs have to cover all of their overhead costs from contributions.

4. This assumes efficient capital markets. For a discussion, see R. Kenneth Godwin, Edward J. Lopez, and Barry J. Seldon, "Incorporating Policymaker Costs and Political Competition into Rent-Seeking Games," *Southern Economic Journal* 73, no. 1 (2006): 37–54.

5. For a discussion of how citizen groups simplify and publicize issues, see Kenneth Godwin, *One Billion Dollars of Influence: The Direct Marketing of Politics* (Chatham, NJ: Chatham House, 1988).

6. Ibid., chap. 3–4.

7. Scott R. Furlong and Cornelius M. Kerwin, "Interest Group Participation in Rule Making: A Decade of Change," *Journal of Public Administration Research and Theory* 15, no. 3 (2004): 353–370; Cornelius M. Kerwin, ed., *Rulemaking: How Government Agencies Write Law and Make Policy,* 3rd ed., (Washington, DC: CQ Press, 2003); and Scott R. Furlong, "Political Influence in the Bureaucracy: The Bureaucracy Speaks," *Journal of Public Administration Research and Theory* 8, no. 1 (1998): 39–65.

8. Furlong and Kerwin, "Interest Group Participation in Rule Making," 357.

9. Reported in Kerwin, *Rulemaking,* 205.

10. Not all agencies and departments indicate how they respond to individual comments. For example, the Department of Education lists broad categories of comments and its response to each category. For this reason, scholars cannot evaluate the success of interest organizations in achieving their desired outcomes for each part of a rule from the Department of Education.

11. Marissa M. Golden, "Interest Groups in the Rule-Making Process: Who Participates? Whose Voices Get Heard?" *Journal of Public Administration Research and Theory,* 8, no. 2 (1998): 245–270.

12. Ibid.

13. See Susan Webb Yackee, "Sweet-Talking the Fourth Branch: Assessing the Influence of Interest Group Comments on Federal Agency Rulemaking," *Journal of Public Administration Research and Theory,* 26 (2006): 103–124; Jason Webb Yackee and Susan Webb Yackee, "A Bias Towards Business? Assessing Interest Group Influence on the U.S. Bureaucracy," *Journal of Politics,* 68, no. 1 (2006): 128–139; and Amy McKay and Susan Webb Yackee, "Interest Group Competition on Federal Agency Rules," *American Politics Research 35,* no. 3 (2007): 336–357.

14. Yackee and Yackee, "A Bias Towards Business?," 134.

15. For the full analyses, see Scott Ainsworth, Erik Godwin, and Kenneth Godwin, "Rulemaking and Interest Group Dominance" (paper presented at the annual meetings of the American Political Science Association, Toronto, Canada, 2009).

16. Public Law No. 92–463 (October 6, 1972).

17. Rebecca J. Long and Thomas C. Beierle, "The Federal Advisory Committee Act and Public Participation in Environmental Policy" (Discussion Paper 99–17, Resources for the Future, Washington, DC, 1999).

18. Ibid., 5.

19. Ibid., 17.

20. Ibid.; Clarence Davies, "Public Participation in Environmental Decision-Making and the Federal Advisory Committee Act," Testimony before the U.S. House of

Representatives Government Reform and Oversight Committee, July 14, 1998, www.rff.org/Publications/Pages/PublicationDetails.aspx?PublicationID=17059

21. Steven Balla and John R. Wright, "Interest Groups, Advisory Committees, and Congressional Control of the Bureaucracy," *American Journal of Political Science* 45, no. 4 (2001): 799–812.

22. Ibid.; Joseph A. Pika, "Interest Groups and the Executive: Presidential Intervention," in *Interest Group Politics*, ed. Allan Cigler and Burdett Loomis (Washington, DC: CQ Press, 1983); and Mark P. Petracca, "Federal Advisory Committees, Interest Groups, and the Administrative State," *Congress and the Presidency* 13, no. 1 (1986): 83–114.

23. Among the best known of these studies are Mathew McCubbins and Thomas Schwartz, "Congressional Oversight Overlooked: Police Patrols Versus Fire Alarms," *American Journal of Political Science* 28, no. 1 (1984): 165–179; Terry Moe, "Control and Feedback in Economic Regulation: The Case of the NLRB," *American Political Science Review* 79 (1985): 1094–1116; Mathew McCubbins, Roger G. Noll, and Barry R. Weingast, "Structure and Process, Politics and Policy: Administrative Arrangements and the Political Control of Agencies," *Virginia Law Review* 75, no. 2 (1989): 431–482; David Epstein and Sharyn O'Halloran, "Divided Government and the Design of Administrative Procedures: A Formal Model and Empirical Test," *Journal of Politics* 58 (1996): 373–397; and John Ferejohn and Charles Shipan, "Congressional Influence on Bureaucracy," special issue, *Journal of Law, Economics, and Organization* 6 (1990): 1–20.

24. McCubbins and Schwartz, "Congressional Oversight Overlooked."

25. Studies include Daniel P. Carpenter, "Adaptive Signal Processing, Hierarchy, and Budgetary Control in Federal Regulation," *American Political Science Review* 90 (1996): 283–302; Paul Quirk, "The Food and Drug Administration," in *The Politics of Regulation*, ed. James Q. Wilson (New York: Basic Books, 1980); Barry Weingast and Mark Moran, "Bureaucratic Discretion or Congressional Control? Regulatory Policymaking by the Federal Trade Commission," *Journal of Political Economy* 91, no. 5 (1983): 765–800; Dan B. Wood, "Does Politics Make a Difference at the EEOC?" *American Journal of Political Science* 24 (1990): 503–530; Terry Moe, "Control and Feedback in Economic Regulation"; and Dan Morgan, "Pressure on NLRB Turns into a Doubled Budget Cut," *Washington Post*, July 20, 1995, A8.

26. While this would be a "private bad" for Wal-Mart, it was a collective good for traditional banks and savings and loans.

27. David E. Ervin et al., *Land Use Control: Evaluating Economic and Political Effects* (Cambridge, MA: Lexington Books, 1974); Jeffrey M. Berry et al., "Public Involvement in Administration: The Structural Determinants of Effective Citizen Participation," *Nonprofit and Voluntary Sector Quarterly* 13 (1984): 7–23.

28. Berry et al., "Public Involvement," 8, 10.

29. Thomas C. Beierle and Jerry Cayford, "Evaluating Dispute Resolution as an Approach to Public Participation" (Discussion Paper 01–40, Resources for the Future, Washington, DC, 2001).

30. Jim Rossi, "Making Policy Through the Waiver of Regulations at the Federal Energy Regulatory Commission," *Administrative Law Review* 47 (1995): 255–301.

31. Hui Chen, David Parsley, and Ya-Wen Yang, "Corporate Lobbying and Financial Performance," Social Science Research Network Working Paper, 2010, http://papers.ssrn.com/s013/papers.cfm?abstract_id=1014264

32. Edward Wyatt, "S.E.C. Is Avoiding Tough Sanctions for Large Banks," *New York Times*, February 3, 2012, www.nytimes.com/2012/02/03/business/sec-is-avoiding-tough-sanctions-for-large-banks.html?_r=1&pagewanted=print

33. The journals reviewed were the *American Political Science Review*, the *American Journal of Political Science*, the *Journal of Politics*, the *Journal of Public Administration Research and Theory*, and *Public Administration Review*.

Lobbying Alone or Cooperatively

The greatest uncertainty in Washington
is not whether you will win or lose a floor vote,
but whether your issue will be attended to at all.[1]

Our first task [to get policymakers' attention]
was to build a coalition.[2]

My [lobbying] firm does only one thing,
we build coalitions.[3]

The conventional wisdom among Washington lobbyists insists that building and maintaining a **cooperative lobbying** effort is essential for lobbying success. For example, Bruce Wolpe, a longtime Washington insider and lobbyist, wrote, "The exacting measure of success in congressional lobbying is the ability to create, join, or manage **coalitions** united behind a public policy proposal."[4] Many lobbyists and scholars argue that large coalitions provide evidence to policymakers that a policy proposal has widespread support.[5] Recent research, however, finds that the conventional wisdom may be incorrect. In a study of ninety-six issues and more than 1,000 lobbying organizations, Frank Baumgartner and Christine Mahoney discovered that lobbying alone is more likely to yield success than lobbying as a member of a coalition.[6]

Before we examine the effects of interest organizations lobbying together, however, we must distinguish among three terms related to lobbying: (1) coalitions, (2) cooperative lobbying, and (3) **sides.** Coalitions are formal structures that interest organizations join and to which they pledge resources. Formal coalitions often have paid staff, an office, and the coalition members have specified obligations such as allocating personnel to the coalition effort or paying a fee to the coalition mobilizer and coordinator. Coalitions typically seek highly collective goods. For example, the **National Coalition for Women and Girls in Education (NCWGE)** is a nonprofit coalition of more than fifty groups. Its mission is to advocate for the development of national education policies that benefit all women and girls.[7] Some coalitions are long-lasting and are active on multiple issues. The NCWGE is an example of such a coalition.

Other coalitions organize to support or oppose a single policy decision. The Perchlorate Study Group (PSG) was such a coalition.

We use the term *cooperative lobbying effort* to designate lobbying by interest organizations that share similar policy goals and that coordinate their lobbying efforts. Coalitions are a subset of cooperative efforts. Interest organizations, however, often coordinate their lobbying strategies without creating a formal coalition. For example, firms that benefit from defense contracts may coordinate their lobbying to obtain an increase in the appropriations for the Department of Defense (DoD). All of the cooperating interests see a bigger defense budget as a collective good that is likely to increase their profits. These diverse interests, however, may not organize into a formal coalition.

Sides consist of all organizations and individuals who are lobbying on the same side of a proposed bill.[8] The lobbying for the final version of the American Jobs Creation Act of 2004 included several coalitions. One included firms and trade associations in the information technology and financial services industries. Another included various energy producers and their trade associations. These two coalitions coordinated their lobbying efforts. A host of other interests such as the Plano Molding Company joined the side supporting the jobs act when its tax breaks became part of the bill. Plano did not join a coalition or coordinate its lobbying with other interests favored by the bill. The shared policy goal among these diverse interests was to pass a bill that provided a tax break or subsidy to *their* interest. To understand the differences among lobbying strategies, we examine two additional case studies: (1) drug reimportation and (2) the repeal of the estate tax.

DRUG REIMPORTATION[9]

The **Pharmaceutical Research and Manufacturers of America (PhRMA),** the trade association for companies that manufacture prescription drugs, is among the most powerful lobbying organizations in Washington. In many respects, trade associations act as permanent coalitions that lobby for their members and often coordinate the cooperative lobbying efforts of those members. From 2000 through 2010, PhRMA and the individual pharmaceutical firms spent more than $2 billion lobbying the federal government.[10] One result of these political activities is that nongeneric prescription drugs are much more expensive in the United States than in other countries. Unlike most industrialized countries, the U.S. government does not regulate drug prices. Neither does the federal government use its enormous purchasing power to force the pharmaceutical companies to lower their prices to Medicare and Medicaid patients. (The Veterans Administration, however, uses its purchasing power to lower drug costs for veterans.)

Because the same drugs cost substantially less in Canada and Mexico, many U.S. residents travel across the border to purchase their prescription drugs. Consumers also use the Internet to order drugs from other countries. In response to these activities, PhRMA and its members successfully lobbied Congress to pass the Prescription Drug Marketing Act of 1987. That law prohibits any person or institution from importing drugs covered by U.S. patents. As most of these drugs originally were manufactured in the United States, purchasing of these products abroad and bringing them back into the United States is referred to as "drug reimportation."

From 2000 to 2011, Congress considered legislation to allow the reimportation of prescription drugs from other industrialized countries. Initially, reimportation was a bipartisan issue. Republicans who supported the legislation argued that reimportation would encourage greater competition, and this would force greater efficiency in the manufacture and distribution of prescription drugs. Democrats supporting reimportation maintained that high U.S. prices placed an unfair burden on the elderly and the poor. Research showed that these individuals often took less than the dosage prescribed by their doctors because they could not afford to take the prescribed dosage. Republicans who opposed reimportation saw it as a dangerous infringement on the pharmaceutical companies' property rights. Democrats who opposed reimportation generally cited safety concerns, particularly when individuals used the Internet to order drugs. These Democrats maintained that the best way to help the elderly was to include prescription drug coverage in Medicare, and the best way to help the poor was to use the government's buying power to force pharmaceutical drug manufactures to reduce the prices they charged low-income families.

The pharmaceutical industry argued that it was impossible to guarantee the safety of drugs ordered over the Internet and that allowing reimportation would not permit the companies to recoup their research and development costs. The industry provided evidence that although many Internet drug sites had a Canadian address, they dispensed drugs manufactured in China, India, and Mexico. The size, color, and shape of the drugs were the same as their American counterparts, but often they did not contain the medication at the required strength. Drugs obtained through the Internet often had passed their expiration dates or were made for animals. The industry also maintained that Internet drug sales allowed minors easy access to dangerous drugs as the firms selling drugs over the Internet did not require sufficient verification of the buyer's age.

In 2000, Senators Byron Dorgan, D-ND, and Olympia Snowe, R-ME, decided to challenge the 1987 law that prohibits reimportation. They introduced legislation that would allow the reimportation of drugs to the United States and added the legislation as an amendment to the 2000 agricultural appropriations bill. The Dorgan–Snowe amendment would have allowed reimportation only from pharmacies inspected and certified by the U.S. Food and Drug Administration (FDA). The certified pharmacies were located in nineteen industrialized countries.

The cooperative lobbying effort supporting drug reimportation included a wide range of interest organizations. Families USA, a nonprofit organization that lobbies for affordable health care, led a coalition that included citizen action groups representing the interests of low-income families. Trade associations representing Canadian pharmaceutical companies and Internet pharmacies funded a second coalition. A third coalition represented seventeen large corporations that had health care plans for their workers. Finally, associations of state and local governments in the United States used their existing organizations to lobby for reimportation. Reducing prescription drug costs is particularly important to state governments. Medicaid, the government program that provides medical care to low-income families, is one of the largest state expenditures; drugs represent a major portion of these expenditures. In 2000 and 2001, eleven governors came to Washington to lobby in favor of the Dorgan–Snowe amendment. The organizations on the side supporting drug reimportation coordinated their efforts through phone calls, e-mails, and a weekly Internet newsletter.

The fight over reimportation was fierce. PhRMA brought the previous eleven commissioners of the FDA to Washington to testify against the legislation. Janet Hanney, President Clinton's FDA commissioner, testified that a reimportation program "would be totally unworkable without [additional FDA] funding." U.S. Customs Service commissioner Raymond Kelly testified that the Dorgan–Snowe amendment would create a volume of counterfeit drugs that the Customs Service simply could not handle.[11] Finally, Donna Shalala, President Clinton's secretary of the **U.S. Department of Health and Human Services (HHS),** did not support drug reimportation. These government officials became key lobbyists for the anti-reimportation side.

When the bill containing the Dorgan–Snowe amendment reached the floor in the Senate, Sen. Thad Cochran, R-MS, introduced an amendment written by the head lobbyist of one of the largest pharmaceutical companies.[12] The Cochran amendment required the secretary of HHS to certify the safety and effectiveness of reimported drugs. In the absence of such certification, drug reimportation would remain illegal. The wording of the Cochran amendment was critical. It required that the FDA not evaluate whether the benefits of reimportation would be greater than the costs. Instead, the Cochran amendment prohibited an increase in any type of risk. The wording of the Cochran amendment also made it appear that any legislator voting against the amendment was voting for unsafe drugs. Despite the opposition to reimportation, the legislation sailed through Congress, and President Clinton signed the bill on October 30, 2000. Its proponents expected the development of new regulations governing reimportation to take two years. The regulations, however, were never completed. HHS secretary Donna Shalala stated that she could not certify that reimportation would pose *no* additional risk to consumers.

When President George W. Bush came to the White House in 2001, he announced that he would veto any bill that included reimportation. Dorgan and Snowe, however, did not give up. They proposed legislation that would accelerate the process of approving a new drug, an important benefit to the drug companies. The legislation also increased the FDA's budget to provide the staff necessary to certify reimported drugs as safe. The side supporting reimportation added numerous corporations, small business trade associations, and health insurance companies to their cooperative lobbying effort. The American Association of Retired Persons (AARP) committed its full support to reimportation. This increase in lobbying support encouraged the House of Representatives to pass a reimportation bill without the Cochran amendment. Representatives Gil Gutknecht, R-MN, and Rahm Emanuel (then D-IL) put together a veto-proof majority in support of the bill.[13] In the Senate, however, majority leader Bill Frist, R-TN, opposed reimportation, and he blocked Senate consideration of the bill from 2003 through 2006.

The 2006 elections placed Democrats in control of the House and the Senate. Edward Kennedy became chair of the committee that dealt with the drug safety issues. Although Kennedy pushed reimportation through the Senate, he could not prevent Senator Cochran from attaching his amendment. The most Kennedy could accomplish was to pass legislation that prevented HHS from enforcing the Prescription Drug Marketing Act's ban on reimportation if an individual imported less than a ninety-one-day supply of a drug. The effect of this legislation was to allow individuals to reimport a ninety-day supply of a prescription drug, but such institutions as state governments and pharmacies could not reimport drugs. Reimportation passed the House again in 2008. In the Senate, Kennedy tied the reimportation legislation to an Internet safety bill, the Ryan Haight Online Pharmacy Consumer Protection Act of 2008.[14] Senator Frist, by then Senate minority leader, informed Kennedy that the Republicans would filibuster the Internet safety bill unless he dropped the reimportation provision. Kennedy agreed to do so. The passage of the Ryan Haight bill without reimportation was a significant defeat because it ended the connection between increased Internet drug safety and drug reimportation. The separation of the issues made it more difficult for Dorgan and Snowe to claim that their proposal would increase drug safety.

Increasing partisanship over reimportation greatly reduced the chances that it would become law. Interviews with lobbyists for two pharmaceutical companies and with congressional staffers discovered that the Republican leadership in Congress reached an agreement with PhRMA and the large pharmaceutical companies.[15] The drug industry would direct its lobbying resources to Republican candidates and would hire only Republicans as lobbyists. In return, the Republican leadership would oppose any measure that reduced drug prices. Without bipartisan support, drug reimportation had little hope of becoming law while a Republican was in the White House.

When Barack Obama became president, it appeared that drug reimportation had an excellent opportunity to pass. As a senator, Obama had been a cosponsor of reimportation legislation. Rahm Emanuel, his chief of staff, was a leader of the battle for reimportation in the House of Representatives. However, President Obama's top domestic priority was universal health insurance. To gain the support of the pharmaceutical industry for his health insurance bill, President Obama withdrew his support for drug reimportation and promised not to use the government's purchasing power to reduce drug prices.[16] The president requested that Senate majority leader Harry Reid, D-NV, prevent a vote on reimportation, and Senator Reid complied.

The authors of this book interviewed eleven individuals who played key roles in the reimportation battle. These individuals indicated that Senators Dorgan and Snowe made two critical errors when they first introduced the reimportation legislation.[17] First, Dorgan and Snowe focused narrowly on the legislative process. They did not consider the difficulty of implementing the proposed law. The senators did not meet with HHS secretary Shalala before they introduced their bill or before they accepted the wording of the Cochran amendment. The original reimportation legislation provided $23 million to inspect foreign pharmacies, but HHS secretary Shalala estimated that the actual cost would be $90 million.[18] The second mistake was the failure of Dorgan and Snowe to obtain the full support of the AARP, the most influential lobbying group representing older Americans. Although the AARP officially supported reimportation in 2000, it was not a top priority for the group. In fact, an AARP lobbyist indicated that she feared the legislation would harm the elderly if it prevented legislation that would add prescription drug coverage to Medicare. Without the full support of AARP, the supporters of reimportation did not have the political clout necessary to defeat the pharmaceutical industry. Although Dorgan and Snowe rectified these errors in later congressional sessions, the increasing partisanship of the issue allowed the drug companies to continue attaching the Cochran amendment to the reimportation legislation. This meant that the FDA could not implement reimportation.

In summary, drug reimportation demonstrates how a broad collective lobbying effort with multiple coalitions can place an issue on the political agenda. The policy battle also demonstrates the importance of implementation issues when writing legislation. Although the pro-reimportation side contained several coalitions and had substantial resources, it was unable to prevent Senator Cochran from attaching his killer amendment to the legislation. Even when Democrats controlled Congress, the threat of a Republican filibuster prevented the passage of an amendment-free bill.

THE DEATH TAX

"No taxation without respiration" was a favorite line of Steve Forbes, a Republican candidate for president in 1996 and 2000. In 1992, several families whose net worth was billions of dollars began an effort to end the estate tax. Among the families were the Forbes, the Waltons (owners of Wal-Mart), the Gallos (wine family), and the Mars family (candy). The Walton family alone was worth $90 billion in 2011, a net worth equal to the total net worth of the bottom 30 percent of all Americans.[19] How a bill that granted the vast majority of its benefits to the wealthiest two-tenths of 1 percent of Americans gained the support of a president of the United States and a majority of Congress provides important insights into how the few can defeat the many in a democratic society.

Broad changes in tax policy are highly visible and highly partisan issues. The winners and losers usually are clear, and tax issues deal with differing conceptions of fairness. Every government must decide how progressive or regressive its tax structure will be. A **progressive tax** reduces the taxes paid by people with lower incomes and shifts the tax burden to those with higher incomes. A **regressive tax** places a proportionally heavier burden on the poor than on the rich. For example, a sales tax on all goods and services is a regressive tax, but a sales tax on jewelry costing more than $10,000 would be a progressive tax. The estate tax law in place in 2000 taxed only estates worth more than $1.3 million, and the rate of the tax rose as the size of the estate increased. It was, therefore, a highly progressive tax.

In 1987, a group of wealthy families hired contract lobbyist and financial adviser Patricia Soldano to develop and coordinate a lobbying effort to end the estate tax. Soldano hired political strategists, pollsters, and highly regarded Washington lobbying firms to work on the issue. This effort steadily gained support over the next eight years, particularly after pro-repeal forces discovered that using the term *death tax* rather than *estate tax* or *inheritance tax* enormously increased support for their policy proposal. Surveys using the death tax label found that more than three-quarters of Americans supported repealing the tax. Those surveys also showed that 40 percent of Americans believed that the tax would apply to them. The actual percentage of families that would have to pay an estate tax was about 2 percent. Few citizens were aware that the majority of the benefits of the repealing of the tax would go to families worth more than $100 million.[20]

The effort to repeal the estate tax received a huge boost when the **National Federation of Independent Business (NFIB),** a powerful small-business lobby, joined the lobbying effort. The NFIB played an instrumental role in developing the **Family Business Estate Tax Coalition (FBETC).** By 1996, the FBETC included the NFIB, the National Association of Manufacturers, the American Farm Bureau, the Newspaper Association of America, the U.S. Chamber of Commerce, and trade associations representing cattlemen, liquor and beer distributors, and numerous small business and farm groups. By 1998, more than 100 organizations had joined the FBETC.[21]

The pro-repeal side used stories of the estate tax forcing people to sell their family business or farm. The stories received substantial press attention. The FBETC brought owners of small businesses and family farms to Washington to speak to their legislators. The coalition also paid for polls that indicated to legislators that their constituents favored repealing the tax. As Michael Graetz and Ian Shapiro discussed in *Death by a Thousand Cuts,* the pro-repeal side convinced legislators that they could not lose their job by voting for repeal, but voting against repeal could prevent their reelection. A vote against the repeal would lead to substantial campaign contributions to their opponents in the next election.[22]

The FBETC made the estate tax a highly symbolic issue. Rather than a tax on billionaires, the death tax became an example of big government unfairly intruding into the lives of hard-working people—even after they were dead. There are two distinctly different ways to look at the estate tax. One asks, "Is it fair to tax the estate of an individual or a couple who worked their entire life to build something that they could pass on to their children?" The other perspective asks, "Is it fair to tax working people on the income they earn while not taxing the income people receive simply because they had wealthy parents?" Public opinion polls that ask the first question find a majority of Americans oppose the estate tax. If the pollsters ask the second question, a majority favor the tax. The pro-repeal coalition always presented the issue from the perspective of taxing the hard-working parents.[23]

The FBETC funded research by the Heritage Foundation, a conservative think tank. Heritage published the report, "The Case for Repealing the Estate Tax."[24] It argued that the estate tax reduced job growth and was inefficient. The tax was expensive to enforce, and it was expensive for heirs to comply with the difficult-to-understand tax codes. This report became a core component of the repeal effort and spawned other research concerning the negative effects of the tax.

Although the Republican Party made the elimination of the death tax part of their 1994 Contract with America, very little happened until 1999 when Rep. Jennifer Dunn, R-WA, introduced the Death Tax Elimination Act. Dunn's bill raised the amount of an estate exempted from the inheritance tax every year until it disappeared entirely in 2010. Dunn worked with Patricia Soldano to mobilize bipartisan support for the bill. They realized that the demographics of Democrats had changed. The Democratic Party no longer relied solely on the support of blue-collar workers and minorities. The party also received support from many wealthy individuals, a growing professional class, and government workers. The estates of many of these people exceeded the $1.3 million that was exempted from the estate tax in 2000. Dunn appealed to the Congressional Black Caucus to join her efforts while Soldano recruited the National Black Chamber of Commerce to the coalition. Dunn and Soldano argued that the estate tax prevented the first generation of black multimillionaires from creating a class of wealthy African Americans that spanned across generations. Soldano also appealed to groups representing female entrepreneurs.

Surprisingly, liberals did little to counteract the lobbying by the pro-repeal forces. Early in the debate, liberals did not believe that the pro-repeal side could win. Given that most of the benefits would go to a small number of billionaires, liberals expected public opinion to oppose the repeal. In addition, as long as Democrats controlled the White House, President Clinton would veto any bill that repealed the tax. Two of the Democratic Party's traditional allies—environmental organizations and labor unions—did not see the issue as important to their interests. Strangely, public employee unions also were silent on the issue.

In 2000, Dunn's bill passed Congress, and President Clinton vetoed it. When President George W. Bush took office in 2001, his administration made the repeal of the estate tax part of the 2001 Bush tax cuts. With the help of a few Democrats, the repeal of the death tax passed. There was no estate tax in the United States in 2010. The victory of the pro-repeal forces was not, however, complete. A major limitation on the 2001 legislation was that although the size of the estate tax would decline every year and would disappear entirely in 2010, the tax would reappear in 2011. In 2011, the estate tax would have the same $1.3 million exemption and progressive tax rates that were in effect in 2000.

This seemingly odd situation occurred because the pro-repeal side did not want to alert the public to the long-term cost of the bill. If the repeal had been permanent, the cost to the U.S. Treasury would be hundreds of billions of dollars. This would throw the budget wildly out of balance starting in 2011. Pro-repeal forces gambled that between 2001 and 2011 they would be able to pass a permanent repeal of the tax. They lost that bet, but in December 2010, the Republican-controlled House of Representatives reached a budget agreement with President Obama that for 2011 and 2012 the federal government would exempt the first $5 million of an estate from a tax.

THE EFFECTIVENESS OF COOPERATIVE LOBBYING

As the opening quote for this chapter indicates, the most difficult task a lobbyist faces is not winning a floor vote on her issue. Her most difficult task is getting her issue on the political agenda. Competition for policymakers' attention is stiff. Only 20 percent of bills introduced to Congress receive serious attention, and less than 10 percent ever reach a floor vote in the House and Senate. How does an interest group get policymakers to consider its issue? Numerous scholars have argued that mobilizing a large and diverse set of interests is key to getting on the agenda.[25] Our case studies provide some support for this argument.[26] The agenda-setting process of the North American Free Trade Agreement (NAFTA), the energy act, the jobs act, drug reimportation, and the death tax involved large cooperative lobbying efforts that often involved multiple formal coalitions. How did these coalitions form?

Building a Coalition

Past research indicates that policy entrepreneurs play a key role in organizing a coalition. The entrepreneur may be a lobbyist or a public official. For example, lobbyist Patricia Soldano recruited and organized the coalition to end the death tax. The head lobbyist for PhRMA was the key player in organizing and coordinating the opposition to drug reimportation. Vice President Cheney was the policy entrepreneur in the energy Act. Senators Dorgan and Snowe recruited interest groups representing seniors, low-income families, and state and local governments to support drug reimportation. Finally, an official from the DoD joined with a lobbyist from Aerojet Corporation to organize the PSG.

In his insightful book *Lobbying Together,* Kevin Hula demonstrated that not all coalition members have equally important roles. Hula described three types of coalition participants.[27] The first is the **core member**. Core members value a collective good sufficiently to contribute substantial lobbying resources to obtain it. For example, the Business Roundtable was a core member in the pro-NAFTA coalition, and the NFIB was a core member in the FBETC. Hula argued that the policy priorities of core members are typically such collective goods as free trade, energy independence, or a change in tax policy that affects a large number of individuals or organizations.

Hula's second type of coalition member is the **player**. Players place little value on the collective good. They join a coalition to achieve a specific private good. The case study of NAFTA provides many examples of players participating in the Business Roundtable coalition in return for benefits near the private-good end of the private–collective good continuum. For instance, Chrysler, Ford, and General Motors generally supported free trade. They supported the pro-NAFTA coalition, however, only when the agreement contained a provision that limited the percentage of foreign-made parts contained in automobiles assembled in North America. The limitation on foreign-made parts gave the U.S. automakers an advantage over automakers in Canada and Mexico. Core members of a coalition may recruit a player because that player has influence with a key policymaker. For example, the coalition supporting adding the energy act to the jobs act needed the support of Dennis Hastert, R-IL, former Speaker of the House. To obtain Hastert's support, the coalition inserted a specific tax benefit that affected only the Plano Molding Company in the jobs act. The coalition did this because Plano was a major employer in Speaker Hastert's congressional district.[28]

A drawback of adding players to a coalition is that they have limited loyalty to the coalition's collective good goal. Because of this, they may leave the coalition if a better deal comes along. The jobs act provides an example of this problem. When President Bush asked Congress to reduce corporate taxes, three coalitions of business interests formed and introduced competing bills. Each bill favored a different set of corporations.[29] The U.S. Chamber of Commerce organized one of these coalitions and recruited corporations from the financial services industry. The chamber's bill provided the financial services industry a higher tax reduction than it would receive from the other two bills. But the coalition put together by lobbyists from the information technology industry offered the financial services corporations a larger tax break if they switched coalitions. The financial corporations took the offer, and their defection killed the U.S. Chamber of Commerce bill.

Tagalongs constitute Hula's final category of coalition member. Although generally supportive of the coalition's collective good goal, tagalongs do not expend significant resources to help achieve it—they **cheap ride**.[30] Examples of tagalongs are the numerous corporations that added their names to a pro-NAFTA coalition's list of members but did not devote lobbying resources to pass the agreement. Tagalongs believe that their participation is unlikely to affect the coalition's success or failure. They limit their participation to such inexpensive activities as placing their name on the coalition's letterhead, attending a few coalition meetings, and making phone calls to the staff of their congressional representatives.[31]

Coalitions recruit tagalongs because most lobbyists believe that a larger coalition is more likely to be successful. Not only will core members allow tagalong participation but core members sometimes subsidize such participation. Our interviews revealed several examples of this practice. Such dominant firms in an industry as McDonald's, ExxonMobil, and Microsoft typically have the most at stake when an issue affects their industry. For political reasons, however, the larger firms need smaller firms to participate in the lobbying effort. A lobbyist for a large rubber-resin corporation explained that her firm generally is the key player in most coalitions seeking collective goods for her industry. To increase her coalition's size and its attractiveness to members of Congress, her firm sometimes finances the lobbying efforts of smaller firms. As she put it, "Congressmen like to look out for the little guy, but the little guy often does not know what is going on."[32] Her staff determined which smaller producers should lobby particular policymakers and provided them the information they needed to lobby successfully. In some cases, her firm paid the travel expenses of the chief executive officers of smaller firms when they flew to Washington to participate in the coalition's lobbying effort.

Benefits of Joining a Coalition

A benefit for members of coalitions seeking policy changes includes getting their issue on the political agenda, broadening the support for their issue, and reducing lobbying costs. Obtaining political information to keep up with a highly fragmented policy process is another important benefit of coalition membership. If an organization has only one or two lobbyists, it is impossible for them to keep up with all of the congressional committees and subcommittees, regulatory agencies, and executive departments that are making decisions on issues important to their organization. Cooperation among lobbyists allows organizations to share the effort required to cope with this fragmentation. Kevin Hula wrote the following:

> There are a number of developments in the Washington political environment that create strategic incentives for collective action at the coalition level. Chief among these are the decentralization of government, the expansion of the subcommittee system, and the increase in the multiple referrals of bills. Each of these generates additional work for group representatives.[33]

As we pointed out in chapter 1, there often is an "Oh, S——t!" moment in the policy process when an issue begins to move rapidly to its policy outcome. When that moment occurs, lobbyists must be in a position to have their policy preferences considered. Being part of a formal coalition or a communication-rich cooperative lobbying effort is the best way to ensure that you can participate at this critical time.

Players can benefit enormously from coalition. In the absence a coalition, the player is unlikely to get her issue on the political agenda. For example, in the absence of a coalition, the tax subsidy to Plano Molding Company and the huge buyout of tobacco quotas were unlikely to secure a place on the agenda. Adding their issue to the jobs act and then lobbying for the act allowed these interests to achieve their goals. For players, private goods are the goal; which piece of legislation they use to obtain their private good is unimportant.

A key reason tagalongs participate in coalitions is to *appear* active on a collective good issue. The appearance of activity can be important to organizations. During the battle over allowing oil exploration in the Arctic National Wildlife Refuge (ANWR), several environmental groups did not consider ANWR a priority. The lobbyists for these groups wanted to spend their resources on other issues. Many contributors to these organizations, however, saw ANWR as extremely important. By joining the coalition, groups could preserve their resources while appearing to be active on ANWR. Joining the coalition allowed these groups to claim part of the credit for protecting ANWR from oil and gas exploration. Participating in a coalition can provide similar advantages to corporate lobbyists. As Hula pointed out in *Lobbying Together*, corporate lobbyists often receive calls from members of their company's board of directors.[34] A board member might urge the lobbyist to become active on a particular issue. The lobbyist, however, might believe that spending the company's resources on that issue would have little impact on the policy outcome. Simply appearing active through participation as a tagalong is likely to satisfy the board member.

Rogan Kersh has maintained that contract lobbyists often urge their clients to join a coalition. A lobbyist may do this not because joining the coalition helps her client but because it furthers her career.[35] Contract lobbyists are always seeking new clients. Coalitions increase a lobbyist's visibility and her pool of potential clients. In addition, just as coalitions reduce a group's information and monitoring costs, coalitions can do the same for individual lobbyists. Gaining expertise and political contacts in an issue area is costly. Coalition participation is an inexpensive method by which a lobbyist can obtain these resources.

Building a Coalition to Block Policy Change

A number of scholars have argued that it is easier to build a coalition or to mobilize a cooperative lobbying effort to oppose a policy change than to lobby for a proposed change.[36] There are two reasons for this. First, the opponents of change need not agree on their priorities. The members need only agree to oppose any change in the status quo. Second, research in political science and psychology demonstrates that interest organizations and individuals weigh the loss of a current benefit more heavily than the gain from a future benefit.[37] This imbalance between the motivation of potential winners and losers is particularly true when the proposed policy involves a collective good. Research shows that adding a new collective good goal to a policy proposal often leads to a large increase in the size and intensity of the opposition coalition. In contrast, the addition of numerous private goods to a proposal is unlikely to increase opposition to the proposal. This is particularly true if those who will be harmed are not organized.[38] For example, unorganized consumers suffered the collective harm of higher prices each time the NAFTA implementation agreements provided a producer group protection from competition.[39] The consumers, however, were generally unaware of this harm and did not organize to prevent it.

Costs of Participation in Coalitions and Cooperative Lobbying Efforts

Researchers in American government are nearly unanimous that one way to make a policy proposal attractive to more policymakers is to make it multidimensional. In other words, proposals should appeal to multiple organized interests. Such additions, however, have costs.[40] Each time a formal coalition adds an interest group with a different priority it increases the need for negotiation and compromise among coalition members. These negotiations require time. As one of our interviewees stated, "There are more deals made on K Street [the traditional address of many of the largest lobbying offices] than on Capitol Street [the address of Congress]."[41] More important, the numerous compromises and deals may push the proposed policy in a direction that some coalition members oppose. Sandra Suarez in her book *Does Business Learn?* showed that negotiation costs grow rapidly as the size of a coalition increases. Increasing size also reduces the ability of each member to determine the coalition's priorities. These costs often lead larger corporations to abandon a coalition. When a coalition moves too far from the policy position of a large corporation, the corporation's resources allow it to lobby alone. By lobbying alone, the corporation can emphasize *its* priorities; it need not compromise with other interest organizations.[42]

Our case studies demonstrate that building a multidimensional coalition can help get an issue on the congressional agenda. This was true for NAFTA, the energy act, the jobs act, and the death tax. A lobbyist may be playing a dangerous game, however, when she broadens her coalition by making her issue multidimensional. The death tax provides an example of this situation. Patricia Soldano, the chief lobbyist for the extremely wealthy families, was able to get the estate tax issue on the political agenda by adding to her coalition the National Association of Independent Business, the National Farmers Union, the Hispanic Chamber of Commerce, the National Black Chamber of Commerce, and the National Association of Women Business Owners.

By making the issue multidimensional, Soldano gained support for ending the estate tax. The addition of the new coalition partners, however, created stress within the coalition. More than 99 percent of family-owned businesses and farms have a value of less than $10 million. The estates of Patricia

Soldano's original clients were worth billions. When President Clinton realized that Soldano's coalition was likely to succeed in ending the estate tax, he attempted to take advantage of the differences among coalition members. Clinton offered to exempt from the estate tax the first $5 million of an individual's estate. Clinton's offer meant that a married couple could leave an estate of $10 million to their heirs without paying any estate tax. A $10 million exemption would accomplish relatively little from the perspective of Soldano's original clients. Soldano was able to convince her coalition partners to reject Clinton's offer and to wait until 2001 when Clinton would no longer be in office. Her coalition continued to support the bill that gradually reduced the estate tax until it disappeared for one year in 2010. The downside of the legislation was that the estate tax would reappear in 2011.

In December 2010, time was running out for Soldano and her coalition. In 2011, the estate tax would return to only a $1.3 million exemption. The Republicans in the House of Representatives decided to make the estate tax part of a budget deal with President Obama. Obama refused to end the estate tax, but he offered to exempt the first $5 million of an individual's estate from the tax for 2011 and 2012.[43] This time, the anti-death tax coalition accepted the compromise. The interests that Soldano had added to her coalition decided that a $5 million exemption was a better deal than a $1.3 million exemption. Although Soldano's wealthiest clients disagreed, they no longer controlled the coalition.

In summary, research indicates that coalitions and other cooperative lobbying efforts include not only organizations whose goals are collective goods but also organizations that are seeking private goods. Furthermore, formal coalitions may include organizations that simply wish to appear active on an issue and lobbyists who join coalitions to advance their careers. Cooperative lobbying efforts can benefit an organized interest by getting its issue on the political agenda, by increasing an organization's information about the policy process, and by reducing an organization's monitoring and lobbying costs. But joining a formal coalition has costs as well as benefits. Principal among these is the likelihood that the coalition's negotiated priorities will diverge from those of some coalition members.

EMPIRICAL ISSUES CONCERNING COOPERATION AND LOBBYING SUCCESS

"Will joining a coalition help me achieve my organization's lobbying goals?" is a critical question for a lobbyist choosing her strategy. Although the conventional wisdom supports joining a coalition, there is little empirical evidence supporting that wisdom. Most studies of coalition participation and lobbying success examine only a single case or a relatively small number of cases.[44] Even fewer studies measure the success or failure of coalition lobbying. In the following section, we examine the evidence concerning participation in cooperative lobbying efforts and the relative success of lobbying cooperatively and of lobbying independently.

To examine empirically participation in cooperative lobbying efforts and the success of those efforts, we categorize the level of cooperation that an organization chooses. When lobbying, there are three broad categories of cooperation and coordination. Examine Figure 6.1. It represents all of the organizations that lobbied on a given side of a policy proposal. In area C, the outermost ring, the organizations choose to lobby alone. They do not cooperate or coordinate their lobbying efforts with other organizations. At most, they may share information with organizations that share their interests. The organizations in area B, the middle ring, cooperate with other organizations lobbying on their side, but they do not join a formal coalition. The organizations in area A, the center of the figure, decide to join a formal coalition and to enter into policy negotiations with other members of that coalition.

FIGURE 6.1   Lobbying Efforts on a Side

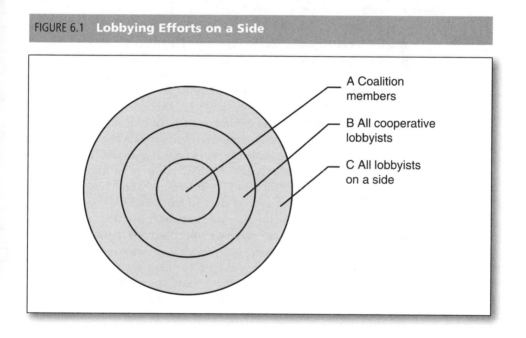

We use the research from *Lobbying and Policy Change* and research carried out for this book to compare the three strategies in Figure 6.1. Frank Baumgartner and Christine Mahoney summarized *Lobbying and Policy Change* research in their paper "The Determinants and Effects of Interest Group Coalitions."[45] Their paper analyzed coalition participation patterns on ninety-six issues and examined the coalition participation and success of more than 400 organizations. The data collected for this book was from interviews we conducted with a stratified random sample of sixty-two lobbyists for the largest 1,000 firms in the United States.[46] These data report the lobbying strategies and policy outcomes for sixty-two firms on 386 issues.

There are some important differences in the two datasets. The scholars who wrote *Lobbying and Policy Change* interviewed only those lobbyists who played a major role in the policy process for their random sample of issues. Baumgartner and Mahoney used those interviews to compare who joined a coalition (those organizations in area A of Figure 6.1) with the organizations that did not join a coalition (organizations in areas B and C). The issues contained in the Fortune 1000 dataset consist of all issues the interviewees named as important to their firm over the previous year. For each issue named by a lobbyist, we asked if her firm lobbied on the issue. If the firm lobbied, we asked if it coordinated its lobbying with that of other organizations. We did not ask whether the firm joined a formal coalition. Our comparison of participation strategies compares organizations in areas A and B of Figure 6.1 with organizations in area C.

Other differences in the datasets concern the measurement of policy objectives and policy success. Baumgartner and Mahoney assumed that all participants on one side of the issue have the same policy objectives.[47] In almost all cases, these objectives are collective goods. The measure of policy success is a comparison of what the organizations indicated they wanted with the final policy outcome.[48] Baumgartner and Mahoney examined who participated in a formal coalition and who did not on each issue. They then compared the success of those organizations in a formal coalition with the lobbying success of organizations that were not members of a formal coalition. Baumgartner and Mahoney examined whether coalition participation is associated with the following variables: type of organization, organizational resources, the size and salience of an issue, the level of conflict over an issue, and the strength of the opposition. Table 6.1 shows the results of their analysis.

Baumgartner and Mahoney found that neither the type of organization nor its resources have an important effect on whether it joins a coalition. The only variables that significantly influence joining a coalition are the salience of an issue and the level of conflict over it. Higher issue salience increases coalition participation while higher conflict over an issue decreases coalition participation. It is important to remember, however, that Baumgartner and Mahoney examined only the core members of coalitions. Their analysis cannot tell us whether salience and conflict affect participation by players and tagalongs.

Perhaps the most interesting aspect of the Baumgartner and Mahoney analysis is its finding that coalition participation is negatively associated with policy success. In addition, the larger the size of the coalition, the less likely it is to be successful. Baumgartner and Mahoney pointed out that this association may not be causal. Figure 6.2 shows two possible causal relationships between coalition participation and policy failure. One way of interpreting their findings (A) is that following a strategy of coalition lobbying reduces the effectiveness of an organization's lobbying efforts. In the second situation (B), many interest groups perceive

TABLE 6.1	The Determinants of Coalition Participation in All Types of Organizations		

Organizations	B	S.E.	P > z
Group types			
Citizen	−0.341	0.228	0.135
Foundation	−0.656	0.685	0.338
Union	0.480	0.322	0.137
Professional association	−0.166	0.253	0.511
Trade	0.262	0.222	0.238
Governmental unit	**−0.819**	**0.438**	**0.062***
Membership size	**−0.000**	**0.000**	**0.076***
DC office	0.581	0.400	0.147
Number of professional staff	0.003	0.008	0.733
Hired outside counsel	−0.034	0.019	0.075
Number of PACs	−0.057	0.141	0.686
Budget resources index	−0.073	0.051	0.154
Organizational age	−0.003	0.002	0.165
Issue-characteristics			
Issue size	−0.003	0.004	0.538
Outside salience index	−0.081	0.053	0.123
Inside salience index	**0.102**	**0.039**	**0.010***
Conflict 1	**−0.537**	**0.283**	**0.057***
Conflict 2	**−0.705**	**0.234**	**0.003***
Presence of opposing coalition	−0.204	0.174	0.240
Constant	−0.157	0.481	0.743
N	527		
Log likelihood	−276.0		
Pseudo R2	0.0922		

*<.10; **<.05; ***<.01 probabilities

Source: Frank R. Baumgartner and Christine Mahoney, "Gaining Government Allies, Groups, Officials, and Alliance Behavior" (paper presented at the annual meeting of the Midwest Political Science Association, Chicago, April 25–28, 2002), Table 10.

that a policy proposal is going to pass that will negatively affect them. This leads the groups to join a coalition to minimize the loss. In other words, coalitions do not cause failures; they are a response to an expected policy failure.

FIGURE 6.2   **Two Possible Causal Relationships Between Coalition Participation and Policy Failure**

A. Join a coalition   ⟶ Less effective lobbying

B. Realization that a policy is likely to   Organizations join a coalition to
    pass that will harm the organization ⟶ reduce the expected policy harm

In our analysis of the Fortune 1000 firms, we first separated the firm's advocacy efforts into those lobbying Congress and those lobbying regulatory agencies. We asked our respondents whether in the past year they had participated in a cooperative lobbying effort of Congress. If they had, we asked whether they had participated as a leader of the effort and whether they had participated in an effort in a secondary role. We repeated these questions for cooperative lobbying efforts aimed at regulatory agencies. Table 6.2 shows that 95 percent of the firms had lobbied as part of a cooperative effort directed at Congress, and 84 percent had participated in such efforts directed at regulatory agencies. Firms lobbying Congress were almost equally likely to participate as a leader as they were to play a secondary role. When lobbying regulatory agencies, however, firms were more likely to be minor players in the cooperative effort.

TABLE 6.2   Overall Rates of Fortune 1000 Firms Lobbying Congress and Regulatory Agencies

	Lobbied Congress	Lobbied Regulatory Agency
Total	95%	90%
Coalition leader	84%	50%
Minor player	82%	76%

The left-hand side of Table 6.3 shows that the top priority for leaders of cooperative lobbying efforts was more likely to be a collective good than a private good. The difference, however, is not large. When firms lead a cooperative effort lobbying Congress, 54 percent of lobbyists name collective goods as their first priority. Private goods are the primary goal for 46 percent of the lobbyists. When a firm takes a secondary role in the cooperative lobbying effort, private goods are the primary motivation for 67 percent of the firms. When we examine the lobbying of regulatory agencies, private goods are the dominant motivation. This is true for situations in which the firm is a leader and when the firm is a minor play in the cooperative lobbying effort.

TABLE 6.3 The Relationship Between a Firm's Role in a Coalition and Its Lobbying Objective

	Lobbied Congress		Lobbied Regulatory Agency	
Primary Goal	Coalition Leader	Minor Player	Coalition Leader	Minor Player
Collective goods	54%	20%	23%	15%
Private goods	46%	67%	71%	72%
Other	0%	12%	6%	13%
Number of cases	52	51	31	47

Our discussions with respondents reveal that if all of the firms in an industry supported a similar position with respect to a regulatory policy, lobbyists see their trade association as the appropriate leader of cooperative lobbying efforts. This is particularly true when the lobbying involves public statements such as filing of a regulatory comment or giving testimony at a public hearing. Firms fear negative publicity. Their lobbyists do not want the public to perceive the firm as attempting to weaken a rule that protects public safety or reduces pollution. One lobbyist commented, "We don't want our fingerprints on [an effort to relax a clean water regulation]." Another stated, "Our trade association gives us cover. We don't want consumers to quit buying our product because of our politics."[49]

Corporations will take a leadership role when trade association members do not share the same policy preference on an issue. For instance, a lobbyist for one of the largest chemical companies explained that her firm and two similar corporations often gain a competitive advantage from a regulation that required new spending on pollution abatement equipment. This advantage occurs because the average per unit cost of pollution abatement often is lower for the larger firms than for their smaller competitors. The perchlorate case study provides an example of this situation. Reaching a contamination level below six parts per billion (ppb) is much less expensive for larger producers than for smaller producers. Because of this, after the PSG succeeded in defeating the EPA's proposed standard of one ppb, smaller producers proposed a much higher ppb for perchlorate than did larger producers.

Regulatory lobbying often concerns such specific private goods as seeking a waiver for a single plant or a particular production process. For example, one firm wanted a ten-year waiver to phase out a coal-fired power plant that would be replaced by a plant with cleaner technology. The value to the firm of this waiver was between $25 million and $50 million. Some waivers, however, are relatively trivial. For example, an automaker wanted a waiver to use a blue light rather than a red light on the interior panels of its cars. Our interviews probably underestimated the prevalence of lobbying for waivers as some respondents saw efforts to obtain waivers as "compliance issues" rather than as "lobbying issues." The firm's attorneys rather than its lobbyists typically pursued regulatory waivers.

We asked our interviewees to rate on a scale of one to five, the importance of four goals when they lobbied in cooperative efforts. A score of five indicated that the firm places that goal as its highest priority. Table 6.4 shows the results. When lobbying regulatory agencies, Fortune 1000 companies tend to value private goods over collective goods. In fact, when firms participate in coordinated lobbying efforts of regulatory agencies, the collective good benefits often are a by-product of a firm's attempt to secure private goods. To pursue their desired private good, firms often had first to secure a collective good that was not as valuable as the private good.

Table 6.4   Average Ranking of Goals When Joining Cooperative Lobbying Efforts

Motivation	Average Ranking
To obtain a benefit for only my firm or my firm and two or three other firms	4.18
To obtain a benefit for many firms	2.53
To obtain information and share monitoring costs	2.45
To maintain good relations	2.03

A multivariate analysis of the factors affecting cooperative lobbying shows that the pursuit of private goods (the desired policy outcome benefits only the client's firm) and intermediate goods (the desired policy outcome benefits the client's firm and two or three others) reduces cooperative lobbying. Cooperative lobbying increases when firms lobby Congress and when they face strong opposition. In contrast to Baumgartner and Mahoney's results for coalition participation, we did not find that firms defending the status quo were more likely to participate in cooperative lobbying. As Table 6.5 shows, neither firm size nor the importance of an issue to the firm affected coalition participation. We discuss the factors that lead to policy success in chapter 7, but we did not find any association between lobbying cooperatively and policy success or failure.

Table 6.5   Determinants of Cooperative Lobbying by Firms

Variable	Coefficient	Robust Standard Error	$P > |z|$	Significance
Private benefit	−2.418	.283	−8.54	P < .001
Intermediate benefit	−1.320	.254	−5.20	P < .001
Opposition strength	.370	.192	2.68	P < .01
Protect status quo	−.204	.203	−1.06	P = .29
Lobbying Congress	.515	.192	2.68	P < .01
Firm size	.0002	.0004	0.54	P = .59
Importance to firm	.168	.146	1.15	P = .25
Constant	.876	.249	3.52	P < .001

N = 278

Wald chi^2 (7) = 88.07, p < .001

Pseudo R^2 = .46

In Table 6.5, we used a logistic regression to explore the decision to lobby cooperatively. Consider the type of good the firm is seeking. The first two variables, private benefit and intermediate benefit, are contrasted with an excluded variable—collective benefit. The negative coefficients for the first two variables indicate that when a firm is pursuing a private or intermediate benefit, it is more likely to avoid cooperative lobbying efforts. As firms seek more public or collective benefits, they are more likely to join a cooperative lobbying effort. Firms are more apt to join cooperative efforts when they face a large or powerful opposition or when they are lobbying the U.S. Congress. Late stage, bureaucratic lobbying is less apt to be tied to cooperative lobbying efforts. This issue will be explored in greater detail in chapter 9.

SUMMARY

Our analysis of coalitions indicates that when interest organizations are pursuing a collective good, they frequently participate in cooperative lobbying efforts. Our case studies are replete with examples of interest organizations building broad-based cooperative lobbying efforts to convince policymakers of the importance of their policy proposals. The drug reimportation and estate tax case studies illustrate the importance of coalitions and cooperative lobbying to agenda setting. Our interviews and statistical analyses cooperative lobbying indicate that past research substantially overestimated the resources that firms devote to achieving collective goods and underestimated the importance of private goods.

ENDNOTES

1. Beth Leech et al., "Drawing Lobbyists to Washington: Government Activity and Interest Group Mobilization," *Political Research Quarterly* 58, no. 1 (2005): 19–30.
2. Personal interview with the authors.
3. Personal interview with the authors.
4. Bruce Wolpe and Bertram Levine, *Lobbying Congress: How the System Works*, 2nd ed. (Washington, DC: CQ Press, 1996), 42.
5. Ibid., 42–44; Kevin W. Hula, *Lobbying Together: Interest Group Coalitions in Legislative Politics* (Washington, DC: Georgetown University Press, 2000); and John W. Kingdon, *Agendas, Alternatives, and Public Policies*, 2nd ed. (Reading, MA: Addison-Wesley, 1995).
6. Frank R. Baumgartner and Christine Mahoney, "The Determinants and Effects of Interest Group Coalitions" (paper prepared for the annual meetings of the American Political Science Association, Chicago, August 31–September 4, 2004).
7. The National Coalition for Women and Girls in Education homepage, www.ncwge .org/
8. Frank R. Baumgartner et al., *Lobbying and Policy Change: Who Wins, Who Loses, and Why* (Chicago: University of Chicago Press, 2009), 6.
9. The authors of this book interviewed congressional staff members and lobbyists from the major interest organizations involved in the issue as well as journalists who had covered the issue for major news organizations. We interviewed fourteen respondents in 2004 and re-interviewed several in 2008.
10. OpenSecrets.org: Center for Responsive Politics. "Lobbying: Top Industries," www .opensecrets.org/lobby/top.php?indexType=i
11. Michael E. Dalzell, "Prescription Drug Reimportation: Panacea or Problem?" *Managed Care*, December 2000, www.managedcaremag.com/archives/0012/0012 .reimport.html
12. Personal interview with the lobbyist who wrote the legislation.
13. Rahm Emanuel was President Obama's first chief of staff. Late in 2010, he left the White House to run (successfully) for mayor of Chicago.

14. Ryan Haight was a teenager who bought Vicodin on the Internet without a prescription and died from an overdose of the drug. His mother was one of many individuals who testified against allowing individuals to order a drug without a prescription from their own doctor. Ryan had claimed to have a medical condition that created pain, and he claimed to be over twenty-one.

15. The lobbyists specifically mentioned Republicans Tom Delay, Trent Lott, and Bill Frist as making the issue partisan. PhRMA agreed to support Delay's "K Street Project" as part of the deal. The K Street Project attempted to force lobbying firms and corporations to hire only Republicans as lobbyists.

16. Dana Milbank, "President Obama Writes a New Health Reform Prescription," *Washington Post,* December 16, 2009, 2A.

17. Interviewees included congressional staff members of the leading legislators who supported or opposed the legislation, lobbyists from the organized interests most involved in the legislation, and newspaper reporters who covered the issue.

18. Internal FDA memoranda were made available to the authors.

19. Jeffrey Goldberg, "Goldberg: Wal-Mart Heiress's Museum a Moral Blight," Bloomberg View, December 12, 2011, www.bloomberg.com/news/2011–12–13/ wal-mart-heiress-s-museum-a-moral-blight-commentary-by-jeffrey-goldberg .html

20. Michael J. Graetz and Ian Shapiro, *Death by a Thousand Cuts: The Fight over Taxing Inherited Wealth* (Princeton, NJ: Princeton University Press, 2005).

21. Ibid., 21.

22. Ibid.

23. In 2009, the last year of the estate tax, the money that an estate had accumulated through increases in the value of stock or other assets was never taxed or was taxed at a much lower rate than most income.

24. William Beach, "The Case for Repealing the Estate Tax," The Heritage Foundation, August 21, 1996, www.heritage.org/Research/Reports/1996/08/BG1091nbsp-The -Case-for-Repealing-the-Estate-Tax

25. Kevin W. Hula, *Lobbying Together;* Mayhew, David. *Congress: The Electoral Connection* (New Haven, CT: Yale University Press, 1974); John W. Kingdon, *Congressmen's Voting Decisions,* 3rd ed. (Ann Arbor: University of Michigan Press, 1989); Nelson W. Polsby, *Political Innovation in America: The Politics of Policy Initiation* (New Haven, CT: Yale University Press, 1984); and Virginia Gray and David Lowery, "To Lobby Alone or in a Flock: Foraging Behavior among Organized Interests," *American Politics Quarterly* 26 (1998): 5–34.

26. We used three strategies to identify our interviewees. Kenneth Godwin, John Green, and Nancy Kucinski conducted the first set of twelve interviews. The interviewees were lobbyists from corporations and trade associations in three economic sectors: (1) passenger airlines, (2) rubber-resin, and (3) publishing. The second set of interviews are from a random sample of sixty-two lobbyists for Fortune 1000 firms stratified by whether the interviewee was an in-house or contract lobbyist. Erik Godwin and Kenneth Godwin conducted these interviews. Scott Ainsworth, Erik Godwin, and Kenneth Godwin conducted the final set of thirty-one

interviews. The third set of interviews come from our case studies of drug reimportation, the American Jobs Creation Act of 2004, the Energy Policy Act of 2003, the Data Quality Act (DQA), and perchlorate regulation. We conducted interviews with congressional staff members, regulatory agencies, and lobbyists for corporations, trade associations, and citizen action groups. Our statistical analyses of interview responses include only the sixty-two corporate interviewees selected through probability sampling.

27. Hula, *Lobbying Together*.

28. Frederick W. Mayer, *Interpreting NAFTA: The Science and Art of Policy Analysis* (New York: Columbia University Press, 1998), 316–317.

29. As discussed in Chapter 1, the three coalitions were (1) manufacturers whose production was largely in the United States, (2) multinational corporations that outsourced most of their manufacturing work to locations outside of the United States, and (3) service industry corporations such as banking, insurance, restaurants, and hotels. The National Association of Manufacturers led the first coalition, the largest information technology companies led the second coalition, and the U.S. Chamber of Commerce led the third coalition.

30. Hula, *Lobbying Together*, 25.

31. Ibid.; Marie Hojnacki, "Organized Interests' Advocacy Behavior in Alliances," *Political Research Quarterly* 51, no. 2 (1998): 437–459.

32. Personal interview with the authors.

33. Hula, *Lobbying Together*, 123.

34. Ibid., 34.

35. Rogan Kersh, "Corporate Lobbyists as Political Actors: A View from the Field," in *Interest Group Politics*, 6th ed., ed. Burdett Loomis and Allan Cigler (Washington, DC: CQ Press, 2002), 225–248.

36. E. E. Schattschneider, *Politics, Pressure, and the Tariff: A Study of Free Enterprise in Pressure Politics as Shown in the 1929–1930 Revision of the Tariff* (New York: Prentice Hall, 1935); Amos Tversky and Daniel Kahneman, "Loss Aversion in Riskless Choice: A Reference-Dependent Model," *Quarterly Journal of Economics* 106 (1991): 1039–1061; and Baumgartner et al. *Lobbying and Policy Change*.

37. Tversky and Kahneman, "Loss Aversion in Riskless Choice."

38. Theodore Lowi, *The End of Liberalism: Ideology, Policy and the Crisis of Public Authority* (New York: Norton, 1969).

39. Hula, *Lobbying Together*; Thomas T. Holyoke, "Interest Group Competition and Coalition Formation," *American Journal of Political Science* 53, no. 2 (2009): 360–375; Marie Hojnacki et al., "Goals, Salience, and the Nature of Advocacy" (paper presented at the annual meeting of the American Political Science Association, Philadelphia, August 31–September 3, 2006; Theodore Lowi, *The End of Liberalism*; and William P. Browne, *Private Interests, Public Policy, and American Agriculture* (Lawrence: University of Kansas Press, 1988).

40. Holyoke, "Interest Group Competition and Coalition Formation."

41. Personal interview with the authors.

42. Sandra Suarez, *Does Business Learn? Tax Breaks, Uncertainty, and Political Strategies* (Ann Arbor: University of Michigan Press, 2000).

43. Paul Sullivan, "Estate Tax Will Return Next Year, but Few Will Pay It," *New York Times*, December 17, 2010, www.nytimes.com/2010/12/18/your-money/taxes/18wealth.html

44. Baumgartner and Mahoney, "The Determinants and Effects of Interest Group Coalitions."

45. Ibid.

46. Stratified on whether the lobbyist was an in-house or contract lobbyist. We were unable to complete one of the interviews. For this reason, many of the analyses presented include only sixty-one lobbyists.

47. Personal communication with Frank Baumgartner.

48. To measure success, Baumgartner and Mahoney, in "The Determinants and Effects of Interest Group Coalitions" (pp. 26–27), constructed a summary variable assessing the level of success that each group had across six possible goals that an organization might have, such as changing or maintaining federal spending, changing or maintaining policies within an established program, creating a new program, affecting or protecting state and local budgets, etc. For each of these separate and clearly defined goals, a group may have achieved no success (scored 0), partial success (1), or it may have fully achieved its goal (2). Summing each of these leads to an overall index of policy success. The variable has a hypothetical maximum score of twelve.

49. Personal interview with the authors.

The Case for Neopluralism

[T]he determinants of [a lobbyist's] success are situation specific. The [policy] outcomes appear to turn less on the presence or absence of resources . . . than on much more particular factors that vary from issue to issue.[1]

Comparing the sets of actors active on the same issue, we simply ask whether the side with the most resources won. The results are striking in that the usual types of resources that are often assumed to "buy" public policy outcomes—PAC donations, lobbying expenditures, membership size, and organizational budgets—have no observable effect on the outcomes. . . . [T]here seems to be no relationship between the level of these types of resources that a side controls and whether it obtains its preferred outcomes. The wealthier side sometimes wins and sometimes loses.[2]

We saw in chapter 1 of this book that past studies of interest-group influence reached highly inconsistent findings. Some studies showed that lobbying and campaign contributions influence the behavior of public officials and policy outcomes; other studies show little or no impact. In this chapter and the next, we will concentrate our analysis on three large studies that included a total of almost 500 issues and more than 1,200 interviews. Using the data and results from these studies, we show when the neopluralist framework best describes patterns of influence and when the exchange framework provides the more accurate description.

The quotes at the start of this chapter are from analyses of the two largest studies of interest-group influence ever conducted in the United States. The first quote is from *The Hollow Core: Private Interests in National Policy Making* by John Heinz, Edward Laumann, Robert Nelson, and Robert Salisbury. They based their conclusion on interviews with 776 lobbyists and 301 public officials conducted in 1983 and 1984. Their study covered 77 issues. The second quote comes from *Lobbying and Policy Change* by Frank Baumgartner and his colleagues. *Lobbying and Policy Change* based its conclusions on in-depth studies of ninety-eight randomly chosen issues and interviews with almost 300 lobbyists. The studies' conclusions fit well the neopluralist expectations concerning lobbying and influence. There was substantial competition over issues, an organization's resources did not predict its policy success, and policy outcomes were contingent upon factors unique to a particular time and situation.

LIMITATIONS OF PREVIOUS STUDIES OF LOBBYING

In their review of fifty years of interest-group scholarship, Frank Baumgartner and Beth Leech identified three characteristics of past studies that limited their usefulness:

1. Researchers concentrated more on the political action committee (PAC) contributions and roll call votes in Congress than on behaviors where lobbying was more likely to make a difference.

2. Researchers often studied a single issue or single policy area rather than multiple issues and policy areas.

3. Researchers typically focused on highly visible and highly partisan issues rather than examining a representative sample of issues.[3]

How did these characteristics impede our understanding of lobbying impact and interest-group influence?

Concentrating on Campaign Contributions and Roll Call Votes

Congressional scholars maintain that many of the most critical policy decisions typically occur during committee and subcommittee deliberations.[4] Scholars also agree that the least likely time for groups to influence the legislative process is at the roll call vote.[5] Studying only the effects of PAC contributions on roll call votes, however, views lobbying and policymaking as if lobbying takes place immediately before a roll call vote and that such votes are the major policymaking decision.[6] Concentrating on roll call votes excludes the influence of interest organizations on the agenda setting, formulation, and implementation stages of the policy process.

Using campaign contributions as the measure of lobbying creates a measurement problem. PAC campaign contributions are only a fraction of total lobbying expenditures. According to the Center for Responsive Politics, total lobbying expenditures for 2010 were almost $4 billion.[7] Federal PAC contributions in the same year were less than 10 percent of that amount. In addition, lobbying expenditures and campaign expenditures are not highly correlated. Many organizations that lobby do not have PACs, and many organizations with PACs do not hire lobbyists.

Measuring lobbying impact by a legislator's roll call vote also has measurement problems. A vote has only three possible values: (1) the legislator votes to support an interest group's preferred outcome, (2) the legislator votes against the group's preferred outcome, or (3) the legislator abstains from voting on the issue. Looking only at a legislator's vote fails to consider whether the legislator worked to weaken or strengthen a bill in committee or whether the legislator encouraged other legislators to support or oppose the bill. The outcome of a roll call vote also fails to indicate the extent to which a group achieved its objectives. For example, it makes a huge difference to corn producers whether Congress eliminates, reduces, leaves the same, increases slightly, or increases substantially the subsidy for ethanol made from corn.

Examining Single Issues

The tendency of past research to focus on a single issue or a single policy domain also limits its usefulness. For example, professors Michael Graetz and Ian Shapiro provided an excellent case study of the lobbying and policymaking process that surrounded the temporary elimination of the estate tax.[8] By concentrating on a single issue and studying the entire the policymaking process, Graetz and Shapiro overcame the problems of looking only at campaign contributions and roll call votes. Their study showed how groups affected agenda setting and policy formulation as well as the final roll call votes. The authors also were able to analyze the extent to which different interests achieved their objectives.

Looking only at a single policy, however, increases the possibility that the causal relationships they saw as important actually were unimportant. Limiting their analysis to a single case limits the generalizability of their findings. Despite their in-depth knowledge of the policy and their analytic skills, Graetz and Shapiro's account of the causes of the estate tax outcome might be incorrect. Factors they interpreted as essential to deciding the policy outcome might actually have been unimportant. Graetz and Shapiro argued, for instance, that an important factor in the success of the pro-repeal lobby was its reframing of the issue from an "estate tax on wealthy heirs" to a "death tax on hardworking couples." Because of their knowledge of the policy process and their research skills, we might be convinced that the successful reframing was critical. We cannot know, however, whether the same outcome would have occurred without the reframing. An alternative explanation of the policy outcome could be that once voters gave control of Congress to the Republican Party and elected a president whose top priority was to cut taxes, the repeal of the estate tax was inevitable.

Throughout this book, we show that case studies are important in discovering relationships and in testing explanations of social phenomena. Nevertheless, generalizing from one case or from a small number of cases can lead to incorrect conclusions. We believe that Graetz and Shapiro are correct about the importance of reframing to the estate tax outcome, but we cannot conclude that issue reframing leads to changes in the status quo. Researchers would need to examine many issues to determine whether success in reframing correlates with lobbying success. Frank Baumgartner and his colleagues showed in their study of ninety-eight issues that successfully reframing an issue is a rare occurrence and that reframing generally is unnecessary to lobbying success.[9]

Studying Only High-Conflict and Highly Visible Issues

A third problem that limits the value of many studies of interest-group influence is the tendency of researchers to consider only issues that were salient to the public or highly partisan. Andrew McFarland maintains that interest-group influence is weaker when issues are highly salient to the public and when partisanship is greater.[10] When issues are salient, political parties, citizen action groups, the media, and government agencies constrain the influence of producer groups.[11] After a time, however, the public loses interest and media coverage declines. Political parties and elected officials move to other issues and the activity of citizen groups declines, but producer groups with an economic stake in the issue remain active. When only producer interests are lobbying, politics can become "routine" as congressional committees and the bureaucracy allocate resources to the groups that continue to pay attention to the issue. Suppose McFarland is correct, and scholars have focused more on the most salient and partisan issues. In those instances, business influence is lessened. Therefore, the (typically salient and partisan) issues selected to study might have led researchers to underestimate the impact of business lobbying.

SOLUTIONS TO THE RESEARCH PROBLEMS

Both *Lobbying and Policy Change* and *The Hollow Core* constituted a decade-long efforts by teams of researchers. The two studies included large numbers of lobbyists and issues. The *Hollow Core* interviewed more than 1,000 lobbyists and policymakers in the areas of agriculture, energy, labor and health. The study included seventy-seven issues. The strengths of *The Hollow Core* were that it incorporated legislative and bureaucratic lobbyists and it included interviews with those who lobbied and those who were the targets of that lobbying. The study's weaknesses were that it focused almost exclusively on highly salient issues, and its measure of policy success came solely from the evaluation of the lobbyists interviewed rather than from a more objective measure of policy change.[12]

Three aspects of *Lobbying and Policy Change* make it a unique study. First, the study used a weighted random sample of 98 issues selected from more than 19,000 issues reported in the lobbying disclosure reports that lobbyists must file with Congress. For this reason, the sample included not only highly salient and partisan issues but also those issues that were less salient and less partisan.[13] Second, the study consisted of ninety-eight well-researched cases. In addition to the data on each issue from interviews with policy advocates, the research project collected data on each issue from media reports, congressional hearings, congressional and White House reports, policy papers, and archival documents produced by interest organizations. The result was a study that has many of the advantages of both qualitative case studies and quantitative analyses. Third, the researchers compared each policy outcome with the policy prior to the initiation of the lobbying effort. This provided a more objective measure of success than simply asking the lobbyists to evaluate their own success.

The design of *Lobbying and Policy Change* had two shortcomings. First, using the lobbying disclosure reports filed with Congress led the authors to concentrate on legislative issues and congressional lobbying. We do not know whether we can generalize its findings to bureaucratic lobbying and policymaking. Second, although the researchers used random sampling to select their issues, their selection of lobbyists to interview about those issues was not random. The research team interviewed only those lobbyists who were the leaders of their side of the issue. To use the language of Kevin Hula in *Lobbying Together,* the study examined only lobbyists who represented the core member organizations. The interviews did not include lobbyists representing the players seeking private goods or tagalongs who engaged in cheap riding. By interviewing only core members, the authors unintentionally excluded most private goods from their study.

TESTING NEOPLURALIST EXPECTATIONS

The neopluralist perspective includes seven central propositions:

1. Policymaking and lobbying are lengthy processes that involve multiple decisions.

2. Major policy changes (high politics) involve multiple competing groups.

3. Government officials are not neutral but are themselves effective lobbyists.

4. Political ideologies, political parties, and elections reduce interest-group influence.

5. The free rider problem does not prevent effective competition.

6. Institutions matter.

7. Interest-group influence is highly contingent of particular characteristics of the political environment and of the issue.

We examine the evidence for neopluralism using the data and findings from *The Hollow Core* and *Lobbying and Policy Change*. We supplement those with the data from the case studies in this book.

Policymaking and Lobbying Are Lengthy Processes Involving Multiple Decisions

A central finding of *Lobbying and Policy Change* was that "lobbying is a long-term commitment requiring steady and methodical effort."[14] Almost 90 percent of issues studied by Baumgartner and his colleagues involved lobbying activity that extended two years after the initial interview. Most of the issues studied also had been on the political agenda for two years prior to the interviews.[15] *The Hollow Core* interviews asked whether the lobbyists' issues typically were long lasting and whether their issues typically involved the same players or different players. Three-quarters of the lobbyists saw their issues as persisting for many years. Similarly, 62 percent of their respondents reported that the issues on which they lobbied involved repeat players from stable cooperative lobbying enterprises.[16]

All of our case studies—the North American Free Trade Agreement (NAFTA), the Energy Policy Act of 2003, the American Jobs Creation Act of 2004, the Data Quality Act (DQA), drug reimportation, atrazine, perchlorate, and the estate tax—are consistent with neopluralism's contention that policymaking typically takes place over a long period and involves multiple decisions. Among our eight issues, only the jobs act took less than two years to move from agenda setting to implementation. Despite the brevity of the DQA, the rules implementing the legislation took more than four years to write. The DQA continued to face legal challenges ten years after it became law. The NAFTA debate lasted over three years; atrazine, drug reimportation, and perchlorate have all been on the political agenda for more than a decade.

Our case studies that involved congressional decision making entailed multiple congressional committees and subcommittees as well as the White House.[17] *The Hollow Core* and *Lobbying and Policy Change* found similar patterns of fragmented and decentralized decision making. This fragmentation of policymaking extended the time necessary to complete the policy process, and it encouraged cooperative lobbying efforts.

Major Policy Changes Involve Competitive Lobbying

A consistent finding in interest-group research has been that the rise of citizen action groups and the expansion of issue networks have increased the number of head-to-head competitions over the past forty years.[18] University of Michigan political scientist John Kingdon's study of congressional voting on issues in 1969 found interest groups active on both sides of an issue for only 12 percent of the cases he examined.[19] *The Hollow Core* and *Lobbying and Policy Change* found the opposite pattern. Over 90 percent of the lobbyists interviewed for *The Hollow Core* reported that their key policy issues involved substantial competition.[20] In eighty-one of the ninety-eight issues studied in *Lobbying and Policy Change,* there were two or more competing sides.[21] Interestingly, the policy proposals that were most likely to fail were those on which only one side lobbied. Baumgartner and his colleagues argued that this finding indicated that opponents of a policy change did not become active unless a proposed policy change had a reasonable chance of becoming law.

Our case studies also showed competitive lobbying. With the exception of the legislative action on the DQA, the presence of competing interests characterized all of the cases. The case studies also supported the Baumgartner et al.

finding that many different types of organizations compose each side of an issue. For example, all major sides on NAFTA, the energy act, the jobs act, and drug reimportation included corporations, trade associations, citizen action groups, and government officials.

Government Officials Are Effective Policy Advocates

One of the important contributions of *Lobbying and Policy Change* is their documentation of the role of government officials as advocates for or against policy proposals. Neopluralism recognizes that government officials rarely are neutral in the policy process. The study also shows that when officials are active on an issue, they are effective advocates. One of the first tasks of a lobbyist is to mobilize their allies within the government.[22] Lobbyists believe this is critical because having government officials on your side significantly increases your likelihood of winning the policy battle. *Lobbying and Policy Change* demonstrates that this belief is correct and reinforces substantial earlier research showing that legislators and government bureaucrats are effective lobbyists.[23]

Our case studies also demonstrate the importance of government officials as advocates. Officials in the White House played a major role in organizing the lobbying effort in support of NAFTA and the 2003 energy act. In the regulatory cases of perchlorate and atrazine, the Department of Defense (DoD) and the U.S. Department of Agriculture (USDA) were important advocates in preventing policy changes. Drug reimportation provides the clearest case of government officials successfully defeating a proposed policy change. The opponents of reimportation brought the past and present commissioners of the U.S. Food and Drug Administration (FDA) to testify that they could not guarantee the safety of reimported drugs. This effectively killed reimportation because it prevented the secretary of Health and Human Services (HHS) from certifying that the reimported drugs constituted no new threat to drug safety.

Political Parties, Ideology, and Elections Constrain Interest-Group Influence

Beginning with E. E. Schattschneider and Robert Dahl, a substantial body of research indicates that competitive political parties, ideology, and elections constrain the influence of interest organizations.[24] Parties and elections limit interest-group influence because unorganized individuals have the opportunity to vote for political parties and candidates whose preferences match their own. Elected officials who stray too far from their constituents' preferences are unlikely to gain reelection. Ideology curbs the demands of interest groups by providing a normative framework that policymakers and the public can use to evaluate policy proposals.

When a new president comes to office or there is a change in which party controls Congress, the battlefield in the tug-of-war between interest organizations shifts. Numerous issues studied in *Lobbying and Policy Change* show the importance of elections. That study found that the election of a new president affected more than 15 percent of the cases in their sample.[25] Our case studies also demonstrated that elections matter. The elimination of the "death tax" favored the wealthy and had the strong backing of the powerful small business trade association the National Federation of Independent Business (NFIB). The elimination of the tax could not pass, however, while a Democrat was in the White House. Once a Republican became president, the battlefield tipped in favor of the interest groups supporting the measure. The energy act displayed a similar pattern. Republicans preferred policies that increase energy production while the Democrats were more likely to emphasize energy conservation. An energy bill with large subsidies for the oil and gas industries had little chance of becoming policy while the Democratic Party controlled the White House. This changed radically when the 2000 election resulted in the Bush–Cheney White House.

Although elections can change the political agenda in favor of some groups over others, *Lobbying and Policy Change* showed that, on average, highly partisan policy proposals are less likely to become law regardless of the electoral environment. Only 33 percent of partisan issues experienced significant change while 50 percent of nonpartisan issues experienced significant change.[26] Partisanship tends to reflect an ideological split, and policymakers are less willing to negotiate and compromise when ideology is important. Ideology tends to trump pragmatic politics as ideological interest groups see any compromise as a forsaking of principle.

The Power of Inertia

Organized interests are acutely aware that public policies create winners and losers. Proposed policy changes that will reduce or eliminate benefits for certain groups are likely to mobilize those very same groups. The fragmented nature of policymaking gives defenders of the status quo numerous opportunities to stop a proposed change. The inertia due to fragmentation is exacerbated when different parties control the House and the Senate.[27] These factors suggest that defenders of the status quo will experience greater success than supporters of policy change.

The authors of *Lobbying and Policy Change* used the metaphor of a heavy object on a sticky surface to characterize the inertia of the status quo. Moving that object (the current policy) in any direction takes substantial effort, and this makes policy change difficult. The study found that the single best predictor of which side would win a policy battle was which side was defending the status quo. On only seventeen of the ninety-eight issues studied in *Lobbying and Policy Change* did the proponents obtain a significant policy change within two years. Even after four years, proponents achieved a significant change on only twenty-seven issues. *Lobbying and Policy Change* also showed that if the side with greater resources was defending the status quo, it was more effective in achieving its goal than was the side with fewer resources. This was one of the few situations where the authors found that greater resources led to greater policy success.[28]

Our case studies also found inertia to be a powerful force, and the cases demonstrated that inertia was greatest when producer groups were defending the status quo. Drug reimportation presents an example of the difference between the ability of producer interests and consumer interests to overturn the status quo. We saw in chapter 6 that, prior to 1987, it was legal for individuals to reimport pharmaceuticals. This led the Pharmaceutical Research and Manufacturers of America (PhRMA) and the drug companies to propose a policy change that banned drug reimportation by any entity other than the U.S. manufacturer of that drug. The only interest organizations testifying on the bill were PhRMA and the pharmaceutical companies, and they had little difficulty in achieving their proposed change. Consumer groups did not organize to oppose the change.[29] Predictably, the new policy increased the price of prescription drugs and consumers broke the law by traveling to Canada and using the Internet to fill their prescriptions. Public support for reversing the 1987 law led Congress to pass legislation that allowed drug reimportation. A lobbyist for a major pharmaceutical producer, however, convinced Sen. Thad Cochran, R-MS, to add an amendment to that legislation that required the secretary of HHS to certify the safety of reimported drugs. The secretary of HHS was unwilling to make such a certification. The Cochran amendment meant that substantial reimportation would not occur. Despite losing the roll call vote that allowed drug reimportation, producer interests had successfully blocked the implementation of that decision.

Inertia also is a powerful force in policymaking by regulatory agencies, particularly when producer interests are protecting their current privileges. The case studies of atrazine and perchlorate illustrate the ability of organized producer interests to protect the status quo. Substantial peer-reviewed research in the United States and Europe indicated that atrazine was an endocrine disruptor that might harm humans, especially the youngest agricultural workers. Nevertheless, for over a decade, the Syngenta Corporation successfully blocked regulations that would eliminate atrazine use in the United States. Similarly, the Perchlorate Study Group (PSG) coalition worked with the DoD and the National Aeronautics and Space Administration (NASA) to prevent the Environmental Protection Agency (EPA) from reducing the reference dose (RfD) for perchlorate below twenty-four parts per billion (ppb) despite the agency's belief that a twenty-four ppb standard endangered the health of infants.

The authors of *The Hollow Core* did not find inertia to be a powerful force. The lobbyists whom they interviewed reported greater success when they were proposing a policy change than when they were opposing change.[30] Heinz and his colleagues suggested that this unexpected finding might have occurred because the lobbyists preferred to discuss issues on which they achieved policy change. Nevertheless, this result is the opposite of what the researchers expected.[31]

Overcoming the Free Rider Problem

For almost fifty years prior to the publication of *Lobbying and Policy Change*, researchers had not written a major book on lobbying without discussing the collective action dilemma and the free rider problem. *Lobbying and Policy Change*, however, did not mention these concepts. Previous work by the book's authors explained this omission. Two of the five authors, Frank Baumgartner and Beth Leech, had published an extensive review of the previous fifty years of research on special interests. The authors concluded that the collective action dilemma is only relevant *if* the free rider problem prevents citizen groups from forming and lobbying, and numerous authors had previously shown that citizen groups form and they lobby effectively.[32] Baumgartner and Leech concluded, therefore, that the collective action dilemma is largely irrelevant to the study of group influence.[33]

A second reason that *Lobbying and Policy Change* omitted discussing the free rider problem was that citizen groups constituted almost half of the interest organizations identified as major players in the ninety-eight issues. Baumgartner and his colleagues wrote, "The most striking feature of this distribution of interest-group lobbying is the predominance of citizen groups in these debates."[34] Given that the collective action dilemma should be greater for citizen groups than for other organizations, this finding indicated that the collective action dilemma was unimportant. Baumgartner et al. also found that on most issues the sides of the issue were heterogeneous. Each side of an issue was likely to have a mix of citizen groups, corporations, trade associations, and government advocates. This heterogeneity helped ensure that all sides had sufficient lobbying resources.

One of the authors of *The Hollow Core*, Washington University political scientist Robert Salisbury, also saw the collective action problem as generally unimportant to lobbying conflicts. Most lobbying entities were not membership-based groups; rather, they were institutions such as universities, hospitals, and corporations.

> [W]hen a corporation seeks to affect public policy—regarding pollution standards, for example—it does not justify its effort by alleging that it is reflecting the values of its employees. Nor does a university seek increased student loan funds on the grounds that its student body has expressed its desire for the money. It is not member interests as such that are crucial, but the judgments of organizational leaders about the needs of the institution as a continuing organization.[35]

Leaders of such organizations have no group maintenance concerns, so it is easier for them to engage in lobbying activities without fearing internal backlash from members. The interests of the institution stand separate from those people associated with the institution.

Institutions Matter

A critical characteristic of the neopluralist approach is its recognition that governmental institutions matter. Andrew McFarland has argued that the institutional arrangements that give policymaking authority to committees and subcommittees often favor producer interests over citizen groups.[36] There are multiple reasons for his expectation. A citizen group typically is active on many more issues than is a corporation or trade association. At the same time, however, the citizen groups generally have fewer resources than producer organizations. Because multiple committees and subcommittees often have shared jurisdiction over an issue,[37] it is difficult for a citizen's group to attend all the important meetings concerning the group's many issues. In contrast to citizen groups, producer groups tend to have greater resources and tend to lobby on fewer issues. The narrower focus and greater resources allow producer interest organizations to attend these committee hearings and markup sessions as well as to monitor the activity of bureaucrats engaged in an issue. The producer groups' greater resources allow them to hire policy specialists who possess substantial knowledge of particular issues. The producer groups also have the resources to hire lobbyists who have excellent access to committee and subcommittee members and their staffs. Another reason McFarland gives for the advantage of producer interests is that bureaucratic policymaking and decisions made in committee markup often involve technical arguments. Producer interests are more likely than citizen groups to have the resources to gather the necessary technical information.[38]

The authors of *Lobbying and Policy Change* tested the arguments concerning the institutional advantages of producer interests and found them relatively unimportant. In their case studies of the ninety-eight issues, Baumgartner et al. found that the lobbying tug-of-war generally was not between producer organizations on one side and citizen groups on the other. Rather, the competing sides of issues included lobbyists representing producer, citizen, and government organizations.[39] We observed the same pattern in most of our case studies. When Congress debated NAFTA, the jobs act, and drug reimportation, each side contained producer, citizen, and government groups. Coalitions and cooperative lobbying arrangements allowed the diverse groups to share resources, lobbying costs, and information.

Although *Lobbying and Policy Change* found that heterogeneous coalitions reduced the institutional advantages of producer groups, the authors of *The Hollow Core* found that producer and citizen organizations were on opposite sides of the issue when bureaucracies and subcommittees were making policy.[40] Our case studies of perchlorate and atrazine found a similar pattern. It may be that coalition heterogeneity is more characteristic of congressional lobbying than lobbying in the bureaucracy. If so, this would indicate that producer organizations maintain an institutional advantage when policymaking moves to the bureaucracy.

Amy McKay's reanalysis of the data from *The Hollow Core* suggests that producer interests have an advantage when policymaking is fragmented. A group's resources allow it to lobby in more venues and lobbying more venues leads to greater lobbying success.[41] McKay also found that interest organizations with greater resources are more likely to lobby unopposed than are organizations with fewer resources. This favors producer interests in their pursuit of narrow private goods.

WHAT RESOURCES ARE IMPORTANT TO LOBBYING SUCCESS?

While *Lobbying and Policy Change* provides support for almost all of the arguments of neopluralism, the book's most surprising finding was that the relative resources available to competing lobbying organizations appeared not to matter. The side with greater material resources was only slightly more likely to win than the side with fewer resources. Table 7.1 provides the summary of the relationships Baumgartner et al. found between particular types of resources and policy success. Many of the resources exchange theory expects to influence policy outcomes did not. Neither a side's lobbying expenditures nor its campaign contributions appear to matter. The table does show that *who* lobbies for a side matters a great deal. For more than three-quarters of the issues studied, the side with more high-level governmental advocates was victorious. Baumgartner et al. wrote that when high-level government officials, particularly congressional leaders and the president, become involved in pushing an issue forward, their side is likely to win.[42]

Another human resource also matters: **covered officials**. Covered officials are the employees who formerly had jobs as members of Congress, high-ranking congressional staff members, or high-level agency officials during the previous two years. As the authors of *Lobbying and Policy Change* pointed out, these are people who themselves likely were lobbied only a short time ago. Covered officials are a resource that money can buy, and the influence of covered officials on policymaking appears to be worth their price. This supports the finding from *The Hollow Core* data that although money itself may not buy outcomes, money indirectly affects outcomes by purchasing the types of lobbyists who are most likely to achieve policy success.[43]

Almost a decade ago, two of the major proponents of neopluralism summarized the argument that interest-group influence is contingent on factors unique to a given policy at a given time and place:

> We have argued that recent research based on large and midsize-*n* samples provides a much more *contingent* assessment of the nature and impact of the influence enterprise. . . . Simply put, the environment in which organized interests operate is a very complex one, one

TABLE 7.1   The Relationship Between Lobbying Resources and Policy Outcomes

Type of Resource	Percentage of Cases in Which the Side Having Greater Levels of This Resource Achieved its Preferred Outcome	Number of Cases
High-level government allies	78**	23
Covered officials lobbying	63**	35
Mid-level government allies	60**	48
Business financial resources	53	34
Lobbying expenditures	52	58
Association financial resources	50	58
Membership	50	58
Campaign contributions	50	58

** Difference statistically significant at p < .01.

Cell entries are the percentage of issues that the side with the greater level of this type of resource achieved its policy goal.

Source: Frank R. Baumgartner et al., *Lobbying and Policy Change: Who Wins, Who Loses, and Why* (Chicago: University of Chicago Press, 2009), 208.

in which competition for survival is multifaceted and complicated by significant linkages and feedbacks between the stages of the influence production process.[44]

This expectation fits the findings of *The Hollow Core* and *Lobbying and Policy Change.* These large studies concluded that the factors unique to a given issue along with the political constraints created by elections, political parties, and political ideology far outweigh the impact of resources on policy outcomes.

WHY DO RESOURCES APPEAR NOT TO MATTER?

The absence of relationships between policy outcomes and most resource variables raises two critical questions: (1) "Why don't most resources matter?" and (2) "If resources don't matter, why do interest organizations continue to use them?" Baumgartner and his colleagues argued that the total resources available to a side *do* matter, but we do not observe a relationship between resources and outcomes for two reasons. First, lobbying Congress is extraordinarily competitive. Although some individual organizations have greater resources than others, when the resources of all the organizations lobbying on a side of an issue are added up, each side has sufficient resources to lobby effectively. The authors of *Lobbying and Policy Change* maintained that if one side withdrew its resources, it would lose the policy tug-of-war.

The second reason that resources appear not to matter is that current policy reflects previous differences in resources. Most policy issues are continuing in nature. The existing policy reflects the results of past lobbying efforts.

> Changing policy from the status quo involves justifying a *shift* in the allocation of resources, moving it from a status quo position to a new position. But the status quo position was already the object of the mobilization of interest groups, members of the public, and political leaders in previous years. *So to see that money cannot automatically purchase shifts in the status quo does not mean that the status quo might not already reflect important biases in politics.*[45]

Using our tug-of-war metaphor, the current location of the policy already reflects the relative resources of the opposing sides. Unless new organizations join a side, existing organizations drop out of the struggle, or an external event tilts the playing field, there is no reason to expect that a continued struggle will change the policy's position.

Current policy is the result of both current and previous lobbying efforts. In such a situation, both sides in the tug-of-war must maintain their current efforts to prevent the other side from moving the policy toward its preferred position. If one side reduces its lobbying effort, interest organizations on the other side will pull the policy their way. In short, Baumgartner and his colleagues appear to have solved the paradox of why interest organizations continue to expend resources on lobbying even though that spending does not *appear* to matter. Political scientists David Lowery and Virginia Gray used the metaphor of an arms race to describe how this continuing battle affects PAC contributions. Arms races are terribly wasteful, but all sides must increase their expenditures to avoid losing the policy war.[46]

We suggest that there are three additional reasons that *Lobbying and Policy Change* did not find a relationship between having greater material resources and winning policy outcomes. First, by adding all of the resources of all interests on each side of the issue, Baumgartner et al. assumed that every member of the side was acting as a core member of a coalition. All members of the side were equally willing to use their resources to obtain the collective good. We saw in chapter 6 that this assumption is false. A second reason the study might not have found relationships between lobbying resources was the study's exclusive focus on Congress rather than Congress and the bureaucracy. Baumgartner et al. suggest at the beginning of their book that this may be a problem.[47] Given that corporations, trade associations, and professional associations engage in lobbying of regulatory agencies as frequently as they engage in congressional lobbying,[48] the bias in the sampling process may have created a problem for the generalizability of the study. We saw in chapter 5 that in battles over the rule-making process corporations win more frequently than other organizations. A third reason that *Lobbying and Policy Change* may not have found a relationship between lobbying resources and policy outcomes stems from the study's concentration on collective goods. By interviewing only the major players on issues decided by Congress, *Lobbying and Policy Change* missed many of the lobbying situations where private goods are important.

SUMMARY

The Hollow Core and *Lobbying and Policy Change* provide excellent empirical support for the neopluralist model. The authors showed empirically that if a significant proposed policy change reaches the political agenda, those organizations that would be harmed by the proposed change generally have the resources to lobby effectively against it. Baumgartner et al. showed that for issues decided by Congress, citizen action groups are effective lobbyists and have sufficient influence to offset the producer group advantages hypothesized by exchange theory. For Baumgartner and his colleagues, the free rider problem is too insignificant to mention and parties and elections play their expected role in constraining interest-group influence. The major fly that *The Hollow Core* and *Lobbying and Policy Change* found in the neopluralist ointment was that wealthier groups have greater resources to hire covered officials. Having these officials does make a statistically significant difference in policy outcomes. Even that advantage, however, is relatively weak.

Lobbying and Policy Change made numerous methodological advances in the studying of interest-group influence. Rather than examining lobbying at a single point in time, the study examined issues over a multiyear period. Rather than studying only PAC contributions, the research team examined the impact of the numerous resources that organizations use in lobbying. Rather than having a dichotomous measure of policy success (the group either won or it lost the roll-call vote), *Lobbying and Policy Change* created a measure of policy success that captured the extent to which each side of an issue achieved its goals. Rather than studying a single issue or a single policy area, *Lobbying and Policy Change* examined ninety-eight issues from numerous issue areas. These multiple methodological advances allowed the authors to study the relative importance of issue-level variables such as salience, partisanship, and competition. The breadth and depth of their data also allowed the study to compare the relative impact of numerous types of group resources on policy outcomes.

The results of *Lobbying and Policy Change* improved our understanding of lobbying in many ways. Among the more important of these advances were its findings concerning the heterogeneity of different sides lobbying on an issue, the effectiveness of lobbying by current and past government officials, and its discovery of broad support for the neopluralist framework. Baumgartner and his colleagues also provided an explanation for the paradox that organizations continue to spend more and more on lobbying despite the appearance that such expenditures appear unrelated to policy outcomes.

ENDNOTES

1. John Heinz et al., *The Hollow Core: Private Interests in National Policy Making* (Cambridge, MA: Harvard University Press, 1993), 351.

2. Frank R. Baumgartner et al., *Lobbying and Policy Change: Who Wins, Who Loses, and Why* (Chicago: University of Chicago Press, 2009), 208–209.

3. Frank R. Baumgartner and Beth L. Leech, *Basic Interests: The Importance of Groups in Politics and in Political Science* (Princeton, NJ: Princeton University Press), 136–137.

4. Richard Hall and Frank Wayman, "Buying Time: Moneyed Interests and the Mobilization of Bias in Congressional Committees," *American Political Science Review* 84 (1990): 797–820; and Ken Kollman, "Inviting Friends to Lobby: Interest Groups, Ideological Bias, and Congressional Committees," *American Political Science Review* 41 (1997): 519–544.

5. Scott E. Adler and John S. Lapinski, "Demand-Side Theory and Congressional Committee Composition: A Constituency Characteristic Approach," *American Journal of Political Science*, 41, no. 3 (1997): 895–918.

6. Baumgartner and Leech, *Basic Interests.*

7. Michael Beckel, "Federal Lobbying Expenditures Plateau After Years of Rapid Growth," OpenSecrets.org, February 4, 2011, www.opensecrets.org/news/2011/02/federal-lobbying-expenditures-plateau.html

8. Michael J. Graetz and Ian Shapiro, *Death by a Thousand Cuts: The Fight over Taxing Inherited Wealth* (Princeton, NJ: Princeton University Press, 2005).

9. Baumgartner et al., *Lobbying and Policy Change,* Chapter 9.

10. Andrew S. McFarland, "Interest Groups and Political Time: Cycles in America," *British Journal of Political Science* 21, no. 3 (1991): 257–284; and Andrew McFarland, *Neopluralism: The Evolution of Political Process Theory* (Lawrence: University of Kansas Press, 2004), 59–61.

11. In his study of business interests, Mark Smith makes a similar claim. Mark Smith, *American Business and Political Power: Public Opinion, Elections, and Democracy* (Chicago: University of Chicago Press, 2000).

12. Georgia State University political scientist Amy McKay reanalyzed the data from *The Hollow Core* using improved statistical methods and more objective measures of policy success. Her results are published in Amy M. McKay (2010), "The Decision to Lobby Bureaucrats," *Public Choice* 147, no. 1–2 (2011): 123–138; and Amy M. McKay, "Buying Policy? The Effect of Lobbyists' Resources on Their Policy Success," *Political Research Quarterly* (forthcoming 2012).

13. For a discussion of the lobbying disclosure reports and their use in research, see Frank R. Baumgartner and Beth L. Leech, "Studying Interest Groups Using the

Lobbying Disclosure Reports," *VOX POP: Newsletter of the Political Organizations and Parties Section of the American Political Science Association* 17 (1999): 1–3.

14. Baumgartner et al., *Lobbying and Policy Change,* 106, 218.

15. Ibid., 106.

16. Heinz et al., *The Hollow Core,* 250.

17. Although the atrazine and perchlorate regulations did not involve congressional legislation, numerous legislators were active lobbyists on the issue.

18. Jeffrey Berry, *Lobbying for the People: The Political Behavior of Public Interest Groups* (Princeton, NJ: Princeton University Press, 1977).

19. Cited in Michael T. Hayes, "The Semi-Sovereign Pressure Groups: A Critique of Current Theory and an Alternative Typology," *Journal of Politics* 40, no. 1 (1978): 134–161.

20. Heinz et al., *The Hollow Core,* 250.

21. Baumgartner et al., *Lobbying and Policy Change,* 58.

22. Ibid., 151–164.

23. Scott Ainsworth, "The Role of Legislators in the Determination of Interest Group Influence," *Legislative Studies Quarterly* 22 (1997): 517–533; Robert Salisbury and Kenneth Shepsle, "U.S. Congressman as Enterprise," *Legislative Studies Quarterly* 6 (1981): 559–576; Heinz et al., *The Hollow Core*; Hall and Wayman, "Buying Time"; and Richard L. Hall and Alan V. Deardorff, "Lobbying as Legislative Subsidy," *American Political Science Review* 100 (2006): 69–84.

24. E. E. Schattschneider, *The Semi-Sovereign People* (New York: Holt, Rinehart & Winston, 1960); and Robert Dahl, *Who Governs? Democracy and Power in an American City* (New Haven, CT: Yale University Press, 1961).

25. Baumgartner et al., *Lobbying and Policy Change,* Table 5.3, 104.

26. Ibid., Table 5.4, 105.

27. Barbara Sinclair, *Unorthodox Lawmaking: New Legislative Processes in the U.S. Congress,* 3rd ed. (Washington, DC: CQ Press, 2007).

28. Baumgartner et al., *Lobbying and Policy Change,* 232.

29. 100 CIS Legis. Hist. P.L. 293 (100 PL 293).

30. Heinz et al., *The Hollow Core,* 241–242.

31. Ibid., 242.

32. Berry, *Lobbying for the People.*

33. Baumgartner and Leech, *Basic Interests,* 81–82.

34. Baumgartner et al., *Lobbying and Policy Change,* 10.

35. Robert H. Salisbury, "Interest Representation: The Dominance of Institutions," *American Political Science Review* 78, no. 1 (1984): 67.

36. For McFarland, a countervailing group would be any group that opposed the goals of the organized producer group. See McFarland, *Neopluralism,* 15.

37. Sinclair, *Unorthodox Lawmaking.*

38. McFarland, *Neopluralism,* 51, 55.

39. Frank Baumgartner and Christine Mahoney, "Gaining Government Allies: Groups, Officials, and Alliance Behavior" (paper presented at the annual meeting of the Midwest Political Science Association, Chicago, April 25–28, 2002).

40. Heinz et al., *The Hollow Core,* 39, 51, 277.

41. McKay, "Buying Policy?," 12.

42. Baumgartner et al., *Lobbying and Policy Change,* 209.

43. McKay, "Buying Policy?," 12.

44. Virginia Gray and David Lowery, "A Neopluralist Perspective on Research on Organized Interests," *Political Research Quarterly* 57, no. 1 (2004), 171.

45. Baumgartner et al., *Lobbying and Policy Change,* 213–214, emphasis added.

46. Virginia Gray and David Lowery, "Reconceptualizing PAC Contributions: It's Not a Collective Action Problem and It May Be an Arms Race," *American Politics Quarterly* 25 (1997): 319–346.

47. Baumgartner et al., *Lobbying and Policy Change,* 5. They write that their sampling procedures "focus on issues that in some way involved Congress and issues relating to the judiciary and that are solely agency-related may be undercounted." The authors further indicate that their sampling procedures would miss lawyers, engineers, and other specialists who work on regulatory issues and are not required to register as lobbyists or file their contacts with policymakers.

48. Scott R. Furlong, "Political Influence in the Bureaucracy: The Bureaucracy Speaks," *Journal of Public Administration Research and Theory* 8, no. 1 (1998): 39–65; and Cornelius Kerwin, ed., *Rulemaking: How Government Agencies Write Law and Make Policy,* 3rd ed. (Washington, DC: CQ Press, 2003).

Evidence for the Exchange Model

C hapter 7 provided support for the neopluralist model of interest-group influence. This chapter reviews research that buttresses the exchange model. An important point to remember is that the neopluralist and exchange models are not mutually exclusive. If all sides of an issue have sufficient resources to compete for policy support, the predictions of the two models will be similar. The models make different predictions when one side does not have sufficient resources to bid for policymakers' support. When this occurs, the exchange model predicts that the unorganized and members of groups with few resources will not be well represented.

The *Lobbying and Policy Change* and *The Hollow Core* studies[1] demonstrate that the total resources currently available to different sides of an issue do not predict which side will win a policy battle. These results reinforce earlier research that found little or no effect of campaign contributions on policy outcomes. *Lobbying and Policy Change* does not conclude, however, that resources do not matter. The authors argued instead that the current policy reflects the inequalities in the resources that were available to each side in past policy struggles. In other words, the tug-of-war over an issue had reached an equilibrium that reflects the past strength of the opposing sides. Unless one side gains *additional* resources, the policy outcome will not change. For example, the current perchlorate policy at the Environmental Protection Agency (EPA) is the result of past battles between those interests that want a lower allowable level of perchlorate contamination and those interests that oppose lower levels. Each side must continue lobbying to prevent the other side from moving the policy, but unless there is a change in the strength of one side or the other, the perchlorate policy will remain the same.

Although *Lobbying and Policy Change* finds little relationship between current resources and policy outcomes, a growing body of research shows that firms are successful rent seekers. Studies of corporate political activity show that more politically active firms receive substantial political benefits. Firms that increase their lobbying expenditures achieve higher profits, increase their market share, pay fewer taxes, experience less regulatory oversight, and achieve greater increases in stock prices.[2] These findings indicate that lobbying creates specific economic and political benefits to firms that lobby. The findings also support the hypothesis that exchanges occur between lobbying organizations and policymakers. What is involved in this exchange process?

THE SUPPLY AND DEMAND FOR POLICY SUPPORT

We saw in chapter 2 that one way to understand the exchange model is with the metaphor of a Middle Eastern bazaar. In the bazaar, an organized interest buys public officials' support for a desired policy outcome. If this exchange occurs, what does the policymaker want from the group? Some exchange models assume that public officials have only one goal: to increase their wealth. More frequently, however, authors using the exchange approach assume that public officials have multiple goals including advancing one's career, gaining political power, making good policy, and representing their constituents.[3] *All models assume that reelection is the predominant objective of elected policymakers.* Defeated legislators cannot pursue career advancement, political power, or good policies. They certainly are in no position to represent their constituents.

The Price Officials Charge

The price policymakers will charge organized interests depends on four aspects of the interest group's policy objective:[4] (1) its congruence with the policy preferences of the official's voting constituency, (2) its salience to those constituents, (3) its fit with the objectives of the legislator's political party, and (4) its compatibility with the legislator's own policy preferences.

Suppose a bill concerning the rights of citizens to buy automatic weapons comes before Congress. Two groups, Handgun Control and the National Rifle Association (NRA), bid for a legislator's support. Handgun Control wants a policy that restricts the sale of automatic weapons; the NRA wants a policy that guarantees a citizen's access to those same weapons. If we assume that officials who support policies favored by their constituents are more likely to win reelection, then officials will charge a lower price to support a policy that their constituents favor. If the policymaker's constituency favors greater restrictions on gun ownership, he will charge Handgun Control a lower price for his support than he would charge the NRA. After all, the legislator expects to gain votes by supporting gun restrictions. If the policymaker is willing to support the NRA's policy goal, he will charge the organization a high price. To purchase the legislator's support, the NRA must provide him sufficient resources to gain enough new votes to offset the votes the legislator will lose by opposing greater restrictions. In short, policymakers will act to improve the chance they will win reelection. One way of achieving this is to support policies favored by one's constituents; another tactic is to trade policy support for resources that will aid one's reelection.

The salience of an issue to the public can increase or decrease the price the legislator charges a group. If an official's constituents favor a group's preferred policy, then greater salience of an issue will reduce the price the group must pay. If, however, an interest group seeks a policy the official's constituents oppose, higher salience will increase the price the group must pay. This situation demonstrates an important implication of exchange theory: *the more important the issue is to constituents, the more costly it will be for an interest group to move a policymaker away from the constituents' preferred policy.*

In their important book, *The Party Decides,* Marty Cohen, David Karol, Hans Noel, and John Zaller showed that some interest organizations form long-term coalitions with a political party. For example, the Republican Party's coalition includes groups representing small and large businesses, medical doctors, pharmaceutical companies, evangelical Christians, gun advocates, and anti-abortion groups. The Democratic Party's coalition includes organizations representing public school employees, unions, environmentalists, African Americans, Latinos, and trial lawyers. In their analysis of the presidential nomination process, Cohen and his colleagues showed how these groups influence the outcome. Groups such as the NRA can mobilize a donor network of hundreds or even thousands of people. An environmental group might ask its members to support a particular candidate. The groups supply the thousands of citizen activists who make phone calls, canvass door-to-door, and drive voters to the polls. Group endorsements show a candidate's strengths with core constituents.[5] The critical importance of interest-group support means that a party's nominee must demonstrate to the groups that his policy preferences are acceptable to them and that they can count on him to further their interests.

Parties are critical to a candidate's obtaining office, and they remain important after the candidate is in office. To gain greater political power within a legislature, an elected official normally requires the backing of his political party. Legislators who support their party's desired policies are more likely to rise to leadership positions. For this reason, a legislator will charge an interest group a lower price if its desired policy is congruent with the policy preferences of the legislator's political party. The Democratic Party favors greater restrictions on gun control; the Republican Party opposes them. We would expect, therefore, that Democratic legislators would charge Handgun Control a lower price than would Republican legislators. Conversely, Republican legislators will charge a lower price to the NRA than will Democratic legislators.

The fit of a group's desired policy with an official's own policy preferences also affects the price the official will charge. One reason officials run for office is to move public policies closer to their own preferences. Groups asking a policymaker to act contrary to his policy goals must pay a higher price than groups whose goals are consistent with the legislator's policy preferences.[6]

The Price Groups Pay

Organized interests pay legislators based on three factors: (1) the value of the policy to their organization, (2) the ability of the policymaker to produce that policy, and (3) the price other legislators charge for a similar level of policy productivity. More productive public officials obtain higher prices than their less productive colleagues.[7] Exchange theory hypothesizes that an interest organization will pay higher prices to a legislator who (1) holds a leadership position in the legislature, (2) is the chair of a committee that is relevant to the group's goals, (3) is a member of a committee relevant to the group's goals, and (4) is a member of the majority party.[8] The same logic applies to exchanges with bureaucrats. Interest organizations will provide more support to those officials who have decision-making power over issues important to the interest. In short, the better placed an official is to provide the group's desired policy, the more the group will pay for his or her support.[9]

If a policymaker and an interest group agree on a price, how do interest organizations and legislators enforce the bargains they make? If an interest organization makes a campaign contribution before the legislator acts on an issue, what keeps the legislator from breaking his promise to the group? If the group promises to reward the legislator after he has given his support, what prevents the group from reneging on its promise? Legislators and lobbyists do not walk the hallways of Congress randomly associating with one another. Legislators and lobbyists *choose* to interact with one another. One part of that choice process considers the incentives that either party has to renege on the agreements they make.

Enforcing Exchange Agreements

Even in the strongest personal relationships, defections or broken promises occur. The major factor that prevents officials and interest organizations from breaking their promises is the continuing nature of their relationship. For example, legislators have repeated contacts with corporations in their districts. These interactions create recurring opportunities for exchanges. Corporate headquarters seldom move lock, stock, and barrel from a state or city. Incumbency advantages lead to long tenures among elected officials. These realities mean that key interactions will be ongoing. If participants in the legislator–lobbyist interaction have long time horizons then they are less apt to break their promises. Organized interests that want a policymaker's support in the future cannot afford to ruin the present relationship.[10]

Some of the best-known formal work related to these issues is by Robert Axelrod. Axelrod studied strategic behaviors in repeated prisoners' dilemmas games (see Box 8.1). If a game is played only once, each player has an incentive to defect on the other player. If both defect, each player is left with a suboptimal outcome. If the players play the game repeatedly and they expect play to continue then each player has an incentive to cooperate with the other. If the expectation of continued interactions decreases, the incentive to renege on promises of cooperation increases. Political and social interactions are replete with examples of this sort of strategic dynamic. Presidents and legislators who have lost their reelection bids or who have stated their intent to retire typically have at least two more months left to serve. Between a failed reelection bid and the inauguration of the newcomers, outgoing officeholders are referred to as "lame ducks." With lame ducks, there will be no long-term interactions. Legislators and lobbyists are sensitive to the likelihood of their continued interactions and act accordingly.

BOX 8.1   **A Prisoners' Dilemma**

For many decades, scholars have been intrigued with different aspects of a simple, two-person prisoners' dilemma game. As presented here, a prisoners' dilemma is a good model of favor exchange. Consider two people, say Bob and Ray, who are interested in exchanging favors. Bob and Ray each face a set of two options. They may choose to cooperate with the other or they may chose to defect. Bob and Ray are not able to choose outcomes; they can only choose among their options—cooperate or defect.

		Ray Chooses Either	
		Cooperate	Defect
Bob Chooses Either	Cooperate	3, 3	0, 5
	Defect	5, 0	1, 1

Depending on the options chosen by Bob and Ray, one of four outcomes will occur. If they both cooperate, each will receive a payoff of three, as seen in the northwestern cell. If they both defect, they will each receive a payoff of just one, as seen in the southeastern cell. If one chooses to cooperate while the other chooses to defect, the cooperator is penalized and receives zero while the defector is rewarded and receives five.

How do Bob and Ray choose to play the game? Consider the following: Bob does not know what Ray will choose, and Ray does not know what Bob will choose. But suppose that Bob *thinks* that Ray will choose to cooperate. In that case, Bob looks at the payoffs he could receive from cooperating or defecting. Cooperating would yield three but defecting would yield five. If Bob thinks that Ray will cooperate, Bob should defect. Suppose, however, that Bob *thinks* that Ray will choose to defect. Bob, once again, considers whether he is better off cooperating or defecting if he thinks that Ray will defect. A payoff of one is better than a payoff of zero, so Bob will defect if he thinks that Ray will defect.

Bob's best option is to defect, regardless of the choice made by Ray. Of course, the game is perfectly symmetric, so Ray will use the same reasoning as Bob. Each will defect on the other. Indeed, the only equilibrium outcome in the prisoners' dilemma game is defined by mutual defection. An equilibrium occurs whenever no one can change his or her strategy and secure a higher payoff.

Now suppose Bob and Ray know that they are likely to see each other again and again. A one-shot prisoners' dilemma game does not reflect the fact that Bob and Ray anticipate interacting in the future. If the probability of future interactions is very high then Bob and Ray have an incentive to cooperate with one another at each game in the repeated interaction. A long string of ones is not nearly as favorable as a long string of threes. Why would Bob resist the temptation to defect on Ray from time to time? If the interaction is likely to continue, Bob would be vulnerable to Ray's retaliation. Ray could start to defect on Bob. Although Bob or Ray might secure a payoff of five every now and then, they might also get stuck with zero. Alternating between zero and five is less rewarding than a string of steady threes. As long as the probability of future interactions is high, cooperating is the best option.

Suppose that Bob and Ray know that their interactions will end, but they are not quite sure when. Because interactions are less likely to continue, each will be enticed to defect on the other. Political examples abound. Suppose Bob and Ray are legislators who like to cooperate with one another on an important committee but Bob lost his reelection bid. Lobbyists are likely to treat Bob and Ray differently based on the fact that interactions will end with Bob and continue with Ray. Indeed, Bob and Ray are likely to treat each other differently. Ray will seek out other legislators with whom to work, and Bob will spend more time making contacts with prospective employers in the private sector. Bob and Ray might still exchange some small favors, but each will have his eye on an exit strategy and the incentive to defect will be strong.

Source: See Robert Axelrod, *The Evolution of Cooperation* (New York: Basic Books, 1984).

Legislators and lobbyists work assiduously to form long-term relationships so they can work together to achieve shared policy objectives. These long-term relationships reduce the legislator's **transaction costs**. An ongoing relationship reduces the legislator's uncertainty concerning the quality and truthfulness of the information provided by a lobbyist. The legislator and lobbyist may choose to participate in larger alliances of like-minded lobbyists and legislators as well as with agency personnel who share their policy preferences. The legislator's willingness to coordinate efforts with a wide range of individuals signals the legislator's strong commitment to the lobbyist's cause. Extensive, ongoing relationships assure the lobbyist that the legislator is not simply paying lip service to the cause. The lobbyist's willingness to organize a coalition of interest organizations to support the legislator signals her commitment to the legislator. These coalitions of legislators, lobbyists, and agency officials compose "lobbying enterprises" that provide a structure for coordinated policy action.[11]

The Resources Interest Organizations Provide Policymakers

Interest organizations and the lobbyists who represent them have important resources that policymakers need. Although most of the media attention focuses on campaign contributions, information and political connections are more likely to be a lobbyist's primary resources. To win elections, to increase their political power, and to achieve their policy goals, legislators need substantive information and timely political information on numerous issues. Legislators also need assistance in identifying and mobilizing potential allies on issues.

Elected public officials are generalists. They must make decisions concerning numerous policies that affect the nation and their constituents. The policymaking process regularly confronts extremely complex and highly technical issues, so legislators' need for expertise is easy to appreciate. Even straightforward language in bills can have implications of which few legislators are aware. As the passage of the Data Quality Act (DQA) made clear, legislators often do not read, much less understand thoroughly, the numerous provisions in bills. Although members and senators have staff to assist them, it is impossible for legislators and their staffs to obtain all the information they need to make good decisions.

In contrast to members of Congress, in-house lobbyists are specialists. They focus on one or two issue areas that are relevant to their employer. It is not surprising, therefore, that public officials turn to lobbyists for information.[12] All legislators report using lobbyists to obtain information, and more than 90 percent of lobbyists who work with Congress prepare research reports on policy issues for legislators.[13] In their survey of individuals who lobby Congress, Kay Lehman Schlozman and John Tierney found that 85 percent of lobbyists report that they drafted legislation for legislators.[14] The drafting and redrafting of bills is not a well-understood process. Very little legislation is written from scratch. Committee rooms are filled with "rough drafts" of earlier failed legislative efforts. Recall how the Energy Policy Act of 2003 went through several formulations as sections were attached or detached. Writing legislation is more like cutting and pasting than drafting an entirely new document. Legislators can always count on lobbyists for assistance in doing the difficult work of writing and rewriting a bill.

Another way that lobbyists assist legislators is by helping them plan their legislative strategy. Lobbyists participate in complex issue networks that include members of Congress and their staffs, the staff of the relevant congressional committees, agency personnel, other lobbyists specializing in the issue area, and scholars in universities and think tanks.[15] Lobbyists who support similar policy goals often work together to organize coalitions and to reach decisions concerning what the coalition's policy priorities will be. We saw in the case study of the "death tax" that lobbyists Patricia Soldano and Grover Norquist sponsored research reports that justified eliminating the estate tax. These two lobbyists also put together the coalition of organizations that lobbied for changing the tax. They helped Sen. Bob Dole, R-KS, and Rep. Jennifer Dunn, R-WA, write estate tax bills, and the two lobbyists developed legislative strategies for achieving the policy change. Finally, the lobbyists worked out compromises among the coalition members concerning what the coalition's priorities would be. Soldano and Norquist helped to coordinate the outside and the inside games. For policymaking to be successful, the inside game with legislators and agency officials and the outside game with voters and organized interests must be addressed simultaneously. Policy entrepreneurs like Soldano and Norquist are able to assist officials in winning both games.[16]

Interest groups provide campaign resources that include money, campaign volunteers, polling services, campaign consultants, and independent spending.[17] As political campaigns have become increasingly expensive, the role of interest groups in raising money also has increased. For example, lobbyists and organized interests sponsor fund-raising dinners for candidates and assist them in soliciting donations from other organized interests. The Supreme Court decision *Citizens United v. Federal Election Commission* greatly enhanced the ability of organized interests to influence electoral outcomes.[18] The decision allowed corporations and unions to spend unlimited amounts in advertisements for or against a candidate. *Citizens United* also led to the formation of so-called "super PACs," organizations that generate huge sums to assist candidates.

Legislators who want to achieve leadership positions not only must finance their own elections but they also must provide financial assistance to other candidates in their party. Public officials do this through their leadership political action committees (PACs). The greater a legislator's contributions to other campaigns, the more quickly that member or senator will rise to a leadership position.[19] Interest organizations can enhance a legislator's power in the legislature by ensuring that the legislator's leadership PAC has substantial funds to contribute to his party's candidates.

Resources provided by interest groups influence not only the legislators who receive the resources but also other officials involved in the policymaking process. Lobbying and campaign resources send important signals to policymakers in the courts and federal agencies. When a group provides friendly legislators substantial resources, it is signaling its willingness to become politically active to achieve its policy goals.[20] Spending also alerts regulatory agencies that the interest group will fight regulations that harm its interests and will go to court to achieve its goals. Signaling activity helps us understand why firms that are active in politics have fewer problems with regulatory agencies than similar firms that are not active politically.[21]

Exchanges With Unelected Policymakers

Researchers have not given much attention to exchanges between organized interests and policymakers in the bureaucracy. This oversight is unfortunate because lobbying the bureaucracy constitutes approximately half of all lobbying activity. In this book, we assume that unelected policymakers also desire career advancement, increased political power, and good policy. These goals are consistent with the basic analyses of bureaucracies by scholars such as Anthony Downs, William Niskanen, and James Q. Wilson.[22] Positing clear goals for bureaucrats allows us to develop hypotheses concerning the possible exchanges between these officials and interest groups.

One resource that lobbyists can provide is a job. The most widely discussed career assistance is a job at the lobbyist's interest organization. Often described as a "revolving door," government workers frequently move to better paying positions in the private sector. They then may move back into the public sector at a position with a higher salary and greater responsibility. Some individuals move through this process multiple times. A lobbyist also can recommend that a bureau or agency hire an individual currently working in a different bureau or agency or as a congressional staff member. The career assistance that lobbyists give unelected officials can be helpful to both the lobbyist and the official. For example, assume for a moment that you are a lobbyist for a firm that produces chemicals used in medicine. One of those is the perchlorate used for medical tracing. Through your lobbying on the perchlorate issue, you get to know an official in the Department of Energy (DOE). You and that official have very similar policy preferences concerning chemical regulation. As part of your lobbying activities, you interact frequently with officials in the U.S. Food and Drug Administration (FDA). A high-level position becomes available there. You may choose to use your connections with the FDA to encourage the agency to interview (if not hire) the individual from the DOE. If the person obtains the job, you now have a friend within the FDA.

Although lobbyists might assist agency personnel in finding higher paying jobs, the primary resource that lobbyists provide unelected officials is information. As the case studies of atrazine, perchlorate, and the implementation of the DQA made clear, information is critical to bureaucratic policymaking. Cornelius Kerwin wrote in his book *Rulemaking* that information provides key leverage with bureaucrats:

> Interest groups could find few modes of government decision making better suited to their particular strengths than [bureaucratic] rulemaking. . . . Rulemaking often requires a considerable amount of substantive, often technical, information. Agencies are rarely in possession of all the information or insights they require to write sound, defensible rules. Frequently, interest groups and the individuals or firms they represent have ready access to the information that agencies need. This gives such groups a considerable amount of leverage.[23]

Bureaucrats are not neutral about policy decisions.[24] Public officials and the agencies they work for want to win policy battles. If the official is a presidential appointee, she also has a strong interest in implementing the president's preferred policies. Although agencies such as the Forest Service, the EPA, and the Nuclear Regulatory Commission produce their own information, producer interests have the best information concerning the safety of their products, the cost of reducing pollution, and the long-term needs of their industries. Providing a policymaker with information or analyses increases substantially the likelihood that she will win the policy battles she fights. Bureaucrats who win policy battles that increase the reputation of their agency advance more rapidly than bureaucrats who lose policy battles and harm their agency's reputation.

To summarize the arguments so far, exchange theorists predict that elected policymakers make trade-offs between their competing goals of reelection, increased power, and good policy. When all is said and done, a policymaker will weigh the benefits and costs of supporting a group's policy preferences. The policymaker will set a price for supporting a group based on the congruence between the group's policy preference and the preferences of the official, the official's constituency, and the official's political party. Interest groups will determine the price they will pay based on the policymaker's productivity. Officials and lobbyists whose goals are congruent are likely to participate in long-term lobbying enterprises that help the public officials and the lobbyists achieve their goals.

IMPLICATIONS OF EXCHANGE MODELS FOR POLITICAL REPRESENTATION

Some political scientists object to the exchange model because it makes legislators and lobbyists appear selfish, crass, and Machiavellian. The model appears to leave little room for public officials to pursue the public good. Instead, the model appears to predict that policy decisions go to the highest bidder. Our previous analyses, however, indicate that the exchange model actually predicts effective linkage between policymakers and their constituents.[25] If an official fears electoral defeat then he is unlikely to support a policy that his constituents oppose. If the official were to support such a policy, his opponent in the next election would make voters aware of his action. The *potential* for opponents to make voters aware means that elected officials have a substantial incentive to support only those policies supported by their constituents. The fear of alienating one's constituents is particularly strong for highly salient issues.

Neopluralists argue that the American political system provides effective representation for unorganized as well as organized interests.[26] We agree so long as issues are salient and visible to the public. In this situation, the official's desire for reelection ensures effective representation. But many (if not most) policy decisions are not salient and visible. Organized groups and unorganized voters interact very differently with elected officials because of a key information asymmetry.[27] Unorganized voters know little about how their elected officials vote on issues and even less about their behavior in committees, whereas organized groups thrive on that very same information. Elected officials have substantial freedom of action on most issues because unorganized voters have less information to counter the actions and arguments of organized groups.[28]

The ability of constituents to monitor policymakers is especially restricted when an issue does not receive media coverage or when the policy decision occurs away from the public eye. The American Jobs Creation Act of 2004 provides an example of this problem. When three coalitions proposed different sets of tax cuts for corporations, all three sides had the resources to present their cases and to monitor policymakers' decisions. Up until this point, the neopluralist framework accurately described the policymaking process. Once the jobs act went to the House–Senate conference committee, however, committee members added subsidies and tax breaks for numerous special interests. Because these decisions occurred in conference committee, legislators had no opportunity to vote on individual additions to the bill. It certainly was not possible for citizens to know which legislators to credit (or to blame) for giving $140 billion to holders of tobacco quotas, tackle box manufacturers, racetrack owners, producers of nuclear energy, and other recipients of the act's largess.

Neopluralists argue that political parties and ideology restrain the likelihood that policymakers will take advantage of the unawareness of unorganized voters. Michael Hayes summarized this position: "any party capable of mobilizing a majority and capturing control of the government will inevitably possess enormous leverage over any individual interests, for it can always go elsewhere for support."[29] Hayes cited E. E. Schattschneider who argued, with only two parties and thousands of interests, the parties will not offer too much to any one interest. As "purchasers of political support, parties have a buyers' market."[30] Cohen and his colleagues presented a different view of how parties act toward their supporting interest organizations. They wrote that because unorganized voters have little information about most issues, political parties often encourage their public officials "to pull policy toward what their interest and activist groups want, even if that is not what most voters want."[31]

Although a legislator's political party is certainly a good predictor of his roll call votes, we are not sanguine about the likelihood that parties restrict the pork barrel, earmarks, and private goods attached like Christmas tree ornaments to many bills. Diana Evans made a strong case that party leadership uses pork barrel projects to buy legislators' votes on the most important issues facing the country.[32] We will show, however, that the provision of private goods by Congress and the bureaucracy extends well beyond earmarks attached to such collective goods issues as free trade and energy independence.

IMPLICATIONS OF EXCHANGE THEORY FOR LOBBYING STRATEGIES

The importance of issue visibility for holding representatives accountable also has implications for lobbying strategies. First, when requesting a public official's support on an unpopular issue, interest groups should request that the policy provide them benefits in ways that will not attract the attention of voters. Policy requests that are narrow in scope and technical in nature seldom attract much attention. Issues decided in committees or in conference seldom attract attention.[33] The vast majority of issues addressed in bureaucratic agencies virtually are guaranteed protection from prying eyes. Even the structure of a policy win can lessen its salience among erstwhile opponents. For example, corn growers will find it easier to obtain government subsidies if the government's payments are indirect rather than direct. A payment produced by a complicated formula for obtaining and repaying guaranteed loans from the

U.S. Department of Agriculture (USDA) is less likely to draw public attention than a policy that makes a direct payment to all corn growers.

Second, interests should form a broad-based coalition. Research by James Q. Wilson and Michael Hayes finds that coalitions should sponsor a single bureaucratic proposal or bill that contains numerous narrow requests rather than sponsoring many separate requests.[34] Corn growers are likely to obtain their desired policy if their representatives join legislators from soybean, wheat, sugar, and tobacco-growing districts and put all of their demands into a single agricultural appropriations bill. **Universalism,** the practice of insuring that everyone secures some rewards, embodies several strategic advantages.[35] The ability to secure a broad-based coalition depends partly on institutional structures. At various times since the Civil War, the U.S. House of Representatives has either combined or separated the education and labor committees. The 112th Congress (2011–2012) had a combined Committee on Education and the Workforce. When education and labor issues are addressed in separate committees, it is harder for advocates working in those areas to coordinate cross-issue coalitions. But when the education and labor committees are collapsed into one committee, it is easier to construct cross-issue coalitions.[36]

Third, producer interests should be most active at the committee and subcommittee stages of the policy process. To a large degree, legislators' actions in committee are invisible to the public. Officials are, therefore, more likely to trade policy support for resources when an unpopular decision occurs in committee than when the decision occurs on the floor of the House or the Senate. In their article "Buying Time: Moneyed Interests and the Mobilization of Bias in Congressional Committees," Richard Hall and Frank Wayman found that although the relationship between campaign contributions and legislators' recorded floor votes was weak, the relationship between a group's contributions and a legislator's support for the group in committee was quite strong.[37] Randall Kroszner and Thomas Stratmann demonstrated that interest groups provide greater resources to legislators on committees relevant to the group's interests. If a legislator leaves the relevant committee, past contributors dramatically reduce their support to that legislator.[38]

THE ROLE OF PRIVATE GOODS IN LOBBYING

The difficulty of testing exchange models empirically is that the long-term lobbyist–public official relationships rarely involve a specific exchange of a campaign contribution or other resource for supporting a particular policy. Even if such exchanges were common, however, policymakers are unlikely to admit that an interest group "purchased" their support. Lobbyists who have long-term relationships with legislators would be foolish to speak of specific exchanges of resources for policies. Diana Evans showed in *Greasing the Wheels* that specific private goods are difficult to track. They do not appear in the legislation passed. Instead, legislators hide these benefits in directives to the agencies that will administer the benefits.[39] For reasons discussed in the previous chapter, PAC contributions and roll call votes are not good measures of an organization's support for a policymaker or of a policymaker's support for an interest group. In addition, these variables tell us little about the behavior of agency personnel.

A second reason that exchanges are difficult to track is that the lobbying organizations often send broad signals to policymakers. Signaling theory tells us that interest organizations use lobbying to show their willingness to support or to challenge an agency's decisions. We saw in chapter 5 that almost 90 percent of firms lobby Congress in order to influence agency behavior. Obtaining a private good was the firm's objective in 63 percent of those lobbying efforts. If the legislators pressured the agencies in return for support from the interest group, it is almost impossible to identify this exchange. Similarly, when a regulator who attained her position because of a recommendation from an interest group grants a waiver to that group or makes a change in a proposed rule, that exchange is well outside the public eye.

We noted at the beginning of this chapter that firms with greater lobbying expenditures increase their profits, pay fewer taxes, experience less regulatory oversight, and achieve greater increases in stock prices. These relationships exist even after controlling for a firm's industrial sector. [40] This pattern indicates that the benefits firms receive from lobbying are largely private to the firm rather than collective to the industry. We accept the arguments of Theodore Lowi, Michael Hayes, and Robert Salisbury and John Heinz that the distributive policies that supply private benefits rarely are in the public interest. Rather, the policies are products of client politics where the organized groups win and unorganized citizens lose.[41] We believe that the extent to which organizations lobby for private goods provides a reasonable, if indirect, test of the exchange model. As the percentage of lobbying resources spent on private goods increases, the evidence of exchanges also increases.

A number of studies have investigated the importance of private goods to lobbying organizations. Kenneth Godwin, John Green, and Nancy Kucinski examined the effects of government regulation on lobbying by firms and their trade associations.[42] The authors found that greater regulation in an industry was correlated with increased lobbying expenditures. The increased lobbying expenditures occurred for lobbying the bureaucracy and the legislature. Godwin and his colleagues found that firms lobbied as frequently for private goods as for collective goods, and the pursuit of private goods was by far the dominant reason for lobbying regulatory agencies and the executive branch.

When Godwin et al. asked lobbyists what factors led them to provide resources to a legislator, the lobbyists stressed five factors: (1) the legislator sits on a committee important to the firm, (2) the legislator is from a state or district where the firm has facilities, (3) the legislator previously assisted the firm in its dealings with regulatory agencies, (4) the legislator holds a leadership position, and (5) the legislator previously had lobbied other legislators on behalf of the firm.[43] All of these factors fit the expectations of the exchange model.

In a study of 101 firms that lobbied the Federal Communication Commission, economists John de Figueiredo and Emerson Tiller found that private goods were an important objective of regulatory lobbying.[44] A firm was more likely to lobby when it would receive a private good and was less likely to lobby when benefits were collective. The results also showed that firms often were free riders when they shared interests with many other firms in the industry. Again, all of these findings fit the expectations of the exchange model.

An important paper by Wendy Hansen, Neil Mitchell, and Jeffrey Drope studied the relative importance of private and collective goods in corporate lobbying.[45] The authors found that the best predictors of a firm's political activity included the following factors: (1) the level of government regulation in the firm's industry, (2) the level of government regulation of the individual firm, (3) the importance of government contracts to the firm, (4) the number of lawsuits in which the firm was involved, and (5) the number of times the firm had been cited in the press as having a negative impact on public welfare. All but the last of these factors indicate the importance of private goods.

The case studies in this book provide additional evidence that interest groups request private goods and that policymakers provide them. When we examine the goals of individual firms involved in the case studies, we see an important pattern. Firms lobby not only for collective benefits, but they also lobby for benefits specific to their firm or organization. On the North American Free Trade Agreement (NAFTA), for example, the Ford Motor Company and the Chrysler Corporation lobbied for the collective benefit of freer trade, but they also lobbied for a very specific benefit. The two companies wanted the trade agreement to define "cars produced in North America" as having at least 70 percent of their parts manufactured in Mexico, Canada, or the United States. Cars assembled with more than 30 percent of their parts manufactured outside of North America would be subjected to substantial import duties.[46] This provision benefitted Ford and Chrysler while it harmed automakers manufacturing in Mexico and Canada. We observe the same pattern in our other case studies. The firms that lobbied on the jobs act, NAFTA, perchlorate, atrazine, and the energy bill often were requesting benefits that were specific to their firm or to a small number of firms. Even in the case of the estate tax, the vast majority of the tax benefits went to a small set of families.

A TEST OF THE EXCHANGE MODEL

To examine the relative value of private and collective benefits, the authors of this book interviewed lobbyists for sixty-two firms in the Fortune 1000. Using the lobbying disclosure reports, we identified the firms with representation in Washington, DC. We then drew two random samples of 100 firms. For one sample, we mailed a firm's chief lobbyist a short letter requesting a thirty- to forty-five-minute appointment to discuss her firm's lobbying activities. For the other sample, we contacted a contract lobbyist whom the firm had hired and sent her the same letter. We then telephoned the lobbyists to request a forty-five-minute appointment. Once we had thirty-three appointments from each sample, we stopped the contacting. We made eighty-five calls to obtain the sixty-six appointments. Of the sixty-six appointments, we completed sixty-two interviews. To help us assess the generalizability of our findings, we employed the same questions as John Heinz and his colleagues used in *The Hollow Core*.[47] Our study added questions concerning the extent to which a lobbyist's objective was private or collective, whether the respondent lobbied cooperatively on that issue, and the monetary value of the policy decision to the firm.

We asked each lobbyist to think of the issues that had been important to her firm or client over the previous year and asked her to list up to five issues on which her firm lobbied and five issues on which the firm chose not to lobby.[48] We then asked the respondent a series of questions about her lobbying strategy and the strategies of other lobbyists on those issues. Following Godwin, Green, and Kucinski, we asked the respondent to categorize the desired benefit into three categories: (1) issues that benefitted only her firm, (2) issues that benefitted her firm and one to three other firms, and (3) issues that benefitted many firms. In our analysis, we label these categories *private, intermediate,* and *collective* benefits.

We asked our respondents to describe the lobbying that took place on each issue. If the lobbyist's response to this open-ended question did not include information on certain aspects of the lobbying, we asked her several follow-up questions about the issue. Those questions included the following: (1) which branch of government she lobbied, (2) whether her firm lobbied alone or coordinated with other organizations, (3) the strength of the opposition to her firm's desired outcome, and (4) the extent to which the lobbyist achieved her objectives. For issues on which firms chose not to lobby, we asked the lobbyist why her firm chose not to lobby.

Our sixty-one respondents (one interview was incomplete, so it is not counted) described 386 issues. The firm's primary interest was a collective good in 185 cases, an intermediate good in 80 cases, and a private good in 97 cases. Although the lobbyists named more collective goods issues, the probability that a firm would lobby on an issue was highest for private goods. Firms lobbied on more than 90 percent of the private-good issues, but they lobbied on only 58 percent of the collective good issues.

We asked respondents to rank the importance of each issue to the firm on a scale of one to five where five indicated the highest level of importance. Looking only at the issues on which firms lobbied, the average score for a good that benefitted only one firm was 3.66, the average score for an issue that benefitted two or three firms was 3.87, and the average score for a good that benefitted many firms was 4.24. These results indicate that for a firm to spend lobbying resources on a collective good, its value to the firm must be significantly higher than the value of an intermediate good or a private good. One reason for this difference was the strength of the opposition. For each good that benefitted only one firm, respondents ranked the opposition to policy objective as "very strong" in only 26 percent of the cases. The corresponding figures for intermediate and collective benefits were 30 percent and 76 percent respectively.[49] Respondents indicated that they achieved most of their objectives 89 percent of the time when they lobbied for private goods. In contrast, respondents reported that they received most of their collective good objectives on only 51 percent of the issues.

Our study of Fortune 1000 lobbying found mixed results for the power of the status quo. If the firm's objective was a collective good, firms opposing change were more likely to succeed than were firms proposing change. This result was stronger for regulatory lobbying than for congressional lobbying. As we discussed in chapter 5, we found similar results when examining comments on proposed rules. When a commenter requested the agency not to change its proposed rule, the organization's success rate was 94 percent. When the commenter requested that the agency change its proposed rule, its success rate was only 31 percent. When our Fortune 1000 lobbyists were pursuing a private good or intermediate good from Congress, there was no statistically significant relationship between defending the status quo and lobbying success. For private goods, the key variable predicting policy success was the strength of the opposition. Stronger opposition reduced lobbying success.

In contrast to the expectations of neopluralists, our case studies and interviews with Fortune 1000 companies found substantial evidence of free riding and cheap riding. For instance, our interviews concerning the energy act discovered several environmental organizations that admitted cheap riding during the battle over the Arctic National Wildlife Refuge (ANWR). We observed a similar pattern in our interviews with Fortune 1000 corporations. Nineteen of the sixty-two lobbyists indicated that their firm had been a free rider on issues important to their firm, and 35 percent indicated that they had limited their participation in a cooperative lobbying effort to such cheap riding activities as phone calls to the staff of their home legislators. When many other interest organizations were active, firms were more likely to free ride.

SUMMARY

In this chapter, we examined the key features of the exchange model and reviewed evidence supporting it. We saw that although elected policymakers may have multiple goals, ultimately the benefits they gain from their exchanges must assist their reelection. This dependence on voters encourages effective representation of unorganized voters when issues are visible and salient to the electorate. When elected policymakers choose to support policies that reduce the probability that they will win reelection, they prefer to make their policy decisions in forums that are not visible to the public. Unelected policymakers also have multiple goals, but their success in reaching these goals generally requires information and assistance that organized interests provide. The studies of private goods by Evans, Godwin et al., de Figueiredo and Tiller, and Hansen et al. provide evidence for the exchange model. So, too, did our analysis of the lobbying activities of Fortune 1000 firms.

ENDNOTES

1. Frank R. Baumgartner et al., *Lobbying and Policy Change: Who Wins, Who Loses, and Why* (Chicago: University of Chicago Press, 2009); and John Heinz et al., *The Hollow Core: Private Interests in National Policy Making* (Cambridge, MA: Harvard University Press, 1993).

2. Brian Shaffer, Thomas J. Quasney, and Curtis M. Grimm, "Firm Level Performance: Implications of Nonmarket Actions," *Business & Society* 39, no. 2 (2000): 126–143; Brian Richter, Krislert Samphantharak, and Jeffrey Simmons, "Lobbying and Taxes," *American Journal of Political Science* 53, no. 4 (2009): 893–909; Stanford C. Gordon and Catherine Hafer, "Flexing Muscle: Corporate Political Expenditures as Signals to the Bureaucracy," *American Political Science Review* 99, no. 2 (2005): 245–261; and Hui Chen, David Parsley, and Ya-Wen Yang, "Corporate Lobbying and Financial Performance," Social Science Research Network Working Paper, 2010.

3. Richard Fenno, *Congressmen in Committees* (Boston: Little, Brown, 1973).

4. For a review of the economic literature on the two sets of models, see Joseph P. Kalt and Mark A. Zupan, "The Apparent Ideological Behavior of Legislators: Testing for Principal-Agent Slack in Political Institutions," *Journal of Law and Economics* 33, no. 1 (1990): 103–113.

5. Marty Cohen et al., *The Party Decides: Presidential Nominations Before and After Reform* (Chicago: University of Chicago Press, 2008).

6. Morris P. Fiorina, *Representatives, Roll Calls, and Constituencies* (Lexington, MA: Lexington Books, 1974); and David R. Mayhew, *Congress: The Electoral Connection* (New Haven, CT: Yale, 1974).

7. Richard Hall and Frank Wayman, "Buying Time: Moneyed Interests and the Mobilization of Bias in Congressional Committees," *American Political Science Review* 84 (1990): 797–820. Also see Kevin M. Esterling, "Buying Expertise: Campaign Contributions and Attention to Policy Analysis in Congressional Committees," *American Political Science Review* 101, no. 1 (2007): 93–109.

8. Cox and Magar found that the loss of majority party status could be linked to a $60,000 decrease in PAC contributions for the typical Democratic legislator. Gary W. Cox and Eric Magar, "How Much Is Majority Status in the U.S. Congress Worth?" *American Political Science Review* 93, no. 2 (1999): 299–309.

9. Hall and Wayman, "Buying Time"; Roger Congleton, "Committees and Rent-Seeking Effort," *Journal of Public Economics* 25 (1984): 197–209.

10. The ongoing nature of the relationship also encourages interest organizations to provide the policymaker with full and accurate information. If one is caught providing heavily biased information to a policymaker, that would reduce the likelihood of future access to the policymaker.

11. Scott Ainsworth, "The Role of Legislators in the Determination of Interest Group Influence," *Legislative Studies Quarterly* 22 (1997): 517–533.

12. A large number of scholars have explored the opportunities for lobbyists to dissemble. Credible information transmission is always a concern for legislators.

13. Hugh Heclo, "Issue Networks and the Executive Establishment," in *The New American Political System,* ed. Anthony King (Washington, DC: American Enterprise

Institute, 1978); and Kay Lehman Schlozman and John T. Tierney, *Organized Interests and American Democracy* (New York: Harper & Row, 1986), 290.

14. Schlozman and Tierney, *Organized Interests and American Democracy,* 274.

15. Ibid.; Ainsworth, "The Role of Legislators"; and Heinz et al., *The Hollow Core.*

16. Scott Ainsworth and Itai Sened, "The Role of Lobbyists: Entrepreneurs with Two Audiences." *American Journal of Political Science* 37 (1993): 834–866. A lobbyist entrepreneur must coordinate the efforts of individuals outside of the legislature and convince legislators that an issue is worthy of attention.

17. Independent spending is spending that helps a candidate win an election, but the spending is not coordinated with the candidate's campaign organization. For example, a group might purchase television time to explain why Candidate A should be elected or why Candidate B should not be elected. The Supreme Court decision *Citizens United v. Federal Election Commission,* 558 U.S. 08–205 (2010), 558 U.S. ——, 130 S.Ct. 876 (January 21, 2010) increased substantially the role that corporations and wealthy individuals play in campaigns. The Supreme Court's decision allows corporations to spend corporate funds to finance campaign advertisements so long as these messages were not coordinated with a candidate's campaign. Unions and wealthy individuals also can spend as much as they are willing to fund these messages. The *Citizens United* decision spawned the so-called "super PACs" that pool donations and spend them on behalf of their favored candidates. The court maintained that such expenditures do not give rise to corruption or the appearance of corruption. Some of the unintended consequences of the decision include the financing of presidential primary candidates by huge donations from a single individual. For example, gambling casino mogul Sheldon Adelson and his wife gave $10 million to support Newt Gingrich. This gift allowed Gingrich to continue his presidential bid in South Carolina and Florida despite his early defeats in Iowa and New Hampshire. Gingrich ended his campaign in the late spring of 2012, but those contributions allowed him to campaign for an extended period. James V. Grimaldi, "Billionaire Adelson Gives Millions to Gingrich Super PAC," *Washington Post,* January 7, A-1, www.washingtonpost.com/politics/billionaire-adelson-gives-millions-to-gingrich-super-pac/2012/01/07/gIQAXI6rhP_story.html

18. The text of the *Citizens United* decision can be found at www.scotusblog.com/wp-content/uploads/2010/01/citizens-opinion.pdf.

19. Eric Heberlig, Mark Hetherington, and Bruce Larson, "The Price of Leadership: Campaign Money and the Polarization of Congressional Parties," *Journal of Politics* 68 (2006): 992–1005; and Eric Heberlig, "Congressional Parties, Fundraising, and Committee Ambition," *Political Research Quarterly* 56 (2003): 151–161.

20. For examples of signaling models, see Ainsworth and Sened, "The Role of Lobbyists"; John M. de Figueiredo and Charles M. Cameron, "Endogenous Cost Lobbying: Theory and Evidence" (paper presented at the CELS 2009 4th Annual Conference on Empirical Legal Studies Paper, Los Angeles, August 3, 2009), http://ssrn.com/abstract=1443559; and Susanne Lohmann, "Information, Access, and Contributions: A Signaling Model of Lobbying," *Public Choice* 85 (1995): 267–284.

21. Gordon and Hafer, "Flexing Muscle."

22. Anthony Downs, *Inside Bureaucracy* (Boston: Little, Brown, 1967); and William Niskanen, *Bureaucracy and Representative Government* (Chicago: Aldine, 1967). The best known of these three works in political science is probably James Q. Wilson, *Bureaucracy: What Government Agencies Do and Why They Do It* (New York: Basic Books, 1989).

23. Cornelius M. Kerwin, ed., *Rulemaking: How Government Agencies Write Law and Make Policy,* 3rd ed. (Washington, DC: CQ Press, 2003), 35.

24. Andrew S. McFarland, *Neopluralism: The Evolution of Political Process Theory* (Lawrence: University of Kansas Press, 2004). For recent work that develops specific ideal points for agency heads, see Anthony M. Bertelli and Christian R. Grose, "Secretaries of Pork? A New Theory of Distributive Public Policy," *Journal of Politics* 71, no. 3 (2009): 926–945.

25. Formal models that make similar assumptions to those in this chapter include Arthur T. Denzau and Michael C. Munger's "Legislators and Interest Groups: How Unorganized Interests Get Represented," *American Political Science Review* 80 (1986): 89–106. For a model that relies on strong, responsible political parties for linkage, see Gene M. Grossman and Elhanan Helpman, *Special Interest Politics* (Cambridge, MA: MIT Press, 2002).

26. David Lowery, "Why Do Organized Interests Lobby? A Multi-Goal, Multi-Context Theory of Lobbying," *Polity* 39 (2007): 29–54.

27. One of the most eloquent analyses of organized and unorganized groups remains: Earl Latham, *The Group Basis of Politics: A Study in Basing-Point Legislation* (New York, Octagon Books, 1965).

28. Cohen et al. *The Party Decides;* and William T. Bianco. *Trust: Representatives and Constituents* (Ann Arbor: University of Michigan Press, 1994).

29. Michael Hayes, *Lobbyists and Legislators: A Theory of Political Markets* (New Brunswick, NJ: Rutgers University Press, 1981), 148.

30. E. E. Schattschneider, *Party Government: American Government in Action* (Westport, CT: Greenwood Press, 1977), 86, cited in Hayes, *Lobbying and Legislators,* 148.

31. Cohen et al., *The Party Decides,* 7.

32. Diana Evans, *Greasing the Wheels: Using Pork Barrel Projects to Build Majority Coalitions in Congress* (New York: Cambridge University Press, 2004).

33. William P. Browne, "Organized Interests and Their Issue Niches: A Search for Pluralism in a Policy Domain," *Journal of Politics* 52 (1990): 477–509.

34. Wilson, *Bureaucracy;* and Hayes, *Lobbyists and Legislators.*

35. Barry Weingast, "A Rational Choice Perspective on Congressional Norms," *American Journal of Political Science* 23, no. 2 (1979): 245–262.

36. Richard A. Smith, "Agenda Defection and Interest," in *Agenda Formation,* ed. William H. Riker (Ann Arbor: University of Michigan Press, 1993).

37. Hall and Wayman, "Buying Time."

38. Randall S. Kroszner and Thomas Stratmann, "Interest-Group Competition and the Organization of Congress: Theory and Evidence from Financial Services' Political Action Committees," *American Economic Review* 88 (1998): 1163–1187.

39. Evans, *Greasing the Wheels,* 43.

40. See Note 1.

41. Robert Salisbury and John Heinz, "A Theory of Policy Analysis and Some Preliminary Applications," in *Policy Analysis and Political Science,* ed. Ira Sharkansky (Chicago: Markham, 1970).

42. R. Kenneth Godwin, John Green, and Nancy Kucinski, "Home Cooking: The Things Interest Groups Want and How They Get Them" (paper presented at the annual meetings of the Southwest Social Science Association, New Orleans, 2006).

43. Ibid., Table 3.

44. John M. de Figueiredo and Emerson H. Tiller. "The Structure and Conduct of Corporate Lobbying: How Firms Lobby the Federal Communications Commission," *Journal of Economics and Management Strategy* 10, no. 1 (2001): 91–122.

45. Wendy L. Hansen, Neil J. Mitchell, and Jeffrey M. Drope, "The Logic of Private and Collective Action," *American Journal of Political Science* 49, no. 1 (2005): 150–167.

46. The 70-percent figure was not accidental. The General Motors Company (GM) wanted the percentage of parts manufactured in North America to be only 60 percent as many of its parts came from GM plants outside of North America. A 70 percent rule would give a competitive advantage to Ford and Chrysler over GM; the reverse would be true with the 60 percent rule.

47. The late Robert Salisbury helped us with the development of our interview questions. He provided information concerning the reliability and validity of the questions used in *The Hollow Core* and suggested where in the interview protocol we should add our questions concerning private and collective goods, cooperative lobbying, and lobbying strategies.

48. Contract lobbyists generally are unwilling to discuss their lobbying activity for a specific client. We therefore asked the contract lobbyist to choose one of their corporate clients and, without identifying the client, to discuss the issues that affected that firm. Three contract lobbyists with whom we had made appointments ultimately were unwilling to discuss specific issues.

49. R. Kenneth Godwin, Edward J. Lopez, and Barry J. Seldon, "Incorporating Policymaker Costs and Political Competition into Rent-Seeking Games," *Southern Economic Journal* 73, no. 1 (2006): 37–54.

chapter 9

Building a Model of Lobbying

N eopluralists David Lowery and Virginia Gray argue that adopting an economic perspective of interest-group influence and using deductive models of interest representation is inadvisable for three reasons. First, such models cannot readily handle the complexity of human motivations and the uncertainty of the policy process. Yet complexity and uncertainty are core traits of the policy process. Second, the models are static and inattentive to the multiple stages of the policy process. Third, the models are "typically only episodically and weakly constrained by data." The real world requires theories that correspond to the dynamic, complex, and uncertain world of policymaking.[1] Lowery and Gray acknowledge that the complexity of the neopluralist perspective means that their models are less parsimonious than might be desired, but they argue that scholars must make this trade-off in order to understand the complex relationships between interest organizations and policy outcomes.

This chapter presents a deductive model that addresses Lowery and Gray's criticisms. The model explains how lobbying organizations choose the issues on which they will lobby and how the different stages of the policy process require changes in lobbying objectives and strategies. The model is highly intuitive, and the chapter uses metaphors and thought experiments rather than mathematics to explain it. We present the math in a separate section at the end of the chapter and invite more mathematically inclined readers to examine our assumptions and proofs.

An advantage of exchange-based models is that their mathematical formulation encourages logical coherence. A complex perspective that is rich in detail may appear to allow a better description of the process of politics. But adding more and more detail risks the inclusion of entirely coincidental information and a greater likelihood that the hypotheses contained in the perspective are overlapping or contradictory.[2]

There are four key features of the proposed model. First, our model has multiple stages to capture the dynamic, multistage nature of the policy process. It captures how lobbying strategies are likely to differ in the various stages of the policy process. Second, the model includes the trade-offs organizations make between private and collective good goals. Third, the model includes the biases that policymakers have that favor their constituents, political party, and own policy preferences. Fourth, the model includes coalition formation and dissolution; it reflects the fact that today's coalition members can be tomorrow's competitors. We test the model using real-world data.

THE MOOSE HUNT[3]

Rather than start with a dry mathematical presentation, let us start with a thought experiment. Pretend for a moment that you are an anthropologist observing primitive hunters in search of game. You observe that hunters from different villages fight for control of hunting grounds. Only after a village wins control of an area can its members hunt for game. There are two types of hunters. One type consists of hunters from the same village who usually hunt together. These hunters pursue game in the areas under their control. If the hunters kill large game, usually a moose, they can provide meat for their entire village. The second type of hunter consists of individuals who are unattached to a village. You have discovered that young men must leave their village and support themselves. When they are sufficiently proficient hunters, another village may invite a young hunter to join their village.[4] By tradition, all villages allow these individual hunters to pursue small game in the villages' hunting grounds. The individual hunters may hunt alone for small game or temporarily join hunters from a village to pursue larger game.

As was the case in Rousseau's famous story of the stag hunt, members of a hunting party surround large prey and slowly close in upon it. (A full-grown moose often weighs over 1,000 pounds and stands six to seven feet tall!) To succeed in killing the animal, no hunter can leave his position in the circle and chase after a rabbit (or go off and pick berries). If hunters leave their position in the circle, the moose will escape. If the hunting party holds together, it is more likely to be successful. After killing the moose, the hunters will bring the meat back to their village and divide the other parts of the animal among themselves. Some hunters may want the antlers, others the hooves, and still others the hide.

Larger and better-armed hunting parties are more likely to gain control of the best hunting grounds and to succeed in a moose hunt. To achieve these goals, a village hunting party may recruit individual hunters. Which individual hunters will the village recruit? The village hunters would prefer to add individuals who are brave and effective hunters but who do not want parts of the moose that the village hunters desire. For example, the village hunters might recruit archers who need sinew to construct bowstrings or who want the organ meat that is taboo for the village hunters to eat.

An individual hunter will join the group that offers him the best combination of low personal risk and valuable parts of the moose. From the perspective of the individual hunter, the best time to join a hunting party is after it has gained control of the hunting ground. If he can do this, the individual hunter does not risk injury or death in battles between villages to control a hunting ground. Although the individual hunter is not a member of the village, he may wish to cooperate with the village hunters again, and he may want to join the village. The village hunters may be evaluating the individual hunter to determine if they should invite him to join their village. The possibility of future cooperation between the village and the individual hunter reduces the probability that the individual will abandon his position in the circle. It also reduces the likelihood that the village hunters will renege on their promise to share the moose.

The moose hunt story illustrates the multistage nature of lobbying. In the first stage, villages compete for control of the best hunting grounds. To ensure their success, villages recruit individual hunters because larger, better-armed groups are more likely to obtain the best hunting grounds. In our metaphor, the control of the hunting ground and the meat for the village are collective goods. The parts of the moose that the hunters divide among themselves are private goods. As the hunting party gets larger, the benefits available to each hunter will decline. If the individual hunters demand a portion of the meat that would otherwise go to feed the village, the size of the collective good declines as a village recruits more hunters.[5] The division of the parts of the moose among the hunters is the second stage of the hunting metaphor. The applicability of the metaphor to most of our case studies is straightforward. The first stage comprises the development of a coalition working to move the policymaking process forward. Fast-forward from the moose hunt to today's policy disputes. The producers and users of perchlorate formed a coalition to defeat the Environmental Protection Agency's (EPA) efforts to set a reference dose (RfD) of one part per billion (ppb). The coalition succeeded in this effort, and all of the coalition members enjoyed the benefit of a higher RfD. But lobbying by the coalition members did not stop. After defeating the one ppb RfD proposal, the various corporations then competed among themselves to have the EPA set the RfD at the level that would most benefit their firm. No coalition member desired the EPA's initial proposal of 1 ppb, but several coalition members desired a level well below the status quo RfD of 24.5 ppb. Recall that Massachusetts had a five ppb restriction and California a six ppb. Manufacturers and users in California and Massachusetts did not want their competitors in other states to benefit from weaker standards.

The American Jobs Creation Act of 2004 also fits the metaphor. In the first stage of the policy process, three coalitions competed to determine which industries would receive the greatest benefits from the corporate tax cut. Each coalition recruited allies to assist its winning the first stage. The coalition that ultimately won at the first stage recruited individual firms such as Plano Molding Company to obtain the support of specific powerful legislators. The North American Free Trade Agreement (NAFTA) also fits the moose hunt metaphor. When the president of Mexico wanted to place NAFTA on the agenda, he went to the Business Roundtable, an organization made up of the chief executive officers of the largest corporations in America. The Business Roundtable and the White House tried to build the largest possible coalition to lobby for the agreement. The opposition also consisted of a large coalition made up of organized labor, numerous environmental groups, civil rights organizations, and large portions of the Democratic Party leadership in Congress. Once again, passing the treaty (securing the hunting grounds) required building a sufficiently large coalition to overcome the opposition. Building this coalition, however, reduced substantially the free trade benefits the agreement would provide. Each corporation or trade association that joined the coalition wanted free trade for every product but its own. All of the special provisions to sugar growers, corn growers, vegetable growers, the auto industry, and to numerous individual companies reduced the overall economic efficiency of the agreement.

Building Coalitions

A coalition forms because its members believe that by coordinating their efforts they are likely to achieve greater success than they would by lobbying separately. But today's coalition partners readily become tomorrow's lobbying opponents. Policymaking is a process with multiple stages. Even such highly collective goods as national defense and clean water lead to firm-level competition over contracts and cleanup costs. As with the hunting metaphor, policy decisions involved multiple stages in which an organization's success at stage one affects the private goods opportunities at stage two. How do coalitions form and decide which potential members to recruit?

For insight, we return to the metaphor of the moose hunt. How do the hunters put together a coalition that succeeds in killing the moose but does not result in the members of the hunting party killing each other as they fight over the carcass? One way is to have a long-term coalition. Village hunters illustrate this. They have kinship ties and other positive interactions with other hunters from their village, and they expect to continue to hunt together in the future. We see this in lobbying with the development of lobbying enterprises. Interest organizations form long-term relationships in which the members can reach broad agreements as to the goals of the coalition and rules for the division of private goods.

To have a sufficient number of hunters, however, a village sometimes must recruit individual hunters. We have suggested how this occurs. The hunting party will recruit persons that can make important contributions to the success of the hunt and whose price for participation costs the group less than the benefit they bring to the hunting party. The same calculus occurs for interest organizations that are recruiting coalition members. For example, the winning coalition in the jobs act recruited Plano Corporation because the participation of Plano ensured the support of House Speaker Dennis Hastert, R-IL. Another strategy is to recruit hunters who want parts of the moose that the villagers do not want. If some hunters favor the hide, others the hooves, others the antlers, and still others the organ meat, then the hunting party can grow larger because everyone recognizes that there will be less direct competition after the kill. The members of the coalition who are not part of the lobbying enterprise are free to take their parts of the moose and go their own way. To use Kevin Hula's coalition terminology, these individual hunters are coalition *players* who seek only private goods that do not conflict with the goods that core members desire.

We discussed in chapter 6 that groups often form multi-issue coalitions that pursue broad, collective goods. They do this because larger coalitions are more likely to gain a place on the agenda than smaller coalitions. Larger coalitions also are more likely to achieve success during policy formulation. At some point, however, members of the winning coalition are likely to compete for private goods. The work of Barry Weingast and Kenneth Shepsle and research by Douglas Arnold illustrate situations explained by our two-stage model. These works show that the production of public goods creates competition among firms seeking government contracts.[6] For example, defense contractors may form a coalition to lobby for a large increase of the defense budget. The coalition members lobby for the increase because they hope to obtain some of the Department of Defense (DoD) contracts the budget increase makes possible. National defense, of course, is a collective good. The contracts, however, are private goods. What would a model of this multistage process look like?

BUILDING A MODEL OF LOBBYING

To introduce models of the lobbying process, we begin with perhaps the simplest model, that of economist Gordon Tullock. Tullock and his Nobel prize–winning colleague James Buchanan were instrumental in the development of public choice, an approach to studying politics that uses microeconomic tools and game theory to model political institutions and policy decisions. These models consistently show that when the political system provides protective tariffs, tax breaks, or subsidies to economic groups, this decreases a nation's economic efficiency. Prices are artificially propped up and valuable resources and talents are poorly utilized. The resilience of tariffs even in the face of economic inefficiencies led Tullock to pose this question: "Although lobbying creates economic waste and inefficiency for society, is lobbying profitable for interest organizations?"

To answer this question, Tullock conceptualized lobbying as a raffle in which firms buy tickets to win a prize. The tickets are lobbying expenditures, and the winning firm receives the private good of a government contract. Only one firm can win the prize. Each firm buys the number of raffle tickets that maximizes its expected profits, and the probability that a firm will win equals the number of tickets it buys divided by the total number of tickets purchased by all firms. For example, if only Firm A and Firm B buy raffle tickets, and each buys fifty, then the probability that Firm A will win is 50 divided by 100, or .5. If, however, Firm A were to buy 100 raffle tickets and Firm B bought only 50, then Firm A would have a .67 chance of winning (100/150) and Firm B would have only .33 chance of winning (50/150). Note that buying more tickets increases a Firm A's probability of winning the contract, but there remains some chance that Firm B will win.

If only two firms buy raffle tickets, then we can use a little shorthand to represent this lottery. For ease of exposition, let the subscripts 1 and 2 represent the first and second firm. Furthermore, we can use b_A and b_B to represent the number of raffle tickets purchased by the first and second firms. More raffle tickets reflect higher bids or greater lobbying effort. Firm A's probability of winning the government contract is equal to this:

$$Pr_A = b_A/ (b_A + b_B).$$

Of course, Firm B's probability of winning is equal to this:

$$Pr_B = b_B/ (b_A + b_B).$$

Tullock demonstrated that once any firm buys a raffle ticket (lobbies to obtain the contract), all other firms that desire the contract also will buy tickets. A lobbying arms race ensues, and the total amount the firms spend lobbying (or buying raffle tickets) exceeds the value of the private good they are seeking. If this portrayal of lobbying is accurate, then lobbying reduces the profits of firms that lobby. Public choice scholars refer to this result as "Tullock's paradox." This paradox has piqued the curiosity of many social scientists. Literally thousands of papers have explored Tullock's paradox, political rent seeking, and other models of lobbying that lead to suboptimal outcomes for society and for the organizations that lobby.

One of the advantages of Tullock's simple model is that it is easy (and fun) to consider altering it in various ways. Rather than thinking of Tullock's model as *right* or *wrong*, think of it as a tool that can help us better understand lobbying. As with any tool (such as wrenches, cars, or computers), we can change it in the hope of improving it. The challenge is to alter the model so that it reflects better the realities of the lobbying and policymaking processes without making it so complex that it loses its usefulness.

Tullock's model of lobbying deviates from real-world lobbying situations in four important ways. First, the model excludes political institutions and policymakers' costs. Stated differently, Tullock excluded such factors as the partiality that elected officials show for policies preferred by their constituents or that bureaucrats display toward programs that might further their careers. Second, because there are no institutions, the model is static. Firms simply decide the number of raffle tickets they will purchase. There is no ongoing policy process. Third, the model assumes that all policy decisions have one, and only one, winner. Stated differently, each policy proposal contains only one benefit. There are no side payments to Florida fruit and vegetable growers to gain support for NAFTA. There is no logrolling or adding riders to appropriations bills. Fourth, the model does not reflect the possibility that organizations can lobby for collective goods.[7] The only lobbying objective is a private good. Even with these shortcomings, Tullock's model remains appealing because it is intuitive and easy to understand. Therefore, rather than trying to build a model from scratch, we modify the Tullock model. Our goal is not to create *the* model of lobbying. Instead, we demonstrate that a relatively simple model can reflect the key aspects of lobbying and the policymaking process.

The Role of Political Institutions and Policymakers' Costs

When a policymaker chooses to use his resources to support Group A on issue X, he cannot spend those same resources to support Group B on issue Y. The policymaker's resources are finite; therefore, he must decide whether supporting Group A will improve his chance of reelection more than supporting Group B. The cost of supporting Group A is the benefit foregone by not supporting Group B. Why are these costs important? If policymakers incurred no costs when supporting a policy proposal, then all proposals would secure a spot on the political agenda. We know, however, that there is intense competition for space on the agenda. This competition is costly, and an interest organization is more likely to fail than to succeed.[8] Tullock's model assumes that the issue already is on the political agenda. If organized interests seeking private goods must compete to get their issue on the agenda before they can compete for a set of private goods then the lobbying model must have at least two stages. During the first stage, several groups might join their issues and form a coalition to increase the chances of their issues reaching the agenda. For instance, several large defense contractors may form a coalition to encourage a higher defense budget. The struggle among the contractors for the contracts the larger budget allows can wait until the coalition achieves the collective goods of getting the issue on the agenda and obtaining a budget increase.

One way to represent the competition to get onto the issue agenda is to use a fixed parameter between zero and one to represent the probability that an interest organization will get its issue on the agenda. That is, we can multiply the numerator of the Tullock basic model by a term that reflects the probability that a policy proposal will reach the agenda. The value of this term can range from near zero for a proposal that has no real hope of getting on the agenda to close to one for a proposal that is almost guaranteed to be addressed. For example, a proposal to eliminate all private property would have a value near zero. A proposal to respond to an armed attack on the United States would have a value near one. A proposal that a majority of legislators' constituents favor has a higher probability of getting on the agenda than a proposal that most legislators' constituents oppose. The counterintuitive implication of requiring interest groups lobby at two stages rather than one is that it lowers total lobbying expenditures by the groups.[9]

Suppose policymakers charge different groups different prices. Both the neopluralist and exchange approaches argue that policymakers charge their constituents a lower price than they charge interests located outside their district. Policymakers also charge a lower price if a group's policy goal is congruent with the goals of the legislator and his political party. Bureaucratic policymakers charge lower prices to interests whose goals are congruent with those of the agency. Using the language of the Tullock model, some groups can buy raffle tickets more cheaply than can other groups. If policymakers charge different prices to interest organizations, then this also lowers the lobbying expenditures of both firms.[10]

To see why this occurs, imagine that Donald Trump is building a new casino in Atlantic City. Suppose you own a plumbing firm, and you plan to bid on the contract to install the plumbing in the casino. You know, however, that a plumbing firm owned by Trump's niece also will bid on the contract. Her firm has worked for Trump previously, and he likes using it. Given Trump's preference to work with his niece, you understand that to win the contract your bid must be significantly lower than that of Trump's niece. The presence of Trump's niece reduces your potential profits from the job. Because the contract is worth less, you will spend less time and effort preparing your proposal. The bias by policymakers to favor their constituents or to prefer policy proposals by groups that share their ideology works in the same way. The more the political process favors some groups over others, the less organized interests will spend on lobbying.[11]

Allowing Multiple Winners and Allowing No Winners

Our case studies demonstrate that Congress and regulatory agencies provide multiple goods in a single statute or regulation. For example, NAFTA and the jobs act provided private benefits to numerous organizations. Ideally, a model of the policymaking process would include the possibility that no organization will win and the possibility than many organizations will win. To reflect these possibilities, we can use a fixed parameter between zero and one. If Firm A's winning has no impact on Firm B's chance of winning, then the competition term equals zero. If Firm A's win reduces but does not eliminate the likelihood that Firm B also will win, the competition term is greater than zero and less than one. Finally, if Firm A's win means that Firm B must lose (as in the case with Tullock's government contract), then the competition term equals one.[12] How does including a term that reflects the directness of the competition level affect lobbying? Our model shows that the more direct the competition among organizations, the less each organization will spend lobbying.

Although making these changes makes Tullock's model more realistic, they also increase the model's complexity. In the article, "Incorporating Policymaker Costs and Political Competition into Rent Seeking Games," Kenneth Godwin, Edward Lopez, and Barry Seldon investigated various scenarios in which the values of the lottery prize, policymakers' costs, and the level of competition vary. Their results show that for most values of a private-good benefit, increasing the policymakers' cost of supporting a group and increasing competition among groups reduce an organization's lobbying expenditures. The only exception to this occurs when the value of the prize is exceptionally large relative to lobbying costs. In that situation, greater competition can increase lobbying expenditures.[13]

Briefly summarizing, making the private-good model more dynamic by adding an agenda-setting stage to the lobbying process reduces total lobbying expenditures. Second, if policymakers favor some interests over others, this also reduces lobbying expenditures. Third, for most values of the desired private good, greater competition among interests generally reduces lobbying expenditures. When a benefit is extremely valuable relative to policymakers' costs, however, competition can increase lobbying expenditures.

Models of Lobbying for Collective Goods

We have thus far discussed lobbying for private goods. If organizations lobby only for collective goods, the model is similar to the private-good model. The collective–good model includes parameters for the probability the firms seeking the collective good will reach the political agenda, the lobbying resources spent by each organization lobbying for the collective good, the total resources spent by organizations lobbying opposing the collective good, and the policymakers' costs of supplying the collective good. The model also considers the degree of competition among firms lobbying for alternative collective goods.

As with private goods, increases in policymakers' costs, institutional and policymaker bias in favor of some groups over others, and political competition all lead to declines in an organization's lobbying expenditures. The major difference between the private-good model and a collective goods model is that organizations seeking the same collective good may share some lobbying costs. When this occurs, each firm will prefer to spend less and have its partners pay more. An organization's ideal position would be to have its lobbying partners pay all of the lobbying costs while it partially or fully free rides as a tagalong coalition member.

A Model That Includes Private and Collective Goods

Almost all previous rent-seeking models assumed that organizations lobbied only for private goods or only for collective goods. But a key question for this book concerns the trade-offs organizations make when they can lobby for both types of goods. When will an organization pursue a collective good, and when will it pursue a private good? The model developed by Godwin, Lopez, and Seldon predicts that when collective and private goods are equally valuable, organizations will pursue the private good. The exception to this occurs when an organization can partially or fully free ride on the efforts of other organizations. Two factors account for the preference for private goods. Scholars from E. E. Schattschneider to the present have stressed that interest groups pursuing narrow private goods can logroll their proposals into a single bill that satisfies them all. Logrolling coalitions focused on private goods engender little opposition. The politics surrounding the provision of these goods are likely to be routine and to have low visibility and partisanship. When a coalition includes multiple collective goods, however, competition from organized interests increases substantially.[14] Unless the value of the good is extremely valuable, increases in competition encourage an organization to lower its lobbying expenditures. The second factor that discourages interest organizations from seeking collective goods is the cost of reaching agreement among coalition members. Sandra Suarez, Thomas Holyoke, Marie Hojnacki, and others have shown that the costs of hammering out agreements among coalition members discourage coalition participation.[15]

A final factor encouraging lobbying for prefer private goods is that organizations find it easier to add a private good than a collective good to an issue already on the political agenda. Adding an amendment to an existing proposal is similar to an individual hunter joining a village hunting group after the village hunters have secured the hunting grounds. By adding a desired objective to an existing proposal, the lobbying organization spends fewer resources in the first stage of the lobbying process. Although it is possible to add a collective good as an amendment to a policy proposal already on the agenda (e.g., addition of the Data Quality Act [DQA] to an appropriations bill), the research reviewed in this book indicates that these amendments are more likely to add private goods.

NONTECHNICAL SUMMARY OF THE LOBBYING MODELS

Gordon Tullock's model suggests that lobbying is like a lottery, and those who buy the lottery tickets are interest organizations. Assume that the prize is a government contract to build a highway and that the contract will create a $100 profit to the winning firm. Firms can buy as many lottery tickets as they like. Assume that each ticket costs $10, and there are only two firms competing for the contract (buying lottery tickets). Firm A buys two tickets and Firm B buys four tickets. In this situation, Firm A has a .333 probability of holding the winning ticket (2/6); Firm B's probability is .667 (4/6). Given that the contract is worth $100, each firm is behaving rationally. However, if more firms enter the lottery and buy tickets, the probability that Firm A or Firm B will win the contract declines. For example, if Firm C enters the lottery and buys four tickets, Firm A's probability drops from .333 to .2 (2/10). Firm B's probability drops from .667 to .4 (4/10), which is equivalent to Firm C's situation. The paradox in Tullock's lottery model is that once one firm buys a lottery ticket, all of the other firms will also buy tickets. The total expenditures firms make for all of the tickets will exceed the value of the prize.

Tullock's model makes four important simplifications of the policy process. First, he assumes there are no politics involved in deciding whether to spend money on a highway or on some other government provided good such as education. Of course, there always are battles over government budgets. If we assume that this budget battle—the decision to spend money on the highway or spend money on a new school—is the first stage of the policy process, then adding the first stage changes the expected benefits of lobbying for the firms. For example, the first stage of a lobbying battle might pit a coalition of the firms that will bid on the highway contract against the firms that will bid on the school contract. For simplicity, assume that the probability that the highway coalition will win is .5. What does this do to the willingness of Firms A and B to buy tickets? It cuts the value of each ticket in half. If Firm A buys four tickets, now the expected value of those tickets is not $33.33 but $16.67 ($33.33 x .5). When we add this first stage to the political process, Firm A is no longer willing to spend $40. It will spend substantially less.

The second simplification in Tullock's lottery is that the policymakers charge the same price to all ticket buyers. We know, however, that this assumption is false. If, for example, the chair of the Committee on Transportation represents the district in which Firm A resides, Firm A will have to bid less for the chair's support than Firm B. Put differently, Firm A might pay only $5 for a lottery ticket while Firm B must pay $10. This bias by policymakers in favor of one interest organization over another reduces the amount each firm is willing to spend for tickets. Recall the discussion of Donald Trump, his niece, and the plumbing contract.

Tullock's third simplification is that firms always are in direct competition with one another. In other words, only one firm can win the prize, and one firm will win the prize. While this may be true of lotteries, it is not true of politics. For example, when the legislature is deciding how to allocate money to education and transportation, every dollar given to education does not necessarily reduce the transportation budget by one dollar. The government may choose to take the money from health care, law enforcement, or some other category and give it to highways. The government may also choose to borrow money and thereby increase the available funding for highways and education. Therefore, firms belonging to a coalition favoring highway expenditures are not always in direct competition with firms favoring education expenditures. The model previously described makes allowances for varying levels of competition between competing interests. The models demonstrate that the more direct the competition between two interest organizations, the less each of those organizations are willing to spend lobbying.

The final simplification of Tullock's model is that interest organizations lobby only for private goods. Interest organizations, however, lobby for goods all along the private–collective good continuum. Our model predicts that if the desired private good and the desired collective good are of equal value, the organization will choose to lobby for the private good. For instance, say that a firm is choosing to use its lobbying resources either in coordinated lobbying effort to reduce the perchlorate RfD or to lobby alone for a contract from the DoD to clean up a site contaminated by perchlorate. The lower RfD is a collective good; the contract is a private good. If the goods are equally valuable to the firm, our model predicts that it will lobby for the cleanup contract.

The two-stage model allows us to examine which interest organizations are likely to join a coalition. When an interest organization builds a coalition, it evaluates the trade-off between how much adding a particular interest group will improve the likelihood of winning the first stage of the lobbying process. The coalition members will also assess how much adding the new member will reduce the benefits to existing coalition members in the second stage. In the moose hunt metaphor, the hunters from a village will add individual hunters whose skills and bravery help the village obtain a hunting ground and kill a moose. The village hunters also prefer that the individual hunter not demand parts of the moose desired by members of the village. In our case study of the jobs act, the coalition of multinational and informational technology (IT) companies added Plano Molding Company to their coalition because adding the company guaranteed the support of the Speaker of the House. The cost of adding Plano had only a minor impact on the tax cut available to the multinational and IT companies, but it increased significantly the likelihood that the jobs bill would pass. The model that was previously described allows several testable hypotheses concerning an organization's lobbying behavior. We turn now to those hypotheses and their tests.

RESOURCE ALLOCATION BETWEEN PRIVATE AND COLLECTIVE GOODS

To test the implications of the model, we analyze the interviews with the lobbyists for Fortune 1000 firms. As discussed in chapter 7, the lobbyists were asked to identify which government actions and decisions over the past year were most important to their corporation. The interviewer indicated to the lobbyist that the issues could be from any branch of government. The respondent named which legislative issue and which agency issue were the most important to her firm. For those two issues, the respondent estimated the approximate dollar value of the issue to her firm. Unlike earlier studies of lobbying, the respondents listed the important issues on which they chose not to lobby as well as the issues on which they lobbied.

For every issue a lobbyist named as important to her firm, she estimated on a scale from one to five its relative importance. She also indicated the strength of the opposition to her firm's preferred policy. The respondent then indicated whether the outcome of the policy decision affected only her firm, her firm and two or three others, or many firms. These responses were categorized as private, intermediate, or collective. If her firm lobbied on an issue, the respondent indicated whether she lobbied alone or as part of a coalition. If she lobbied as part of a coalition, she indicated whether her firm was a major player or a minor player.

What Firms Want and the Value of Policy Decisions

Table 9.1 shows the expected value of the most important legislative and agency issues. If these estimates of the lobbyists are accurate, many policies are worth more than $50 million dollars to a single firm. Given these high values, it is not surprising that firms spend thousands of dollars pursuing publicly provided goods.

TABLE 9.1   Estimated Expected Value of Most Important Government Actions

Value of the Decision	Legislative Actions	Agency Actions
Less than $10 million	15%	37%
$10–$50 million	22%	25%
Over $50 million	63%	38%
N	55	53

When we asked respondents what portion of their lobbying resources they devoted to private, intermediate, and collective goods, the results supported our theoretical model. Firms spend more of their lobbying resources on benefits near the private good end of the private–collective good continuum. Table 9.2 shows that corporate lobbyists report spending almost two-thirds of their resources pursuing goods that benefit four or fewer interest organizations (goods near the private end of the continuum). Table 9.2 also indicates that the probability of pursuing goods that benefit more than four firms (goods nearer the collective end of the continuum) is significantly higher for lobbying Congress than for lobbying agencies.

TABLE 9.2   The Allocation of Lobbying Resources to Benefits

Activity	Benefits Accrue to Four or Fewer Firms	Benefits Accrue to More Than Four Firms or Interests
All lobbying	64%	36%
Lobbying Congress	60%	40%
Lobbying agencies	69%	31%

The roughly 60–40 division of resources between private and collective goods seen in Table 9.2 is consistent throughout our analyses. Respondents identified 362 issues as important to their firms. Of these, a majority concerned collective goods. When the analysis includes only issues on which the firms lobbied, 58 percent involved private or intermediate goods. When asked to identify their biggest lobbying win, 59 percent of the lobbyists named a private or intermediate good issue. Seventy-eight percent of their most important losses, however, dealt with a collective good. This pattern supports the earlier findings of Mahoney and Baumgartner that firms are more likely to lose when they participate in lobbying coalitions than when they lobby alone.[16] As we discussed in chapter 6, the relationship between lobbying as a coalition member and losing is probably spurious. Organizations are more likely to join coalitions when the opposition to their preferred policy is strong, and stronger opponents are more likely to win than are weaker opponents. The reason that members of coalitions lose is not because they are lobbying in a coalition; they lose because their opponents are strong.

A Multivariate Analysis of Lobbying Decisions

The model of interest-group lobbying decisions generates four hypotheses.

1. **As the value of the desired good increases, the probability that a firm will lobby also increases.** For each issue that the lobbyist named as important to her firm, she ranked its importance on a scale of one to five, where five represents the greatest importance.

2. **As competition over a desired good increases, the probability that the firm will lobby decreases.** For each issue that the lobbyist named as important to her firm, she ranked the level of competition from one to five. A score of one indicates that there was no active opposition; a score of five indicates very strong opposition.

3. **The higher the policymakers' cost of supporting a group's issue, the lower the probability the firm will lobby.** Unfortunately, we have no direct measure of policymakers' costs. Our indirect measure is whether the firm is lobbying for a policy change or is lobbying to maintain the status quo. We assign the value of one to issues for which the firm desires a policy change. We assign the value zero to issues for which the firm wants to maintain the status quo. This assignment of costs is rough, but it reflects the relative ease of maintaining the status quo and the difficulty of obtaining a policy change.

4. **Firms are more likely to lobby for private and intermediate goods than for collective goods.** The benefit sought can be in one of three categories. A good is *private* if it benefits only the lobbyist's firm. A good is *intermediate* if it benefits not only to the lobbyist's firm but also to two or three other firms. All other benefits are *collective*. We use two dummy variables to distinguish among the three categories. A collective benefit is the omitted category so a positive sign on private and intermediate goods indicates greater lobbying for those categories.

To predict whether a firm chose to lobby, we used a logistic regression model. Logistic regressions predict the probability an event will occur. Table 9.1 shows that, when two goods are equally valuable to a firm, the firm is less likely to lobby Congress than to lobby the bureaucracy. Therefore, we con-trolled for whether the firm was lobbying Congress or the bureaucracy.

The results shown in Table 9.3 support all four hypotheses. Firms were more likely to lobby when (1) the value of the good was greater, (2) competi-tion decreased, (3) lobbying to maintain the status quo, and (4) the desired benefit was a private or an intermediate good. *Ceteris paribus*, firms were more likely to lobby the bureaucracy than Congress. Table 9.3 shows the results of the statistical analysis.

TABLE 9.3   A Multivariate Logistic Regression Analysis of the Decision to Lobby

Variable	Coefficient	Robust Standard Error	$p > |z|$
Importance of the issue to the firm	1.611	.391	.000
Strength of the opposition	-.828	.222	.000
Lobby Congress	-.913	.373	.014
Lobby to maintain the status quo	-1.133	.391	.004
Private-good benefit	1.437	.597	.016
Intermediate good benefit	1.150	.447	.010
Constant	-1.677	1.015	.098

N = 362

Wald chi sq (6) = 110.31

Prob > chi sq < .0001

Pseudo R^2 = .37

CONCLUSION

The model we developed and the statistical analysis that tested it led to four major conclusions. First, the model and its tests show that lobbying is rational and strategic. Interest organizations free ride, avoid competition, and participate in coalitions when the expected benefits outweigh their costs. Previous research that omitted issues on which organizations did not lobby have seriously flawed research designs. This defect may have led the authors of *The Hollow Core* and *Lobbying and Policy Change* to ignore collective action problems and to conclude that institutions do not face a free rider problem. The design flaw almost certainly led some scholars to place too much emphasis on the uncertainty of lobbying outcomes and encouraged other scholars to suggest that lobbying is not a rational activity.[17]

The second implication of our model is that competition reduces lobbying expenditures. This implication departs from previous lobbying models, but the Fortune 1000 data confirm the hypothesis. The lower level of direct competition over private goods helps to explain why firms are more likely to lobby for private rather than for collective goods of similar value. The third implication of the model is that the biases of policymakers and such institutions as subcommittees reduce lobbying expenditures. It is largely the biases of policymakers toward their constituents, their party, their ideology, and their agency's mission that prevents Tullock's paradox from occurring. Institutional arrangements such as subcommittees and allowing riders to appropriations bills reinforce these biases while lowering policymakers' costs.[18]

The final implication of our model is firms prefer to lobby for less visible private and intermediate goods. Goods close to the private end of the private–collective good continuum are extremely important in understanding lobbying and the policy process. Firms, of course, comprise just part of the interest-group environment, but they are the most numerous and the most active organized interests.

A MORE FORMAL PRESENTATION

This section has a more rigorous mathematical exposition of a two-stage lobbying model. Again, we do not suggest that this is *the* model of lobbying. Instead, we want to illustrate how one might begin to formalize a model of lobbying. We start our discussion with the final stage of the struggle for benefits because strategic actors often choose an action based on what they envision following that action. Game theorists refer to this type of reasoning as **backward induction.** (To see how backward induction works, playing a game or two of tic-tac-toe with a young child will illustrate the process. Every move is evaluated with an understanding of how the game is apt to conclude if that particular move is made.)

Recall that the lobbying process occurs in stages. First stage competitors may be individual firms working alone or coalitions of firms. Let W_c, consisting of one or more firms from the set of interested firms N, represent the winning coalition from the first stage. In a basic rent-seeking model, the probability of the firm or group in W_c winning at the second stage is simply

$$\frac{b_i}{b_i + \sum\limits_{j \in W_c | i} b_j},$$ where b_i represents firm i's lobbying efforts and $\sum\limits_{j \in W_c | i} b_j$

represents the sum of the lobbying efforts of all other firms in W_c except i.[19] Although the second stage rewards are private goods, the extent of competition among the members of W_c may vary considerably.

For any two firms, i and j, in the winning coalition, let $\alpha_{ij} \in (0,1)$ represent the degree of competition in the second stage between i and j. The values

α_{ij} are always greater than zero and less than or equal to 1, and larger values of α_{ij} indicate greater competition between the firms i and j. We envision this competition to be entirely symmetric, so $\alpha_{ij} = \alpha_{ji}$ meaning that firm i competes with j to the same extent that j competes with i. If there were only two members of W_c, the probability of i's success, ρ_i, would be $\dfrac{b_i}{b_i + \alpha_{ij} b_j}$. More generally, for any size of Wc, we have

$$\rho_i = \frac{b_i}{b_i + \sum\limits_{j \in W_c \mid i} \alpha_{ij} b_j} . \tag{1}$$

Aside from the α terms and the i and j subscripts, the rent seeking in the second stage is similar to the model in the main text.[20] Rather than focusing on only two firms, A and B, we shift to the more traditional i and j index and allow multiple firms to lobby. We also allow for varying levels of competition (as represented by α) among the lobbying firms.

Given $\rho_i = \dfrac{b_i}{b_i + \sum\limits_{j \in W_c \mid i} \alpha_{ij} b_j}$ and the value U_i of the rent, for any $i \in W_c$, we can

determine a firm's expected utility from the second stage interaction. Of course, the efforts in b_i imply a cost as well. We use

$$V_i = \rho_i \times U_i - c_{bi} \tag{2}$$

to represent the expected value of the second stage for firm i, where c_{bi} represents the costs incurred from b_i.[21] Of course, the expected value of the second stage affects the willingness of an individual firm to commit resources to the first stage. As more firms compete in the second stage, V_i decreases for all $i \in W_c$. When there are fewer firms and groups in the winning coalition, coalition members secure greater second stage rewards.

Now that we have a sense of what might happen at the second stage, consider the first stage. The first stage of the policymaking process is all about getting on to the issue agenda. Generally, the larger a coalition is the better its chances are of securing a spot on the issue agenda. However, as the winning coalition from the first stage gets larger and larger, there are fewer perquisites to distribute among winning coalition members in the second stage. Lobbying entities balance their interests in securing a spot on the issue agenda, which requires collective effort, with their desires to preserve as many spoils from the lobbying as possible for themselves.

The government's attention to an issue is a collective good, so the lobbying is fundamentally different in the first stage as opposed to the second. Consider a set of N firms and groups. Any firm or group may make a bid $\beta_i \geq 0$ for the attention of the government. In the simplest rent seeking models, bids by additional lobby groups reduce the chances of any other particular lobby group being successful. That is, if $\dfrac{\beta_i}{\beta_i + \sum\limits_{j \in N|i} \beta_j}$ determines the chances of i's success, then bids by firms $j \neq i$ depress those chances. Firms may, however, have an incentive to form a coalition so that their chances of success in the first stage are not in direct competition with one another. We use B_c to indicate a collection of bids from a coalition. That is, $B_c = \sum\limits_{j \in C} \beta_j$. The chance of coalition C succeeding in the first stage is $\dfrac{B_c}{B_c + \sum\limits_{j \in N|C} \beta_j}$. In other words, coalition C's success at the first stage is still affected by all of the other firms bids as represented by the second term in the denominator.

If there are n firms, then there are $2^n - 1$ possible coalitions. What determines the composition of a coalition? At this point, we highlight two **individual rationality** (IR) requirements to help us assess the viability of any particular coalition. Coalitions do not miraculously appear, so—like other interest-group scholars such as Burdett Loomis and Kevin Hula—we start with a coalition broker or leader.[22] Now consider the entire set of α_{ij}s. Let A be the set of every α_{ij} for all of the different groups and firms. The expression min$A$ identifies the two firms that would be least competitive with one another in the second stage. Based on a coin flip, one of those two firms becomes the first-stage leader l. The first IR requirement is that the leader of the coalition is better off after he adds a partner i, and the coalition expands. The question for the coalition leader l is whether $\dfrac{\beta_l}{\beta_l + \sum\limits_{j \in N|l} \beta_j}$ is greater or less than

$\dfrac{\beta_l + \beta_i}{\beta_l + \beta_i + \sum\limits_{j \in N|l,i} \beta_j}$, where β_i is the bid of the potential coalition partner. If a firm simply focused on the first stage of lobbying, the larger coalition would always be favored over the smaller because

$$\frac{\beta_l + \beta_i}{\beta_l + \beta_i + \sum\limits_{j \in N|l,i} \beta_j} \geq \frac{\beta_l}{\beta_l + \sum\limits_{j \in N|l} \beta_j} \text{ for any } \beta_i > 0. \tag{3}$$

Given that we restrict all bids to be positive, the larger coalition always has a better chance of securing a spot on the government's issue agenda than the smaller coalition. Given the inequality in (3), the limits on the size of the coalition a leader might try to construct are not immediately apparent—unless one considers the second stage of policymaking.

Of course, the attention of the government is only part of any firm's concerns. The lead firm and all other firms are also concerned about the second stage because an increase in the coalition size in the first stage decreases their rewards in the second stage. Size helps the coalition secure the attention of government officials, but that size also makes the competition for second stage rents more intense. The coalition leader seeks to balance the increased chances of success in the first stage with the decreased expected payoffs in the second stage. Clearly, the coalition leader prefers attracting those firms to the coalition with the lowest second stage $\alpha_{li} b_i$ and the largest first stage β_j. In other words, the coalition leader wants to attract those interests that can contribute resources to first stage lobbying—high β_i —and that provide little direct competition during the second stage of lobbying—low $\alpha_{li} b_i$. Revisiting the moose hunt for just a moment, the best coalition member is a superb hunter whose only interest in the hunt is entirely mystical. That is, this coalition member covets no tangible part of the moose whatsoever. If the only reward is the ritual of the hunt, then in the second stage there is less competition over the division of the spoils.

Let $\upsilon_i = (B_c)$ represent the expected value for firm i of some coalition B_c that includes i.

$$\upsilon_i (B_c) = \left[\left(\frac{B_c}{B_c + \sum\limits_{j \in N|C} \beta_j} \right) \times \left(V_i | \frac{B_c}{B_c \sum\limits_{j \in N|C} \beta_j} \right) - c_i (B_c) \right] \qquad (4)$$

The first term within the square brackets is the likelihood of the coalition's success in the first stage. The second term within the square brackets is a bit more complicated. It is the value (V_i) of the second stage given that the winning coalition in the first stage, B_c, included i. The last term represents the cost of maintaining B_c for firm i. The argument, B_c, in the last term, indicates that these costs may be affected by the actual makeup or size of B_c. Of course, the product of the first two terms minus the costs yields the expected values of this coalition for firm i.

The leader can use an algorithm to find the best coalition partners.

$$\upsilon_i^* (\beta_l + \beta_i)$$

$$\begin{array}{l} ARGMAX \\ = \forall_i \in N | l \end{array} \left[\left(\frac{\beta_l + \beta_i}{\beta_l + \beta_i + \sum\limits_{j \in N|i,l} \beta_j} \right) \times \left(V_l | \frac{\beta_l + \beta_i}{\beta_l + \beta_i + \sum\limits_{j \in N|i,l} \beta_j} \right) - c_l (\beta_l + \beta_i) \right]$$

$$(5)$$

What is the single best firm for the leader to add to the coalition? The first and second terms are identical in function to the first and second terms in (4). Of course, the product of the first two terms minus the costs yields the expected value of this coalition for the leader. The ARGMAX notation indicates that the leader makes this same calculation for each of the firms in N, and then chooses the single best firm for maximizing the terms inside the square brackets.

Recall that a larger coalition increases the chances of winning at the first stage. Those chances are represented by the first term in the square brackets. Recall also that V_l, the second stage rewards, will decrease as a coalition increases in size because $V_l = \rho_l \times U_l - c_{bl}$ and $\rho_l = \dfrac{b_l}{b_l + \sum\limits_{j \in W_c \,|\, l} \alpha_{lj}\, b_j}$ so any increase in the coalition size increases the denominator in ρ_l. The calculations in (5) allow the coalition leader to sort all of the other firms by υ and then select the best possible partner. Finally, the leader must ascertain whether the value of the enhanced coalition, $\upsilon_l^*\,(\beta_l + \beta_i)$ is greater than the value of the smaller coalition $\upsilon_l\,(\beta_l)$.

Of course, if a firm is asked to consider joining forces by the lead firm, then that firm must also be made better off by the coalitional effort. The IR condition for the potential partner requires that $\upsilon_i\,(\beta_l + \beta_i) > \upsilon_i\,(\beta_i)$ where

$$
\upsilon_i(\beta_l + \beta_i) = \left[\left(\frac{\beta_l + \beta_i}{\beta_l + \beta_i + \sum\limits_{j \in N|i,l} \beta_j} \right) \times \left(V_i \left| \frac{\beta_l + \beta_i}{\beta_l + \beta_i + \sum\limits_{j \in N|i,l} \beta_j} \right. \right) - c_i\,(B_c) \right]
$$

$$(6)$$

If the IR conditions for the leader and the potential coalition partner are met, then the coalition forms. If the leader and firm i collaborate, then the algorithm can be repeated to seek additional firms.

Models are particularly helpful when they allow one to derive propositions that can be tested empirically. We now state two simple propositions, very briefly sketch their proofs, and discuss their implications. At this point, we assume that the game is symmetric, so that all bids and costs in all stages are equivalent.

Proposition 1: If a partnership forms within the first stage, it will be stable.

Proposition 1 indicates that cycles of the following sort cannot occur. Suppose there are three firms, and Firm A seeks to partner with Firm B, and Firm B seeks to partner with Firm C, and Firm C seeks to partner with Firm A. Such a cycle is not possible because of the symmetry of α_{ij} If Firm A sought B because $\alpha_{AB} = \Delta$, and Firm B sought C because $\alpha_{BC} = \Delta - \varepsilon$, and Firm C sought A because $\alpha_{CA} = \Delta - \varepsilon - \varepsilon$, then A's initial overtures to B would contradict the algorithm detailed in (5).

Partnerships are not automatically stable; consider divorce statistics in the United States. Why are these lobbying partnerships stable during the first stage? The organized interests all know the α_{ij}s, so the sorting process to find the most desirable partners is quite easy. Another way to consider the implications of Proposition 1 is to consider what happens when legislative content shifts, thereby jostling the α_{il} terms. If we see instability, we should explore whether there were shifts in the set of α_{il} terms.

Proposition 2: Suppose α_{il} is the same for lobbying firms and organized interests. The optimal coalition size is affected by $c_i(B_c)$ and if $c_i(B_c) > 0$, then no coalition forms.

Absent costs, Proposition 2 indicates that every coalition yields the same expected payoffs for its members. If α_{ij} is the same for all lobbying firms and organized interests, then the only reason to favor some coalition over a situation with no coalitions is if $c_i(BC)$ is negative, meaning that breaking up the coalition is more costly than maintaining it. Recall that some organized interests have long-standing partnerships with other interests. To maintain those partnerships might be costly in the short term, but they are still worth maintaining because of their long-term rewards. Think about all of those marriages in the United States that survive rough spells. Maintaining the relationship might be costly, but breaking off the relationship is even costlier.

Cross subsidization of lobbying efforts can make sense especially when legislators are sensitive to patterns in lobbying behaviors. For instance, excessively large bids from a single firm may appear untoward or be legally limited. To obtain the participation of smaller firms, larger firms and the trade associations may be willing to pay the lobbying expenses of smaller firms. As reported earlier, "Legislators love to say they represent the 'little guy.'" This orientation toward smaller firms was especially evident in our discussions with officials in regulatory agencies where the career bureaucrats often saw protecting the "little guy" as a part of their mission. Under such circumstances, a coalition leader may choose to subsidize another firm's coalition presence.

The model explained in this section is more advanced than the models introduced in the text, but the foundation of the models is identical. The mathematical rigor allowed us to derive propositions that suggested new ways to evaluate coalition formation and stability. If one is interested in how coalitions form, then the additional details and rigor might be reasonable. If coalition behavior is not a primary concern of the researcher, then it is best to consider other ways to tweak the basic model.

ENDNOTES

1. David Lowery and Virginia Gray, "A Neopluralist Perspective on Research on Organized Interests," *Political Research Quarterly* 57, no. 1 (2004): 164–175.
2. Consider your experience with reading philosophy or literature. How many times did the intuitions embedded in a philosopher's language or a novelist's prose require reading, rereading, listening to teacher's explanations, and using SparkNotes before you understood it? To be fair, complexity is judged through the eyes of the beholder. Just as some people prefer reading William Faulkner over Ernest Hemingway, social scientists have different preferences in regard to perspectives and models.

3. Our apologies to Rousseau. The French philosopher Jean-Jacques Rousseau (1712–1778) used a stag hunt to illustrate certain problems associated with collective efforts.

4. Those readers caught up in this extended metaphor may enjoy reading Sir George Frazer's controversial classic, *The Golden Bough*, first published in 1890.

5. The collective good in this instance has rivalrous consumption, so as some consume the good others have less to consume.

6. Kenneth Shepsle and Barry Weingast, "Political Preferences for the Pork Barrel," *American Journal of Political Science* 25 (1981): 96–111; Barry Weingast, "A Rational Choice Perspective on Congressional Norms," *American Journal of Political Science* 23, no. 2 (1999): 245–262; Barry R. Weingast, Kenneth A. Shepsle, and Christopher Johnsen, "The Political Economy of Benefits and Costs: A Neoclassical Approach to Distributive Politics," *Journal of Political Economy* 89 (1981): 642–664; and Douglas Arnold, *Congress and the Bureaucracy: A Theory of Influence* (New Haven, CT: Yale University Press, 1980).

7. Kenneth Godwin, Edward J. Lopez, and Barry J. Seldon, "Incorporating Policymaker Costs and Political Competition into Rent-Seeking Games," *Southern Economic Journal* 73, no. 1 (2006): 37–54; and Kenneth Godwin, Edward J. Lopez, and Barry J. Seldon, "Allocating Lobbying Resources between Collective and Private Rents," *Political Research Quarterly* 61, no. 2 (2008): 345–359.

8. Frank R. Baumgartner and Beth L. Leech, "Interest Niches and Policy Bandwagons: Patterns of Interest Group Involvement in National Politics," *Journal of Politics* 63, no. 4 (2001): 1191–1213.

9. For the full explication of this result and the associated proof, see Godwin et al. "Incorporating Policymaker Costs."

10. Interested readers can find the explication of the model in Godwin et al., "Incorporating Policymaker Costs," and Godwin et al., "Allocating Lobbying Resources."

11. For the full explanation of this conclusion, the associated proofs, and comparative statics, see Godwin et al. "Incorporating Policymaker Costs."

12. It is likely that the competition parameter is never zero in that issues must compete, however indirectly, for agenda space.

13. In the Godwin et al. model, competition can increase total lobbying expenditures, but the total amount that lobbying organizations spend never exceeds the value of the private good.

14. E. E. Schattschneider, *Politics, Pressures, and the Tariff: A Study of Free Enterprise in Pressure Politics as Shown in the 1929–1930 Revision of the Tariff* (New York: Prentice Hall, 1935); Theodore Lowi, *The End of Liberalism: Ideology, Policy and the Crisis of Public Authority* (New York: Norton, 1969); and William Browne, *Cultivating Congress: Constituents, Issues, and Interests in Agricultural Policymaking* (Lawrence: University of Kansas Press, 1995).

15. Sandra Suarez, *Does Business Learn? Tax Breaks, Uncertainty, and Political Strategies* (Ann Arbor: University of Michigan Press, 2000); and Thomas T. Holyoke, "Interest Group Competition and Coalition Formation," *American Journal of Political Science* 53, no. 2 (2009): 360–375.

16. Christine Mahoney and Frank Baumgartner, "Converging Perspectives on Interest Group Research in Europe and America," *West European Politics* 31 (2008): 1253–1273.

17. See for example, Rogan Kersh, "Corporate Lobbyists as Political Actors: A View from the Field," in *Interest Group Politics,* 6th ed., ed. Burdett Loomis and Allan Cigler (Washington, DC: CQ Press, 2002).

18. Shepsle and Weingast, "Political Preferences for the Pork Barrel"; and Weingast, "A Rational Choice Perspective on Congressional Norms."

19. One can think of this sort of model as a lottery, where b_i represents the number of tickets purchased by i. Of course, auction-based models of rent seeking have a different formulation. The most general functional form simply requires that one's efforts have a positive but diminishing marginal effect on success.

20. Different levels of competition have been incorporated in rent seeking models by other scholars, including Joan Esteban and Debraj Ray, "Conflict and Distribution," *Journal of Economic Theory* 87, no. 2 (1999): 379–415.

21. In the rent seeking literature, b_i is typically a straightforward monetary bid, so there is no distinction between b_i and c_{b_i}, the cost of b_i.

22. Burdett Loomis, "Some Expressions of 'Interest,'" *Political Research Quarterly* 39, no. 4 (1986): 736–741; and Kevin Hula, *Lobbying Together: Interest Group Coalitions in Legislative Politics* (Washington, DC: Georgetown University Press, 2000).

Conclusions and Implications

Including Alexis de Tocqueville's famous study *Democracy in America*, social scientists have commented on Americans' tendency to organize political and civic groups for over 150 years. Business interests, citizen groups, unions, and other organized interests have proliferated rapidly in the past fifty years, and their presence has profoundly affected our political, social, and economic lives. This book has attempted to improve our understanding of the effects organized interests on policymaking by focusing on four broad questions: (1) What do organized interests want? (2) What strategies do they use? (3) How successful are they? and (4) What do the answers to these questions mean for democracy in America? To answer those questions, the authors examined and tested the neopluralist and exchange perspectives. What have we learned?

Interest-group and policy scholars have used increasingly rigorous approaches over the past quarter century. Case studies of individual policies and individual interest groups are increasingly analytical in nature. Recent studies of lobbying state their hypotheses more clearly, and the research is logically structured and empirically grounded. Even with these advances, however, considerable room for improvement remains.[1] Frank Baumgartner and Beth Leech's analysis of fifty years of interest-group research suggested that future lobbying and interest-group studies should address three concerns. First, studies should focus more on policymakers' actions beyond roll call votes. Second, the issues studied should include political issues that are less visible and less partisan. Third, studies should move away from focusing on a single issue, as these studies have limited the ability to make comparisons across issues.

The 2009 publication *Lobbying and Policy Change: Who Wins? Who Loses? and Why?* by Frank Baumgartner and colleagues attempted to overcome the three problems identified by Baumgartner and Leech.[2] Using the neopluralist approach and investing tens of thousands of hours of research, *Lobbying and Policy Change* examined whether interest groups with greater resources win the majority of policy struggles.[3] The answer, in one word, was "no." The authors made a strong case that interest-group participation in the policy process is highly competitive and that most sides are represented. This central finding of Baumgartner and his coauthors is a powerful critique of the idea that interest groups have undue influence in American politics.

As we have discussed throughout this book, however, the advantages purchased by greater resources become apparent once we include private goods and regulatory politics in the analyses. Obtaining a private good or a change in a proposed regulation requires intimate knowledge of the policy process so that the lobbyist chooses the right moment and right policymaker to obtain the desired good. Obtaining the good also requires the technical and legal expertise to write a rider to a bill, to submit an effective comment during the rulemaking process, or to obtain a waiver from the appropriate agency. This access and expertise are expensive, and as we showed in chapter 5, producer interests are far more likely to have the resources necessary to intervene in these ways.

Baumgartner and Leech were not the only scholars to make recommendations for improving interest-group research. Preeminent neopluralist writers David Lowery and Virginia Gray have recommended that the way forward to better studies is to avoid exchange-based models. They argued that the rationality assumption applied to lobbying is unrealistic. There simply are too many variables in the policy process, and there is too much information that must be processed for lobbyists and policymakers to act *rationally*. In addition, policymaking is too contingent on unpredictable factors for the successful use of rational choice models.[4]

Our study challenges Lowery and Gray's recommendation by demonstrating the rationality of lobbyists' decision making. Of course, no one operates with complete information, but limited information does not preclude rational actions. Rational actions are based on the information one has available. Rationality does not imply omniscience. As we showed in chapter 9, it is possible to adapt a relatively simple model of lobbying to capture the most important contingent variables. These include the stage of the policy process, the costs and benefits to policymakers and interest groups, the biases of policymakers, the strength of the opposition, and whether the interest is pursuing a private or a collective good. Using that model, we were able to predict when an interest organization would expend lobbying resources. The model also predicted whether an interest organization would lobby Congress or the bureaucracy to achieve its goals.[5]

This book has included the neopluralist and exchange approaches. Without meaning to be wishy-washy, we believe that there are considerable advantages to each. The neopluralist perspective is less static and more appreciative of the contextual aspects of the lobbying process. The perspective encourages scholars to connect the research on lobbying to the policymaking process. As we saw in our case studies, policymaking—and the lobbying that accompanies it—involves much more than the legislators' floor votes that often constitute the empirical tests of exchange models. Policymaking starts long before the House and Senate floor votes. Organized interests and (often unanticipated) events persuade policymakers that a problem exists. Recognizing a fortuitous turn of events, policy entrepreneurs push policy options forward. Interests bargain among themselves to develop policy alternatives that can

overcome the inertial advantage of the status quo. Even with a legislative success, policymaking does not end. When Congress passes a new statute, policymaking moves to the bureaucracy. As we stressed in chapters 4 and 5,
policymaking within the bureaucracy is a complex process that provides
numerous opportunities for interest-group influence. The complexity of all of
the decisions that go into making *a policy* suggests that scholars should share
the neopluralists' appreciation of the convoluted nature of lobbying strategies
in the legislative and bureaucratic arenas.

Scholars using the exchange approach argue that the immense complexity
of the policymaking process shows the necessity of models that simplify the
policymaking process. Exchange-based models have two powerful advantages.
First, they build from the assumption of goal-oriented behavior. That is, lobbyists and policymakers engage in goal-oriented behavior and act rationally as
they try to secure their favored policy outcomes. Rational, goal-oriented
behavior is a powerful assumption. It allows one to develop models of strategic
behavior by interests whose goals conflict. Second, exchange models allow the
deduction of hypotheses that generally are straightforward in their predictions
and, therefore, allow empirical testing.

Some scholars prefer detail to generalizability. This encourages them to
reject exchange-based models. Models, however, are simplifications of the real
world, which means they purposefully ignore certain aspects of that world.
Adding detail can be very helpful for understanding a particular situation, but
the addition of more and more details specific to one situation means that it
has less applicability to other situations. As we have shown, however, even a
relatively simple model can include the most important of these variables. The
remaining sections of this chapter show why integrating pluralist concerns into
exchange models helps us answer the four questions with which we began this
book.

WHAT DO INTERESTS WANT, AND
WHAT STRATEGIES DO THEY USE?

Interest organizations seek collective and private goods. The policymaking
process is complex, but there are clear patterns in lobbying behavior. Lobbyists
recognize the interplay between high politics, routine politics, and lobbying
strategies. They also realize that they must adopt different lobbying strategies
for different stages of the policy process. Finally, lobbyists remain sensitive to
coalitional efforts and long-term cooperative relationships.

Interest Organizations Want Private As Well As Collective Goods

If we were to make a single criticism of interest-group scholarship, it would be
that research generally has omitted private goods. This omission holds across
a wide range of scholarship, including neopluralists and exchange theorists.
Almost all case studies of interest-group influence on policymaking focus
on what Andrew McFarland calls issues of high politics—issues on which

lobbying efforts involve broad and competitive coalitions, sweeping across the entire legislative branch and often involving the White House as well as the bureaucracy. One way to distinguish routine politics from high politics and highly visible issues from less visible ones is to consider whether the issues at hand focus on collective goods or private goods. Distinguishing high politics from routine politics can be problematic as tautologies sometimes emerge. Issues are highly visible when everyone knows about them, and everyone knows about them when issues are highly visible. Considering where policies lie on the collective to private spectrum helps us avoid such tautologies. When interest organizations seek collective goods, lobbying is more competitive, involves more coalitions, and attracts more attention from the media and the public. When interests focus more on private goods, there will be less competition among groups, less coalitional lobbying, and less public attention. Our research indicates that where an interest group's objective lies on the private–collective continuum strongly affects lobbying strategies and policy outcomes.

How important are private goods? The case studies in this book revealed numerous incidents of interests lobbying to add private goods to legislation and attempting to gain a competitive advantage by changing a proposed rule. Sometimes the organizations lobbied for private goods during the policy formulation stage when interest groups were bargaining among themselves. Sometimes groups lobbied to add private goods at the decision stage when additional votes were needed to pass a bill, and sometimes an interest lobbied agency personnel to add the private good during the implementation stage. NAFTA, the jobs act, and the energy act provide examples of adding private goods to legislation at the decision stage. The example with which we began this book, adding a $50 million price increase to a missile during committee markup, is one of thousands of cases that occur in every congressional session. One of the most important reasons that organized interests hire contract lobbyists is to gain access to a key decision maker whose support or acquiescence the group needs to achieve its desired private good.

From the perspective of corporations, private goods are enormously important. As we discussed in chapter 9, research concerning corporate lobbying found that the availability of private goods predicts firm lobbying behavior.[6] Our interviews with Fortune 1000 corporations indicate that 63 percent of all the issues on which firms lobbied provided benefits or imposed costs on four or fewer firms. Although some issues, such as the American Jobs Creation Act of 2004, the Energy Policy Act of 2003, and the North American Free Trade Agreement (NAFTA) attract hundreds (even thousands) of lobbyists, the bread-and-butter issues for corporate lobbyists concern relatively narrow benefits and costs. Lobbyists typically deal with these issues through direct contact with policymakers and their staffs. NAFTA and the jobs act demonstrate that even when hundreds of organizations are lobbying, many of the interest organizations involved in these efforts are lobbying for private goods.

Analyses of participants in regulatory issues indicate that producer interests lobby for goods along the private–collective continuum appropriate to the lobbying organization. Corporations focus a majority of their efforts on obtaining relatively narrow private goods. A chemical company might lobby for a regulatory waiver for one of its plants or for a longer phase out of a particular pesticide. Trade associations concentrate on benefits that include their entire membership or large sections of it. When an issue has major implications across an entire industry, corporations frequently join coalitions led by their trade associations.

As we move from the private to the collective end of the continuum, we find greater activity by lobbying organizations specializing in collective goods. The American Chemistry Council, a trade association for chemical companies, was extremely active when the Environmental Protection Agency (EPA) was developing its data quality guidelines for reviewing toxic substances. Peak associations such as the Business Roundtable, the U.S. Chamber of Commerce, and the AFL-CIO lobby for highly collective goods. NAFTA provides the obvious example. The Business Roundtable led the lobbying effort to obtain an extraordinarily broad trade agreement that would increase opportunities for most U.S. businesses. The Business Roundtable faced opposition from the AFL-CIO, the peak association for union workers in the United States. In the debate over the jobs act, the U.S. Chamber of Commerce lobbied for tax cuts for the entire service sector of the economy while the National Association of Manufacturers lobbied on behalf of all manufacturers.

Citizen groups often have obtaining such broad collective goods as cleaner air, lower taxes, or safer streets as their stated mission. These groups recruit donors and new members by demonstrating that the group is an effective lobbyist for such collective goods. Lowery and Gray have shown, however, that citizen groups seek particular niches to reduce their competition with other citizen action groups in the same general area. In other words, even organizations set up to lobby for collective goods find it useful to focus narrowly.[7] So, for example, the National Audubon Society focuses on saving bird habitats and preserving wetlands for migrating waterfowl. The National Wildlife Federation concentrates on saving mammals, and the Wilderness Society focuses on saving and expanding wilderness areas. In this way, they avoid competing with one another directly. When dealing with much broader issues such as clean air or clean water, these citizen action groups may choose to enter a long-term formal coalition such as the Coalition for Clean Air.[8]

Coalitions present difficulties when scholars are trying to determine what organized interests want. How can we determine the goals of individual coalition members? Not all members of a coalition share the same goals and not all members devote the same proportion of their resources to influence the policy outcome. To use Kevin Hula's language, some coalition members are core members, some are players, and some are tagalongs.[9] The priority of some members may be the collective good. For other members, the priority may be a private good. And, for still others, the goal may be to appear active on the issue. To know what each interest wants would require the researcher to interview each coalition member. On issues where there were hundreds of participants on each side, such an approach is beyond the resources of even the best-funded team of scholars.

Jim Tozzi probably cared nothing about the thousands of items in the appropriations bill to which Rep. Jo Ann Emerson, R-MO, attached the Data Quality Act (DQA). The holders of the tobacco quotas who received a $10 billion buyout in the jobs act probably did not care whether all corporations or only manufacturing corporations received tax breaks. In both of these cases, an interest was looking for a legislative vehicle to which it could attach its private good.

To reach their conclusion that the relative resources of competing sides does not predict which side will win, the authors of *Lobbying and Policy Change* added up all of the resources of all organizations that lobbied on each side of an issue. This summation meant that they treated each interest organization as a core member, pursuing the side's collective good objective and contributing all of its lobbying resources to the side's success. We know that this assumption is incorrect. The question, of course, is whether that simplification of reality led to incorrect conclusions. Did the failure to consider private goods lead Baumgartner and his colleagues to conclude incorrectly that resources do not predict lobbying success?

Campaign Contributions

One strategy that organized interests use to pursue their lobbying goals is to become active in elections. Electoral efforts appear especially promising for organized interests because if they can ensure that the *right people* are elected then there is less need for subsequent lobbying. Interest groups, especially those that ally closely with one party, can have substantial influence in picking the right people to run for office. Interest groups that prefer not to align themselves with one party can influence who wins general elections by providing support for their preferred candidate. After the release of Federal Election Commission data in the mid-1970s, there was a flood of studies on political action committees (PACs) and their contributions to legislators. Election scholars had great data. This facilitated careful, analytical studies of interest groups and elections. Some of the strongest work in PACs and campaign contributions links those contributions to lobbying access or considers campaign contributions as only one of the ways interest groups influence elections and policymaking. As valuable as that work is, organized interests spend much more money on lobbying. By some counts, lobbying expenditures are ten times greater than PAC contributions. Although studies of campaign contributions by organized interests outnumber lobbying studies, the *real money* that interest groups spend is on lobbying. As we discussed in chapter 8, it remains to be seen whether the *Citizens United v. Federal Election Commission* decision will increase significantly the impact of campaign contributions.[10]

The Decision to Lobby, Cheap Ride, or Free Ride

The first issue facing an interest is choosing the issues on which it will lobby and the issues it will ignore or act as a cheap rider. If an issue involves a purely private good such as a regulatory waiver or a tax loophole that would benefit only a single corporation, there is no opportunity to free ride. In this situation, our model predicts that an interest organization simply will compare the expected benefits from lobbying on that issue with the expected benefits of lobbying on other issues. If the desired benefit is collective, however, then numerous other considerations come into play. In deciding whether to lobby or to free ride, the lobbyists consider the size of the benefit their firm would receive if the lobbying effort is successful, the strength of the opposition, and the likelihood the lobbying effort will succeed. Our research demonstrates that a firm is less likely to free ride when the value of the collective good is extremely high, the proposed legislation or rule has a private good provision for the firm, when the firm has access to the key policymakers such as a committee chair, and when it regularly cooperates with other members of the cooperative lobbying effort.

One clear finding from our interviews is that organizations—whether they are firms, citizen action groups, or trade associations—engage in free riding and cheap riding. Almost every respondent in our interviews with Fortune 1000 lobbyists indicated that her firm sometimes engaged in free riding and cheap riding. The interviews conducted for the case studies also found significant levels of such behavior. For example, the American Association of Retired Persons (AARP) decided to cheap ride on drug reimportation until its coalition partners pressured it to take a more active role. Several citizen action groups that were asked to participate actively in pro-reimportation coalitions limited their participation to placing their name on a coalition letterhead. All organizations have limited lobbying resources, and their resources rarely allow them to lobby on every issue important to their organization.

POLICYMAKING IN THE BUREAUCRACY

Most studies of lobbying focus exclusively on congressional lobbying, but a narrow focus on Congress loses sight of the fact that policymaking neither begins nor ends in the legislature. Legislative success does not ensure policymaking success as bureaucratic agencies have considerable leeway in the manner in which they choose to implement law. Remember, "Congress handicrafts new law while the bureaucracy mass produces it."[11] Bureaucratic rulemaking is intertwined with the policymaking efforts of hundreds of legislators and numerous organized interests. Congressional oversight reduces agency discretion, and our interviews with Fortune 1000 firms found that lobbyists spend substantial resources lobbying legislators to pressure agencies. Ideally, future studies of lobbying will pay greater attention to how lobbying strategies relate to the stages of the policy process and the location of the decision maker.

How do lobbying strategies change when we move from legislation to rulemaking and implementation? The biggest change concerns the increasing importance of expertise and technical information and the decreasing relevance of votes and elections. These changes create an advantage for wealthier interests because they are best able to obtain the expertise and information that bureaucrats need and use. The interviews for this book, as well as previous work on bureaucratic policymaking, show that business interests are the predominant participants not only in making comments on rules but also as participants in advisory committees and public hearings.

Another aspect of bureaucratic policymaking that deserves attention is the frequent contact between lobbyists and agency personnel. For example, interviews with lobbyists for passenger airlines found that the lobbyists speak with Federal Aviation Administration civil servants at least once each week. Lobbyists in the rubber-resin industry reported talking with EPA officials at least twice each month. External lobbyists also maintain frequent contacts with officials in the agencies most relevant to their field of expertise. These contacts help firms and trade associations know what issues regulatory agencies are considering for future action. A lobbyist hired by a major pesticide firm indicated that her EPA contact had informed her that the agency was moving quickly into nanotechnology issues that would affect her client. In response, the lobbyist set up a meeting with the EPA officials in charge of the new initiative. One of the major contributions of *The Hollow Core* was its attention to the substantial resources lobbyists must devote to developing and maintaining contacts with policymakers.

WHAT FACTORS LEAD TO LOBBYING SUCCESS?

Three factors stand out when we consider who wins and who loses. First, those who oppose policy change win more frequently than those who support change. This relationship is much stronger for collective goods than for private goods. Second, winning support for a private good is easier than winning support for a collective good. Finally, interests that have long-established relationships with policymakers are more successful than those who do not have such relationships.

Defend the Status Quo

Studies across at least three disciplines have found that it is easier to mobilize people who fear losing a government-provided benefit than to mobilize people to obtain a new benefit. Therefore, mobilizing to protect the status quo is easier than mobilizing to achieve a policy change. In addition, to defeat a policy proposal an interest group may need to win at only one point in the policymaking process. For example, a presidential veto (or even the threat of a veto) can defeat a policy proposal. Similarly, a committee chair who refuses to hold hearings on a bill or who allows a killer amendment can derail a policy proposal. The same is true in the regulatory arena. Presidential appointees can decline to write a rule, or the Office of Management and Budget (OMB) can slow down the rulemaking process by forcing an agency to withdraw a proposed rule. To change the status quo, an interest has to win at *every* stage of the policymaking process—both in the legislature and in the agencies. The authors of *Lobbying and Policy Change* found that the single best predictor of a side's likelihood of winning was whether it was protecting the status quo or trying to change it.

Seek Private Goods Rather Than Collective Goods

Perhaps the clearest finding from our interviews with Fortune 1000 lobbyists is that they are more likely to succeed when their objective is a private good or a good that benefits only a small number of firms. At first, this seems counterintuitive as past scholarship on coalitions indicates that to get a new policy proposal on the political agenda often requires a broad coalition. The difficulty with generalizing from the past studies, however, is that the issues they studied involved benefits that were collective goods. This was true not only for the in-depth case studies but it was also true for the research carried out for *The Hollow Core* and *Lobbying and Policy Change*. Getting a new collective good issue on the agenda is difficult, but interest groups often can attach their desired private good to a policy proposal already on agenda. The case studies included in this book, interviews with lobbyists, and our model of the lobbying process all indicate that it is easier to attach a private good than a collective good to an existing proposal. These results reinforce considerable research covering a wide swath of scholarship. Scholars as diverse as Theodore Lowi, John Kingdon, James Q. Wilson, Barry Weingast, and Kenneth Shepsle note that logrolling numerous narrow benefits together makes obtaining these policies much easier. The ability to add a private-good rider to an appropriations bill is a common practice in the U.S. Congress. Adding broad collective goods to such bills is not.[12]

Participate in Established Lobbying Relationships

A strategic decision for an organized interest concerns whether it will lobby alone or as part of a coordinated effort. Lobbyists tend to view coalitions and cooperative lobbying positively as they allow interest organizations to reduce their lobbying costs.[13] The research for this book demonstrates the importance of lobbying enterprises. Corporations, trade associations, and citizen groups have long-term relationships with other lobbying organizations. In addition, these lobbying enterprises have regular participants who are government officials. These participants may represent executive departments, regulatory agencies, congressional committees, or the White House.[14] The repeated interactions among the members of lobbying enterprises greatly facilitate organizing for effective action. Participation in these enterprises is one reason that firms lobby when we might expect them to free ride. The expectation of continuing cooperation among the participants keeps lobbying enterprises together. For example, when asked to explain why they participated as minor players in a coalition, 23 percent of Fortune 1000 interviewees indicated that their participation was in response to a request from organizations with which they frequently cooperated. The lobbyists expected that on future issues the lobbyist who made the request would reciprocate.

In summary, organized interests use multiple strategies across multiple venues to achieve their goals. Some strategies work better when an organization is attempting to preserve the status quo while other strategies are more effective when attempting to achieve policy change. Similarly, a lobbyist pursuing a benefit near the private good end of the private–collective good continuum will employ a different strategy than a lobbyist seeking a collective good. For example, she may attempt to join a coalition as a player rather than as a core member. Other strategies such as organizing a coalition or long-term participation in lobbying enterprises are necessary for pursuing collective goods. One conclusion is clear from our research: lobbyists' strategic choices are rational. Lobbyists select their tactics based on the type of good they are pursuing, the current stage of the policy process, and whether Congress or the bureaucracy is making the decision.

WHAT ARE THE IMPLICATIONS OF OUR FINDINGS FOR AMERICAN DEMOCRACY?

Madison in the *Federalist* No. 10 worried about the "tyranny of the majority," but most observers of politics today worry about the ways in which lobbying by a special interest subverts the will of the majority. It is unlikely that citizens would worry as much about undue lobbying influence if the perceived majority interest always prevailed. Organized interests need not subvert a majority, however, when the information they provide results in more efficient policies and fewer unintended negative consequences. More important, some organized interests appear necessary for American democracy. Long-term relationships between interest organizations and political parties provide the funding, campaign workers, and other party activists necessary for parties to inform and mobilize unorganized voters. These interest organizations are not acting out of altruism, but their activities are not necessarily subverting the will of the majority. Similarly, presidents and congressional leaders often have provided special benefits to interest groups to obtain the votes necessary to pass bills supported by the majority of citizens.

When majorities are large and readily noted, public opinion holds considerable sway, and elections greatly influence policy outcomes. But majorities are not always clear. In fact, majorities need not exist. When majorities are unclear or when there is no majority on an issue, there are greater opportunities for manipulating the agenda, logrolling, and vote trading. Lobbyists and organized interests thrive in these circumstances.

The examples of NAFTA, the jobs act, perchlorate, and drug reimportation demonstrate clearly how the resource advantages of producer interests can place them in a position to exploit situations where clear majorities do not exist or where the majority remains unorganized. Fruit and vegetable growers in Florida, holders of tobacco quotas, producers of perchlorate, and pharmaceutical companies had the access to policymakers, political clout, substantive knowledge of the policy issue, and expertise in the policy process to obtain their desired objectives. Whether we are looking at lobbying Congress, the White House, or the bureaucracy, producer interests make up the largest percentage of lobbying organizations and spend the most resources to achieve their goals. Given the dominance of business interests, do business interests generally win policy battles?

Measuring business wins and losses is not straightforward. Businesses face opposition from numerous camps. Public opinion can counter business interests quite successfully when an issue is salient and important.[15] It is critical to remember that business is rarely unified in its support or opposition to a policy proposal. For example, consumer and environmental interest groups frequently oppose business interests during the regulatory process, but the most frequent opposition to one business interest group comes from another business interest group. For example, the jobs act pitted corporations in the service industry against corporations in the manufacturing sector. Key findings of Baumgartner and his colleagues in *Lobbying and Policy Change* were the heterogeneity of competing sides on most issues and the fact that producer interests often were on opposite sides.[16]

It also is useful to remember that politics and policymaking are not necessarily zero-sum games. We saw in chapter 5 that when comments from businesses are unopposed in the rulemaking process, the commenter often is seeking a clarification of policies and practices. Requesting clarification about the meaning or intent of a rule is unlikely to harm the general public or to shift costs onto unorganized interests. Similarly, we suspect that the vast majority of regulatory waivers do not harm the public, but the waivers may enhance economic efficiency. Such waivers can decrease prices to consumers as well as increase the profits of the firm receiving the waiver.

To be certain, lobbying often reduces social efficiency. The various tariffs, subsidies, and tax loopholes involved in trade policy clearly reduce economic efficiency. Recall the NAFTA debates and the wheeling and dealing necessary to ensure its passage. Reducing tariffs would enhance efficiency, and buying legislators' support with narrow projects reduces those efficiency gains. In the end, however, the United States might be better off with NAFTA in place. The payments that President Clinton gave individual legislators (e.g., protections for vegetable growers and more purchases of C-17 planes) were the costs necessary to secure the collective benefit of freer trade. Economists sometimes refer to first-best and second-best outcomes.[17] Even if a first-best outcome is not achievable, a second-best outcome can still yield considerable gains. NAFTA without side payments for legislators' votes is more efficient than NAFTA with many additional projects and benefits tied to it. That said, President Clinton clearly believed that the second-best NAFTA was a major improvement over the status quo.

Unorganized voters know little about how their elected officials vote on issues, less about their behavior in committees, and still less about bureaucratic policymaking. For voters to be informed about policymaking is costly, and voters tend to be rationally ignorant. But in a world where the federal government's budget provided more than $4 trillion in private and collective benefits during fiscal year 2011, countervailing interest groups, combined with bureaucracies with missions to protect "the public interest," are essential.[18] Competing interests can provide a check on other interest groups in the policy process. In addition, political parties, elections, and public opinion constrain the power of all special interests, including business.

Unfortunately for American democracy, the constraints on special interests are less likely to apply to the government's provision of private goods. Interest organizations lobbying for private benefits are less likely to face countervailing powers, and private goods are rarely the types of issues that political parties place in their platforms or that are salient to voters.

If we examine the incentives facing organized interests, we see that the American political system encourages them to ask for private goods and to reward policymakers for providing those goods. Congress often rails against pork barrel politics and earmarks. But unless there are major changes in the U.S. Constitution, the institutions of federalism, separation of powers, and the election of individuals to represent geographic constituencies will continue to encourage policymakers to provide private goods.

QUESTIONS YOU MUST ANSWER

So what is the state of American democracy when viewed through the lens of interest-group influence on policymaking? The answer depends on your answers to two questions. First, *if parties, elections, public opinion, and competition among interest groups constrain major policy decisions that provide collective goods, is this sufficient to give a positive evaluation to the political system?* An indisputable finding from *Lobbying and Policy Change* is that there are countervailing powers when governments make decisions about collective goods. The research in this book buttresses that finding. If policymakers are considering such issues as the size of the federal government, whether to adopt universal health care insurance, or whether to increase or reduce the scope of environmental regulations, then public opinion, political parties, elections, and countervailing interest groups limit the power of special interests.

Second, *if the government continues to provide billions of dollars in private benefits to organized interests, does this force one to make a negative evaluation of American politics?* Perhaps the most important contribution of this book is to draw attention to the private benefits that organizations, particularly producer organizations, seek and receive. Interest organizations lobbying for private benefits are less likely to face countervailing powers and are more likely to obtain their desired policy outcome. This is particularly true when the decisions concern private goods and are products of logrolling in congressional committees or of bureaucracies allocating benefits to favored constituencies. Given the value that technical expertise and information have in bureaucratic decision making, this imbalance is unlikely to change. It may be sufficient for democratic governance, however, that many agencies have as their mission the protection of the unorganized and that elected officials have substantial oversight of the bureaucracies.

We cannot answer these questions for you, but your answers indicate how *you* evaluate the American political system.

ENDNOTES

1. Frank R. Baumgartner and Beth L. Leech, *Basic Interests: The Importance of Groups in Politics and in Political Science* (Princeton, NJ: Princeton University Press, 1998).

2. Frank Baumgartner et al., *Lobbying and Policy Change: Who Wins, Who Loses, and Why?* (Chicago: University of Chicago Press, 2009).

3. Ibid.

4. David Lowery, "Why Do Organized Interests Lobby? A Multi-Goal, Multi-Context Theory of Lobbying," *Polity* 39 (2007): 29–54; David Lowery and Virginia Gray, "A Neopluralist Perspective on Organized Interests," *Political Research Quarterly* 57, no. 1 (2004): 164–175. For the classic critique of rational choice theory, see Donald Green and Ian Shapiro, *Pathologies of Rational Choice Theory: A Critique of Applications in Political Science* (New Haven, CT: Yale University Press, 1994). For a series of essays concerning the strengths and weaknesses of the rational choice approach to political science, see Jeffrey Friedman, ed., *The Rational Choice Controversy: Economic Models of Politics Reconsidered* (New Haven, CT: Yale University Press, 1995).

5. R. Kenneth Godwin, Edward J. Lopez, and Barry J. Seldon, "Allocating Lobbying Resources Between Collective and Private Rents," *Political Research Quarterly* 61, no. 2 (2008): 345–361.

6. Wendy L. Hansen, L. Neil, J. Mitchell, and Jeffrey M. Drope, "The Logic of Private and Collective Action," *American Journal of Political Science* 49, no. 1 (2005): 150–167.

7. Virginia Gray and David Lowery, *The Population Ecology of Interest Representation: Lobbying Communities in American States* (Ann Arbor: University of Michigan Press, 1996).

8. For information concerning this coalition, see http://action.sierraclub.org/site/MessageViewer?em_id=194321.0

9. Kevin W. Hula, *Lobbying Together: Interest Group Coalitions in Legislative Politics* (Washington, DC: Georgetown University Press, 2000).

10. The text of the *Citizens United v. Federal Election Commission* decision can be found at www.scotusblog.com/wp-content/uploads/2010/01/citizens-opinion.pdf.

11. Commissioner of the Federal Communications Commission, quoted in Lee J. Fritschler, *Smoking and Politics* (New York: Appleton-Century Crofts, 1969), 94.

12. Sidney A. Shapiro, "The Information Quality Act and Environmental Protection: The Perils of Reform by Appropriations Rider," *William and Mary Environmental Law Review* 28, no. 2 (2004): 339; and Jacques B. LeBoeuf, "Limitations on the Use of Appropriations Riders by Congress to Effectuate Substantive Policy Changes," *Hastings Constitutional Law Quarterly* 19 (1992): 457–493.

13. Bertram J. Levine, *The Art of Lobbying: Building Trust and Selling Policy* (Washington, DC: CQ Press, 2009).

14. Paul Sabatier and Hank Jenkins-Smith, *Policy Change and Learning: An Advocacy Coalition Approach* (Boulder, CO: Westview Press, 1993). Although we have not discussed the advocacy coalition framework in this volume, research concerning advocacy coalitions in the regulatory process supports the importance of lobbying enterprises not only in legislatures but also in the bureaucracy. This source provides a discussion of advocacy coalitions.

15. Gary Mucciaroni, *Reversals of Fortune: Public Policy and Private Interests* (Washington, DC: Brookings Institution, 1994).

16. Baumgartner et al., *Lobbying and Policy Change*, pp. 204–212.

17. R. G. Lipsey and Kelvin Lancaster, "The General Theory of Second Best," *Review of Economic Studies* 24, no. 1 (1956): 11–32.

18. President Obama's budget called for *only* $3.83 trillion in spending. However, many billions more went to so-called "tax expenditures."

Students frequently ask the question, "What kind of training do I need to become a lobbyist?" This is an important question because the answer reveals a great deal about the relationship between lobbying and the policy process. There are several good articles available to students concerning congressional and local government lobbyists' career patterns and work habits.[1] Here, however, we examine how lobbying firms that target the White House and bureaucratic agencies recruit and train their personnel. The information included in this appendix comes from interviews with the heads of four lobbying firms plus the personal experience of coauthor Erik Godwin.[2] We do not claim that the information presented here is representative of all types of executive branch lobbying. In particular, it is not as representative of procurement lobbying.[3] The information does, however, shed light on the types of career paths that executive branch lobbyists follow and the techniques that they rely upon when influencing federal policy.

A GENERAL BLUEPRINT OF LOBBYING

Whether lobbying the legislature, the president, or the bureaucracy, lobbyists must understand and account for three streams of information about the policy they seek to influence: they must know the *substance* of the issue, the *process* that governs the policy, and the *people* who will make key decisions along the way. Every successful lobbying effort requires correctly moving the substance, process, and people at the right time. Substantive knowledge refers to an understanding of the technical aspects of a policy and the political environment surrounding the issue. Lobbyists who lack substantive expertise are unable to provide quality information, generate accurate analyses, or request realistic policy adjustments for their clients. Lobbyists must also know the process by which the policy decision will be made. This includes when the process is vulnerable to outside influence, where in the process the critical decisions will be made (and by whom), what types of information will be most persuasive at those times, and how to structure the policy outcome so that its impact will be long lasting. Finally, a lobbyist must know the people who will decide the policy. Better yet, she should know these policymakers personally. The decision makers must trust that the lobbyist will protect their interests, is telling the truth, and can deliver what she promises. For example, if a lobbyist is attempting to convince a policymaker at the Nuclear Regulatory Commission that changing a proposed regulatory rule will not jeopardize safety, the policymakers must have confidence in the lobbyist's expertise and information. Most importantly, the policymakers must have confidence in the integrity and truthfulness of the lobbyist herself.

Failing to account for any of the three streams of information leaves a lobbying strategy vulnerable to unexpected obstacles at inopportune times. Every lobbyist interviewed by the authors explicitly stated the importance of addressing each of the three categories, although different lobbyists and/or firms weight the three aspects differently. In other words, some lobbyists and firms specialize in substantive expertise, others concentrate on influencing a specific subset of policy processes, and still others rely upon key contacts within government to move policy. Regardless of specialization, however, a firm must possess or purchase a sufficient degree of control over all three categories to have sustained policy influence. We now examine how the search for the three skill sets drives the hiring and training of executive branch lobbyists.

SUBSTANTIVE EXPERTISE

There was a consensus among the heads of lobbying firms that individuals who lobby the executive branch should have sufficient expertise in a substantive area to present a client's case to knowledgeable decision makers. Executive branch lobbyists tend to have advanced degrees in law, business, economics, public policy, or in a substantive area such as agriculture, water resources, or engineering. After completing his or her formal education, a future lobbyist gains further substantive expertise by working in government, in a consulting firm, or for industry. The preparation of Erik Godwin, the coauthor who worked for the executive lobbying firm the EOP Group, is typical of executive branch lobbyists. He did graduate work in environmental science at Oxford University in England, earned a master's degree in public policy at the University of Michigan, worked for the environmental consulting firm Industrial Economics Inc., and then worked on environment and energy issues in the Office of Information and Regulatory Affairs (OIRA) in the Office of Management and Budget (OMB). Only after all of that training and job experience did he join the EOP Group, where he lobbied on environmental issues.

The heads of contract lobbying firms saw substantive knowledge as the easiest type of expertise for the firm to acquire. Firms can have their existing lobbyists learn the substance of an issue, they can partner with other interest groups, or they can simply hire someone who already has the necessary expertise. A recent example of how corporations and trade associations hire substantive expertise is the eruption of hiring that followed the passage of the 2010 Dodd–Frank Wall Street Reform and Consumer Protection Act.[4] Hailed as the most important financial regulation since the Great Depression, the law is 851 pages long and contains 1,601 provisions, almost all of which will result in new rules and regulations from the Securities and Exchange Commission (SEC), the Commodity Futures Trading Commission, and other federal agencies. The act immediately became the "Financial Lobbyist Full Employment Act" as banks and other financial institutions rushed to hire the legal and financial expertise necessary to lobby the regulatory agencies working on the new rules.[5]

Lobbying firms can also obtain substantive expertise by taking advantage of the work conducted by the numerous think tanks that specialize in particular fields. For example, Resources for the Future (RFF) is a think tank located in Washington, D.C., that focuses on environmental economics. RFF produces excellent issue-specific analyses that are designed to resonate with federal decision makers. Some think tanks are clearly partisan and ideological. For instance, the American Enterprise Institute (AEI) is a conservative think tank that favors the Republican Party, the Brookings Institution is more liberal and favors the Democratic Party, and the Cato Institute supports the libertarian ideology. The partisan affiliations of think tanks often serve as useful cues that help decision makers evaluate the political implications of the work products. For example, our estate tax case study showed how Patricia Soldano used an economic report prepared by AEI to convince Republican lawmakers that the estate tax reduced jobs and economic growth. Because of AEI's conservative stance, the Republican audience had greater confidence that the information was consistent with the preferences of the conservative agenda.

Substantive expertise is often the fastest route into lobbying for newly minted college graduates. Lobbying firms often hire within such defined areas of policy knowledge as renewable energy, biotechnology, labor economics, or aerospace engineering. Students spend their collegiate careers acquiring significant technical skills that make them attractive to firms that need to increase technical knowledge. Note, however, that new substantive specialists generally have a very limited initial role in the lobbying process. They are technical resources and are good for answering technical questions. Joining a lobbying firm or interest organization as a substantive specialist is one of the fastest and easiest ways into lobbying, but you must still develop expertise in process and people.

In summary, there are lobbying firms that specialize in every major substantive area in which the federal government is active. These firms supply expertise to corporations, trade associations, citizen action groups, and to other lobbying firms. If you are thinking of becoming such a lobbyist, look at Figure A.1. It provides a short synopsis of the education and career paths of Dan Barolo, James Aidala, and Linda Fisher, three lobbyists who specialized in pesticides.

FIGURE A.1   **The Career Paths of Three Pesticide Lobbyists**

Daniel M. Barolo is currently president of Dan Barolo, LLC, and currently is a partner in Bergeson and Campbell, a firm specializing in lobbying on pesticides. He attended Vanderbilt University where he earned a bachelor's degree in civil engineering in 1966 and a master's degree in sanitary engineering in 1967. Barolo is a former director for the U.S. Environmental Protection Agency's (EPA) Office of Pesticide Programs (OPP), Office of Prevention, Pesticides, and Toxic Substances (OPPTS) (1994–1998). Prior to 1994, he was director of the Special Review and Reregistration Division within OPP. In the ten years before joining the EPA, Barolo served as director of the Division of Water, New York State Department of Environmental Conservation (NYSDEC). Immediately prior to directing the state's water office, Dan served as associate director, Air Pollution Control Program, Division of Air Resources, NYSDEC, among other positions.

Linda J. Fisher is vice president—DuPont Safety, Health & Environment and chief sustainability officer. She has responsibility for advancing DuPont's progress in achieving sustainable growth; DuPont safety, health, and environmental programs; the company's product stewardship programs; and global regulatory affairs. She joined DuPont in July 2004. Prior to joining DuPont, Ms. Fisher has served in a number of key leadership positions in government and industry including Deputy Administrator of EPA; EPA Assistant Administrator—Office of Prevention, Pesticides and Toxic Substances; EPA Assistant Administrator—Office of Policy, Planning and Evaluation; and Chief of Staff to the EPA Administrator. Fisher, an attorney, was also vice president of Government Affairs for Monsanto and was "Of Counsel" with the law firm, Latham & Watkins. Ms. Fisher received a law degree from Ohio State University, a Master's of Business Administration from George Washington University, and a B.A. from Miami University. Ms. Fisher serves as liaison to the Environmental Policy Committee of the DuPont board of directors. She serves on the board of directors of the Covanta Holding Corporation and the boards of several nonprofit organizations, including the National Parks Foundation and Resources for the Future.

James V. Aidala is vice president for Policy and Governmental Affairs of the Acta Group, L.L.C. The Acta Group lobbies to gain governmental approvals of chemicals, biocides, biotechnology, and nanotechnology. Aidala completed undergraduate and graduate studies at Massachusetts Institute of Technology, Brown University, and Harvard University. He was the former assistant administrator for the U.S. Environmental Protection Agency's (EPA) Office of Prevention, Pesticides, and Toxic Substances (OPPTS) (2000–2001); former associate assistant Administrator for OPPTS (1993–2000); worked on the Subcommittee on Environment, Energy, and Natural Resources in the U.S. House of Representatives, where he was in charge of oversight of EPA's implementation of the Federal Insecticide, Fungicide and Rodenticide Act (FIFRA) and the Toxic Substances Control Act (TSCA) (1991–1993); director of Policy Development at the Wallace Institute for Alternative Agriculture (1990–1991); policy expert on FIFRA and TSCA at the Congressional Research Service (1983–1990), which is part of the U.S. Library of Congress; professional staff member for the U.S. Senate Committee on Government Affairs, Subcommittee on Energy (1981–1983). Prior to joining Bergeson and Campbell, Aidala worked as a lobbyist with Jellinek, Schwartz & Connolly.

Sources for Barolo: Adapted from Emily Headen, *From Bureaucrats to Fat Cats: EPA Pesticide Program Is a "Farm Team" for the Pesticide Lobby* (Washington, DC: Environmental Working Group, n.d.), www.ewg.org/files/fatcats.pdf; and Spoke, "Daniel M. Barolo," www.spoke.com/info/p6KGomB/DanielBarolo.

Source for Fisher: DuPont, "Linda J. Fisher," www2.dupont.com/Government/en_US/gsa_contracts/our_team/fisher.html.

Sources for Aidala: Adapted from ZoomInfo, "The ACTA Group, L.L.C.," www.zoominfo.com/company/The+Acta+Group+%2C+L.L.C.-806583; and Spoke, "James Aidala," www.spoke.com/info/p6msk8Y/JamesAidala.

PROCESS EXPERTISE: INSTITUTIONS MATTER

There is a consensus among the heads of the contract lobbying firms that a lobbyist who thoroughly understands the political structures and the policy processes surrounding a given issue is a vital part of a successful firm. We have seen throughout this book that policy change is dynamic, with key decisions occurring at different times in the policy process. Successful lobbyists know when these decisions will occur, which procedural stages are vulnerable to influence, and what types of lobbying are most persuasive at each stage. One head of a lobbying firm stated that more than 50 percent of his firm's business involved using bureaucratic processes to speed up, slow down, or stop a given policy change. Political scientists have long recognized the importance of process mastery to lobbyists. Stanford political scientist Terry Moe, perhaps the preeminent bureaucracy scholar over the past 25 years, wrote the following:

> The most fundamental task for political actors is to find and institute a governance structure that can protect their political organizations from control by opponents.[6]

> Structural choices have all sorts of important consequences for the content and direction of policy, and, because this is so, choices about structure are implicitly choices about policy. They are part and parcel of the same thing.[7]

> [Voters do not care about structure.] Organized interests, on the other hand do care. They are active and informed in their own policy domains, and they understand the advantages they seek from government depend crucially on precisely those fine details of structure that cause voters' eyes to glaze over. Structure is valuable to them, and they have every incentive to mobilize their political resources to get what they want. They are very likely, as a result, to be the only source of political demands and pressures when structural issues are at stake. *Structural politics is interest group politics.*[8]

Who is most likely to understand the political structures and policy processes? The answer is those individuals who have worked in the government. A major reason that there is a constant movement of government officials to lobbying organizations is that ex-bureaucrats understand where in the policy process structural decisions are made, where in the decision process to devote lobbying resources, and how a policy should be written to ensure that its implementation is effective (or ineffective). For instance, environmental organizations want the Environmental Protection Agency (EPA) not the U.S. Department of Agriculture (USDA) to be in charge of pesticide registration and review. Interest organizations that oppose a regulation, conversely, will want its implementation assigned to an agency whose mission opposes the regulation's goals. For example, imagine how different safety in the workplace might be if the U.S. Department of Commerce and Industry rather than the

Occupational Safety and Health Administration (OSHA) were in charge of regulating worker safety.

Our case studies demonstrate the value of using process knowledge to either facilitate or undermine policy changes. In the case of the Data Quality Act (DQA), lobbyist Jim Tozzi wanted the DQA to serve industry's preference for stringent evaluation of information. He made sure that OIRA would oversee the implementation of the new law. OIRA's statutory mandate calls for the office to maximize the societal benefits of new regulations. The result of the agency's mandate was a bureaucracy in which economic efficiency was the dominant value. Efficient outcomes are extremely difficult to generate when policy decisions are made using poor quality data, and OIRA had a long history of turning back agencies' attempts to collect and/or generate substandard information. By placing the implementation of the DQA within OIRA, Tozzi ensured that an agency committed to information quality and economic efficiency would oversee agencies' compliance with the new law.

Skilled lobbyists can also use their knowledge of the policy process to prevent new policies from being successfully implemented. When the pharmaceutical company lobbyist wrote the Cochran Amendment to the Prescription Drug Reimportation Act, she knew that the U.S. Food and Drug Administration (FDA) was unlikely to certify that all imported drugs were safe. The FDA's mission to protect consumer safety made it functionally impossible for the agency to certify the safety of all reimported drugs. The lobbyist also knew that legislators would be wary of voting against an amendment that ostensibly was designed to increase consumer safety.

The need for process expertise creates endless opportunities for individuals to enter into the lobbying profession. Because government structures and policy processes are so complex, numerous lobbying agencies specialize in particular parts. So, for example, some firms can specialize in the regulatory process of a specific agency such as the EPA, the SEC, or the Nuclear Regulatory Commission. As a lobbying firm increases the number of issue areas on which it is active, the firm must hire individuals who understand the institutional structure and policy process of each substantive issue area. To be hired as a process specialist, however, a prospective lobbyist will ideally have worked within the policy processes that she seeks to influence. In the case of the DQA, for example, Jim Tozzi had directed OIRA earlier in his career. He therefore not only had exhaustive knowledge of the processes but he also understood how the economic preferences of OIRA as an institution shaped its discretionary application of those processes.

That level of process expertise is extremely expensive for firms to develop in-house, and all of the firms interviewed stated a preference for hiring lobbyists who were already procedural experts. Hiring out of the agencies has another key advantage in terms of process knowledge—accuracy. Government processes inevitably evolve over time as they respond to changes in the policy environment. By hiring recent government practitioners, lobbying firms can stay current on the procedural stages and exploit new procedural opportunities.

In fact, bureaucrats often have substantial discretion to change federal decision-making processes. This makes them the world's experts on the new processes that they designed.

Finally, one lobbying firm founder stated that the principal reason he liked to hire process specialists out of the bureaucratic ranks is that they typically make far fewer mistakes than those who had not spent time in government. When asked why, he said, "Lobbyists can't afford to ask for the impossible. Some things simply cannot be done at certain times in an agency's process. Ex-bureaucrats are sensitive to this, and ask the right person, for the right thing, at the right time, in the right way." Notably, a comprehensive knowledge of the process depends upon identifying who is making the key decisions and what the policy preferences of those individuals look like. We turn now to how people expertise factors into the hiring decisions of lobbying organizations.

PEOPLE EXPERTISE

During an interview with the head of a lobbying firm, one of the authors of this book was permitted to observe a job interview between the firm partner and a candidate seeking to join the firm as a lobbyist. At one point, the partner slid a legal pad across the desk to the applicant and said, "Write down the name and position of everyone at the EPA who will take your call without pushing it to voice mail." When the author asked about the question later, the partner replied, "I need to know who this guy can reach out and touch. Substance and process are vital, but people are where we make our money." All of our interviews confirmed that the worth of lobbyists is strongly related to their access to decision makers. In this age where every bureaucrat has caller ID, the ability of agency personnel to systematically ignore an interest organization makes access increasingly difficult.

Interest-group scholars and journalists tend to discuss this type of expertise when writing about the legislative branch. It is quite common, for example, for lobbying firms to hire ex-congresspersons and senators, a legislator's key staff member, or a staff member from an important legislative committee. For example, the lobbying firm Greenberg Traurig gives the following biography for Nancy Taylor, one of their partners:

> Nancy Taylor has over 20 years of legislative and regulatory experience in advising clients on health care related matters, having served 10 years in her capacity as Health Policy Director for the Senate Committee on Labor and Human Resources [this committee considers health issues in the Senate]. She has also served as CEO of a start up medical device company where she was successful in obtaining eight product clearances and reimbursement coverage for the products.[9]

Taylor, an attorney, was listed in 2007 by the *Washingtonian* as the thirty-third most influential lobbyist in Washington with revenues of well over $1 million per year. The *Washingtonian* reports that Taylor's close relationship with Sen. Orrin Hatch, R-UT, a member of the Senate Labor and Human Resources Committee, accounts for much of her success in lobbying on health care.[10] Out of the fifty top lobbyists listed by the *Washingtonian,* thirteen are previous members of Congress, twenty-one are ex-congressional or ex-agency staffers, and three are family members of serving members of Congress.[11] The lobbyists listed at the very top of the list were Hale Boggs and Bob Dole. Boggs's mother and father were members of Congress, and his sister is an important journalist in the Washington community. His lifelong connections with key personnel throughout the Democratic Party provide him with unmatched access to Democrats in Congress. Similarly, Bob Dole was the Senate majority leader and a Republican nominee for president. Until 2008, his wife was a senator from North Carolina.

In an important paper, Jordi Vidal, Mirko Draca, and Christian Fons-Rosen examined the income of lobbyists who joined a contract lobbying firm after serving as congressional staffers. The authors found that lobbyists connected to U.S. senators have an annual income that averages more than $300,000. These lobbyists suffer an initial loss of $160,000 in their annual revenue when their previous employer leaves the Senate. Although these lobbyists regain about half of this annual income after a five-year period, they are unable to reach their previous income level. Many ex-staffers leave lobbying shortly after their senator leaves.[12] Vidal et al. interpreted this finding as evidence that a key determinant of the revenue that a congressional lobbyist can generate is her close relationship with a congressperson. In other words, lobbyists "cash in on their connections."[13] Although no one has collected similar data on lobbyists who specialize in lobbying the executive departments and regulatory agencies, a quick examination of Figure A.1 and the websites of powerful executive-branch lobbying firms shows that government connections are a key attribute of the lobbyists. You will find a similar pattern if you go to the web pages of major trade associations and examine the personal pages of their government relations staff.

Why are these relationships so important? The answer is partly structural and partly reputational. Structurally, the most obvious answer is that a person who has worked closely with other members within a policy system is more likely than an unknown outsider to have her phone call accepted, to meet the policymakers for lunch, and to receive time to discuss an issue. This effect is particularly powerful if the lobbyist used to work within the agency and hired, trained, or promoted the people she now seeks to influence. Several of our case studies also showed the importance of forming coalitions with other lobbying organizations. This is much easier to do if you know the lobbyists in those organizations and you have developed a high level of interpersonal trust. These individuals often have political information that will be extremely useful to your lobbying efforts. They also can assist you in developing lobbying strategies and monitoring what an agency is doing.

The importance of personal contacts, however, goes far beyond a lobbyist simply knowing the players on an issue. A lobbyist who is personally familiar with the individuals involved also has knowledge of their policy preferences. The decision processes used by each individual tend to follow predictable patterns—patterns that lobbyists must account for when crafting a strategy. For example, if a lobbyist knows that a key decision maker believes strongly in market incentives then the lobbyist will approach the bureaucrat with economic arguments. Conversely, a lobbyist would take a different approach with a bureaucrat who is more concerned with equity issues.

Finally, no conversation of lobbying would be complete without recognizing the importance of reputation when dealing with the people making decisions. Lobbyists are more successful when they know decision makers, but lobbyists are also much more successful when decision makers know and trust lobbyists. Building this trust often takes repeated interactions in multiple venues. Trust is difficult to gain but easy to lose. The reputation of a lobbyist is one of her most precious possessions because lobbyists rely upon access so heavily. Executive branch personnel rarely grant access to lobbyists who have proven themselves untrustworthy in the past. As the head of one lobbying firm stated, "If you have to choose between sinning against God or the bureaucracy, choose God. He forgives."

In summary, having good relationships with policymakers and with other lobbyists is critical in lobbying agencies. As we saw in our case studies, important issue areas such as corporate taxation, agriculture, energy, pesticides, transportation, and health care have issue networks made up of government officials, lobbyists, and others who have sufficient substantive knowledge to participate. The success of a lobbyist in representing her client's interest may depend on her personal relationships with other participants in an issue network, both government officials and other lobbyists.

SUMMARY

In every contract lobbying firm and in every effective lobbying organization, there must be all three types of expertise: (1) substance, (2) process, and (3) people. Obviously, these three sets of skills are related. Persons who have process expertise on an issue also will know a great deal about the substance of that issue, and they will know many of the policymakers. This helps to explain why ex-government officials are sought after by lobbying firms. Say, for instance, the Natural Resources Defense Council (NRDC) or Dow Chemical Company wants expertise concerning the renewal of a particular pesticide. It can hire specialists from such lobbying firms as Jellinek, Schwartz & Connolly or Bergeson & Campbell. These firms hire ex-bureaucrats who dealt with pesticides while working at the EPA. For example, Jellinek, Schwartz & Connolly hired Daniel Barolo, the ex-director for the EPA's Office of Pesticide Programs, and James V. Aidala, the ex-assistant administrator for EPA's Office of

Prevention, Pesticides, and Toxic Substances. Barolo had done graduate work in environmental engineering at Vanderbilt, and Aidala had done graduate work in chemistry at Harvard.[14] These individuals understand the scientific information about pesticides, know what types of information are most important to the EPA officials who will make the policy decisions, and Barolo and Aidala probably recruited many of the policymakers in the EPA whom they later lobbied.

Lobbyists who command the highest salaries and lobbying fees are those who can bring all three types of expertise to bear on issue quickly and cleanly. Dr. Jim Tozzi provided the clearest example of how having all three types of knowledge increases a lobbyist's value. First, the bureaucratic process that he was seeking to change was not specific to any one department or agency. To change it, therefore, required more than simply convincing a single agency to amend its process for evaluating the quality of data; all of the agencies would have to accept the new system. Since some agencies were quite happy with the existing process, Tozzi needed to use Congress to force widespread change. Tozzi's relationships with the right people were critical to DQA's success. Specifically, he successfully convinced two policymakers to help him: Rep. Jo Ann Emerson, R-MO, in the House and Sen. Richard Shelby, D-AL, in the Senate. Emerson attached two short paragraphs to an appropriations bill. Tozzi understood the substance of the issue perfectly, and he knew precisely how to word the two seemingly innocuous paragraphs. The two paragraphs caused a dramatic shift in the types of information that the executive departments and regulatory agencies could use in licensing and renewing products. This changed the tug-of-war between industry and citizen groups by tilting the playing field in favor of industry. Senator Shelby then ensured that the amendment remained part of the appropriations bill in the Senate. Tozzi had the information necessary to convince these two key legislators that the regulatory process was rigged against industry and that this imbalance created economic harm to the nation. Most important, because he had served as the director of OIRA, Tozzi understood how to restructure the process of federal information gathering in a way that favored producers. He made use of OIRA's existing infrastructure, personnel, and preferences to ensure that the implementation stage was successful.

Similarly, Mexican president Carlos Salinas knew that the best approach for getting the North American Free Trade Agreement (NAFTA) on the political agenda was not to approach President George H. W. Bush directly but to convince the American business community that a free trade agreement was in its interests. Salinas also knew that the most influential business lobby was the Business Roundtable, and he had close personal relationships with several members of that organization. Patricia Soldano was able to lobby successfully for a temporary end to the estate tax because she knew how to create a coalition, frame the issue in a way that would appeal to the public, and generate the information necessary to justify the legislation. Finally, the chief lobbyist for a major pharmaceutical company convinced Sen. Thad Cochran, R-MS, to add an amendment she wrote to the drug reimportation legislation. The amendment required the secretary of Health and Human Services (HHS) who represented the FDA, to certify that *all* pharmaceutical drugs imported to the United States would be *completely* safe. The lobbyist understood that this would be impossible for the FDA to guarantee, and the Cochran Amendment totally eviscerated the drug reimportation legislation. In each of these cases, the lobbyists had all three types of knowledge. They knew the policymakers who could make the decisions, understood what political and substantive information would convince them, and understood how to write the proposed policy so that it would have the desired effect. Often, however, the interest group wanting to make a policy change must hire several lobbyists to achieve all three types of expertise.

As Figure A.1 indicates, becoming a super-lobbyist of the bureaucracy is difficult. It requires graduate training, often requiring multiple graduate degrees. It requires working in a firm or in a government agency to gain further substantive knowledge of a policy area. It also requires service in government at a sufficiently high level to develop personal relationships with policymakers and to gain the knowledge of government structure and process necessary to be effective. So, do you really want to become a lobbyist? It is a long road from graduating with a degree in political science to becoming an effective lobbyist.

ENDNOTES

1. See, for example, Bertram J. Levine, *The Art of Lobbying: Building Trust and Selling Policy* (Washington, DC: CQ Press, 2009); Ed Ingle, "Government Relations," in *Reputation Management*, ed. John Doonley and Helio Fred Garcia (New York: Routledge, 2007), 159–182; Anthony J. Nownes, *Total Lobbying: What Lobbyists Want (and How They Try to Get It)* (New York: Cambridge University Press, 2006); and Jordi Blanes i Vidal, Mirko Draca, and Christian Fons-Rosen, "Revolving Door Lobbyists," CEP Discussion Paper No. 993 (London: Centre for Economic Performance, August 2010).

2. None of the four interest organizations is the EOP Group, the firm that employed Erik Godwin.

3. For a discussion of the differences between procurement lobbying and policy lobbying, see Nownes, *Total Lobbying*, chapter 6.

4. Public Law No. 111-203, 2010, www.gpo.gov/fdsys/pkg/PLAW-111publ203/pdf/PLAW-111publ203.pdf

5. To keep track of these hires, go to the DealBook website of the *New York Times*, and see www.opensecrets.org/lobby/lookup.php?type=i&q=Dodd-Frank to see the number of lobbying disclosure reports related to the Dodd–Frank Act.

6. Terry M. Moe, "The Politics of Structural Choice: Toward a Theory of Public Bureaucracy," in *Organization Theory: From Chester Barnard to the Present and Beyond*, ed. Oliver E. Williamson (New York: Oxford University Press, 1995), 119.

7. Ibid., 127.

8. Ibid., 129, emphasis added.

9. Greenberg Traurig, www.gtlaw.com/People/NancyETaylor

10. Kim Eisler, "Hired Guns: The City's 50 Top Lobbyists," *Washingtonian,* June 1, 2007. www.washingtonian.com/articles/mediapolitics/4264.html

11. Ibid.

12. Blanes i Vidal et al., "Revolving Door Lobbyists," 4–6. These losses are the median loss. The average loss is much larger as numerous lobbyists have incomes well over $1 million.

13. Ibid., 5.

14. Later Barolo and Aidala left Jellinek, Schwartz & Connolly and moved to Bergeson & Campbell. www.spoke.com/info/p6KGomB/DanielBarolo

AARP (formerly called the American Association of Retired Persons): The AARP is a nonpartisan organization for members over the age of fifty. AARP is one of Washington's most powerful lobbying organizations.

Advisory Committee on Trade Policy and Negotiations (ACTPN): The ACTPN coordinated the activities of thirty advisory committees focused on U.S. trade policy. The ACTPN was cochaired by CEOs Jim Robinson and Kay Whitmore during the NAFTA policy process.

Agenda setting: Agenda setting is one of the five stages of public policymaking. Agenda setting considers how an issue comes to the attention of public officials and how public officials decide whether or not to address the issue.

Arctic National Wildlife Refuge (ANWR): ANWR is the largest wildlife refuge in the United States. It is located in Alaska. The opening of ANWR to oil and gas exploration was a major component of the Energy Policy Act of 2003 that failed to pass Congress.

Backward induction: This is a type of reasoning in which strategic actors choose an action based on what they envision will follow that action. The process is used to determine the optimal course of action.

By-product: To reduce free riding, Mancur Olson argued that interest groups used selective incentives to entice contributions to collective efforts. As private goods, selective incentives are not vulnerable to free riding. Therefore, groups can use the profits from the sale of the selective incentives to finance the provision of the collective good. The collective good is provided as a by-product of the sale of private goods.

Cheap ride: Contrast a cheap ride with a free ride. When corporations or individuals in a coalition limit their participation to small acts, such as allowing the use of their name on the coalition's letterhead, this is a cheap ride. They limit their participation to these activities because they see the issue as relatively unimportant to them or because they believe that their participation is unlikely to affect the coalition's successes or failures.

Coalition: Coalitions are formal lobbying institutions that interest organizations join and to which they pledge resources. Coalitions often have paid staff and an office, and the coalition members have specified obligations such as allocating personnel to the coalition effort or paying a participation fee to the coalition. Coalitions typically seek highly collective goods. (See cooperative lobbying and sides [or lobbying sides] as well.)

Collective action problem: Also called the "free rider problem," collective action problems occur when rational, self-interested people free ride and cheap ride rather than help provide the collective good.

Collective goods: These are goods with nonrivalrous consumption and non-excludability.

Comment letters: When individuals and organizations comment on proposed bureaucratic rules, their communications are typically referred to as comment letters. Also see comments.

Comment period: A mandated period of time during which the full text of a proposed regulation is open to public view and comment is a comment period. Proposed regulations must be published in the *Federal Registrar* for easy public access. A comment period formalizes bureaucratic oversight. It is designed to reduce the information asymmetries hampering Congress, the president, and interest groups as they seek to control or influence bureaucratic actions.

Comments: During the rulemaking process, affected individuals and organizations are allowed to offer comments in letters to the agency officials who will write the final rule. Also see comment letters.

Cooperative lobbying: Cooperative lobbying occurs when interest organizations coordinate their lobbying efforts on a policy issue but do not form a formal coalition. (See coalition and sides [or lobbying sides].)

Core member: Core members of lobbying coalitions are active in organizing and directing a coalition's lobbying efforts. Contrast core members with players, tagalongs, and free riders.

Covered officials: Covered officials are policymakers as recognized by the Lobbying Disclosure Act of 1995. Covered officials include members of Congress, congressional staff members, and executive branch officials.

Crowding effects: Crowding effects occur when a collective good has some rivalrous consumption. Roads are collective goods, but they are vulnerable to crowding effects.

Data Quality Act (DQA): The DQA directed the Office of Management and Budget (OMB) to write general data quality guidelines for data used by the federal government.

Decision making: See policy legitimation.

Department of Defense (DoD): The DoD is a cabinet level department in the executive branch.

Economic rents: Economic rents are any payment for goods or services beyond the actual costs of those goods and services. (Also see political rents.)

Energy Policy Act of 2003 (108th Congress, H.R. 6): This was a comprehensive energy proposal supported by President George W. Bush to increase energy production in the United States. It contained several controversial features including the opening of the Yucca Mountain Nuclear Repository and the opening of the Arctic National Wildlife Refuge (ANWR) to oil exploration and extraction. The bill died in the Senate, but portions of the bill later were included in the American Jobs Creation Act of 2004, which became law.

Equilibrium: When a system reaches a steady state it is in equilibrium. In policy, an equilibrium position occurs when no entity can pull the policy away from its current position.

European Union (EU): The EU is a confederation of over twenty European nations. The EU maintains a single economic market and a shared currency.

Exchange model: This is a political process in which organized interests *buy* or *bid* on policies by providing resources to policymakers in exchange for favorable policy decisions.

Excludable: A good is excludable if the owner of the good can prevent others from benefitting from it. Private goods are excludable. Collective goods are nonexcludable.

External (or contract) lobbyists: External lobbyists (also called contract lobbyists) work for firms whose primary business is lobbying. External lobbyists work for hire for other firms but are not direct employees of the organizations for whom they are lobbying. (Also see internal lobbyists.)

Family Business Estate Tax Coalition (FBETC): The FBETC included the National Federation of Independent Business (NFIB), the National Association of Manufacturers, the American Farm Bureau, the Newspaper Association of America, the U.S. Chamber of Commerce, and trade associations representing cattlemen, liquor and beer wholesalers and distributors, and a host of other small business and farm groups. The goal of this coalition was to end federal estate taxes.

Fast track: One of several means of unorthodox lawmaking, fast track procedures require the House and Senate to follow preset rules governing debate and amending procedures. Fast track procedures circumvent the House Committee on Rules and unanimous consent agreements in the Senate.

Feedback: Feedback is the final stage of the policymaking process. Continuous evaluation of a policy by those affected provides feedback to decision makers who might then choose to revise the policy.

Fire alarm: Fire alarm is a metaphor to describe after the fact means of bureaucratic oversight. When organized interests feel they are being treated unfairly by bureaucratic decisions, a "fire alarm" can be pulled, thereby alerting congressional policymakers to the problem. Rather than addressing problems in the bureaucracies proactively, members of Congress respond when fire alarms are pulled.

Foreign Sales Corporation and extraterritorial income (FSC/ETI): These are provisions in the U.S. tax code that gave tax benefits to U.S. corporations. These benefits violated provisions of the World Trade Organization (WTO).

The laws creating the benefits were repealed as part of the American Jobs Creation Act of 2004.

Free rider: This is a person who enjoys a collective good but does not help provide the collective good.

Free rider problem: Also called the "collective action problem," a free rider problem occurs when rational, self-interested people free ride rather than help provide the collective good.

General Agreement on Tariffs and Trade (GATT): GATT was a multilateral trade agreement that reduced tariffs and other barriers to international trade. GATT was replaced with the World Trade Organization (WTO) in 1995.

Grassroots campaign: Grassroots efforts are thought to be from the ground up rather than the top down. Genuine grassroots campaigns are citizen based and have little support from elite policymakers.

High politics: High politics are politics involving nonincremental policy changes and modifications in who participates in an issue network. (Also see routine politics.)

Hold: A hold is an informal communication from a senator to the Senate majority leader. By placing a hold, a Senator can keep a motion from reaching a vote.

Implementation: Legislative statutes are not self-implementing. Bureaucrats in executive branch agencies and departments develop rules to put a legislative policy into practice.

Individual rationality: When considering interactions between individuals, game theorists consider whether the individuals involved would have a rational basis for maintaining their interactions. Outcomes or events that depend on individuals violating rationality principles are less stable than those outcomes that maintain individual rationality conditions.

Information asymmetry: In most interactions between people, there is an information asymmetry in which some people are better informed and others are less well-informed. Whenever one hires an expert, there is an information asymmetry. For instance, a dentist knows more about a patient's teeth and the cost of fixing a problem than the patient.

Intense (high) demanders: Individuals or organizations that secure very large relative benefits from a good are typically intense demanders of that good. In the case of collective goods, intense demanders might fund the entire good or coordinate a collective effort to secure the good. Intense demanders in political parties are interest groups that demand a role in the selection of the party's nominees for office.

Interest-group liberalism: This is Theodore Lowi's term to describe the government's distribution of benefits to numerous unrelated organized interests while it imposes the costs on an unaware public.

Internal (or in-house) lobbyists: These are lobbyists who work full-time for one client. That client also is their employer. The employer is not itself in the lobbying business. For example, an internal lobbyist for GE would be an employee of GE. (Contrast this with external lobbyist.)

Iron triangles: The policymaking relationships among Congress, government agencies, and interest groups are sometimes referred to as iron triangles because participation from those beyond the triangles is limited. Participants in iron triangles share similar policy goals.

Issue arena: An issue arena is a broad substantive policy category such as urban policy, tax policy, defense policy, environmental policy, or trade policy.

Issue networks: Issue networks are more expansive policy subsystems than iron triangles, with many more participants. Issue networks are likely to include interest groups, representatives from federal agencies, congressional committee staff, and policy experts in universities and think tanks. Whereas all participants in iron triangles share similar policy objectives, participants in issue networks often have divergent policy objectives.

Lobbying: Any attempt to influence the decisions and policies of government officials is considered lobbying.

Lobbying enterprises: An informal group of lobbyists and legislators who have repeated interactions and share common goals is a lobbying enterprise. The repeated interactions reduce a legislator's uncertainty when dealing with lobbyists.

Lobbyist: A lobbyist is someone who lobbies as part of her job. There are internal (in-house) and external (contract) lobbyists.

Maquiladora: These are firms in one country that use tariff-free inputs from another country for their manufacturing. The term refers largely to United States firms located on Mexico's side of the U.S.–Mexico border. These firms can produce goods using tariff-free inputs from both countries and then export the manufactured goods to United States without paying export duties to Mexico or import duties to the United States.

Marginal benefits: Marginal benefits are the benefits yielded from the last dollar or the last unit of effort invested.

Marginal costs: Marginal costs are the costs associated with the last unit of effort invested.

Methyl tertiary-butyl ether (MBTE): MBTE is a gasoline additive.

Mobilization on Development, Trade, Labor, and the Environment (MODTLE): MODTLE was a coalition of environmentalist, human rights, family farm, food safety, worker rights, and civil rights organizations that joined labor unions to oppose any trade agreement with Mexico.

National Coalition for Women and Girls in Education (NCWGE): The NCWGE is a nonprofit coalition of more than fifty groups. Its mission is to advocate for the development of national education policies that benefit women and girls.

National Federation of Independent Business (NFIB): The NFIB is a powerful small-business lobby that played an instrumental role in developing a coalition of business and farm organizations that pushed for repealing the estate tax.

Neopluralism: One of the approaches to understanding interest-group influence, it is a view of politics that sees multiple groups competing for political influence.

Nonrivalrous: See rivalrous consumption.

North American Free Trade Agreement (NAFTA): NAFTA created a trading bloc between the United States, Mexico, and Canada.

Office of Information and Regulatory Affairs (OIRA): OIRA's main job is to review proposed federal regulations and to determine whether a regulation's benefits outweigh its costs. OIRA also oversees the quality of data collected or used by federal agencies.

Office of Management and Budget (OMB): The OMB assists the Executive Office with preparing the federal budget and with reviewing rules and regulations.

Omnibus bills: Omnibus bills are single bills that address a wide range of issues and programs. Omnibus bills are frequently used to address budget issues.

Parts per billion (ppb): This is a unit of measurement used by the Environmental Protection Agency (EPA) in determining water standards.

Peak association: A peak (or umbrella) association is comprised of related firms or other organizations. Peak associations work to coordinate their affiliated organizations' political activities. Examples of peak associations are the National Association of Manufacturers, which represents manufacturing interests in the United States, and the AFL–CIO, which is a federation of labor unions.

Perchlorate Study Group (PSG): The PSG was the primary lobbying coalition opposing stricter standards for perchlorate in water. The organization had four core members from the private sector: (1) Aerojet, (2) American Pacific Corporation, (3) Kerr-McGee Chemical, and (4) Lockheed Martin.

Personal contacts: Personal contacts include individuals in positions of power who one knows well enough to contact for favors, including information sharing.

Pharmaceutical Research and Manufacturers Association (PhRMA): PhRMA is a trade association of companies that manufacture prescription drugs. PhRMA is among the most powerful lobbying organizations in Washington.

Player: A player is a member of a lobbying coalition who places little value in the collective good the coalition is seeking. Players seek private goods. They are apt to move in and out of coalitions as their interests change.

Police patrols: Police patrols is a metaphor used to describe a preemptive form of bureaucratic oversight. Oversight triggered by fire alarms occurs after a problem is uncovered. Police patrol oversight is meant to prevent problems from occurring in the first place.

Policy formulation: Policy formulation is the second stage of the policymaking process. After a problem reaches the agenda, policymakers must develop ways to address the problem.

Policy legitimation: Policy legitimation is the policymaking stage when decision makers choose one among various policy proposals.

Policy subsystems: See iron triangle and issue networks.

Policy window: A policy window is a metaphor to illustrate the fact that opportunities to address policy problems vary considerably. A policy window is open when public opinion and elites see an issue as important to solve, when a viable policy alternative is available, and when political conditions favor the adoption of that alternative.

Political rents: Political rents are the additional profits that firms receive when they improve their economic position through favorable government actions.

Principal–agent dilemma: In a principal–agent model, the principal hires an agent to work on the principal's behalf. The principal secures the agent's expertise but loses some authority. Typically, information asymmetries characterize principal–agent models. That is, the agent has expertise and information that the principal does not. Recognizing that the agent has an informational disadvantage, the principal strives to write contractual agreements to bring the agent's preferences as close to his or her own as possible.

Private goods: Two features characterize private goods. They have rivalrous consumption, and they are excludable.

Problem definition: Problems can be defined or framed in various ways. How a problem is defined affects how government officials address the issue.

Procedural knowledge: Knowledge of the arcana associated with congressional lawmaking and bureaucratic rulemaking is considered procedural knowledge.

Progressive tax: Any tax that burdens wealthier individuals more than poorer individuals is a progressive tax. A tax on yachts—or any other luxury tax—is progressive because poor people seldom buy yachts.

Public policy: Any course of action taken by a government to address economic, social, or political problems is a public policy.

Reference dose (RfD): The RfD of toxic chemicals is an estimate of the daily exposure to the human population that is likely to be experienced without an appreciable risk of harmful effects during a lifetime.

Regressive tax: A tax that falls more heavily on lower income earners is regressive. For instance, taxes on grocery store items are regressive. Poor people spend a greater portion of their income on grocery store items than do rich people.

Rent seeking: Rent seeking is lobbying the government to improve an interest's economic position by securing political rents.

Rivalrous consumption: If a good's value is diminished by consumption, then that good has rivalrous consumption. Rivalrous consumption is a feature of private goods. Collective goods such as national defense are nonrivalrous.

Routine politics: Routine politics occur when policymakers follow standard operating procedures and make incremental changes in policies. Contrast routine politics with high politics.

Rules: Executive branch departments charged with implementing congressional statutes develop rules to flesh out congressional intent. In contrast to vaguely written congressional statutes, rules tend to be finely detailed. Most federal law stems from rules.

Safe Drinking Water Act (SDWA): The SDWA requires the Environmental Protection Agency (EPA) to determine the safe level of exposure to toxic chemicals in tap water.

Selective incentives: Selective incentives are benefits provided only to members of an interest group. Unlike a group's collective goods, selective incentives are private goods, so they are not vulnerable to free riding.

Sides (or Lobbying Sides): A lobbying side consists of all organizations lobbying for a given policy outcome. The organizations may be members of a formal coalition, may coordinate their lobbying efforts, or may lobby independently. (See coalition and cooperative lobbying.)

Substantive expertise: Substantive expertise includes and depends upon substantive knowledge of a policy issue. For example, substantive knowledge of pesticide policy would include knowledge of how various chemicals affect living organisms. See procedural knowledge.

Sunset provisions: Sunset provisions establish a date at which a policy or program will conclude unless Congress chooses to make an extension. Absent an extension, sunset provisions end programs and policies.

Tagalongs: Tagalongs are members of lobbying coalitions who are happy to cheap ride. They might lend their names to the coalition effort, but they seldom contribute very much.

Transaction costs: Any costs associated with individuals making a deal or coming to an agreement are transaction costs. Using an old cell phone with an old carrier because everyone knows the number makes sense if the transaction costs of switching to a new carrier, plan, and number are too great.

Unified Agenda of Federal Regulatory and Deregulatory Actions, or Unified Agenda: Each agency must publish all upcoming regulatory activities in the Unified Agenda.

Universalism: Universalism is the term used to describe a means of allocating legislative benefits in which every legislator secures rewards for some of his or her constituents.

USA*NAFTA: USA*NAFTA was a lobbying coalition with the purpose of organizing business lobbying for NAFTA.

U.S. Department of Agriculture (USDA): The USDA is a cabinet-level department of the executive branch responsible for policy on food, farming, and agriculture.

U.S. Department of Health and Human Services (HHS): HHS is a cabinet-level department in the executive branch. HHS is the principal federal agency for protecting the health of all Americans.

U.S. Food and Drug Administration (FDA): The FDA is an agency within the Department of Health and Human Services (HHS). The FDA is primarily charged with ensuring food and drug safety.

U.S. Trade Representative (USTR): The USTR is responsible for developing trade policy for the U.S. government and works to resolve trade disputes between the United States and other countries. The USTR also meets with governments, business groups, members of Congress, and public interest groups to gather input on trade issues and to discuss the president's trade policy positions.

World Trade Organization (WTO): The WTO supervises international trade. It provides a forum for governments to negotiate trade agreements and operates the system of trade agreements among the member nations.

World Wildlife Fund (WWF): WWF is an interest group working for the protection and restoration of the environment.

Bibliography

Abramowitz, Michael, and Steven Mufson. "Papers Detail Industry's Role in Cheney's Energy Report." *Washington Post,* July 18, 2007. www.washingtonpost.com/wp-dyn/content/article/2007/07/17/AR2007071701987.html

Adler, E. Scott, and John S. Lapinski. "Demand-Side Theory and Congressional Committee Composition: A Constituency Characteristics Approach." *American Journal of Political Science* 41, no. 3 (1997): 895–918.

Ainsworth, Scott. *Analyzing Interest Groups.* New York: Norton, 2002.

———. "Regulating Lobbyists and Interest Group Influence." *Journal of Politics* 55 (1993): 41–56.

———. "The Role of Legislators in the Determination of Interest Group Influence." *Legislative Studies Quarterly* 22 (1997): 517–533.

Ainsworth, Scott H., Erik Godwin, and Kenneth Godwin. "Measuring Interest Group Influence in Bureaucracies: The Impact of Simpson's Paradox." Paper presented at the annual meeting of the American Political Science Association, Washington, DC, 2010.

Ainsworth, Scott H., Erik Godwin, and Kenneth Godwin. "Rulemaking and Interest Group Dominance." Paper presented at the annual meeting of the American Political Science Association, Toronto, Canada, 2009.

Ainsworth, Scott H., and Thad E. Hall. *Abortion Politics in Congress: Strategic Incrementalism and Policy Change.* New York: Cambridge University Press, 2011.

Ainsworth, Scott H., and Itai Sened. "The Role of Lobbyists: Entrepreneurs with Two Audiences." *American Journal of Political Science* 37 (1993): 834–866.

Allison, Graham. *Essence of Decision: Explaining the Cuban Missile Crisis.* Boston: Little, Brown, 1971.

Alt, James E. "Thoughts on Mancur Olson's Contribution to Political Science 1932–1998." *Public Choice* 98 (1999): 1–4.

Amegashie, J. Atsu. "The number of rent-seekers and aggregate rent-seeking expenditures: An unpleasant result." *Public Choice* 99, no. 1/2 (1999): 57–62.

"American Public Says Government Leaders Should Pay Attention to Polls." World Public Opinion. org. March 21, 2008. http://www.worldpublicopinion.org/pipa/articles/governance_bt/461.php?lb=btgov&pnt=461&nid=&id=

Anderson, James F. *Public Policymaking,* 7th ed. Boston: Wadsworth, 2010.

Arnold, Douglas. *Congress and the Bureaucracy: A Theory of Influence.* New Haven, CT: Yale University Press, 1980.

Atkins, Chris. "FSC/ETI Transition Relief in the New JOBS Act: Does the U.S. Have to Quit Cold Turkey?" Tax Foundation Special Report, no. 133 (2005): 1–8.

Austen-Smith, David, and John R. Wright. "Competitive Lobbying for a Legislator's Vote." *Social Choice and Welfare* 9, no. 3 (1992): 229–257.

Bacheller, John M. "Lobbyists and the Legislative Process: The Impact of Environmental Constraints." *American Political Science Review* 71 (1977): 252–263.

Bachrach, Peter, and Morton S. Baratz. "The Two Faces of Power." *American Political Science Review* 56, no. 4 (1962): 947–952.

Baik, Kyung Hwan, and Lee Sanghack. "Strategic Groups and Rent Dissipation." *Economic Inquiry* 39, no. 4 (2001): 672–664.

Baldwin, Robert E., and Christopher S. Magee. "Is Trade Policy for Sale? Congressional Voting on Recent Trade Bills." *Public Choice* 105 (2000): 79–101.

Balla, Steven, and John R. Wright. "Interest Groups, Advisory Committees, and Congressional Control of the Bureaucracy." *American Journal of Political Science* 45, no. 4 (2001): 799–812.

Bauer, Raymond A., Ithiel de Sola Pool, and Lewis Anthony Dexter. *American Business & Public Policy: The Politics of Foreign Trade.* Chicago: Aldine Atherton, 1972.

Baumgartner, Frank R. *Advocacy and Public Policymaking.* http://lobby.la.psu.edu/

Baumgartner, Frank R., Jeffrey M. Berry, Marie Hojnacki, David C. Kimball, and Beth L. Leech. *Lobbying and Policy Change: Who Wins, Who Loses, and Why.* Chicago: University of Chicago Press, 2009.

Baumgartner, Frank R., and Beth L. Leech. *Basic Interests: The Importance of Groups in Politics and in Political Science.* Princeton, NJ: Princeton University Press, 1998.

———. "Interest Niches and Policy Bandwagons: Patterns of Interest Group Involvement in National Politics." *Journal of Politics* 63, no. 4 (2001): 1191–1213.

———. "Studying Interest Groups Using the Lobbying Disclosure Reports." *VOX POP: Newsletter of the Political Organizations and Parties Section of the American Political Science Association* 17, no. 3 (1999): 1–3.

Baumgartner, Frank R., and Christine Mahoney. "The Determinants and Effects of Interest Group Coalitions." Paper prepared for the annual meetings of the American Political Science Association, Chicago, August 31–September 4, 2004.

———. "Gaining Government Allies, Groups, Officials, and Alliance Behavior." Paper presented at the annual meeting of the Midwest Political Science Association, Chicago, April 25–28, 2002.

Baye, Michael R., Dan Kovenock, and Casper G. de Vries. "The All-Pay Auction with Complete Information." *Economic Theory* 8, no. 2 (1996): 291–305.

Beach, William. "The Case for Repealing the Estate Tax." The Heritage Foundation. August 21, 1996. www.heritage.org/Research/Reports/1996/08/BG1091nbsp-The-Case-for-Repealing -the-Estate-Tax

Beaulieu, Eugene, and Christopher Magee. "Four Simple Tests of Campaign Contributions and Trade Policy Preferences." *Economics and Politics* 16, no. 2 (2004): 163–187.

Beckel, Michael. "Federal Lobbying Expenditures Plateau After Years of Rapid Growth." OpenSecrets.org: Center for Responsive Politics. February 4, 2011. www.opensecrets.org/ news/2011/02/federal-lobbying-expenditures-plateau.html

Becker, Gary. "A Theory of Competition Among Pressure Groups for Political Influence." *The Quarterly Journal of Economics* 98 (1983): 371-400.

Beierle, Thomas C., and Jerry Cayford. "Evaluating Dispute Resolution as an Approach to Public Participation." Discussion Paper, Resources for the Future, Washington DC, 2001.

Bennedsen, Morten, and Sven E. Feldmann. "Informational Lobbying and Political Contributions." *Journal of Political Economics* 90, no. 4/5 (2006): 631–656.

———. "Lobbying Bureaucrats." *The Scandinavian Journal of Economics* 108, no. 4 (2006): 643–668.

Bentley, Arthur Fisher. *The Process of Government: A Study of Social Pressures.* Bloomington, IN: Principia Press, 1949.

Berry, Jeffrey M. *The Interest Group Society.* New York: Longman, 1997.

———. *Lobbying for the People: The Political Behavior of Public Interest Groups.* Princeton, NJ: Princeton University Press, 1977.

———. *The New Liberalism: The Rising Power of Citizen Groups.* Washington, DC: Brookings Institution, 1999.

Berry, Jeffrey M., Kent E. Portney, Mary Beth Bablitch, and Richard Mahoney. "Public Involvement in Administration: The Structural Determinants of Effective Citizen Participation." *Nonprofit and Voluntary Sector Quarterly* 13 (1984): 7–23.

Bertelli, Anthony M., and Christian R. Grose. "Secretaries of Pork? A New Theory of Distributive Public Policy." *Journal of Politics* 71, no. 3 (2009): 926–945.

Bianco, William T. *Trust: Representatives and Constituents.* Ann Arbor: University of Michigan Press, 1994.

Blanes i Vadal, Jordi, Mirko Draca, and Christian Fons-Rosen. "Revolving Door Lobbyists." CEP Discussion Paper No. 993. London: Centre for Economic Performance, August 2010.

Box-Steffensmeier, Janet M., Laura W. Arnold, and Christopher J. W. Zorn. "The Strategic Timing of Position Taking in Congress: A Study of the North American Free Trade Agreement." *American Political Science Review* 91, no. 2 (1997): 324–338.

Browne, William P. *Cultivating Congress: Constituents, Issues, and Interests in Agricultural Policymaking.* Lawrence: University of Kansas Press, 1995.

———. "Organized Interests and Their Issue Niches: A Search for Pluralism in a Policy Domain." *Journal of Politics* 52 (1990): 477–509.

————. *Private Interests, Public Policy, and American Agriculture*. Lawrence: University of Kansas Press, 1988.

Buchanan, Patrick. "Remarks Made to the Conservative Political Action Conference." Paper presented at the Conservative Political Action Conference, Omni Shoreham Hotel, Washington, DC, 1992.

Carpenter, Daniel P. "Adaptive Signal Processing, Hierarchy, and Budgetary Control in Federal Regulation." *American Political Science Review* 90 (1996): 283–302.

Chen, Hui, David Parsley, and Ya-Wen Yang. "Corporate Lobbying and Financial Performance." Social Science Research Network Working Paper, 2010.

Chubb, John E. *Interest Groups and the Bureaucracy: The Politics of Energy*. Stanford, CA: Stanford University Press, 1983.

Chubb, John. E., and Paul Peterson, eds. *Can the Government Govern?* Washington, DC: Brookings Institution, 1998.

Cigler, Allan and Burdett Loomis. *Interest Group Politics*. 6th ed. Washington DC: CQ Press, 2002.

Clayton, Mark. "BP Oil Spill: MMS Shortcomings Include 'Dearth of Regulations.'" *Christian Science Monitor*, June 17, 2010. www.csmonitor.com/USA/Politics/2010/0617/BP-oil-spill-MMS-shortcomings-include-dearth-of-regulations

Cohen, Marty, David Karol, Noel Hans, and John Zaller. *The Party Decides: Presidential Nominations Before and After Reform*. Chicago: University of Chicago Press, 2008.

Colburn, Jamison E. "Agency Interpretations." *Temple Law Review* 82, no. 3 (2009): 657–702.

Cooper, Joseph, and William F. West. "Presidential Power and Republican Government: The Theory and Practice of OMB Review of Agency Rules." *Journal of Politics* 50, no. 4 (1988): 864–895.

Copeland, Curtis W. "Federal Rulemaking: The Role of the Office of Information and Regulatory Affairs." *CRS Report for Congress*. June 9, 2009. www.fas.org/sgp/crs/misc/RL32397.pdf

————. "The Unified Agenda: Implications for Rulemaking Transparency and Participation." *CRS Report for Congress*. July 20, 2009. www.fas.org/sgp/crs/secrecy/R40713.pdf

Copeland, Curtis W., and Michael Simpson. "The Information Quality Act: OMB's Guidance and Initial Implementation." *CRS Report for Congress*. September 17, 2004. www.fas.org/sgp/crs/RL32532.pdf

Corn, David. "How a Clean Water Advocate and Senator Became a Chemical Industry Lobbyist." *Mother Jones*. February 23, 2009. www.alternet.org/water/128471/how_a_clean_water_advocate_and_senator_became_a_chemical_industry_lobbyist/?page=1

Cornell University Law School, Legal Information Institute. "CITIZENS UNITED v. FEDERAL ELECTION COMM'N (No. 08-205)." www.law.cornell.edu/supct/html/08-205.ZS.html

Cox, Gary W., and Eric Magar. "How Much Is Majority Status in the U.S. Congress Worth?" *American Political Science Review* 93, no. 2 (1999): 299–309.

Dahl, Robert. *Who Governs? Democracy and Power in an American City*. New Haven, CT: Yale University Press, 1961.

Dalzell, Michael E. "Prescription Drug Reimportation: Panacea or Problem?" *Managed Care*. December 2000. www.managedcaremag.com/archives/0012/0012.reimport.html

Dash, Eric, and Julie Creswell. "Too Big to Fail, or Too Trifling for Oversight?" *New York Times*, June 11, 2011.

Davidson, Roger H., and Walter J. Oleszck. *Congress and Its Members*. 8th ed. Washington DC: CQ Press, 2002.

Davies, J. Clarence. "Public Participation in Environmental Decision-Making and the Federal Advisory Committee Act." Testimony before the U.S. House of Representatives Government Reform and Oversight Committee, July 14, 1998. www.rff.org/Publications/Pages/PublicationDetails.aspx?PublicationID=17059

de Figueiredo, John M., and Charles M. Cameron. "Endogenous Cost Lobbying: Theory and Evidence." Paper presented at the CELS 2009 4th Annual Conference on Empirical Legal Studies Paper, Princeton, NJ, August 3, 2009. http://ssrn.com/abstract=1443559

de Figueiredo, John M., and Emerson H. Tiller. "The Structure and Conduct of Corporate Lobbying: How Firms Lobby the Federal Communications Commission." *Journal of Economics and Management Strategy* 10, no. 1 (2001): 91–122.

Denzau, Arthur T., and Michael C. Munger. "Legislators and Interest Groups: How Unorganized Interests Get Represented." *American Political Science Review* 80 (1986): 86–106.

Downs, Anthony. *An Economic Theory of Democracy.* New York: Harper, 1957.

———. *Inside Bureaucracy.* Boston: Little, Brown, 1967.

Dreiling, Michael. "The Class Embeddedness of Corporate Political Action: Leadership in Defense of NAFTA." *Social Problems* 47 (2000): 21–48.

Dreiling, Michael, and Brian Wolf. "Environmental Movement Organizations and Political Strategy: Tactical Conflicts over NAFTA." *Organization and Environment* 12 (2001): 34–54.

DuPont. "Linda J. Fisher." www2.dupont.com/Government/en_US/gsa_contracts/our_team/fisher.html

Edsall, Thomas B. "NAFTA Debate Reopens Wounds in the Battle of the Democratic Party: Arguments Pit Traditional Coalition, Centrists in Battle for Soul." *Washington Post,* October 23, 1993, 4A.

Edwards, George C. III. "Strategic Choices and the Early Bush Legislative Agenda." *Political Science and Politics* 35, no. 1 (2002): 41–45.

Eggen, Dan. "The Influence Industry: Buchanan Dogged by Allegations in FEC Contributions Case." *Washington Post: Post Politics,* 2011.

Eisler, Kim. "Hired Guns: The City's 50 Top Lobbyists," *Washingtonian,* June 1, 2007. www.washingtonian.com/articles/mediapolitics/4264.html

Engel, Steven T., and David J. Jackson. "Wielding the Stick Instead of the Carrot: Labor PAC Punishment of Pro-NAFTA Democrats." *Political Research Quarterly* 51, no. 3 (1998): 813–828

Environmental Working Group. "Tobacco Subsidies in the United States Totaled $1.1 billion From 1995-2010." http://farm.ewg.org/progdetail.php?fips=00000&progcode=tobacco

Epstein, David, and Sharyn O'Halloran. *Delegating Powers: A Transaction Cost Politics Approach to Policy Making Under Separate Powers.* New York: Cambridge University Press, 1999.

———. "Divided Government and the Design of Administrative Procedures: A Formal Model and Empirical Test." *Journal of Politics* 58 (1996): 373–397.

———. "The Nondelegation Doctrine and the Separation of Powers: A Political Science Approach." *Cardozo Law Review* 20 (1999).

Ervin, David E., James Fitch, Kenneth Godwin, Bruce Shepard, and Herbert Stoevener. *Land Use Control: Evaluating Economic and Political Effects.* Cambridge, MA: Lexington Books, 1974.

Eskridge, William, and John Ferejohn. "Super-Statutes." *Duke Law Journal* 50 (2001): 1215–1276.

Esteban, Joan, and Debraj Ray. "Conflict and Distribution." *Journal of Economic Theory* 87, no. 2 (1999): 379–415.

Esterling, Kevin M. "Buying Expertise: Campaign Contributions and Attention to Policy Analysis in Congressional Committees." *American Political Science Review* 101, no. 1 (2007): 93–109.

———. *The Political Economy of Expertise: Information and Efficiency in American National Politics.* Ann Arbor: The University of Michigan Press, 2004.

Eulau, Heinz, John Wahlke, William Buchanan, and Leroy Ferguson. "The Role of the Representative: Some Empirical Observations on the Theory of Edmund Burke." *American Political Science Review* 53, no. 3 (1959): 742–756.

Evans, Diana. *Greasing the Wheels: Using Pork Barrel Projects to Build Majority Coalitions in Congress.* New York: Cambridge University Press, 2004.

Executive Order 12291, Paperwork Reduction Act (February 17, 1981, 46 FR 13193).

Executive Order 12866, Regulatory Planning and Review (September 30, 1994, 58 FR 51735).

Executive Order 13132, Federalism (August 4, 1999, 64 FR 43255).

Executive Order 13563. "Improving Regulation and Regulatory Review." *Federal Register* 76, no. 14 (2011).

Federal Register, Vol. 76, No. 14, p. 3821, www.gpo.gov/fdsys/pkg/FR-2011-01-21/pdf/2011-1385.pdf

The Federal Reserve Board. "Testimony of Chairman Alan Greenspan: The Regulation of OTC Derivatives Before the Committee on Banking and Financial Services, U.S. House of Representatives." July 24, 1998. www.federalreserve.gov/boarddocs/testimony/1998/19980724 .htm

Fenno, Richard. *Congressmen in Committees.* Boston: Little, Brown, 1973.

———. *Home Style: House Members in their Districts.* Boston: Little, Brown, 1978.

Ferejohn, John A., and Roger D. Noll. "Promises, Promises: Campaign Contributions and the Reputation for Services." Working Papers in Political Science No. P-85-1, Hoover Institution, Stanford, CA, 1985.

Ferejohn, John, and Charles Shipan. "Congressional Influence on Bureaucracy." Special issue, *Journal of Law, Economics, and Organization* 6 (1990): 1–20.

Fiorina, Morris P. *Representatives, Roll Calls, and Constituencies.* Lexington, MA: Lexington Books, 1974

Friedman, Jeffrey, ed. *The Rational Choice Controversy: Economic Models of Politics Reconsidered.* New Haven, CT: Yale University Press, 1995.

Fritschler, Lee J. *Smoking and Politics.* New York: Appleton-Century Crofts, 1969.

Furlong, Scott R. "Political Influence in the Bureaucracy: The Bureaucracy Speaks." *Journal of Public Administration Research and Theory* 8, no. 1 (1998): 39–65.

Furlong, Scott R., and Cornelius M. Kerwin. "Interest Group Participation in Rule Making: A Decade of Change." *Journal of Public Administration Research and Theory* 15, no. 3 (2004): 353–370.

Gartzke, Erik, and J. Mark Wrighton. "Thinking Globally or Acting Locally? Determinants of the GATT Vote in Congress." *Legislative Studies Quarterly* 23, no. 1 (1998): 33–55.

General Electric. "Products and Services." www.ge.com/products_services/index.html

Godwin, R. Kenneth. *One Billion Dollars of Influence: The Direct Marketing of Politics.* Chatham, NJ: Chatham House, 1988.

Godwin, R. Kenneth, John Green, and Nancy Kucinski. "Home Cooking: The Things Interest Groups Want and How They Get Them." Paper presented at the annual meeting of the Southwest Social Science Association, New Orleans, 2006.

Godwin, R. Kenneth, Edward J. Lopez, and Barry J. Seldon. "Allocating Lobbying Resources between Collective and Private Rents." *Political Research Quarterly* 61, no. 2 (2008): 345–361.

———. "Incorporating Policymaker Costs and Political Competition into Rent-Seeking Games." *Southern Economic Journal* 73, no. 1 (2006): 37–54.

Goldberg, Jeffrey. "Goldberg: Wal-Mart Heiress's Museum a Moral Blight." Bloomberg View. December 12, 2011. http://www.bloomberg.com/news/2011-12-13/wal-mart-heiress-s -museum-a-moral-blight-commentary-by-jeffrey-goldberg.html.

Golden, Marissa M. "Interest Groups in the Rule-Making Process: Who Participates? Whose Voices Get Heard?" *Journal of Public Administration Research and Theory* 8, no. 2 (1998): 245–270.

Goldstein, Jacob. "Reminder: Medicare, Medicaid Are Gobbling up the Budget." *Wall Street Journal: Health Blog,* February 2, 2010. http://blogs.wsj.com/health/2010/02/02/reminder-medicare -medicaid-are-gobbling-up-the-budget/

Goodman, Sara. "Defense Contractors Lobby to Block Perchlorate Advisory." *Greenwire,* June 22, 2009.

Gopoian, J. David. "What Makes PACs Tick? An Analysis of the Allocation Patterns of Economic Interest Groups." *American Journal of Political Science* 28, no. 2 (1984): 259.

Gordon, Stanford C., and Catherine Hafer. "Flexing Muscle: Corporate Political Expenditures as Signals to the Bureaucracy." *American Political Science Review* 99, no. 2 (2005): 245–261.

Graetz, Michael J., and Ian Shapiro. *Death by a Thousand Cuts: The Fight Over Taxing Inherited Wealth.* Princeton, NJ: Princeton University Press, 2005.

Gray, Virginia, and David Lowery. "The Population Ecology of Gucci Gulch, or the Natural Regulation of Interest Group Numbers in the American States." *American Journal of Political Science* 39, no. 1 (1995).

————. *The Population Ecology of Interest Representation: Lobbying Communities in the American States*. Ann Arbor: University of Michigan Press, 1996.

————. "Reconceptualizing PAC Contributions: It's Not a Collective Action Problem and It May Be an Arms Race." *American Politics Quarterly* 25 (1997): 319–46.

Green, Donald, and Ian Shapiro. *Pathologies of Rational Choice Theory: A Critique of Applications in Political Science*. New Haven, CT: Yale University Press, 1994.

Grenske, Janet M. "PACs and the Congressional Supermarket: The Currency Is Complex." *American Journal of Political Science* 33 (1989): 1–24.

Grier, Kevin B., Michael C. Munger, and Brian E. Roberts. "The Determinants of Industry Political Activity, 1978-1986." *American Political Science Review* 88, no. 4 (1994).

Grimaldi, James V. "Billionaire Adelson Gives Millions to Gingrich Super PAC." *Washington Post*, January 7, 2012, A-1. www.washingtonpost.com/politics/billionaire-adelson-gives-millions -to-gingrich-super-pac/2012/01/07/gIQAXI6rhP_story.html

Groseclose, Timothy, and James M. Snyder, Jr. "Buying Supermajorities." *American Political Science Review* 90, no. 2 (1996): 303–315.

Grossman, Gene M., and Elhanan Helpman. *Interest Groups and Trade Policy*. Princeton and Oxford, UK: Princeton University Press, 2002.

————. *Special Interest Politics*. Cambridge, MA: MIT Press, 2002.

Hall, Richard L., and Alan V. Deardorff. "Lobbying as Legislative Subsidy." *American Political Science Review* 100 (2006): 69–84.

Hall, Richard L., and Frank Wayman. "Buying Time: Moneyed Interests and the Mobilization of Bias in Congressional Committees," *American Political Science Review* 84 (1990): 797–820.

Hansen, Wendy L., Neil J. Mitchell, and Jeffrey M. Drope. "The Logic of Private and Collective Action." *American Journal of Political Science* 49, no. 1 (2005): 150–167.

Hardin, Russell. *Collective Action*. Baltimore: Resources for the Future by the Johns Hopkins University Press, 1982.

Hayes, Michael T. *Lobbyists and Legislators: A Theory of Political Markets*. New Brunswick, NJ: Rutgers University Press, 1981.

————. "The Semi-Sovereign Pressure Groups: A Critique of Current Theory and an Alternative Typology." *Journal of Politics* 40, no. 1 (1978): 134–161.

Headen, Emily. *From Bureaucrats to Fat Cats: EPA Pesticide Program Is a "Farm Team for the Pesticide Lobby*. Washington, DC: Environmental Working Group, n.d. www.ewg.org/files/ fatcats.pdf

Heberlig, Eric. "Congressional Parties, Fundraising, and Committee Ambition." *Political Research Quarterly* 56 (2003): 151–161.

Heberlig, Eric, Mark Hetherington, and Bruce Larson. "The Price of Leadership: Campaign Money and the Polarization of Congressional Parties." *Journal of Politics* 68 (2006): 992–1005.

Heclo, Hugh. "Issue Networks and the Executive Establishment." In *The New American Political System*, edited by Anthony King, 87–124. Washington, DC: American Enterprise Institute, 1978.

Heinz, John, Edward O. Laumann, Robert L. Nelson, and Robert H. Salisbury. *The Hollow Core: Private Interests in National Policymaking*. Cambridge, MA: Harvard University Press, 1993.

Hojnacki, Marie. "Interest Groups' Decisions to Join Alliances or Work Alone." *American Journal of Political Science* 41 (1997): 61–87.

————. "Organized Interests' Advocacy Behavior in Alliances." *Political Research Quarterly* 51, no. 2 (1998): 437–459.

Hojnacki, Marie, Frank R. Baumgartner, Jeffrey Berry, David Kimball, and Beth L. Leech. "Goals, Salience, and the Nature of Advocacy." Paper presented at the annual meeting of the American Political Science Association, Philadelphia, August 31–September 3, 2006.

Holyoke, Thomas T. "Interest Group Competition and Coalition Formation." *American Journal of Political Science* 53, no. 2 (2009): 360–375.

Hula, Kevin W. *Lobbying Together: Interest Group Coalitions in Legislative Politics*. Washington, DC: Georgetown University Press, 2000.

Hummel, Patrick. "Buying Supermajorities in a Stochastic Environment." *Public Choice* 141, no. 3/4 (2009): 351–369.

Ingle, Ed. "Government Relations." In *Reputation Management*, edited by John Doonley and Helio Fred Garcia, 159–182. New York: Routledge, 2007.

Ingram, Helen M., and R. Kenneth Godwin, eds. *Public Policy and the Natural Environment.* Greenwich, CT: JAI Press, 1985.

Jenkins, Jeffery, and Nathan Monroe. "Buying Negative Agenda Control in the U.S. House." Paper prepared for the annual meeting of the American Political Science Association, Toronto, Canada, September 2009.

Kalt, Joseph P., and Mark A. Zupan. "The Apparent Ideological Behavior of Legislators: Testing for Principal-Agent Slack in Political Institutions." *Journal of Law and Economics* 33, no. 1 (1990): 103–113.

Kersh, Rogan. "Corporate Lobbyists as Political Actors: A View from the Field." In *Interest Group Politics*, 6th ed., edited by Burdett Loomis and Allan Cigler, 225–248. Washington, DC: CQ Press, 2002.

Kerwin, Cornelius M., ed. *Rulemaking: How Government Agencies Write Law and Make Policy.* 3rd ed. Washington, DC: CQ Press, 2003.

Kilborn, Peter. "The Free Trade Accord: Little Voices Roar in the Chorus of Trade-Pact Foes." *New York Times*, November 12, 1993, 10.

Kingdon, John W. *Agendas, Alternatives, and Public Policies.* 2nd ed. Reading, MA: Addison-Wesley, 1995.

———. *Congressmen's Voting Decisions.* 3rd ed. Ann Arbor: University of Michigan Press, 1989.

Kollman, Ken. "Inviting Friends to Lobby: Interest Groups, Ideological Bias, and Congressional Committees." *American Political Science Review* 41 (1997): 519–544.

Kraft, Michael, and Scott Furlong. *Public Policy: Politics, Analysis, and Alternatives.* Washington, DC: CQ Press, 2004.

Kroszner, Randall S., and Thomas Stratmann. "Interest-Group Competition and the Organization of Congress: Theory and Evidence from Financial Services' Political Action Committees." *American Economic Review* 88 (1998): 1163–1187.

Krutz, Glen S. "Issues and Institutions: 'Winnowing' in the U.S. Congress." *American Journal of Political Science* 49, no. 2 (2005): 313–326.

Lapinski, John S. "Policy Substance and Performance in American Lawmaking, 1877–1994." *American Journal of Political Science* 52, no. 2 (2008): 235–251.

Lasswell, Harold. *Who Gets What, When, and How.* New York: P. Smith, 1950.

Latham, Earl. *The Group Basis of Politics: A Study in Basing-Point Legislation.* New York: Octagon Books, 1965.

Lav, Iris J., and James Sly. "Estate Tax Repeal: A Windfall for the Wealthiest Americans." Report for the Center on Budget and Policy Priorities, June 21, 2000.

LeBoeuf, Jacques B. "Limitations on the Use of Appropriations Riders by Congress to Effectuate Substantive Policy Changes." *Hastings Constitutional Law Quarterly* 19 (1992): 457–493.

Lee, Jennifer. "Second Thoughts on a Chemical: In Water, How Much Is Too Much?" *New York Times*, March 2, 2004, 1F.

Leech, Beth, Frank R. Baumgartner, Timothy M. La Pira, and Nicholas A. Semanko. "Drawing Lobbyists to Washington: Government Activity and Interest Group Mobilization." *Political Research Quarterly* 58, no. 1 (2005): 19–30.

Leininger, Wolfgang. "More Efficient Rent-Seeking—A Munchhausen Solution." *Public Choice* 75, no. 1 (1993): 43–62.

Leiserson, Greg, and Jeffrey Rohaly. "Distribution of the 2001-2006 Tax Cuts: Updated Projections." Washington, DC: Urban-Brookings Tax Policy Center, 2008.

Levine, Bertam J. *The Art of Lobbying: Building Trust and Selling Policy.* Washington, DC: CQ Press, 2009.

Lipsey, R. G., and Kelvin Lancaster. "The General Theory of Second Best." *Review of Economic Studies* 24, no. 1 (1956): 11–32.

Lohmann, Susanne. "Information, Access, and Contributions: A Signaling Model of Lobbying." *Public Choice* 85 (1995): 267–284.

Long, Rebecca J., and Thomas C. Beierle. "The Federal Advisory Committee Act and Public Participation in Environmental Policy." Discussion Paper 99–17, Resources for the Future, Washington, DC, 1999.

Loomis, Burdett A. "Coalitions of Interests: Building Bridges in the Balkanized State." In *Interest Group Politics*, 2nd ed., edited by Allan J. Cigler and Burdett A. Loomis. Washington, DC: CQ Press, 2002.

———."Some Expressions of 'Interest.'" *Political Research Quarterly* 39, no. 4 (1986): 736.

Lovette, William A., Alfred E. Eckles, and Richard L. Brinkman. *U.S. Trade Policy: History, Theory, and the WTO*. 2nd ed. Armonk: M.E. Sharpe, 2001.

Lowery, David. "Why Do Organized Interests Lobby? A Multi-Goal, Multi-Context Theory of Lobbying," *Polity* 39 (2007): 29–54.

Lowery, David, and Holly Brasher. *Organized Interests and American Government*. New York: McGraw-Hill, 2004.

Lowery, David, and Virginia Gray. "A Neopluralist Perspective on Research on Organized Interests." *Political Research Quarterly* 57, no. 1 (2004): 164–175.

———. "To Lobby Alone or in a Flock: Foraging Behavior among Organized Interests." *American Politics Quarterly* 26, no. 1 (1998): 5–34.

Lowi, Theodore. "American Business, Public Policy, Case-Studies, and Political Theory." *World Politics* 16, no. 4 (1964): 677–715.

———. *The End of Liberalism: Ideology, Policy and the Crisis of Public Authority*. New York: Norton, 1969.

———. "How Farmers Get What They Want." *Reporter*, May 21, 1964, 35.

Magazine Publishers of America. "Top 100 Magazines." The New York Job Source. http://nyjobsource.com/magazines.html

Mahoney, Christine, and Frank Baumgartner. "Converging Perspectives on Interest Group Research in Europe and America." *West European Politics* 31 (2008): 1253–1273.

Marcus, Alfred. "Environmental Protection Agency." In *The Politics of Regulation*, edited by James Q. Wilson. New York: Basic Books, 1980.

Mayer, Frederick W. *Interpreting NAFTA: The Science and Art of Political Analysis*. New York: Columbia University Press, 1998.

Mayhew, David R. *Congress: The Electoral Connection*. New Haven, CT: Yale University Press, 1974.

McCubbins, Mathew, Roger G. Noll, and Barry R. Weingast, "Structure and Process, Politics and Policy: Administrative Arrangements and the Political Control of Agencies." *Virginia Law Review* 75, no. 2 (1989): 431–482.

McCubbins, Mathew, and Thomas Schwartz. "Congressional Oversight Overlooked: Police Patrols Versus Fire Alarms." *American Journal of Political Science* 28, no. 1 (1984): 165–179.

McFarland, Andrew S. "Interest Groups and Political Time: Cycles in America." *British Journal of Political Science* 21, no. 3 (1991): 257–284.

———. *Neopluralism: The Evolution of Political Process Theory*. Lawrence: University Press of Kansas, 2004.

McKay, Amy M. "Buying Policy? The Effect of Lobbyists' Resources on Their Policy Success." *Political Research Quarterly* (forthcoming 2012).

———. "The Decision to Lobby Bureaucrats." *Public Choice* 147, no. 1–2 (2011): 123–138.

McKay, Amy, and Susan Webb Yackee. "Interest Group Competition on Federal Agency Rules." *American Politics Research* 35, no. 3 (2007): 336–357.

Milbank, Dana. "President Obama Writes a New Health Reform Prescription." *Washington Post*, December 16, 2009, 2A.

Milligan, Susan. "Energy Bill: A Special-Interests Triumph." *Boston Globe*, October 4, 2004, 1A.

Mills, Joshua. "Business Lobbying for Trade Pact Appears to Sway Few in Congress." *Washington Post*, November 12, 1993, 1A.

Mintrom, Michael, and Phillipa Norman. "Policy Entrepreneurship and Policy Change." *Policy Studies Journal* 37 (2009): 649–666.

Mitchell, William C., and Michael C. Munger. "Economic Models of Interest Groups: An Introductory Survey." *American Journal of Political Science* 35, no. 2 (1991): 512–546.

Moe, Terry. "Control and Feedback in Economic Regulation: The Case of the NLRB." *American Political Science Review* 79 (1985): 1094–1116.

———. "The Politics of Structural Choice: Toward a Theory of Public Bureaucracy." In *Organization Theory: From Chester Barnard to the Present and Beyond,* edited by Oliver E. Williamson. New York: Oxford University Press, 1995.

Mogerman, Josh. "Federal Government Moves Towards Potential Atrazine Phase-Out." Natural Resources Defense Council, October 7, 2009. www.nrdc.org/media/2009/091007.asp

Mooney, Chris. "Interrogations." *Boston Globe,* August 28, 2005. www.boston.com/news/globe/ideas/articles/2005/08/28/interrogations

Morgan, Dan. "Pressure on NLRB Turns Into a Doubled Budget Cut." *Washington Post,* July 20, 1995, A8.

Mucciaroni, Gary. *Reversals of Fortune: Public Policy and Private Interests.* Washington DC: Brookings Institution, 1994.

National Research Council. *Health Implications of Perchlorate Ingestion.* Washington, DC: National Academies Press, 2005.

Natural Resources Defense Council. "The Cheney Energy Task Force." March 27, 2002. www.nrdc.org/air/energy/taskforce/tfinx.asp

———. "Federal Government Moves Towards Potential Atrazine Phase-Out." October 7, 2009. www.nrdc.org/media/2009/091007.asp

———. "How NRDC Brought the Records to Light." www.nrdc.org/air/energy/taskforce/bkgrd.asp

Niskanen, William. *Bureaucracy and Representative Government.* Chicago: Aldine, 1967.

———. "Bureaucrats and Politicians." *Journal of Law and Economics* 18, no. 3 (1975): 617–643.

Nownes, Anthony J. *Total Lobbying: What Lobbyists Want (and How They Try to Get It).* New York: Cambridge University Press, 2006.

Nye, Joseph S., Philip Zelikow, and David King. *Why People Don't Trust Government.* Cambridge, MA: Harvard University Press, 1997.

Office of Information and Regulatory Assessment, Office of Management and Budget. *Report to Congress on the Benefits and Costs of Federal Regulations.* www.whitehouse.gov/omb/inforeg_regpol_reports_congress

Office of Management and Budget. "Guidelines for Ensuring and Maximizing the Quality, Objectivity, Utility, and Integrity of Information Disseminated by Federal Agencies; Notice; Republication." *Federal Register* 67, no. 36 (2002). www.whitehouse.gov/omb/fedreg_final_information_quality_guidelines/

OMB Watch. "The Reality of Data Quality Act's First Year: A Correction of OMB's Report to Congress." July 2004. www.ombwatch.org/files/info/dataqualityreport.pdf

Orbell, John, Oleg Smirnov, Holly Arrow, and Douglas Kennet. "Ancestral War and the Evolutionary Origins of "Heroism." *Journal of Politics* 69, no. 4 (2007): 927–940.

Palfrey, Thomas R., and Howard Rosenthal. "Participation and the Provision of Discrete Public Goods: A Strategic Analysis." *Journal of Public Economics* 24, no. 2 (1984): 171.

———. "Private Incentives in Social Dilemmas: The Effects of Incomplete Information and Altruism." *Journal of Public Economics* 35, no. 3 (1988): 309–332.

———. "Repeated play, cooperation and coordination: An experimental study." *Review of Economic Studies* 61, no. 208 (1994): 545.

———. "A Strategic Calculus of Voting." *Public Choice* 41, no. 1 (1983): 7–53.

Pesca, Mike. "Bill Frist, Blind Trusts and Conflicts of Interest." National Public Radio. Oct. 25, 2005. www.npr.org/templates/story/story.php?storyId=4973742&ft=1&f=17

Petracca, Mark P. "Federal Advisory Committees, Interest Groups, and the Administrative State." *Congress and the Presidency* 13, no. 1 (1986): 83–114.

Phillips, Gretchen A. "Labor PACs and NAFTA Legislators: An Examination of Reward, Punishment, and the NAFTA Vote." Unpublished manuscript. Durham: Duke University, 2000.

Pika, Joseph A. "Interest Groups and the Executive: Presidential Intervention." In *Interest Group Politics*, edited by Allan Cigler and Burdett Loomis. Washington, DC: CQ Press, 1983.

Polsby, Nelson W. *Political Innovation in America: The Politics of Policy Initiation*. New Haven, CT: Yale University Press, 1984.

Potters, Jan, and Randolph Sloof. "Interest Groups: A Survey of Empirical Models That Try to Assess Their Influence." *European Journal of Political Economy* 12 (1996): 403–442.

Potters, Jan, and Frans Van Winden. "Lobbying and Asymmetric Information." *Public Choice* 74, no. 3 (1992): 269–292.

Quirk, Paul. "The Food and Drug Administration." In *The Politics of Regulation*, edited by James Q. Wilson. New York: Basic Books, 1980.

Ricardo, David. *On the Principles of Political Economy and Taxation*. London: John Murray, 1817.

Richter, Brian, Krislert Samphantharak, and Jeffrey Simmons. "Lobbying and Taxes." *American Journal of Political Science* 53, no. 4 (2009): 893–909.

Roscoe, Douglas D., and Shannon Jenkins. "A Meta-Analysis of Campaign Contributions' Impact on Roll Call Voting." *Social Science Quarterly* 86, no. 1 (2005): 52–68.

Rossi, Jim. "Making Policy through the Waiver of Regulations at the Federal Energy Regulatory Commission." *Administrative Law Review* 47 (1995): 255–301.

Sabatier, Paul A., and Hank Jenkins-Smith. "The Advocacy Coalition Framework: An Assessment." In *Theories of the Policy Process*, edited by Paul A. Sabatier. Boulder, CO: Westview Press, 1999.

———. *Policy Change and Learning: An Advocacy Coalition Approach*. Boulder, CO: Westview Press, 1993.

Salisbury, Robert. H. "Interest Groups: Toward a New Understanding." In *Interest Group Politics*, edited by Allan J. Cigler and Burdett A. Loomis. Washington, DC: CQ Press, 1983.

———. "Interest Representation: The Dominance of Institutions." *American Political Science Review* 78, no. 1 (1984): 64–76.

Salisbury Robert H., and John Heinz. "A Theory of Policy Analysis and Some Preliminary Applications." In *Policy Analysis in Political Science*, edited by Ira Sharkansky. Chicago: Markham, 1970.

Salisbury, Robert H., and Kenneth Shepsle. "U.S. Congressman as Enterprise." *Legislative Studies Quarterly* 6 (1981): 559–576.

Sapien, Joaquin. "After Admitting Faults at Hearing, New EPA Head Starts Work." Pro Publica. January 23, 2009. www.propublica.org/article/after-admitting-faults-at-hearing-new-epa-head-starts-work-090123

Schattschneider, E. E. *Party Government: American Government in Action*. Westport, CT: Greenwood Press, 1977.

———. *Politics, Pressures and the Tariff: A Study of Free Enterprise in Pressure Politics as Shown in the 1929–1930 Revision of the Tariff*. New York: Prentice Hall, 1935.

———. *The Semi-Sovereign People*. New York: Holt, Rinehart & Winston, 1960.

Schlozman, Kay Lehman, and John T. Tierney. *Organized Interests and American Democracy*. New York: Harper & Row, 1986.

Schneider, Anne, and Helen Ingram. *Policy Design for Democracy*. Lawrence: University of Kansas Press, 1997.

Schonhardt-Baily, Cheryl. *From the Corn Laws to Free Trade: Interests, Ideas, and Institutions in Historical Perspective*. Cambridge, MA: MIT Press, 2006.

Shaffer, Brian, Thomas J. Quasney, and Curtis M. Grimm. "Firm Level Performance Implications of Nonmarket Actions." *Business & Society* 39, no. 2 (2000): 126–143.

Shapiro, Sidney A. "The Information Quality Act and Environmental Protection: The Perils of Reform by Appropriations Rider." *William and Mary Environmental Law Review* 28, no. 2 (2004): 339–374.

Sharkansky, Ira. *Policy Analysis in Political Science*. Chicago: Markham Publishing, 1970.

Sharp, Elaine B. "The Dynamics of Issue Expansion: Cases from Disability Rights and Fetal Research Controversy." *Journal of Politics* 56, no. 4 (1994): 919–939.

Shepsle, Kenneth, and Barry Weingast. "Political Preferences for the Pork Barrel." *American Journal of Political Science* 25 (1981): 96–111.

Sinclair, Barbara. *Unorthodox Lawmaking: New Legislative Processes in the U.S. Congress.* 3rd ed. Washington, DC: CQ Press, 2007.

Smith, Mark A. *American Business and Political Power: Public Opinion, Elections, and Democracy.* Chicago: University of Chicago Press, 2000.

Smith, Richard A. "Advocacy, Interpretation, and Influence in the U.S. Congress." *American Political Science Review* 78 (1984): 44–63.

———. "Agenda Defection and Interest." In *Agenda Formation,* edited by William H. Riker. Ann Arbor: University of Michigan Press, 1993.

Snyder, James M. "Long-Term Investing in Politicians; or, Give Early, Give Often." *Journal of Law and Economics* 35, no. 1 (1992): 15–43.

SourceWatch. "John D. Graham." November 11, 2008. www.sourcewatch.org/index.php?title= John_D._Graham

Spoke. "Daniel Barolo." n.d. www.spoke.com/info/p6KGOMB/DanielBarolo

———. "James Aidala." www.spoke.com/info/p6msk8Y/JamesAidala

Stein, Robert, and Kenneth Bickers. *Perpetuating the Pork Barrel: Policy Subsystems and American Democracy.* New York: Cambridge University Press, 1995.

Stigler, George. "The Theory of Economic Regulation." *Bell Journal of Economics and Management Science* 2, no. 1 (1971): 3–21.

Stone, Deborah. *Policy Paradox: The Art of Political Decisionmaking.* Rev. ed. New York: W. W. Norton, 2001.

Strolovitch, Dara Z. *Affirmative Advocacy: Race, Class, and Gender in Interest Group Politics.* Chicago: University of Chicago Press, 2007.

———. "Do Interest Groups Represent the Disadvantaged? Advocacy at the Intersections of Race, Class and Gender." *Journal of Politics* 68, no. 4 (2006): 894–910.

Suarez, Sandra. *Does Business Learn? Tax Breaks, Uncertainty, and Political Strategies.* Ann Arbor: University of Michigan Press, 2000.

Sullivan, Paul. "Estate Tax Will Return Next Year, but Few Will Pay It." *New York Times.* December 17, 2010. www.nytimes.com/2010/12/18/your-money/taxes/18wealth.html

Surrey, Stanley S. "How Special Tax Provisions Get Enacted." In *Public Policies and Their Politics: Techniques of Government Control,* edited by Randall Ripley, 51–60. New York: Norton, 1966.

Truman, David B. *The Governmental Process: Political Interests and Public Opinion.* New York: Alfred A. Knopf, 1951.

Tversky, Amos, and Daniel Kahneman. "Loss Aversion in Riskless Choice: A Reference-Dependent Model." *Quarterly Journal of Economics* 106 (1991): 1039–1061.

U.S. Environmental Protection Agency. "Atrazine Updates." September 2011. www.epa.gov/ opp00001/reregistration/atrazine/atrazine_update.htm

U.S. Environmental Protection Agency: Integrated Risk Information System (IRIS). "Perchlorate (ClO4) and Perchlorate Salts Quickview (CASRN 7790-98-9)." April 20, 2012. http://cfpub .epa.gov/ncea/iris/index.cfm?fuseaction=iris.showQuickView&substance_nmbr=1007

Uslaner, Eric M. "Let the Chits Fall Where They May? Executive and Constituency Influences on Congressional Voting on NAFTA." *Legislative Studies Quarterly* 23, no. 3 (1998): 347–371.

Wahlke, John C. "Policy Demands and System Support: The Role of the Represented." *British Journal of Political Science* 1, no. 3 (1971): 271–290.

Walker, Jack L., Jr. "The Origins and Maintenance of Interest Groups in America." *American Political Science Review* 77 (1983): 390–409.

Ward, Hugh. "Pressure Politics: A Game-Theoretical Investigation of Lobbying and the Measurement of Power." *Journal of Theoretical Politics* 16 (2004): 31–52.

Weaver, Kent R. *Automatic Government: The Politics of Indexation.* Washington DC: Brookings Institution, 1988.

Weingast, Barry. "A Rational Choice Perspective on Congressional Norms." *American Journal of Political Science* 23, no. 2 (1979): 245–262.

Weingast, Barry, and Mark Moran. "Bureaucratic Discretion or Congressional Control? Regulatory Policymaking by the Federal Trade Commission." *Journal of Political Economy* 91, no. 5 (1983): 765–800.

Weingast, Barry R., Kenneth A. Shepsle, and Christopher Johnsen. "The Political Economy of Benefits and Costs: A Neoclassical Approach to Distributive Politics." *Journal of Political Economy* 89 (1981): 642–664.

Weisman, Jonathan. "Linking Tax to Death May Have Brought Its Doom." *USA Today*, May 21, 2001.

Weiss, Rick. "'Data Quality' Law Is Nemesis of Regulation." *Washington Post*, August 16, 2004, 1A.

Wilson, Graham K. "Corporate Political Strategies." *British Journal of Political Science* 20 (1990): 281-288.

Wilson, James Q. *Bureaucracy: What Government Agencies Do and Why They Do It*. New York: Basic Books, 1989.

———, ed. *The Politics of Regulation*. New York: Basic Books, 1980.

Wiseman, Alan E. "Delegation and Positive-Sum Bureaucracies." *Journal of Politics* 17, no. 3 (2009): 998–1014.

Wolpe, Bruce C., and Bertram J. Levine. *Lobbying Congress: How the System Works*, 2nd ed. Washington, DC: CQ Press, 1996.

Womach, Jasper. "Tobacco Quota Buyout." CRS Report for Congress RS22046, December 31, 2005. www.nationalaglawcenter.org/assets/crs/RS22046.pdf

Wood, Dan B. "Does Politics Make a Difference at the EEOC?" *American Journal of Political Science* 24 (1990): 503–530.

Wyatt, Edward. "S.E.C. Is Avoiding Tough Sanctions for Large Banks," *New York Times*, February 3, 2012. www.nytimes.com/2012/02/03/business/sec-is-avoiding-tough-sanctions-for-large-banks.html?_r=1&pagewanted=print

Yackee, Jason Webb, and Susan Webb Yackee. "A Bias Towards Business? Assessing Interest Group Influence on the U.S. Bureaucracy." *Journal of Politics* 68, no. 1 (2006): 128–139.

Yackee, Susan Webb. "Sweet-Talking the Fourth Branch: Assessing the Influence of Interest Group Comments on Federal Agency Rulemaking." *Journal of Public Administration Research and Theory* 26, no. 1 (2006): 103–124.

Ziobrowiski, Alan J., Ping Cheng, James W. Boyd, and Brigitte J. Ziobrowski. "Abnormal Returns from the Common Stock Investments of the U.S. Senate." *Journal of Financial and Quantitative Analysis* 39, no. 4 (2004): 661–676.

ZoomInfo. "The ACTA Group, L.L.C." www.zoominfo.com/company/The+Acta+Group+%2C+L.L.C.-806583

Note: n in locator refers to the endnote number.

$SAGE research**methods**

The essential online tool for researchers from the world's leading methods publisher

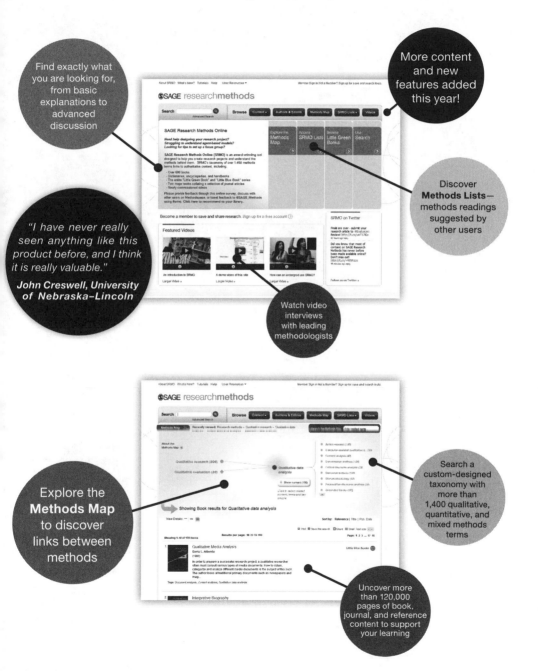

Find exactly what you are looking for, from basic explanations to advanced discussion

More content and new features added this year!

"I have never really seen anything like this product before, and I think it is really valuable."

John Creswell, University of Nebraska–Lincoln

Discover **Methods Lists**— methods readings suggested by other users

Watch video interviews with leading methodologists

Explore the **Methods Map** to discover links between methods

Search a custom-designed taxonomy with more than 1,400 qualitative, quantitative, and mixed methods terms

Uncover more than 120,000 pages of book, journal, and reference content to support your learning

Find out more at
www.sageresearchmethods.com